# Advertising Works 15

Proving the effectiveness of
marketing communications

# Advertising Works 15

Proving the effectiveness of marketing communications

Case studies from the
IPA Effectiveness Awards 2006
Open to all agencies worldwide

**Edited and introduced by**
**Laurence Green**

Convenor of Judges

First published 2007 by World Advertising Research Center
Farm Road, Henley-on-Thames, Oxfordshire RG9 1EJ, United Kingdom
Telephone: 01491 411000
Fax: 01491 418600
Email: enquiries@warc.com

A CIP catalogue record for this book is available from the British Library

ISBN-13: 978-1-84116-193-8
ISBN-10: 1-84116-193-4

DVD of the 2006 IPA Effectiveness Awards winners produced by Xtreme Information Ltd,
London
Typeset by Godiva Publishing Services Ltd, Coventry
Printed and bound in Great Britain by Biddles Ltd, King's Lynn

# Contents

# Foreword

All of us working in advertising know that we can't afford to make any assumptions about anything – least of all, that our advertising ideas have delivered. The joy of these Awards, which we are proud to sponsor, is that forensic analysis of the evidence, isolation of effects and honest attribution to the causes is the only acceptable approach.

Representing television as we do, this depth of analysis is crucial to Thinkbox because, interactive TV aside, television rarely captures the effects and responses it generates, so without robust analysis it is easy to undervalue what brand-building media contribute to the success of a campaign.

Of course, it's perfectly possible to create effective advertising campaigns without television, as four of these 30 papers prove. But the most gratifying aspect for us is not the sheer numerical dominance of TV amongst the winners, but the demonstration and dissection of exactly how TV has delivered: instant breakthrough for Tropicana, drama and interaction for Virgin Trains, driving response into other media for ING Direct and $O_2$, attitudinal change for Teacher Recruitment and the long-term payback for brands like VW Golf, Daz and Felix.

Congratulations to all the winners. Big thanks to you, and to all the people who contributed the work that these Awards celebrate, for proving our assertion that *TV is at the heart of advertising effectiveness.*

Tess Alps
Chief Executive

# Sponsors

The success of the 2006 IPA Effectiveness Awards is in no small part down to its sponsors, and the IPA would like to thank the companies listed here for their continuing support. We are particularly grateful to Thinkbox, its overall sponsor, for their commitment to sponsor this competition until 2008.

IN ASSOCIATION WITH

World Advertising
Research Center

AND

          **campaign**

# Acknowledgements

Many people worked hard to make the Awards a success, especially the following: Sven Olsen, immediate past Chairman of the IPA Value of Advertising Group; Laurence Green, Convenor of Judges and Neil Dawson, Deputy Convenor of Judges.

At the IPA, the core team were: Tessa Gooding, Richard Lambert, Sylvia Ogden, Kathryn Patten, Carey Quarrier, Alex Rogers and consultant Jill Bentley.

We also owe a debt of gratitude to the IPA Value of Advertising Group:

| | |
|---|---|
| Ian Priest (Chairman) | Vallance Carruthers Coleman Priest |
| Les Binet | DDB London |
| Simon Calvert | Draft FCB |
| David Cobban | Wieden + Kennedy |
| Neil Dawson | Hurrell & Dawson |
| Peter Gamble | McCann Erickson Communications House |
| David Golding | RKCR/Y&R |
| Andrew Green | ZenithOptimedia |
| Laurence Green | Fallon London |
| Robert Horler | Diffiniti |
| Louise Jones | PHD Media |
| Sam McIlveen | AV Browne Group |
| Andy Nairn | Miles Calcraft Briginshaw Duffy |
| Sven Olsen | Leo Burnett |
| Gurdeep Puri | Leo Burnett |
| Clare Rossi | Zalpha |
| Charlie Snow | Delaney Lund Knox Warren & Partners |
| Richard Storey | M&C Saatchi |
| Gary Wise | Feather Brooksbank |

# The Judges

**Laurence Green**
*Convenor of Judges*
Founding Partner
Fallon London

**Neil Dawson**
*Deputy Convenor of Judges*
Chairman
Hurrell & Dawson

## STAGE 1: INDUSTRY SPECIALISTS

**John Billett**
Managing Director
Billetts

**Hugh Burkitt**
Chief Executive
The Marketing Society

**Richard Cook**
Managing Director
ACNielsen Analytic Consulting, Europe

**Roddy Glen**
Consultant

**Melanie Howard**
Co-Founder and Director
Future Foundation

**Vanella Jackson**
Chief Executive
Hall & Partners Europe

**John Philip Jones**
Professor of Marketing
Syracuse University

**Amanda Merron**
Partner
Willott Kingston Smith

**Dominic Mills**
Editorial Director
Haymarket Business Publications

**Guy Phillipson**
Chief Executive
Internet Advertising Bureau

**Andrew Sharp**
Director
PricewaterhouseCoopers

**Karl Weaver**
Director
Data2Decisions Limited

**Chris Wood**
Chairman
Corporate Edge

## STAGE 2: CLIENT JURY

**Sir Paul Judge**
*Chairman of Judges*
Chairman of the Marketing Standards Setting Board

**Tess Alps**
Chief Executive
Thinkbox

**Tim Evans**
Director of Customer Insight
BT

**Matthew Howe**
Senior Vice President
Chief Support Officer
McDonald's Restaurants UK

**Alexandra Lewis**
Marketing Director
Sky Networks

**Alison Littley**
Former Global Marketing Procurement
Director
Diageo

**Greg Nugent**
Marketing Director
Eurostar

**Marc Sands**
Marketing Director
*The Guardian*

**Mark Sherrington**
Former Group Marketing Director
SABMiller

**Mike Short**
Vice President, Research and
Development, $O_2$

**Robin Woolcock**
Managing Director
Volkswagen Group UK

# Introduction

Welcome to what we hope loyal readers will agree is a new, improved *Advertising Works*. 'New' because it is the book of record of the freshly minted 2006 Awards. 'Improved', we humbly submit, by trading a little extraneous detail for three overarching perspectives on the winning papers and two best practice guides. By including these – rather than just housing the case studies, good as they are – we are hopeful that this volume might find custom beyond the zealots and prove more complementary to the online larder at WARC.com, already raided by those most eager to read this year's winners.

The IPA Effectiveness Awards enjoy unrivalled currency and boast a rich history. That history has been well documented elsewhere, by this author and others,[1] and we do not intend to dwell on it here, except for a short 2006 'report card' on the initial objectives set at the Awards' birth in 1980. The patient's current health and future prospects are – in this instance – more important than its medical history: it is mission-critical that the Awards at least keep pace with and, at best, set the pace for, the industry they both feed from and feed.

Entry numbers were marginally up this year, which is good, and we received more joint entries than ever, which suggests the industry may be working – or least evaluating its efforts – in a more joined-up way. Also good.

Our crop of winners have used 'old media', new media and often both. If they have dented the fatuous opposition that has been set up between the two, then they have performed a heroic service.

Long-term campaigns and payback also feature, a critical foil to the short-term sales spikes around which effectiveness awards typically coalesce. (Most of what we do as an industry is dedicated to patiently building brands that trade at a premium and command long-term competitive advantage.)

All good.

Less rosily, the Awards remain skewed to creative agencies rather than media agencies, and to domestic UK rather than multi-market campaigns – both are a potentially misleading 'cut' of the value-adding business at large. We might also have expected a more pronounced digital hue to our shortlist, given the seismic changes in the media landscape around us. These issues – and others – form the ongoing 'to do list' for the IPA and future Convenors.

How, then, does the 2006 report card read?

Against a backdrop of client scepticism and agency complacency, the Awards set out at launch to demonstrate that advertising could be proven to work against hard financial criteria and, over time, 'to inculcate ever-improving professional standards' in matters of evaluation and effectiveness.

The Awards have irrefutably delivered against the first of these objectives: the IPA dataBANK now boasts well over 1000 case histories for categories ranging from potatoes to diamonds, for tasks that range from launch to rescue, and over timelines both short and long.

The jury is out, however, on whether the Awards have truly forged an effectiveness culture across the industry. While we have made giant strides in evaluation since the 70s, the revolution is not complete. It seems to me that more time than ever is being spent on front-end inspiration, and less time than ever on back-end evaluation. The Awards have arguably created not so much an effectiveness culture across the industry as an effectiveness awards culture across most, but by no means all, agencies.

It may be, of course, that the 'stretch' objective is simply too audacious, or that the influence of the Awards has been swamped over time by other effects, or even that evaluation is an outmoded concept, as some intellectually responsible commentators argue. But there is also something of the 'law of unintended consequences' about the current state of affairs; a sense, perhaps, in these margin-thin and resource-starved times, that the odd IPA Award confers a sufficient veneer of effectiveness to render unnecessary any root-and-branch commitment to evaluation. Maybe clients – as recent work conducted by the IPA's Value of Advertising Group suggests – now covet a 'responsibility culture' rather than an 'effectiveness' culture from their agencies, secure in the knowledge that they are busy evaluating their campaigns and look to their agencies for ideas above all else.

So what will you find in the pages that follow? No less than 22 inspiring case studies, all recognised for their demonstrations of effectiveness, but each boasting media thinking strategies and creative ideas that we might also learn from.

The Grand Prix and Golds bask in obvious glory, and are reprinted in full here. In the interests of space we have collapsed down to 2000 words each our Silver Award winners, a deep bench that itself comprises various gems: read Felix on consistency; Dero for a contrary take on international marketing; and Monopoly for a seamless example of the 'new creative idea'. Sadly, space dictates that our Bronze winners cannot be reproduced here; all, however, are available at WARC.com. Jamie's School Dinners, Cathedral City and Sony Ericsson especially reward the download.

Beyond the papers themselves, we are keen to table any general themes arising and fast-track any matters for debate provoked by our source material. We have, therefore, included for the first time three bespoke overviews – each attempts to draw general learnings from the papers: I draw creative pointers from this year's winners; Neil Dawson offers up a hymn to 'fresh thinking'; and Iain Jacob calls out the potentially tectonic shift in media practice from 'optimised message distribution' to an emergent model where the consumer does the work.

All are caveated not just by their inevitable subjectivity, but by the overarching requirement for marketers to learn from, but not mimic, competitors and precedent. You may well disagree with the conclusions that Neil, Iain and I have reached; if you do so, they have still done their job.

On a more practical level, this book also introduces two 'modules' dedicated to specific aspects of evaluation where our industry can make further advances. We are truly grateful to Andrew Sharp of PricewaterhouseCoopers and John Philip Jones of Syracuse University, for going above and beyond the already burdensome task of judging to propose best practice on matters of payback and multi-market evaluation respectively. Both pieces are intended to provide a thorough 'route map' for authors, new and old. They are, if you like, an insurance policy against the Awards defaulting to a purely domestic competition and/or one that features well-intentioned but potentially naïve return on investment calculations.

Andrew and John are not alone in over-delivering beyond their original remit. Marc Sands, Marketing Director of the *Guardian*, has generously volunteered a perspective from the judging room that touches not just on the onerousness of the judges' task, but also on the quality of their discussions.

Beyond the submissions themselves, it is the quality of the IPA's judges (not the wordcount, and not the heritage) that truly sustains the Awards' reputation as the global effectiveness gold standard. Remember that our winners have first cleared the industry judging hurdle, where a further 30 or so papers were filtered out before submitting to client scrutiny. Our judges each read between 20 and 30 submissions of some 4,000 words each, and are asked to do so in 'active sceptic' mode. The debates that arise on judging day are a tribute to the seriousness with which they undertake their duty. Most, if not all, decry the wordcount; most, if not all, had read every word. (I shall leave it to others to decide whether we should continue to exploit this goodwill and intellectual curiosity; the ease with which our Silvers were edited suggests to me that shorter papers have much to recommend them.)

Grateful as we are to our judges, the true heroes of this book are the individuals who burnt the midnight oil and the client companies who cooperated. Without such energetic authors and such enlightened clients, these Awards would, quite simply, not exist. And our industry, however broadly you wish to define it, would be a less robust place without them.

My thanks go to Sir Paul Judge, who chaired the client judging with aplomb; to my deputy Convenor, Neil Dawson, whose contribution so outstripped the job spec; and to my PA, Lara, for apparently limitless patience.

Read on, then pass it on.

Laurence Green
Convenor of Judges 2006

---

1   Green, L. (2005). 'Twenty-five years of Advertising Works', *Advertising Works And How – Winning communications strategies for business*. Henley-on-Thames: WARC.

# SECTION 1

# Prize winners

# List of prize winners

**GRAND PRIX**

*RKCR/Y&R* for Marks & Spencer

**GOLD AWARDS**

*DDB London* and *MediaCom* for Volkswagen Golf

*Leo Burnett* for Naturella (Procter & Gamble)

*Proximity London* for TV Licensing (BBC)

*RKCR/Y&R* for Marks & Spencer

*RKCR/Y&R* for Vehicle Crime Prevention (The Home Office)

*Vallance Carruthers Coleman Priest, ZenithOptimedia Group, Archibald Ingall Stretton* and *Lambie-Nairn* for $O_2$

**SILVER AWARDS**

*Abbott Mead Vickers.BBDO* for Nicorette (Pfizer)

*Abbott Mead Vickers.BBDO* and *ROI Consulting* for The Famous Grouse (The Edrington Group)

*Bartle Bogle Hegarty* for Dero (Unilever)

*Burkitt DDB* for Bakers Complete (Nestlé Purina Petcare)

*DDB London* for Felix (Nestlé Purina)

*DDB London* and *MediaCom* for Kwik-Fit

*DDB London* for Teacher Recruitment (Training and Development Agency for Schools)

*DDB London* and *Tribal DDB* for Monopoly Here & Now (Hasbro)

*DDB London* for Tropicana Pure Premium (PepsiCo)

*Delaney Lund Knox Warren & Partners* for Branston Baked Beans (Premier Foods)

*Leo Burnett* for Daz (Procter & Gamble)

*Lowe* for British Heart Foundation – Anti Smoking

*Miles Calcraft Briginshaw Duffy* for Travelocity.co.uk

*RKCR/Y&R* for Actimel (Danone)

*RKCR/Y&R* for Virgin Trains

*Tribal DDB* and *DDB London* for Volkswagen Golf GTI Mk5

## BRONZE AWARDS

*Limitations of space preclude the full publication of the Bronze Award-winning papers. These case studies can be accessed via* www.warc.com

Bartle Bogle Hegarty for Sony Ericsson
*K750i – Take your best shot with a phone/W800i – The soundtrack to your life*
By Martin Smith, Bartle Bogle Hegarty
Contributing authors: Heather Alderson, Bartle Bogle Hegarty and Gavin Bell, Dare Digital

DDB London for More4 (Channel 4 Television Corporation)
*The new adult entertainment channel from Channel 4*
By Dan Ng, DDB London and Julia Wood, DDB Matrix
Contributing authors: Les Binet, DDB Matrix; Sarah Carter, DDB London, and Jonny Mackay, OMD UK

Grey London for Cathedral City (Dairy Crest Group)
*See it, want it*
By Simon White, Grey London

Grey London for Manchester City
*This is Our City*
By John Lowery, Grey London

Grey London for Women's Aid
*Valentine's Day*
By Emma Batho, Grey London
Contributing author: Joanna Bamford, Planning Consultant

Michaelides & Bednash for Jamie's School Dinners
(Channel 4 Television Corporation)
*An integrated campaign which triggered the start of a food revolution*
By Jason Gonsalves, Michaelides & Bednash; Cameron Saunders, Channel 4,
and Joanna Bamford, Planning Consultant
Contributing authors: Rufus Radcliffe and Nick Stringer, Channel 4

Miles Calcraft Briginshaw Duffy for Self Assessment
(HM Revenue & Customs/COI)
*How a change in advertising direction proved that tax doesn't have to be taxing*
By Andy Nairn, Miles Calcraft Briginshaw Duffy

Vallance Carruthers Coleman Priest and Media Planning Group for ING Direct
*UK launch: taking the savings market by storm*
By Dale Gall, Vallance Carruthers Coleman Priest and Martin Stokes, Media
Planning Group
Contributing authors: Victoria Lynch, Vallance Carruthers Coleman Priest;
John Perella, Media Planning Group, and Louise Cook, Holmes & Cook

# Special prizes

**EFFECTIVENESS AGENCY OF THE YEAR**
*DDB London*

**BEST DEDICATION TO EFFECTIVENESS**
Volkswagen UK

**BEST DIGITAL**
*Tribal DDB* and *DDB London* for Volkswagen Golf GTI Mk5

**BEST IDEA**
*Abbott Mead Vickers.BBDO* for Nicorette (Pfizer)

**BEST INTEGRATION**
*Proximity London* for TV Licensing (BBC)

**BEST MEDIA**
*RKCR/Y&R* for Vehicle Crime Prevention (The Home Office)

**BEST MULTI-MARKET**
*Leo Burnett* for Naturella (Procter & Gamble)

**BEST NEW AGENCY (JOHN BARTLE AWARD)**
*Michaelides & Bednash*

**BEST NEW CLIENT**
Channel 4 Television Corporation

**BEST NEW LEARNING (CHARLES CHANNON AWARD)**
*Michaelides & Bednash* for Jamie's School Dinners (Channel 4 Television Corporation)

**BEST READ**
*DDB London* for Felix (Nestlé Purina)

**BEST SMALL BUDGET**
*DDB London* and *Tribal DDB* for Monopoly Here & Now (Hasbro UK)

# Campaign images

**Grand Prix: Marks & Spencer**

The advertising tag-line 'Not Just Food, M&S Food' was coupled with creative executions that emphasised the quality of the product

**Grand Prix: Marks & Spencer**

The 'Your M&S' campaign – which featured figureheads including Twiggy – demonstrated a new confidence and commitment to change in Womenswear

**Gold: Naturella**

Naturella broke from the scientific conventions of the feminine hygiene category, creating a feminine 'world of nature'

## Gold: O$_2$

O$_2$'s 'A World That Revolves Around You' campaign communicated the importance of its existing customers – as demonstrated by this press ad

**Gold: TV Licensing**

By the distinctive use of 'anti-humour', TV Licensing was able to communicate to students just how important it is to buy a licence while at university

**Gold: Vehicle Crime Prevention**

The campaign for Vehicle Crime Prevention used traditional and unusual media – such as this petrol pump nozzle – to communicate its message

**Gold: Volkswagen Golf**

Three TV campaigns for the Volkswagen Golf – 'Changes' (1987), 'Divorce' (1993) and '30 Years in the Making' (2004) – all based around the proposition that whatever else happens in life, you can always rely on your Golf

**Silver: Actimel**

An example of the 'Actimel Challenge', which promised customers their money back if they didn't feel the benefits of drinking Actimel in just two weeks

**Silver: Bakers Complete**

Bakers Complete based its campaign around the notion that 'real dogs would choose Bakers if they could' – as demonstrated in this television commercial, entitled 'TV Dinners'

**Silver: Branston Baked Beans**

The results of the 'Great British Bean Poll' showed that consumers preferred the taste of Branston Beans to the competition, as publicised in this press ad

**Silver: British Heart Foundation – Anti Smoking**

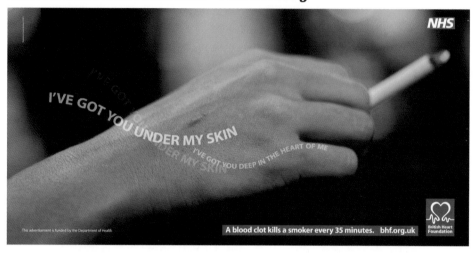

The British Heart Foundation used the song 'I've Got You Under My Skin' alongside images of potentially fatal blood clots to get its anti-smoking message across

**Silver: Daz**

By producing its own soap opera, 'Cleaner Close' – supported on TV, online and in print – Daz was able to reconnect with its target audience

**Silver: Dero**

An outdoor poster showing how Dero translated Surf's highly successful '99 stains' campaign to suit the Romanian market

**Silver: Felix**

Despite facing a number of fresh challenges, Felix kept faith in its long-running and well-loved campaign – typified in this TV ad – with highly positive results

**Silver: Kwik-Fit**

By addressing motorists' concerns rather than focusing on price, Kwik-Fit's 'Recommendations' TV campaign spoke to a new, untapped target audience

## Silver: Monopoly Here & Now

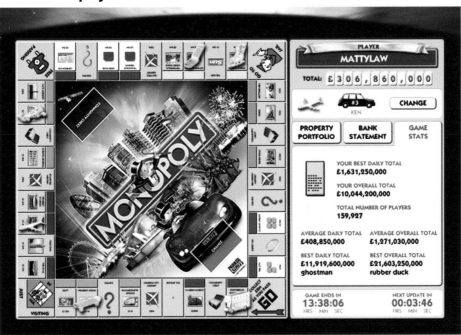

The unique online campaign for Monopoly Here & Now resulted in considerable word of mouth about the game, and boosted sales

**Silver: Nicorette**

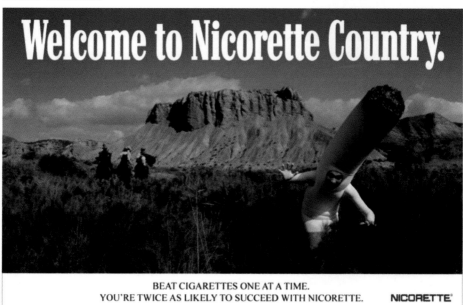

Nicorette's 'Cravings Man' creative focused on helping smokers beat cigarettes one by one, and helped reposition the product as a consumer brand

## Silver: Teacher Recruitment

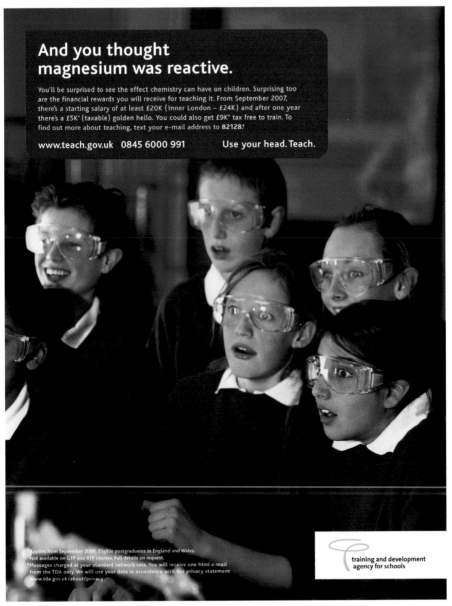

This press ad for the Teacher Recruitment campaign is just one example of how thousands of graduates were driven to enquire about becoming a teacher

**Silver: The Famous Grouse**

THE FAMOUS GROUSE MALT. MAKE AN ENTRANCE.

By producing a brand-based advertising campaign when other leading players were retreating, The Famous Grouse was able to buck the trend in the declining whisky market

**Silver: Travelocity.co.uk**

Alan Whicker was the face of Travelocity.co.uk's 'Hello World' campaign, which aimed to appeal to travel 'aficionados' through a varied media mix

**Silver: Tropicana**

Based on the insight that Tropicana is the most popular grocery brand in New York, this TV campaign successfully fused music and imagery to drive sales

**Silver: Virgin Trains**

Virgin Trains changed commuter behaviour via both emotional and rational appeals, the latter demonstrated by this execution for the back of a lorry

**Silver: Volkswagen Golf GTI Mk5**

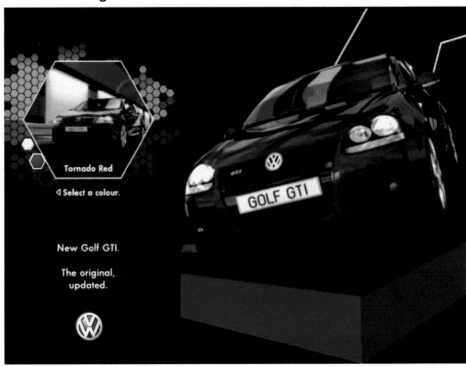

By adopting an innovative online approach, the campaign for the Volkswagen Golf GTI Mk5 made the new model a success even before it was launched

# Tales from the judging room

**By Marc Sands**
Marketing Director, *The Guardian*

Being locked in a room judging the IPA Effectiveness Awards was a real treat. Reading the volume of paperwork was a little less pleasurable, but had to be done. It is nothing like judging creative awards, in which you look at a poster, TV or radio ad and decide whether you like it or not. You actually have to do a lot of work that is based less on your opinion, and more on establishing the truth and separating it from simple assertion. Our leader, Laurence Green, was right when he advised us not to try to read all the case studies in a day, but to stagger them over a few weeks, never trying to read more than four on any given day.

There were real highlights, some lows, and much in between. The roll-call of honour hopefully reflects this. Over and above the detail of the Awards themselves, however, there were issues that left a lasting impression.

## Was it the product or was it the advertising?

To prove beyond reasonable doubt that advertising/marketing works is not that difficult. It is hard to refute the cause and effect that exists at the heart of marketing. We should not be surprised that advertising works, nor should we be apologetic. It is beyond this simple assertion that the problems surface. It is when you get to the what, the how and the why that the fur really begins to fly.

In numerous cases, we were unable to separate whether it was the product that was the hero or the marketing. In the cases where the product really excelled, it proved very hard to isolate the effect of the advertising in the drive to success. It seems fair to say that one can only prove its contribution beyond reasonable doubt in those mature categories in which all other aspects of competitive activity are essentially in a state of stalemate.

Many will argue that at the end of the day it doesn't really matter, that what is important is that the whole worked, and that our obsession with isolating the effect of the individual parts is irrelevant. Yet, and it is a big YET, if you work in one of the 'parts', you want to know that your 'part' has contributed. This understanding will ensure that there can be some carry-over to the next project, ideally in categories beyond the case in hand.

This issue reared its not very pretty head on a number of occasions. There were cases when the totality was clearly seen to work, but the value of the communication was not definitively proven. In the case of Jamie's School Dinners, there was an excellent and protracted debate about the true value generated by the advertising. It was a case of distinguishing and separating what one could describe as the 'intrinsic' value of the programme itself versus the 'added' value generated by the advertising. The case for 'added' value was largely unproven. Does it matter to Channel 4 or Jamie himself? Probably not.

In contrast to this, a number of the case studies clearly worked extremely hard to prove which bits of the marketing mix, from the product to the distribution to the communications, worked, and which bits genuinely added the greatest value. The TV Licensing and Tropicana cases, for example, succeeded in isolating the constituent parts whilst at the same time making a clear, well-argued case for the totality of the success.

Finally, the third camp was that in which the communication was clearly the difference between the campaign just working and the campaign working brilliantly. The judges recognised that Nicorette's highly memorable 'Cravings Man' was central to the memorability of the campaign, and therefore its likely success. One could say the same for the long-running Famous Grouse advertising, which is distinguished and rather brilliant. In a world of equal distribution and price points, it *must* have made the difference. The paper proved that it did, and the product continues to bask in sales success. It would be remiss not to mention the Felix case study in the same breath: a brilliant creative communication that has made the difference.

In summary, the challenge for future authors is to continue the drive towards isolating individual effects in the mix without retreating to the old siloed days.

## What value creativity?

The intangible issue of the explicit value of creativity does not yet feature fully in these Awards. It should. The world is not a rational place, and behind the numbers and correlation coefficients, the success (or not) of many of the case studies was underpinned by an element of true creativity somewhere in the value chain. It may have been in the sphere of consumer insight, media strategy or creative execution. Understanding and appreciating this is, surprisingly, not always well represented in the process. I can give no solutions as to how it should be achieved, but somehow a metric needs to be delivered that recognises the 'magic dust' that is at the heart of many marketing and advertising campaigns.

Many of the campaigns receiving awards are associated with an element of creativity that shines through when reading the case studies, but an association is not sufficient to fulfil the burden of proof; it needs to be a causal relationship. If we could understand this relationship, we would be in a position to ascertain not only that advertising works, but also exactly *why* it works.

I think we are unlikely to ever resolve this dilemma. It is no different to why some books, works of art, types of music, etc., become either critical or commercial successes, while others remain unknown. We may be getting close to the magic formula on the quantitative side of our industry, but on the softer qualitative aspects we remain some distance from exceptional predictive capability.

A number of the case studies illustrated this point, as the excellence of some of them hinged on a truly memorable piece of creativity. Quite how that translates into a success story is always the $64,000 question. But there is clearly, at worst, a correlation and, at best, a causal relationship between creativity that intrudes and is memorable and sales success.

The alternative to a greater understanding of the 'magic dust' of creativity and its contribution to the bottom line is an apocalyptic vision of a beige marketing hell, characterised by white, perfect-toothed families, with perfect hair, starring in dubbed pan-European advertising campaigns.

## A rallying cry for the industry

I am in the fortunate position of having entered the Awards and been invited to be a judge (in different years, I hasten to add), and have found both sides of the fence to be of immense value. The marketing industry at large should be more supportive of these Awards. There were insufficient entries from what one might term the larger, more prestigious marketing organisations. Their entries would lend both credibility and learning to the body of knowledge that has already been accumulated.

As our industry continues to make sense of the seismic changes we are currently confronting, the engagement of the widest audience will benefit us all.

*Case studies referred to, but not featured, can be accessed via www.WARC.com.*

# New learning

# Chapter 1

# The creative multiplier

**By Laurence Green**
Founding Partner, Fallon London

The advertising landscape of the last few years has been dominated by voices and trends from beyond creative shores: at first by the concept of media neutrality, and more recently by the siren call of new media. You could easily be forgiven for concluding that the creative content of communication no longer matters, that successful campaigning pivots solely on smart channel selection and the exploitation of the myriad opportunities afforded not just by the web, but by digital and interactive technologies more broadly.

Dare I say it as one of their number, but that would be a depressing conclusion for creative agencies. And, much more importantly, for the consumer, on whose goodwill we will become ever more reliant in the new world order. It would also be a conclusion much at odds with the evidence around us, not least in the pages of this book and its forebears.

## A brief history of creativity and effectiveness

The IPA Effectiveness Awards have long been a bellwether of both effective communication per se and the specific contribution to results of the creative imagination. Over the years, they have provided ongoing succour to the creative community and the creatively minded client; effectiveness gongs have been won by such critically acclaimed advertisers as Stella Artois, Levi's and, more recently, Honda.

Over three decades the IPA has harvested and published hundreds of case studies that demonstrate not just the power of communications but the superlative effects or greater efficiency of creative communication. All provide distant echoes of John Caples' observation, as long ago as 1932, that 'I have seen one mail order advertisement actually sell not twice as much, not three times as much, but 19 and a half times as much merchandise as another ad for the same product.'[1]

In their own way, then, the Awards have arguably done as much as any agency, campaign or individual to render fatuous the notion that creativity and effectiveness are mutually exclusive.

On occasion, however, the IPA Awards have also inflamed relations between the 'effective' and 'creative' camps by honouring allegedly 'un-creative' campaigns, most famously in the case of BT's 'It's Good To Talk' campaign (Grand Prix winner in 1998). These moments of apparent conflict seem to have sprung historically from one of two quarters – a misunderstanding of the Awards' remit and/or differing perspectives on what we mean when we use the word 'creative'.

## The Awards' remit

The IPA Effectiveness Awards unashamedly exist to reward and lionise our industry's *best demonstrations of effectiveness*. They were conceived to influence the client boardroom and encourage accountability in agencies – roles they still perform almost 30 years on. Judges are instructed to reach verdicts according to each paper's exploration of effectiveness, not each campaign's creative credentials. They have the opportunity to view all relevant creative materials, but are not obliged to do so.

This unswerving dedication to proof of *commercial* effectiveness makes the IPA Effectiveness Awards not only highly distinctive from other awards schemes – plenty of which exist purely to judge creative merit – but also superior to other effectiveness competitions. Credible commercial effectiveness, and this alone, is the benchmark for the IPA judges' decisions.

The Awards are, therefore, a good barometer of the industry's effectiveness state of play but, necessarily, a less good one, except by inference, of the industry's creative state of play. Thus caveated, I intend to infer away ... it would seem churlish not to interrogate the industry's most-heralded effectiveness stories for creative clues.

## What do we mean when we talk about creativity?

Definitions of creativity are as elusive as the quality itself. It is, on occasion, used as a dirty word. This is despite convincing commentary from many beyond our own industry proposing creativity as an essential ingredient of successful brands and businesses in the modern era: an oversupplied 'age of abundance', where needs are broadly met, and only wants remain for marketers to squabble over.[2]

It is probably fair to say, however, that for too long agency creative departments have held a monopoly on the word 'creative', despite the fact that we have long understood that creativity exercised in strategy and media can make a substantial, even definitive, contribution to outcomes. (I would contend that 'It's Good To Talk', for example, advanced from a highly creative *strategy*, which itself accounted for much of its cultural and commercial power.)

## So what can we learn creatively?

This year's shortlist features campaigns that conform to both the broad and narrow definitions of creativity. Accelerated by the popularisation of the internet – and by a growing general awareness of opportunities beyond traditional media – a new breed of creative idea is emerging that blurs the lines of strategy, media and creative. These 'superideas' are less obviously the sole work of the creative department: indeed, they could often be as easily described as media ideas and, at the very least, demand billing as channel-inspired creative ideas.

The majority of cases, however – including the campaign credited by our judges with this year's 'Best Idea' – are more traditional campaign vehicles, with creative ideas and executions still largely divisible from the strategy (and media) that inspired them.

In looking at both camps – and being fully aware that my distinction is drawn not just crudely but also subjectively – I will attempt to draw out some helpful learnings for tomorrow's campaign authors from this year's batch of papers.

It is an exercise that has been approached and should be consumed with caution. My 'sample size' is, of course, a mere 30 campaigns, skewed towards agencies and brands with the sensibility and resources to make compelling effectiveness cases. More generally, it's axiomatic that creativity would be muzzled and its effects muted if we all simply followed the paths shown to us by others.

What, then, do successful creative ideas and executions look like at the beginning of the twenty-first century? What, if any, are the creative rules as channels morph around us?

## The new creative idea

As we would expect, the emergence of new media has inspired and enabled new forms of creative idea. For the purposes of this article, let's define the 'new creative idea' as an idea that lives at least partially beyond 'traditional broadcast', and leverages the fresh creative possibilities afforded chiefly by the web and, to a lesser extent, other 'ambient' new media.

Though many of our winning campaigns have grafted elements of digital and ambient media onto otherwise traditional campaigns, several papers deserve special mention as exemplars of 'the new creative idea':

- Volkswagen's digital pre-launch of the GTI Mk5 Golf is a strategic, creative and commercial triumph both in its own right and as a foundation stone for the Golf's later launch 'proper'.
- Channel 4 and its agencies exploited not just the web but the broader media fabric to turn the *Jamie's School Dinners* TV series into nothing short of a political movement.
- Sony Ericsson challenged category convention by creating a campaign framework that demanded and rewarded consumer participation across a number of platforms.
- Monopoly Here & Now, meanwhile, deserves special mention as the idea that is probably most elusive to those who prefer their campaign development siloed.

Ideas, all, that are creative in the round, not the sole province of the creative department.

### The 'traditional' model

What, though, of the winning campaigns that I have dubbed 'traditional'? These are still in the majority, after all. Are they just instances of solidly effective campaigning, or have they too been catalysed by creativity?

Let's start from the narrowest of creative perspectives: which of our winners this year has, separately, picked up a creative award? Volkswagen Golf, over the years, for sure; the British Heart Foundation and Travelocity.co.uk more recently. Enough, perhaps, to again disprove the notion that creativity and effectiveness are incompatible bedfellows. But not enough to support any contention that a creative award alone is some sort of 'leading indicator' of effectiveness.

A broader creative perspective than a simple 'awards count' is more helpful. Beyond the creativity brought to bear on their respective strategies and media, there is no denying that the success of campaigns such as Vehicle Crime Prevention, Tropicana, Felix and Virgin Trains hinges substantially on their creative delivery. Each has entirely laudable, and occasionally inspiring, strategies at its core; the consumer, of course, connects only with the idea and execution that each has later been clothed in.

Provenance, for example, is a plausible enough 'premiumising' strategy for Tropicana; it is turbo-charged by the beautifully framed vignettes of New York, Dean Martin soundtrack and all.

Felix's insight that catfood advertising had been missing an element of mischief is one thing; the crudely animated but loveable black and white character is what truly won the consumer's heart, and gave the campaign legs.

Plenty of train operators have tried to engage the British public emotionally rather than rationally; few have done so with the panache of Virgin. And so on.

These are brands transformed by communication – as judged by the Awards – and whose strategies have been transformed – as judged by me – from statements of intent to stuff that actually engages, touches and moves the consumer. Each boasts at best an idea, and at least an execution, that the respective agencies have 'layered' onto the product or service in question to create disproportionately favourable marketplace results.

## The agency vanishes

More controversially, perhaps – but no less admirably – the 2006 crop of winners suggests that, on occasion at least, the task of the creative agency is not necessarily to layer new meaning on top of a product or service, but rather to provide the most agreeable frame for products or services that are themselves noteworthy.

From M&S to O$_2$, Jamie's School Dinners to ING, there is compelling evidence that it is sometimes the duty of the creative agency to 'get out of the way' and present the product as simply, attractively and consistently as possible.

At risk of overstating the point, M&S's chocolate pudding, O$_2$'s various product initiatives, the *Jamie's School Dinners* programme, and ING's no-strings high-interest rate are arguably the true creative ideas here, rather than the creative agency's layer of invention. (This is not to diminish the contribution of the creative agencies involved. The discipline and humility required to put 'client' rather than agency creative idea centre stage is admirable.)

Certainly, this emerging brand of product-centric communication chimes with the honesty and transparency that the twenty-first century consumer is clamouring for, and contrasts with previous generations of campaigns where – viewed from the creative village – the agency has added most value.

A tension is immediately apparent for advertisers: whether to hyperbolise or otherwise reframe product or service claims or, more directly, merely to 'package attractively' those same claims. The answer hinges not just on specific circumstances, but now also on a judgement call as to what sorts of commercial messaging will be consumed and passed on by consumers in the future.

## To be (disruptive), or not to be?

Alongside this, another creative debate rages: whether to embrace creative disruption or cherish campaign consistency? This year's winning papers take contrasting positions.

Advertisers like Volkswagen enjoy superior returns by adhering to the principle of consistency, trading short-term fashion for long-term certainties and goodwill. Their work is no less engaging and no less fresh as a result. Others – especially public sector players, whose objectives are rarely well served by inertia – choose disruption.

Some even manage to embrace both philosophies. The Felix paper, for instance, quite persuasively makes the case for campaign continuity over the long haul … albeit for a campaign given initial velocity by its disruptive approach to the category.

## Some less equivocal pointers

Yet again, the IPA Effectiveness Award winners underscore the growing sense that the most effective communication now works not just against the traditional consumer audience, but also against a non-consumer audience (be it staff, stakeholders or the City); and is integrated, at least strategically and at best creatively, as a matter of course.

As we continue to migrate from product to service economy – and as consumers increasingly interrogate the soul of a company – the very best communications inform not just consumer perceptions, but also company delivery. The campaigns for Virgin Trains and Manchester City seem to me to have disproportionately built pride within the organisation, and not just interest beyond.

The creative work for M&S, The Famous Grouse and ING, meanwhile, provides further evidence that tight coordination of activity and execution creates a campaign whose whole is greater than the sum of its parts.

## Celebrity and notoriety

The Awards also remind us that these old creative stalwarts are still alive and well. Whether it's Alan Whicker or Ian Wright, Jamie or Twiggy, or even New York, a carefully judged celebrity endorsement is proven yet again to be a commercially astute investment on the part of the respective advertisers, endorsing and haloing the brands involved.

At the other end of the spectrum a dash of notoriety can still help cut-through and payback, as best demonstrated this year by More 4's 'adult entertainment' launch ruse.

It seems saints and sinners alike can act as a kind of creative multiplier.

## In summary

What, then, is the apparent creative mandate proposed by the 2006 IPA Effectiveness Awards?

■ Embrace creativity in the round. Properly trained – and whether fashioned into an 'old' or 'new' creative idea – it is the ally, not the enemy, of those who chase effectiveness.

■ Reach out for ideas where the join between strategy, media and creative is invisible.

■ Think about whether you have intrinsically interesting product or service information or – more typically – require the transforming qualities of a creative idea 'proper'. Neither course commends itself irrespective of your specific situation.

■ Determine whether you are best served by disrupting your category and position, or by patiently trading off/exploiting existing perceptions and equities. Again, neither course commends itself 'a priori'.

■ Embrace the opinions of – and effects against – internal (and other) audiences; partly because this is a legitimate deployment of communications in its own right, and partly because it increases both the resonance of your promise to consumers and the odds that your promise will be kept.

■ In a fragmenting world – and one where the consumer is investigative not passive – pursue integration and consistency across media and over time, regardless of whether your brand stance is disruptive or continuous.

More generally, and for all the competitive claims of strategic and media initiatives, do not underestimate the transformational power of the creative content of your communication. The planner sees provenance, the consumer sees New York. By this standard, the living room, rather than the boardroom, remains the best frame of reference as you develop communications.

As we look to the future – to the era of pull rather than push, of engagement rather than interruption, of consumers as media and not just audience – it seems entirely plausible that the very best creative work, old or new, will enjoy disproportionate fame and capture disproportionate value for the advertiser and agency involved.

To the creative victor, still, the spoils?

## Notes

1. Caples, J. (1932) *Tested Advertising Methods: How to Profit by Removing Guesswork.* New York: Harper.
2. Pink, D.H. (2005) *A Whole New Mind: Moving from the Information Age to the Conceptual Age.* New York: Riverhead Books.

*Case studies referred to, but not featured, can be accessed via www.WARC.com.*

# Chapter 2

# The media revolution will be televised (and broadcast on the internet, mobile ...)

**By Iain Jacob**
CEO, Starcom MediaVest Group EMEA

There can be little doubt that we are living in revolutionary times. On the one hand, we have never had more control over the information that we consume. Technology-empowered and short on attention, we are enjoying our new-found freedom to edit our media world and act as citizen journalists.

Likewise, the fundamental shift in our clients' commercial environments is re-framing the way we work. Scale and global orientation have become a pre-requisite. Technology and product development life cycles have made differen-tiation a rare asset. The relentless drive to reduce costs in all aspects of the supply chain has focused organisations' attention on immediate and measurable returns from their marketing departments.

Every revolution starts with tension, every revolution is uncomfortable, but ultimately revolutions usually create positive transformations:

> *When consumers [and clients] apply pressure on an industry, whether it's retail or banking, cars or computers [or advertising], it invariably produces a surge of innovation that increases productivity, reduces prices, improves quality and increases choice.*

Professor RE Herzlinger, Harvard Business School

While they are my words in brackets, it is clear that our industry is in a state of positive transition.

Back in our day-to-day world, dominated by hyperbole, where everybody lays claim to having the answers to these emergent challenges, determining real progress in this revolution is tough. Friedrich Engels, during other revolutionary times, said: 'An ounce of action is worth a ton of theory.' Therein lies the value of

11

the IPA Effectiveness Awards. They are, without a doubt, the clearest empirical measure of our collective progress in responding to the new communications challenges facing marketers. In a judging environment largely devoid of hyperbole and where post-rationalisation is easy to spot, they measure real action and consumer reaction. They are the toughest and best measure.

They are a particularly acute measure of real progress in our industry's media thinking and delivery as so much of today's revolution is being fermented by the fundamental shifts in how consumers take on board (or avoid) clients' messages.

In short, these papers both tell us a story of our progress in media and, more importantly, tell us a story of how we need to progress if we are to have any claim to being true strategic partners to our clients. So, how are we doing?

## Bring on the revolution

The consumer is leading this revolution, so I have used the thinking of two exceptional consumer thinkers as my guide in reviewing progress:

> *Everything we've done since we started Wal-Mart has been devoted to this idea that the consumer is our boss.*
>
> Sam Walton, Founder and Chairman, Wal-Mart Stores

> *Strategy is about the basic value you're trying to deliver to customers, and about which customers you're trying to serve.*
>
> Professor Michael Porter, Harvard Business School

We have never had a greater opportunity to better address and serve a brand's most valuable consumers through our use of media and the new technologies available to us. The two questions I have reviewed the papers against are how well does the media thinking genuinely place consumers at the centre, as the boss, and how well does it really serve their needs, rather than simply exposing messaging to a chosen target?

## Two clear schools have emerged

Viewing the IPA Effectiveness Awards through a media lens, there really are two types of entry. No entry is 100% mutually exclusive, but they all fall into one camp or the other. Neither is one approach necessarily 'right' and the other 'wrong'. From a commercial perspective, both routes have delivered results. However, the two approaches come at media from a totally different premise, and I strongly suspect that over the next few years one will emerge as decisively more effective than the other.

## Type 1: the optimal distribution of messaging

The first type of entry is based on using the modern media environment to really optimise the 'distribution of messaging'. These entries have created their media strategies by placing the brand/service message at the centre of their thinking, and working out from this to understand the most appropriate and structured approach to contact their chosen consumer. As such, it will be no surprise to you to hear that this approach was taken by the vast majority of entries.

That said, the level of sophistication and creativity deployed with this approach by the strongest entries truly differentiated them from the norm. The strongest papers showed state-of-the-art analysis and magnificent creativity in using their chosen environments to create an impact. They also clearly highlighted the contribution of individual channels to the end commercial result.

RKCR/Y&R and Mediaedge:cia's campaign for car crime prevention was a perfect example of the success of such an approach. With a clear understanding of the role of individual media in initially 'motivating' people around the problem of car crime, and then constantly 'reminding' them at the point of highest threat, they created a powerful framework of activity around their car driving audience. Their creative use of ambient media to drive (excuse the pun) the message home at the most relevant time, and in the most relevant creative way, was exceptional – car park barriers, parking meters, service station toilets, pump nozzles – most of them media that simply were not available ten years ago.

In a similar way, VCCP & MPG made ING's savings account advertising hard to avoid if you were a potential saver. They worked hard to be the dominant, visible savings brand, while as a direct advertiser still maintaining market-leading cost-per-response and acquisition levels. No mean feat, as any experienced financial marketer would tell you. Whether it involved the tagging of their website visitors to enable future targeting or the domination of the financial 'best buy' tables in the press, they relentlessly pursued the potential saver.

These are strong examples with a record of success.

Throughout the entries in this 'distribution of messaging' category, there were some clear unifying themes. They have all worked from the brand/service out. These are largely brands with a clear idea of what they are going to say, and they use every relevant avenue that they can afford to say it.

However, while the vast majority of entries had a powerful human insight about their chosen consumers and what the brand should say about itself, this insight was often lost in the creation of the media plan. Too often, the plans leant heavily on improving the efficiency of traditional models rather than building a specific media behaviour around an originally identified consumer truth.

These were brands on 'transmit'.

Integration was a common theme amongst the vast majority of cases. However, typically this meant the common use of a message across channels, rather than the identification of a core consumer insight from which all forms of communication content creation and channel thinking naturally fell.

## Type 2: breathing the air of the consumer

This second approach is currently a much rarer beast. These cases do not take a 'brand out' approach; they use retail, media, packaging and technology to actively draw their consumer into their brand proposition.

In fact, all of these case histories have made great use of the biggest, most effective medium available – that is, the consumers themselves. These entries didn't just reach consumers, their approach reached into consumers' worlds, creating active participation with the brand (and not just active participation with its communication – so often an approach labelled 'engagement', where the commercial value of the 'engagement' is rarely clear). In reality, these entries have really gone back to basics: they have created an approach that genuinely places the consumer at its heart, and that creates a programme of communication and active brand participation born out of a unifying human insight.

DDB and OMD reignited interest in a dated, but iconic game: Monopoly. Once they had identified the power of the passionate interest Londoners have in their city and combined this with the human desire to connect and play online, they were well on their way to creating a new phenomenon: Monopoly Live.

Not only was the campaign designed to actively involve people in the thrill of the game through the website and GPS tracking of the 'pieces' (taxis) around the 'real' Monopoly board of London; it placed the game's retail presence at the centre of its communication, in the form of a Hamleys window promotion. This was a powerful clicks-and-mortar approach that, most importantly, created a high volume of 'chat' online about the brand that was, I suspect, the most cost-effective means of communication within the whole programme.

In another example, Tribal DDB went back to the car-buying consumer to really understand how to bring them into the proposition and product detail of the new Golf GTI. Prior to the physical car launch, they created a virtual presence for the car by allowing customers to play with the design of their potential car online. Not only did this create heightened interest in the car, but it also generated a highly motivated group of pre-order customers. Again, this example rejected the conventional car purchase funnel, where the online presence is typically considered as a functional product information tool towards the end of the 'customer journey'. The approach used the flexibility of the medium to create an emotional bond with the car before it even hit the showroom – very smart.

These cases don't have to lay claim to being integrated because they so obviously are. The common theme is that you simply can't identify precisely where the idea came from; the idea is not advertising, media or direct led. In fact, the idea is not channel or discipline led in any way. Rather, the ideas are consumer led: they relate to a clear business model for the brand, and the idea is unified behind a core insight through the communication programme.

Is this approach restricted to brand categories that naturally create more consumer interest and involvement, such as cars or board games? I don't think so: the approach is applicable to any brand, even in the toughest, most competitive, commodity markets, as long as the brand's consumer story is clear. Consider the success (undocumented in these Awards) of Innocent Smoothies, and how it used every means available to involve its consumers in the brand, its formulation, and even its format. Packaging, PR, point of sale, distribution strategy and advertising have all been put to use in building the unifying brand story and to actively involve the consumer.

## So what are the lessons for the future?

Today, pretty much every company claims to put its consumers at the heart of its business. Every IPA Effectiveness paper has the roots of its approach in the consumer; you would expect nothing less.

But in the two approaches to media communication that I have described, there really is a fundamentally different approach.

The first, which creates an optimised approach to message distribution, acts on the consumer. The descriptions are of a controlled monologue where the consumer journey is something you attempt to manage. This may just have been possible in an internet-free world, where blogs hadn't been heard of and the idea that consumers might create their own advertising for brands would seem preposterous. It might just have been possible but, then again, I suspect it probably wasn't. It certainly isn't any more. Consumers have already taken control.

Of course, optimised message distribution still works today, and we are witnessing the best solutions of this type ever seen. They are the most professional, the most targeted, the most highly crafted. But just as with the cartwheel, the best ones were being created just before the demise of the horse and cart as a primary means of transport. Just as the car was to the horse, consumer control is to communications management.

However, the challenge of creating the second approach goes far beyond the creation of a more effective veneer of advertising content and media delivery. Success in this emergent world demands a genuine integration of the consumer into the brand and its communication, not merely the integration of messaging across channels. And while this may sound like motherhood and apple pie, too often the changing client world and fragmented marketing service infrastructure is simply not delivering this. That is a challenge for clients and their agencies alike.

AG Lafley's (CEO of Procter & Gamble) quote from the 75th anniversary edition of *Advertising Age* should be pinned above all our desks:

> It's a consumer revolution – a demanding but liberating shift. The rise of this powerful consumer boss marks one of the most important milestones in the history of branding.

For a step-change in success, way beyond the optimisation of efficiency, a single thread of powerful consumer insight has to run from product to brand to media communication.

## How might the IPA Effectiveness Awards themselves evolve in this environment?

The value of the IPA Effectiveness Awards is that they are rigorous in their review of what actions have been taken by a brand, and what reactions have been created amongst its consumers. The fact that they have done this over a period of years, with a largely consistent methodology, makes them an invaluable database.

That said, what is measured often determines how you behave. Along with the consumer revolution, there is a revolution in how we can go about understanding and measuring consumer behaviour and intention.

As we move from a demand economy to an on-demand economy, all electronic media channels are fast developing enhanced ways to interact with their consumers.

With broadband development, the implications of this go well beyond conventional internet response into areas such as mainstream TV. Advertisers will become increasingly less reliant on surrogate measures for effectiveness, such as tracked awareness, as they start to gain access to live consumer behaviour data. The powerful drug of conventional research tracking data has its benefits in the consistent collection of information over time. However, it will increasingly fail to deliver the rapid consumer knowledge now required to compete.

The availability and reduced cost of customer data are transforming how clients are managing their customers.

For the last ten years, this area has been dominated by direct clients and major retailers. While major retailers have become exceptionally smart at using customer data to develop merchandising, involve customers in new category launches and measure actual outcomes (Tesco Clubcard and Nectar being outstanding examples), many fmcg brands have been left using indirect research methodologies to inform them.

With the rise of digital media, the retailers' position as the 'gateway' to such data is increasingly under threat. Already the likes of Google and Yahoo! have access to much richer data than the retailers, based on live consumer behaviours and insights into how these behaviours can be influenced.

Currently, the IPA Effectiveness papers are still largely focused on long-established research techniques and forms of accountability that are increasingly showing signs of strain in our revolutionary world. Why deploy surrogate measures and modelling when you have access to actual consumer behavioural data to feed both insight and results measurement?

So there is much to learn about media from these papers: they tell us how to do things better, and a few tell us how to do better things.

As with any revolution, the volume of words about change currently outweighs the absolute actions. But the pace of change is accelerating, so to help keep you awake at night, I will leave you with a quote from Stefan Engeseth in his excellent book ONE – A Consumer Revolution for Business:

> Companies acting on yesterday's market expectations may not be here tomorrow. Global media and the internet transforms demand into on-demand.

Bring on the revolution!

---

*Case studies referred to, but not featured, can be accessed via www.WARC.com.*

# Chapter 3

# Fresh thinking works

**By Neil Dawson**
Founding Partner, Hurrell & Dawson

*However beautiful the strategy, you should occasionally look at the results.*

Winston Churchill

The world is full of interesting and original strategies, but how many of them are worthy of your attention? In the case of the 30 IPA Effectiveness Awards 2006 winners, the short answer is simple – they are all based on strategies that, allied to effective execution (both creative and media), led to demonstrable success. And the type of success they demonstrate is that most important to all business endeavour – a return on investment.

These success stories are themselves diverse.

- They showcase a fascinating spectrum of issues, from how to reverse the fortunes of a national institution in a negative PR tailspin, to how to launch a new media brand to an uninterested audience.
- They cover a wide range of categories. Contrary to popular perception, only eight of this year's winners are drawn from traditional fmcg. The rest include financial services, retail, social issues, media (brand and content), charities and 'entertainment' (if Manchester City supporters would describe their club as being in that business).
- They show an increasingly broad range of thinking about media and channels. Alongside the established communications models of TV and print, there are strategies defined and driven by the use of interactive, brand experience and content.

Though diverse in nature, they have a common ingredient: 'fresh thinking'. This is focused in different areas but can be loosely grouped into fresh thinking at the levels of marketing, product/service, creative execution and engagement.

## Fresh thinking about the marketing strategy

*What if we really put customers first?*

The O$_2$ case shows how talking to existing customers with the right messages and tone of voice proved a more effective acquisition strategy than the previous acquisition-driven approach. This ran counter to the value-destroying conventions of the mobile telephone category, which rewarded customers for switching in the quest for headline acquisition numbers.

The role of communications was to highlight a change in marketing approach, a real commitment to customers in the form of service improvements, and a shift in rewards so that loyalty, not defection, was rewarded. By broadcasting this commitment, $O_2$ was highly successful at attracting new customers as well as improving retention of existing customers.

### What if programming was the marketing idea?

Jamie's School Dinners demonstrates how the challenge of improving the nation's school dinners, a subject of national importance, was addressed via an integrated approach that fused television programming into the advertising and marketing mix. There is new thinking here about the role of programming within a campaign, and new learning about how such campaigns work. The 'rainbow coalition' of stakeholders involved is also noteworthy. It included strategists, TV production, website development, press and publicity, a creative agency, media buyer and partner (LEA and schools) – a portent for how strategies and ideas are increasingly being developed.

## Fresh thinking about products and services

### Creating a new magnifying lens for the organisation

The M&S paper highlights how communications changed the public face of a national institution perceived to be in decline. As the paper acknowledges, there were significant improvements to the M&S offering at the store and product level. Womenswear became more stylish, price points had been lowered, service improved and stores were beginning to be refurbished. While product quality and improvement was the inspiration for the campaign, communications played a critical role as a public declaration of confidence and commitment to change. 'Your M&S' had a catalytic role in changing the way the British public viewed M&S products, which has gone well beyond the particular products used as springboards.

### Staging a David and Goliath contest

Product change (albeit unwanted and imposed) drove the Branston Beans thinking. Owing to the loss of the HP licence following its sale to Heinz, Premier Foods was left facing a significant revenue hole. The ingrained nature of consumer behaviour and the dominance of Heinz led to a simple strategy of developing a superior product with the strongest brand name available – Branston. The communications idea, in the form of the Great British Bean Poll, encouraged the nation to try the two brands side by side. Helped by the natural appeal of an underdog, there could be only one winner.

## Fresh thinking about creative execution

*A new perspective on an old problem*

Vehicle Crime Prevention tells how the previous 'demonisation' of the car criminal through various campaigns had left the public both afraid of, and resigned to, the issue of vehicle crime. Overturning this convention by 'humanising' the criminal, giving people an insight into his or her motivations, helped to reduce anxiety, and empowered people to take responsibility for the problem and take preventative action.

*Redefining the 'task' for the consumer*

Smokers typically want to quit, but often see it as an overwhelming challenge. The Nicorette strategy is driven by the insight that smokers can imagine giving up one or two cigarettes or, at best, giving up for a few days – 'winning a battle but not the war'. This more honest and accessible approach inspired the simple idea of 'beating cigarettes one at a time'. It took Nicorette from one of a number of similar pharmaceutical brands designed for a 'problem' to an empathetic and market-leading consumer champion.

*A disruptive approach to the generic category driver*

Protection is the key driver in the feminine care market in emerging markets such as Russia, Poland, Mexico and Venezuela. Products are technological, reliable or affordable, menstruation is portrayed as a 'problem', and communication is rational. Yet women with 'traditional' attitudes also see menstruation as the 'gift of fertility'. The Naturella paper demonstrates how, via the Naturella 'World of Nature', nature itself became a metaphor for protection – not harsh and technological, but natural, soft and feminine.

*Challenging cultural 'norms'*

In Romania (as in most of 'new Europe'), the conventional wisdom ran that 'West is best', hence the natural inclination was to deliver an imported western advertising solution for Unilever's Dero (short for Detergent Romania). In-depth ethnographic research identified that Romanian heritage was in fact a potential strength and differentiator in an increasingly westernised world, and that the key to leveraging this was the uniquely Romanian sense of humour. There is important learning here for global organisations launching into new and developing markets.

*Strategic continuity need not stifle the communication of change*

The Volkswagen Golf story is one of strategic evolution as the brand and the category developed. Superior build quality and reliability born of the German provenance began as mechanical reliability, but moved to emotional reliability in the form of 'whatever happens in life, you can always rely on your VW Golf'. At the time, this strategy of creating an emotional bond between the owner and their car was disruptive for the category. This thinking remained the constant platform for a series of very different expressions of the brand, united by a common tone over the ensuing years.

## Fresh thinking about consumer engagement

*What if we harnessed the 'power of participation'?*

Two cases illuminate this much-discussed but rarely delivered ambition: Monopoly and Sony Ericcson.

■ The launch of an updated version of the old favourite Monopoly was inspired by two thoughts:

   1. What was interesting was not just that Monopoly had been updated, but that London itself had changed.
   2. Getting people to play updated Monopoly would be far more compelling than just telling them about it.

   From this came the idea for Monopoly Live – an online game played with cabs fitted with GPS transmitters driving around the 'real' London. This was designed to both create participation and drive word of mouth.

■ In the mobile phone market, handsets are sold via networks. The dominant convention is to show the product in use in communications, resulting in a lack of differentiation that favoured the dominant brand. The number five player in the market, Sony Ericsson, developed a strategy of participation built on three key pillars:

   1. Rather than simply reflecting what consumers already do with their phones, the opportunity was to open consumers' minds to what they could do.
   2. Channels were deliberately deployed with the objective of driving participation, from the 'invitation' of broadcast TV to 'try this on a real phone' in store.
   3. The brand personality encouraged participation by bringing energy and dynamism to the category.

   The effect of this was to encourage consumers to try Sony Ericsson phones, making the brand different and memorable.

*Maximising the connection with the consumer*

TV Licensing faced the difficult task of educating students about the need for a TV Licence, and convincing them both of the reality of enforcement and the subsequent consequences of evasion. The thinking about the optimum range of channels for a notoriously 'hard to reach' audience resulted in a total of 30 'touch-points'. These ranged from established channels of PR, direct mail and inserts alongside on-the-ground activity on campus. Tactics included targeting drop-off days (the day of arrival), freshers' fairs and sponsoring student TV in union bars, alongside text messaging, online advertising and targeted emails. This innovative approach was supported by a similarly innovative evaluation methodology, which enables isolation of the contribution of various elements of the channel mix.

*Fresh thinking and the continuity vs discontinuity debate*

In an age of ever-increasing discontinuity, there are several cases here based on strategies born out of the need to change or disrupt. In some cases, such as social issues or charities, the public can become immune to certain messages and imagery. Hence change is a constant requirement.

- The British Heart Foundation describes how multi-quitters (hardened smokers who have tried and failed to give up three times or more) were desensitised to the famous, and successful, 'Fatty Cigarette' shock tactics. A new strategy was developed that focused on the cigarette itself, and its dangerous role in everyday life.
- Actimel suffered from a widespread lack of understanding of its role and benefits. 'The Actimel Challenge' asked consumers to try Actimel every day for two weeks, and find out how much better they feel or get their money back. This is strategy directly driving behaviour change.
- In the absence of any funds at all, Women's Aid raised awareness of the issue of domestic abuse, and its role as an organisation that can help, by hijacking Valentine's Day. The juxtaposition of a national celebration of romance and love with the charity's agenda created a powerful strategic and creative platform.

By contrast Vehicle Crime Prevention, Bakers, Felix, O₂, The Famous Grouse and Tax Self Assessment all present a strong case for strategic (and in some cases creative) consistency over significant periods of time. And, looking ahead, M&S looks set to follow a similar path.

While these campaigns are now established and familiar, they were all in their own way disruptive at the point of inception. 'Fresh thinking' can last a long time, and often provides the focus and confidence to maintain a particular course in the face of change and uncertainty. And, although the strategic framework may be tight and clearly defined, the thinking evolves to accommodate different objectives, messages, audiences and channels. Hence, Felix and Volkswagen successfully launched new products, O₂ shifted its focus from new to existing customers, and HM Revenue & Customs offered new services. Only in the case of The Famous Grouse (in a 'no innovation by design' market), where the idea 'per se' is based on strategic/creative consistency, do we see absolute continuity.

There's ample proof in these case histories that 'fresh thinking' is at the root of success, as well as a lot of learnings about the 'how' and the 'why'. There is, of course, the inevitable catch. These cases are history. They cannot be replicated or repeated. There can't, by definition, be such a thing as a formula for fresh thinking. But they do help instil confidence in the necessity for fresh thinking whenever a problem presents itself, as well as a lot of inspiration from how others approach it. They are worth reading if only to see how others think, leaving you better prepared to do it differently yourself.

---

*Case studies referred to, but not featured, can be accessed via www.WARC.com.*

# SECTION 3

# Best practice

# Chapter 4

# Demonstrating payback

**By Andrew Sharp**
Director of Brand Economics & Finance, PricewaterhouseCoopers LLP London

The main purpose of the IPA Effectiveness Awards, and what sets them apart from other awards, is that they clearly set out to encourage marketers and marketing services companies to prove that investing in communications is good business. This doesn't mean 'was it a famous campaign?' (*although it often was*); nor does it just mean 'did sales go up?' (*although they would have had to*). It means 'was it profitable?' Did it 'make more money than it cost to do'? Or, in other words, did it provide positive payback? Because if it didn't, well, nobody summarised it better than Mr Micawber, in Dickens' *David Copperfield*:

> *Annual income twenty pounds, annual expenditure nineteen nineteen six, result happiness. Annual income twenty pounds, annual expenditure twenty pounds ought and six, result misery.*

Or, in our case, increased uncertainty, reduced budgets and troubled career prospects.

Reviewing the papers submitted this year (and some earlier ones), we found that payback clarity was often lacking. Whilst all of the papers unquestionably showed that something significant had happened, not all demonstrated conclusively that true payback had occurred. In fact, there seemed to be a wide variation in understanding about what demonstrating real payback required.

Does this matter? It depends on who we think the ultimate audience for the Awards are. The marketing community itself may be reasonably convinced of the efficacy of communication investment, but even they have their concerns. If, however, it is the wider business community, and within that especially the narrower, specialised community of financially trained executives, that is the intended audience, then they are likely to be both more sceptical and more numerate. Higher standards are required.

What all good effectiveness papers should have, therefore, is clear proof of profit. So the purpose of this chapter is to list the most common problems that seem to arise when 'proving profit', and propose a simple scheme that will enable future judges and readers to understand more precisely what has happened. This will include some simple suggestions as to what can still be said whenever important financial information has to be withheld for reasons of commercial sensitivity.

Please note that throughout this chapter I am going to use the phrase 'marketing communications investment' to describe the money spent in order to avoid, in this modern integrated communications world, any apparent retro bias by just talking about 'advertising investment'. I am also going to use, in this case, the term 'payback' as being synonymous with return on investment, or ROI.

So, I now turn to the review of the problems we encountered.

## Deducting costs

At a very basic level, it appeared that in several cases it was apparently being proposed that if the increased sales revenue value simply exceeded the marketing communications investment cost then that campaign had achieved a positive payback. Would that this were true! Unfortunately, positive payback occurs only when the sum generated after deducting retail margins, sales taxes, cost of extra goods, etc., exceeds the expenditure on marketing communications investment.

A good analogy might be the buying and selling of property. Few of us would think that if we bought a house for £500k, and rapidly sold it for £510k, that it would be likely we had made a profit. We would know that you have to deduct agents' fees and legal fees, etc., from your sale income – and also add legal fees plus stamp duty to your purchase costs. Net result: you would have lost money.

## Defining sales

In some cases, there was uncertainty as to what was actually meant by the term 'sales'. In one case a business that effectively acts as an agent was claiming £5 extra sales for every £1 invested in marketing communications (the actual numbers were different but not wildly different). But what was not clear was what these sales were: the total retail value of items sold, or their 'agent' income? If the former, then the company would need to have had a 20% cut of total sales just to break even on the campaign investment – and this is assuming it had no extra costs arising from those extra sales. Unlikely. On the other hand, if it really was £5 extra actual fee income (their share of the total sale) per £1 invested, then they had probably got a payback rate of several hundred per cent! Sadly, I suspect it was the former case, and this campaign may have – on the basis of the evidence produced at least – actually lost money. In any case, a lack of clarity at a very basic level.

A useful analogy here might be the actual business of ad agencies themselves (or indeed retailers) that can quote revenue at the level of billings, income or net margin. The first is the amount of cash that passed through their hands, the second the amount that they earn in the process and the third the amount left after their costs (e.g. labour) are deducted from the sum earned. Thus you can win a piece of business that increases your turnover (billings), but if it nets you less than you paid to win it, you have lost not gained.

## Timing of revenues

The third problem with revenues, even if they are recognised at the right level, was that of choosing the right time interval to count the revenue over. In most cases the papers choose a simple 12-month timeframe – the normal planning period. But obviously if you choose a longer time period the chance of apparent payback improves dramatically. A simple analogy here is if you are given longer to hit your sales target, it becomes easier to achieve. There are nevertheless often good arguments that returns should be counted over a longer period – customers satisfied or persuaded in one year return in subsequent years, and so forth. In several papers this argument has been advanced – but a number of problems arise, as outlined below.

### Lifetime values

The first, and most common, problem with the extended payback argument is the treatment of all customer acquisitions being valued at their 'lifetime value'. In other words, this is an assumption of likely loyalty times expected revenues, usually discounted at some interest rate. This is typical in contract-based industries like mobile telephony, financial services or even health clubs. It is also often used in public policy cases: cost of lives saved, accidents avoided, etc. Whilst it is a common practice – with the numbers probably being provided by the brand owners themselves – it is also an assumption about the future, and since that is a forecast, it can come unstuck.

In one case, we were presented with a paper that used 'lifetime' revenue values to prove payback when, at the time we were judging, we knew the business was being wound down! Perhaps no one was to know this when the paper was being written or the calculations were being made. The important point is that just being provided with such a single large revenue number as a fait accompli, with no explanation of the detail that went into the sum, does not allow the judges, or indeed the actual people we want to convince, the financial community, to exercise proper judgement, and thus have total confidence in what is being shown to them.

### Selective time periods

The second, but much less common problem, is the use of selective time periods for assessing revenue return. In one paper, the authors removed the investment months from the payback calculation, analysing only subsequent months' revenues, which were, unsurprisingly, more profitable – especially since the product was in a growing market. Creative accountancy indeed!

### Use of adstocks in econometrics

The third timing problem can arise with the use of econometrics. Those of you who are allergic to econometrics should skip this section and move to problem four now!

In principle, econometric analysis is to be highly encouraged; modelling permits a huge reduction in uncertainty as to what caused what in any situation. But there are potential abuses as well as uses. A discussion of these probably deserves its own chapter; suffice to say for now that models should be supplied with all key outputs – coefficients, t-tests and diagnostics – before anyone can draw safe conclusions from them. A little econometrics is a dangerous thing ...

The specific revenue payback time period problem involving econometrics stems from the use of adstocks in modelling. This, again, is a common and correct procedure in principle. If you model advertising, or most marketing communications investment, you will find you get a better 'fit', or explanation, if you adjust the investment to 'flow' over a longer time period beyond the original period in which it was actually made. The principle is that marketing communications effects persist much longer than in just the initial period; there is a carry-over, or echo, effect. Most people would accept this is probably how marketing communications work – we don't immediately forget marketing communications, or good marketing communications at least. The normal technique is to 'flow' the effect by using a decay rate – an assumption that the effect loses a fixed percentage of its effect for each time period measured – say four-week periods.

Some of the models in the papers 'fitted' a very slow decay rate, which implies the investment effects were very long lasting. This increases the amount of sales volume that can be attributed to the investment, and thus improves the apparent payback. There is nothing necessarily wrong with that – but when it was pointed out to less technical judges that a 90% decay rate across four-week periods implies that, by the end of two years, 90% of the total marketing communications investment benefit being counted as payback lay outside the actual period when the marketing communications were being broadcast or distributed (see Figure 1), then there was some doubt. It was rightly seen as an aggressive conclusion – and perhaps an expedient way of multiplying your imputed revenues. I can foresee debate about this issue, but what cannot be argued with, I believe, is that, once again, the fait accompli is not enough – large multiplied revenues need careful explanation.

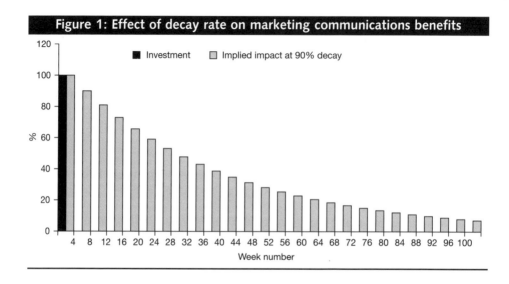

Figure 1: Effect of decay rate on marketing communications benefits

*Returns come from price as well as volume*

A fourth problem is that of a possible bias to new product launches caused by measuring increased revenues only from increased sales. Most papers illustrate the benefit of marketing communications investment in terms of revenue gained from share or volume gained. Yet in highly competitive markets, this can be either impossible or just transient. But marketing investment remains worthwhile. A trip to any supermarket will show many successful brands selling at a considerable price premium to the own-label brands. Some of the best returns (incremental profits) from marketing investment come from price premium growth or protection – yet few papers make that case. It is more tempting to prepare stories of dramatic sales growth, which are typically associated with innovation and launches. This creates its own dilemma. If you invented a cure for the common cold, you would presumably have a highly successful product on your hands – but only as long as people knew about it. So after it inevitably became a massive success, how would you attribute the relative contributions to success made by either the actual product innovation or the marketing of it?

A paper based purely on price premia creation and its protection might be politically difficult for both agencies and clients – but the issue needs to be addressed in papers that seek to demonstrate that investing in marketing communications pays back.

*Integrated communications cost base*

A final, newly emergent problem prompted considerable debate: accounting for integrated communications, particularly when some kind of 'knock-on' effect is being counted. In some cases, free publicity really is free publicity, and the extra exposure generates more communication impacts and thus raises sales. Payback stemming from a small initial 'seed' investment can then appear very large indeed. But there can be difficulties in properly allocating the cost base. If a PR initiative leads to a TV programme and the programme actually delivered the result, then was it 'free'? Should the cost of both activities, PR and TV programme, be netted off the income before declaring positive payback? There is disagreement over this, but no clear answer yet. This field will generate a lot of payback discussion over the coming years.

So, having dwelt on the problems, did anyone get it right? Of course. Several entries demonstrated unambiguous profit from marketing communications investment. One packaged goods entry proved that its campaign was profitable even if you took the worst assumption possible on gross margin. A famous car manufacturer (with a history of effective advertising) was quite open about its profit margins, and thus could prove a very healthy marketing communications investment ROI (in fact it might have been even higher than stated if price premia were also taken into account).

# A few simple suggestions

In this section, I present a few simple suggestions on how best to present the data relating to payback.

*Separate out the 'P&L'*

First, I would advocate that a separate campaign profit and loss (P&L) is laid out on a separate page in the paper. This is where the analysts will start their reading!

*Clarify revenues*

Second, on that page, start by sorting out the amount and definition of the incremental revenues.

- Define revenues clearly. Or, in the case of not-for-profit cases, define the returns carefully. Describe in words, and not just in numbers, what kind of revenue we are talking about. Retail level? Income into company? And so on.
- Consider that revenue gained or retained due to marketing investments comes from two sources: volume *and* price.
- Specify the time period used for the analysis, and explain why it is the right period for the specific market (i.e. something better than 'it is the length of the financial year'). It is legitimate to argue for longer time period effects – but the case should be made explicitly.
- Lifetime values. If they are the currency of the industry in question, then use them – but not in an uncritical way. Find out and quote the assumptions that lie behind these large values in order that judges and business audiences can make their own judgements about the underlying payback.
- Using high adstock decay rates in econometric models of marketing communications effectiveness is also acceptable. But you will need to be prepared to explain in plain English the financial implications of these models, and to argue the case very well for them to be believed without question, given that it will inflate the apparent payback.

*Clarify costs*

Third, sort out the incremental costs associated with the marketing investment.

- Net off retailer margins and taxes (e.g. VAT) – if in doubt, use average values.
- Net off the cost of goods for the extra sales – use an estimated cost if necessary.
- Arrive at the contribution before deduction of marketing expenses. In other words, of every £1 sold at consumer/high-street prices, how many pence does the company keep before it spends money on the communications investment?

*Calculate payback*

Fourth, subtract the marketing investment cost from the above contribution. Divide the remainder by the marketing investment cost – and (ta dah!) you have your marketing communications payback percentage.

*Make it clear*

Fifth, lay it out as a table. Without wishing to be ultra-prescriptive, and accepting that each business situation is unique, the kind of layout that would be clear and useful might look like this:

| Table 1: Separating profit and loss | | | |
|---|---|---|---|
| Campaign 'P&L' | £-Nominal amounts | Percentage | Commentary |
| Incremental retail revenue | 100 | 100% | |
| Incremental company revenue | 50 | 50% | Deductions from retail revenue for VAT, retail margin, etc. |
| Incremental cost of goods | 30 | 30% | Not directly known but estimates – see analyst report X |
| Incremental net return before marketing costs | 20 | 20% | Estimate |
| Marketing communication costs | 15 | | |
| Payback | 5 | 33%* | |

* Denotes return on 'marketing communications' investment

Alternatively, another clear and quick way of showing the same information could be to graph it. Figure 2 displays the same key information as the table above.

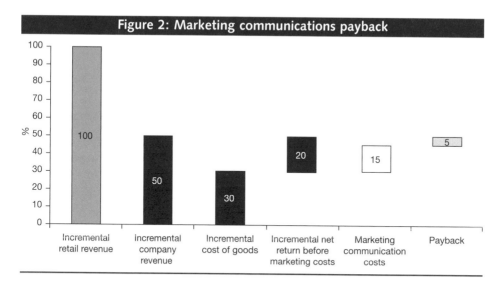

Figure 2: Marketing communications payback

Even if you cannot show this level of information, you can still nevertheless work out the break-even point for the investment. In the case above, it would require an incremental net return before marketing costs of £15 before the marketing communications investment broke even (or a break-even margin – at this level – of 15%, i.e. below the 20% shown). If you can get your client to say that the actual margin is (a) higher and (b) they are currently planning to repeat such investments, then a convincing business argument will have been made without divulging any confidential data.

*Involve the FD*

The sixth and final idea is to get your finance director to have a look over your calculations. Don't just prepare your paper as a planning document; prepare it as a business document.

*Finally …*

The bottom line – literally – is that marketing communications payback is what's left after the right incremental costs have been deducted from the right incremental revenues. Simple to say, a little bit harder to do properly – but not impossible.

# Chapter 5

# Writing multi-national case studies: three practical hints

**By John Philip Jones**
Professor of Advertising, Syracuse University

This chapter is intended to give what I hope is useful advice to people planning to write multi-national case studies. It provides three specific hints, but I want to start by making some overall points about multi-national campaigns in general.

In any country, large or small, the brands sold can be classified into four groups:

1. Brands from local companies that are sold only locally.
2. Brands from multi-national companies that are sold only locally.
3. Multi-national brands from multi-national companies that are sold in many countries, and are supported by locally generated advertising.
4. Multi-national brands from multi-national companies that are sold in many countries, and are supported by multi-national advertising.

In total advertising billing, the fourth group is usually the smallest, accounting for a 'guesstimated' 10%–20% of all advertising expenditure, depending on the country. This is the only group relevant to this chapter. Multi-national advertising was used most widely in the 1960s, after which it retreated to some extent because many advertisers had burned their fingers. But this does not mean that multi-national advertising is unimportant. On the contrary, it includes some of the most striking individual advertising successes. This is because it is now planned strategically, with much greater care than it used to be. It is not a field for the inexperienced.

Note my use of the word *multi-national*, which I believe to be preferable to the alternatives. *Global* implies that the campaign is reaching out geographically further than any such campaigns ever go; they never cover more than a quarter of all countries in the world. The word *international* implies that the campaign was developed for international use, for some undefined international consumer. This is very rarely the way such campaigns are planned: a typical multi-national campaign started in one country and was targeted at a national consumer, then was subsequently rolled out into other markets. The place of origination is almost invariably a large market, e.g. the United States or the United Kingdom, but there are exceptions. The roll-out policy is prudent, but can involve a serious loss of time. It took six years for Timotei to reach out beyond four small markets (three successes and one failure). During such an extended period, competitors are normally able to pre-empt the idea in countries the brand has not reached.

Multi-national campaigns can be found, although not usually in more than a minority of campaigns, in advertising for financial services, technical/electrical/electronic products, many (but certainly not all) fmcg, fast food, gasoline, travel, expensive personal possessions and upmarket clothing. They are rarely used for cars or for direct-response campaigns. They are so uncommon as to be almost unknown in beer, most packaged foods, retail advertising, over-the-counter (OTC) medications, direct-to-consumer (DTC) medical prescriptions (permitted in only two countries), commodity advertising and 'good cause' campaigns. They are also more widely used by some companies (e.g. Unilever and Colgate Palmolive) than others (such as Procter & Gamble (P&G) and Nestlé). Multi-national campaigns are also used occasionally for the same brand sold in different countries, but employing a different name (e.g. Burger King in the United States and Hungry Jack in Australia).

Two demographic groups are important to multi-national advertisers. Both command substantial purchasing power, although the actual numbers of people are not large. The first is the young (the athletic-shoes-and-baseball-cap generation), the ubiquity of whose lifestyles can easily be observed. The second group is the affluent, especially senior business people (the laptops-in-the-business-class-cabin community).

## First hint: be explicit about the objective of the multi-national campaign

By 'objective of the advertising', I exclude anything as general as boosting total sales by entering new markets. It is assumed that the advertiser will have moved forward from this type of objective by setting up a manufacturing or, at least, a selling organisation in each foreign country. With the mechanics of marketing the brand in place, it is important to spell out why a multi-national advertising campaign should be part of the marketing mix, and why this will be better than locally produced advertising.

Every country in the world is different from every other. Advertisers should judge, *as far as their own products are concerned*, the extent to which individual countries might be coalescing, in the way Marshall McLuhan rather fancifully visualised when he talked in the 1960s about the Global Village. As a close observer of the scene, I am sceptical about whether the biggest national differences will ever disappear, or even get much less important than they are today, with the possible exception of the influence of media overlap between countries with similar languages: overlap that will increase because of the proliferation of audio-visual media. But this does not invalidate the potential for multi-national campaigns. There are individual points of similarity between consumers in different countries that can indeed be exploited.

At least six reasons are put forward for using multi-national campaigns. I shall list them below (describing them in typical client language), with my comments.

1. *'I want a uniform multi-national presentation of my brand.'* This is the least relevant argument, because it is important only in cases where individual consumers buy or use the brand in different countries. Such buying is usually trivial (e.g. small purchases during foreign vacations), but there are exceptions (e.g., American Express, used by frequent business travellers).

2. *'As management policy I like to centralise decision-making.'* There are better ways than using advertising to exercise control over satellite operations. For some companies, advertising centralisation strangles initiative. Pan American (Pan Am) used to scrutinise and approve in New York every translation of the company's advertisements, which were all centrally produced in the English language. There are many reasons for the eventual demise of Pan Am, but the rigidity of its operations was one. P&G, a highly centralised organisation and a very successful one, hardly ever uses multi-national campaigns.

3. *'There can be an explosion of publicity if a major product innovation is launched simultaneously and in a similar way in a number of important countries.'* This policy, which has been followed occasionally by Kodak and Gillette, makes some sense. But a word of caution is needed. Most product innovations are failures, so that if the worst comes to the worst, a multi-national launch could become a multi-national disaster.

4. *'I am looking for quality control; it is better to have a single campaign that is reasonably suitable for a number of countries than a patchwork of campaigns, some of which are awful.'* This argument makes some sense, and is related to the last of my six points.

5. *'I want to save money on production costs.'* This argument is substantially valid, but be careful how you interpret it. When a film is used in a number of countries, the production cost is normally divided pro rata (e.g. on the basis of a brand's sales in each country). In addition to the basic production cost, there are usually substantial add-ons for voiceovers, titling, etc. In many countries, the total cost of using a multi-national film is sometimes higher than what would be paid for a local production. The important point, therefore, is that a multi-national film offers far higher quality for the same (or a slightly higher) cost than a locally produced film. This is an important consideration in how the Lux campaign is used. Incidentally, there is often a legal impediment to using television commercials shot in other markets. These are sometimes embargoed because of bans imposed by local trade unions.

6. *'Demonstrably good advertising ideas are rare; if we find one let's use it everywhere we can.'* I believe that this is the most persuasive reason for the use of multi-national campaigns. It is certainly why the campaigns for Dove and Lux have been totally successful, and why the Timotei campaign was a substantial medium-term success, although the brand eventually lacked staying power. And we should always remember Marlboro, the most ubiquitous example of a multi-national campaign.

The point about clarifying the objective(s) of the campaign is that it will make it much easier to judge the group of markets as a whole; for example, country A may require particularly high-quality film productions because of the existence of sophisticated competition; countries B and C may be contiguous, with a substantial overspill of media; countries D, E and F may be managed by the client as a single unit. The purpose(s) of the multi-national (versus a balkanised) approach should run like a red thread through the document.

## Second hint: all case studies need empirical substantiation

All too often, a campaign is deemed successful in one country, and without too much thought is thrown into a number of others. This is simply not good enough for a multi-national case study. Effects must be seriously evaluated. This is a difficult issue, because it is almost unknown for sophisticated data to be provided *on a comparable basis* in a broad range of countries. Here is a list of four types of information that should – in an ideal world – be provided in each market:

1. Econometric studies isolating and quantifying the effects of advertising.
2. Consumer purchasing and related data of varying degrees of complexity and range.
3. Cognitive data to track awareness and image attributes of the leading brands.
4. Cognitive tracking of advertising awareness for the most important brands in the category.

It is unlikely that alternative 1 will ever be available on a multi-market basis. Small countries cannot afford this type of research because of the low sales, and consequently small profit, earned by the brand. Alternatives 3 and 4 are commonly available, at least from intermittent 'dipstick' checks, but they are not enough on their own. Alternative 2 should receive the main priority. Aim to provide reliable and *uniform* data from each country measuring consumer sales, and supported if possible by cognitive information ('dipstick' checks at least) to provided diagnostics.

The IPA has published a total of ten international multi-market cases. This relatively small number from a database of 338 published winners reflects both the UK origins of the Awards, and the challenges of writing such cases to the standards of proof required to win. The first was Levi's 501s in 1988. Recent cases include two foods: Olivio spread in four European markets and Rainbow evaporated milk in a cluster of six countries in the Middle East; an anti-smoking product, Nicorette, sold in seven and later 16 European markets; a women's feminine care product, Naturella, with a campaign in two eastern European countries and two in Latin America; and a mobile telephone, Sony Ericsson, in eight European markets. The two packaged foods are interesting because multi-national campaigns are rarely used for such products.

All these cases were scrutinised by experienced IPA judges, and as expected each is a sound piece of work: well written and based on respectable research. Let me, however, make three general points that apply to some or all of these cases.

1. The authors need to spell out explicitly the reason for using the multi-national campaign (as discussed earlier in this article). This should make it easier to view the campaign as a whole.
2. The research should be presented country by country, as uniformly as possible and preferably tabulated as an appendix. The research can therefore be discussed in the body of the report, and the arguments can be reinforced by references to specific data at the back of the document. It is generally not a good idea to lump groups of countries together, because this conceals internal differences.
3. I strongly advise *against* estimating the (often dramatic) value of incremental sales that have resulted from the campaign: a computation usually derived from an econometric deconstruction of sales. Any such calculation is not only implausible, but is also misleading. This is because it ignores the *additional direct and indirect costs* that had to be incurred in manufacturing the additional volume. The best approach is to make a careful estimate of the additional direct costs, and give these an additional weighting according to the firm's normal ratio of directs to indirects. The total can then be *deducted from the estimate of incremental sales value*. This type of calculation, which is common in the United States and is known as the advertising payback, shows a high degree of uniformity between successful campaigns in different fields: a payback in the range of 50 to 70 cents per dollar invested above the line. This calculation realistically computes the true net cost of the campaign, which is (as explained) normally between 30% and 50% of the space/time budget.

To illustrate what can be achieved with the use of uniform multi-national data, let me list the information I used in the case study I published describing the multi-national campaign for diamond gemstones (De Beers). I confined myself to 'hard' numbers. There was such a wealth of relevant information that I was able to tease out the causes of success and failure from using these alone.

De Beers collects a comprehensive battery of information in all the countries in which it operates. These data include the main economic variables influencing the demand for diamonds, and these formed the basis for my study. I used uniform data from 28 countries: 19 markets where diamond sales were strong, plus nine weaker markets. Here are the data on *diamonds* from each country that I used in my study:

- total retail value of sales
- acquisition of women's diamond jewellery
- average retail price of diamond jewellery
- change (over time) in average retail price of diamond jewellery
- pieces of diamond jewellery sold (indexed over time)
- De Beers' advertising as a ratio of retail sales value.

I also used data on a number of *general market* economic indicators:

- private consumption per capita
- change in private consumption per capita (indexed over time)
- average annual inflation rate.

As a result of looking at all this information in many different ways (although I did not calculate any statistical correlations), I drew three strongly supported conclusions that no one has subsequently disputed. These are as follows: the first influence on sales of diamond jewellery is the affluence of the purchaser (i.e. demand is income-elastic). The second is the price of the stones (i.e. demand is also price-elastic). The third point is that advertising has a demonstrable, although marginal, influence on sales in both the short term and the long term. The last point is remarkable because De Beers' advertising budget represents an extremely small advertising to sales (A:S) ratio, varying in different countries between 0.1% and 1.0%. (In the weaker markets the A:S ratio is much lower than in the stronger markets: a very significant point.)

One characteristic of the diamond market that simplified my analysis is the absence of direct competition. In more normal markets, competition cannot be ignored; and the competitive situation is usually quite different in different countries. This should be explained.

In your paper, be as explicit as you can about any artificial impediments to the success of a multi-national campaign. In my experience, the worst problem has been the resistance of the locals, both client and agency. Good agencies have *amour propre*, an attitude usually described as 'not invented here' (NIH), and they do not enjoy using other people's work. This scepticism is sometimes justified, but not always. The most subtle persuasion is often needed before locals will accept the merits of a multi-national campaign. But it does not help when the local creative talent is seen (from afar) to be made up of 'skilled hacks' (I once heard this phrase used by a top international executive of a major agency).

In the case of De Beers, there are a number of creative centres. Each follows a totally uniform campaign strategy, and creative work is delegated to the agency offices that demonstrate the best specialist abilities. The work from these centres is then syndicated out to a number of markets. We should also remember that very small countries have occasionally originated successful multi-national campaigns, despite the doubts of people in large markets.

## Third hint: write, rewrite and rewrite again

I shall not spell out the obvious need for clarity and economy, and the avoidance of cloudy generalisations, jargon and technical language (unless a few technical terms are absolutely necessary, in which case these need to be translated when they are first used). Assume that you are writing for an educated audience with no knowledge of the product field you are describing.

Here are three pieces of writing you should read and absorb. The way these authors handle the language is more instructive than anything I am able to say.

1. *The Economist*. Read any recent issue. Note the user-friendly and totally lucid use of English; also the way in which even familiar organisations are

identified to make absolutely sure that no readers are puzzled, e.g. 'Analysts at J.P. Morgan, an American investment bank, say ...'.

2. George Orwell. Read his brief essay *Politics and the English Language*. Note Orwell's advice about avoiding stale imagery and mindless clichés. Test every sentence you write by Orwell's criteria.

3. John Kenneth Galbraith. All his books and essays are enjoyable, but I suggest a book whose content is as good as its title, *A Short History of Financial Euphoria*. Note particularly the way Galbraith makes serious points with great raciness, and by inserting his dagger here and there with barbed witticisms.

---

*Case studies referred to, but not featured, can be accessed via www.WARC.com.*

# SECTION 4

# Gold winners

## Chapter 6

# Marks & Spencer

This is not just advertising, this is Your M&S advertising: how confident communications helped restore public confidence in M&S

**By Megan Thompson, RKCR/Y&R**
Contributing authors: Jonathan Neil and Sarah Threadgould, Marks & Spencer, and Sandra Lema Trillo, Walker Media

In spring 2004, consecutive sales declines and continual negative press coverage had left Marks & Spencer (M&S) facing a lack of public confidence in the brand and vulnerable to a second virtual takeover bid. As part of the effort to turn M&S's fortunes around, communications needed to spread the word to lapsed shoppers about the changes being made at store level. It also had to complement those efforts by serving as a public declaration of its confidence and commitment to change, thus helping to turn the tide of negative PR, and increase reappraisal, consideration and footfall.

The resulting 'Your M&S' campaign sought to demonstrate that the public were the rightful owners of M&S, and was intended to apply in equal degree to all M&S products, as well as to everyone from its staff and customers to journalists and analysts in the City.

Together, the various strands of this campaign generated over £6m worth of positive press coverage, and contributed to over 18 million additional customer visits. Womenswear and Food – which together account for over 50% of M&S's turnover – had enjoyed much of the communications focus, and were also among the main success stories. By spring 2006, M&S reported fourth-quarter sales growth of 6.8%, against a backdrop of a total high-street sales decline of 1.4% for the year. The company's share price rose to just below £6, and M&S had the highest P/E multiple of any FTSE 100 retailer.

*In reality, this has been one of the more advertising-led recovery stories we've watched. And it's working.*

Rod Whitehead, Deutsche Bank, 'No Ordinary Recovery'

## Why this paper is worth reading

This is the story of how communications changed the public face of a very public company. M&S is a national institution and speculating on its fortunes is a national pastime:

*The curious thing about M&S is how much we know and care about it. It's more than just another department store. We follow its ups and downs almost as if it were part of our extended family.*

Justine Picardie, the *Telegraph*, 14 April 2006

Back in April 2004, things were looking down at M&S. Consecutive sales declines and continual negative PR had led to a total loss of confidence in the brand. Two years on, and M&S has smashed City expectations by announcing Q4 sales growth of 9.1% against a backdrop of total March UK high-street sales down 1.4% on the year.[1]

This paper explores the role that communications have played in that turn-around. We will show how, as one of the fastest levers new management could pull, communications first acted as a public declaration of corporate intent. We will then show how, as product started to improve, communications changed the lens through which the public (including journalists and City analysts) viewed the product, by restoring confidence in the M&S brand.

## A difficult story to tell …

There have been two challenges to the writing of this paper, both of which stem from the public nature of M&S.

First is that the media has already made advertising the hero of the day (see Figure 1). If anything, this emphasis has been at the expense of a stress on all the improvements to product. In truth, because communications have worked hand in glove with changes in corporate strategy, disentangling their contribution is difficult.

Second is that whilst M&S had announced quarterly sales uplifts for the period ending April 2006, at the time of writing revenue figures were not due to be released until 23 May 2006. M&S could not disclose any data that would breach the requirements of the Financial Services and Markets Act 2004. Therefore, to avoid compromising either the company or the judges, only numbers already in the public domain at the time of writing could be worked with. The good news is that where M&S cannot disclose figures, the equity reports of leading retail analysts provided a rich seam of information to inform our analysis.[2]

Even in the face of such obstacles we believe that the overwhelming wealth of evidence does prove beyond reasonable doubt that communications have contributed significantly more than they have cost.

**Figure 1: Article from the *Daily Express*, Autumn 2005**

## Philip Green makes his move again[3]

Our story begins in July 2004 as Philip Green's Revival Acquisitions makes a proposed final offer for Marks & Spencer of 400p per share, as part of his second attempted bid for M&S (see Figure 2). Unusually for a corporate takeover bid, this story made front-page headlines in both the tabloids and the broadsheets. In fact, during this period, Marks & Spencer was the subject of around 1,000 press articles a month.[4]

Opinions were polarised between those who were 'up in arms'[5] at the thought of Green taking over, and those, including American fund Brandes,[6] who were rumoured to consider 400p an offer worth taking. The M&S Board, backed by the majority of institutional investors, was convinced that the offer significantly undervalued the company, and tasked Stuart Rose with proving what Marks & Spencer was really worth.

**Figure 2: Press coverage during the takeover bid**

Given that this was never a formal bid, and the price seemed to undervalue the company, the M&S Board decided to deny Revival Acquisitions access to company accounts and Revival ultimately withdrew its proposed offer. There was, however, a feeling in the media that Green[7] would come back to the table if the new management failed to deliver. A BBC poll conducted outside the 2004 AGM found that over two-thirds of small shareholders supported Stuart Rose.[8] This support did not, however, translate into increased custom for M&S. In fact, the first set of results that Rose presented to the City showed continued sales declines. The City was willing to forgive in the short term, but the clock was ticking:

> *It would be unfair to judge Rose on these figures – he's only been there for a month or so, so these are not his ranges. The earliest you'll be able to judge is early 2005, when his decisions start to come through.*
>
> Colin Morton, Rensburg Fund Managers, September 2004

## So how had M&S become vulnerable to takeover in 2004?

In the run-up to Green's 2004 bid, it was clear that analysts, journalists and customers alike had lost confidence in M&S (see Figure 3).

**Analyst:**

> *Continual sales declines and a lack of radical impetus for change, suggest that M&S may continue to disappoint on earnings.*
>
> Bruce Hubbard, Citigroup, April 2004

**Journalist:**

> *Fears of further bad news from M&S – one of the worst performing FTSE 100 companies last year – increased last Monday when the retailer launched a mid-season sale that included discounts of up to 50% ... Roger Holmes is understood to have privately concluded that the recovery has run its course.*
>
> Richard Fletcher, *Daily Telegraph*, April 2004

### Figure 3: Projection exercise from Flamingo Qualitative Research

**Customer:**

Those who did continue to visit M&S did so wearing the wrong glasses – they expected to be disappointed:

> *I'll go to M&S as a last resort, I just think of racks of navy blue and fawn.*
>> Core customer, qualitative research, 2003

Worse still, qualitative research amongst core customers at the close of 2003 found:

> *Certain levels of social embarrassment towards being seen to wear M&S clothing and resultant under claiming.*
>> Kirsty Fuller, Flamingo Research, 2003

## Trapped in a vicious PR circle

Even before Green's takeover bid, the troubles at Marks & Spencer were big news (see Figure 4):

> *It was like the papers got hold of a bit of bad news about M&S and they just ran and ran with it. They just wouldn't let things go.*
>> Core customer, qualitative research, 2003

**Figure 4: Press coverage pre-takeover bid**

This negative news flow was exacerbating the public's loss of confidence, and trapping M&S in a vicious circle (see Figure 5).

Figure 5: Negative press coverage was creating a vicious circle

*Due to the bad press, I'd be less likely to go into M&S; there is too much of a stigma.*

Core customer, qualitative research, 2003

## Stuart Rose's vision for M&S: 'A Marks & Spencer seen through Rose-tinted glasses'[9]

At his inaugural AGM, Stuart Rose acknowledged that the old Marks & Spencer had simply not been 'delighting the girls',[10] promising: 'we are going to give M&S back to its customers'.[11] This entailed a return to the core principles upon which Marks & Spencer was founded, and which are still relevant today (see Figure 6).

Citing a previous lack of integration, 'our business units have been operating as if they were stand-alone businesses', Rose promised that Marks & Spencer would once more add up to more than 'the sum of the parts'.[12]

He then placed womenswear at the heart of his recovery strategy: 'I believe womenswear is the key to the whole brand'.[13]

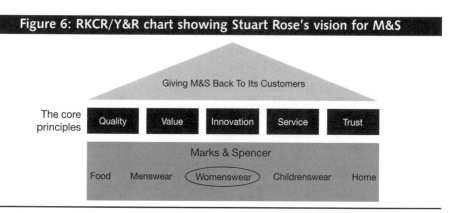

Figure 6: RKCR/Y&R chart showing Stuart Rose's vision for M&S

## The role for communications dictates an overarching brand idea

The importance of changes at store level must not be underestimated. Clothes are becoming more stylish, opening price points have been lowered in line with the competition, service has started to improve and stores are beginning to be refurbished. Without these changes, communications could never succeed, for as Bill Bernbach said, 'a great ad campaign will make a bad product fail faster. It will get more people to know that it's bad'.[14] In other words, the 'Twiggy effect' would not have been the same had Twiggy been modelling any old cardigan. Likewise, we wouldn't have been able to get the nation drooling at the thought of just any old food.

There are some things, however, that only communications could have achieved. As the public face of the organisation, and the fastest lever they could pull, communications needed to serve as a public declaration of M&S's confidence and commitment to change. The perceived threat of a new takeover bid meant that word of mouth alone could not be relied upon to spread news of the changes quickly enough to make them count. Instead communications needed to accelerate awareness of change amongst lapsed shoppers, increasing reappraisal, consideration and footfall. Critically, communications needed to change the lens through which the public viewed M&S products, by turning the tide of negative PR (see Figure 7).

In order to reverse the cycle, communications needed to build positive impressions of M&S (see Table 1). This was particularly important in Food and Womenswear because Food accounts for 50% of M&S's turnover, and Womenswear is the key driver of overall brand perceptions.

Because of the ubiquity of Marks & Spencer (there are five M&Ss within the square mile[15] and Vogue House is a stone's throw from the flagship Marble Arch store) these audiences inevitably overlap and cannot be treated discretely. We needed an overarching brand idea that could appeal to the whole nation.

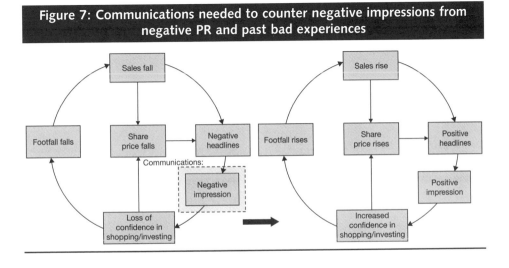

**Figure 7: Communications needed to counter negative impressions from negative PR and past bad experiences**

| Table 1: RKCR/Y&R chart showing role for communications by target audience | |
|---|---|
| **Audience** | **Role for communications** |
| Current shoppers | Make them proud to shop at M&S again, and turn them into vocal brand advocates. |
| Lapsed shoppers | Persuade them that it's worth giving M&S another chance, and change the lens through which they see M&S clothes, creating enough fashion credibility to allow them to act on their interest. |
| Journalists | Convince them that this time the changes M&S promised were for real, giving them enough faith in the brand to recommend it to their readers. |
| City analysts | Demonstrate that investment in marketing campaigns could help to sustain ongoing sales growth. |

## 'Your M&S' gives 'Marks & Spencer back to its customers'

M&S needed to galvanise the business behind change. '*Your* M&S' was the perfect rallying cry, fulfilling a number of vital criteria:

- directly acknowledged the rightful ownership of M&S by the public
- big enough, and true enough, to be relevant when selling anything from a crème brûlée to a man's Autograph suit
- applies to all audiences – customer, shareholder, journalist
- meaningful for staff and employees
- colloquial ('Your **M&S**') not corporate ('Your **Marks & Spencer**').

In design terms the new identity needed to feel contemporary and iconic, premium yet accessible (see Figure 8).

Importantly, 'Your M&S' was flexible enough to unify product-specific campaigns. This gave us the opportunity both to continually surprise the nation with 'new news' and to tap into category motivations.

In particular, 'Your M&S' campaigns were focused around the key areas of M&S Food and Womenswear.

### Figure 8: The new brand idea

## Media choices as confident as Your M&S

The role for communications was to restore confidence in M&S, and so confident media choices underpinned our strategy at every stage (see Figures 9 and 10).

The first step was to redefine the media architecture and unite investment behind a brand-led approach in 'mass' public media. High visibility was essential in giving people a sense that they could have as much confidence in M&S as the company was beginning to have in the product. Nielsen reported that M&S had a total advertising spend of £45m in 2005.

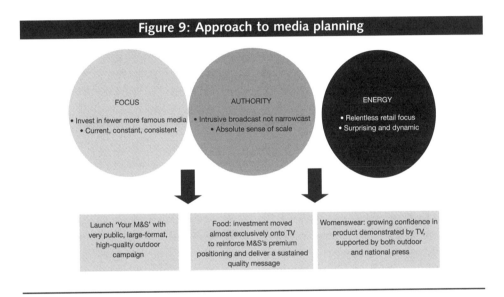

**Figure 9: Approach to media planning**

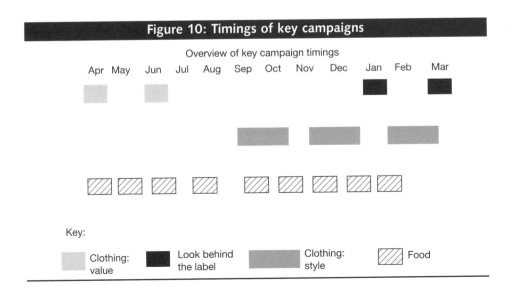

**Figure 10: Timings of key campaigns**

## Launching the brand idea

'Your M&S' was unveiled to the City in August 2004, then publicly launched through a high-profile poster campaign (see Figures 11–15).

**Figure 11: Stuart Rose unveils 'Your M&S'**

**Figure 12: A launch execution, September 2004**

**Figure 13: Large-format outdoor, September 2004**

GOLD
GRAND
PRIX

**Figure 14: Outdoor from the launch of 'Your M&S', September 2004**

**Figure 15: Loyalty mailing to existing customers, September 2004**

## Demonstrating value in clothing: 'Your M&S for Less'

Revising the pricing architecture particularly at opening price points was one of the first changes made,[16] so value was the first area where communications addressed negative impressions (see Figure 16).

**Figure 16: Examples of 'Your M&S for Less' value campaign, April 2005**

## Demonstrating quality in food: 'Not Just Food, Your M&S Food'

M&S Food had always been irresistible, so whilst the clothing team was working behind the scenes to improve product, it made sense to proceed by focusing on the quality of M&S Food. The fact that the supermarkets' premium ranges were beginning to catch up on perceptions of quality added an increased sense of urgency.[17] 'Your M&S' when applied to food meant that M&S understands exactly what gets your taste buds going. The quality difference was summed up as 'Not Just Food, Your M&S Food' (see Figures 17 and 18).

### Figure 17: Examples of 'Your M&S for Less' value campaign, April 2005 and July 2005

VO: This is not just a chicken … this is a farm assured naturally fed extra succulent Oakham chicken

### Figure 18: Examples of how the campaign was used in-store, spring–summer 2005

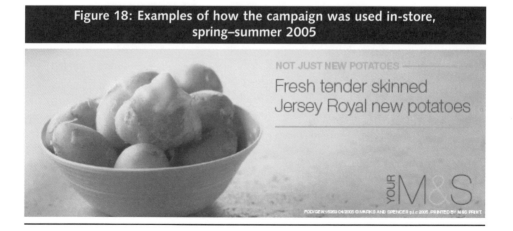

## Demonstrating innovation in style in Womenswear: What's Your M&S?

By September 2005, confident that womenswear was now beginning to be stylish enough to tempt 'every woman, every time',[18] the moment had come for communications to showcase the clothes to the nation.

Since women had been coming into M&S 'wearing the wrong glasses',[19] we needed to give them a fresh lens through which to view the clothes. This lens needed to be technicolor enough to blow away the cobwebs of negative PR, making women proud to wear M&S again. Supermodels were the perfect embodiment of M&S's growing confidence in product, but careful casting was key to finding a balance of women who could appeal to our broad church of customers. Twiggy, in particular, was the perfect metaphor for a national treasure making a spectacular comeback (see Figures 19 and 20).

### Figure 19: Posters, press and TV featuring the 'M&S Girls', September 2005 and February 2006

### Figure 20: The M&S website was integrated with the campaign, September 2005

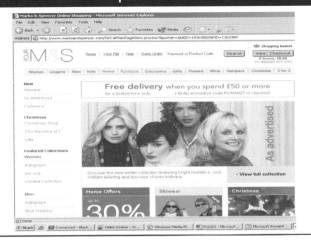

## Building momentum on innovation in style: 'Your M&S' presents Christmas

Christmas is an incredibly important trading period for any retailer, so it was important for us to maintain momentum at this time. The Christmas campaign continued to build style credentials, showing how 'Your M&S' helps you put on a spectacular show at Christmas (see Figure 21).

**Figure 21: Images from 'Your M&S' presents Christmas, November 2005**

## Innovations in style in menswear: 'Your M&S' My Autograph

For the relaunch of Autograph menswear, 'Your M&S' needed to appeal to ordinary men (see Figure 22):

> *We haven't gone for the passing fancy or the current hunk, we've gone for real guys that the M&S chap can relate to. We wanted guys who were respected.*
>
> Steve Sharp, Executive Director, Marketing & Stores, *Drapers*, 8 April 2006

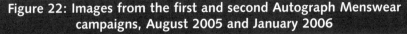

Figure 22: Images from the first and second Autograph Menswear campaigns, August 2005 and January 2006

## Reinforcing trust: 'Look Behind the Label'

Once food and clothing campaigns had created a strong sense of change at M&S, the time had come to reinforce M&S's ongoing commitment to ethical sourcing (see Figure 23):

> *Everything we do, we do with great respect for the environment and the people. We have always done miles more than anyone else in retail but we were failing to get the credit for it.*
>
> Steve Sharp, Executive Director, Marketing & Stores, *Drapers*, 8 April 2006

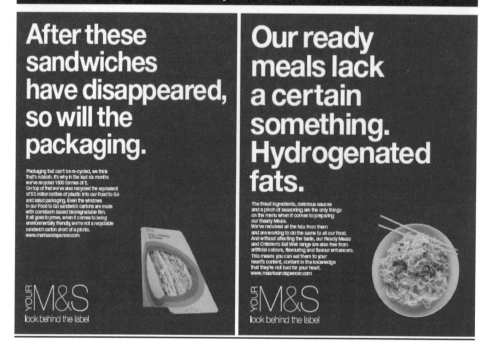

Figure 23: National press advert from the 'Look Behind the Label' campaign, January–March 2006

## Results of the campaign

*PR*

### Communications generate press coverage worth up to £6m

Whilst product PR has improved over the past year, M&S has a policy of not PR-ing advertising, preferring to let communications speak for themselves. Nonetheless recent campaigns have attracted huge amounts of PR coverage (see Figure 24). Since September 2005 communications have generated press coverage that would have cost over £2m to buy as advertising space.[20]

Given the implied endorsement, most PR companies assign a multiplier to ad cost when assessing the value of PR. The actual multiplier varies but can be up to triple the ad value.[21] This positive press could therefore be worth over £6m. In addition to measurable column inches, communications have spawned a national catchphrase, 'this is not just a ...', and become a shared cultural point of reference: 'as lavish as an M&S ad'.[22] Communications have also inspired a sketch on *Bremner, Bird & Fortune*,[23] and two sets of BBC idents.

> That's the best compliment anyone could pay, to get onto the BBC at 8pm on a Saturday night; you can't buy that kind of airtime.

Steve Sharp, Executive Director, Marketing & Stores, *Drapers*, 8 April 2006

Figure 24: The advertising prompts the Daily Telegraph to reassess product, September 2005

Has M&S twigged the art of success?

'I was hyperventilating. Three pairs of boots to choose from!'

'Fun and good value, but it's still a confusing place to shop'

'I had no trouble spotting dozens of things I would buy'

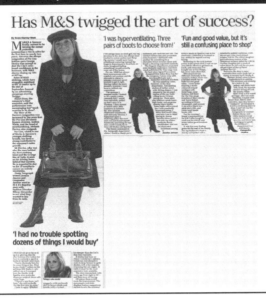

## Communications have turned the tide of PR coverage

This volume of press could be regarded as a simple virtue of being in the public eye. However, past advertising had itself fallen foul of negative PR. In particular, a 2001 M&S womenswear television ad featuring a naked female hill runner had provoked a barrage of negative press coverage. By contrast, a key achievement of the recent advertising has been to provide a focus for much-needed positive PR coverage (see Figure 25).

Figure 25: PR exposure showing an increasingly positive trend

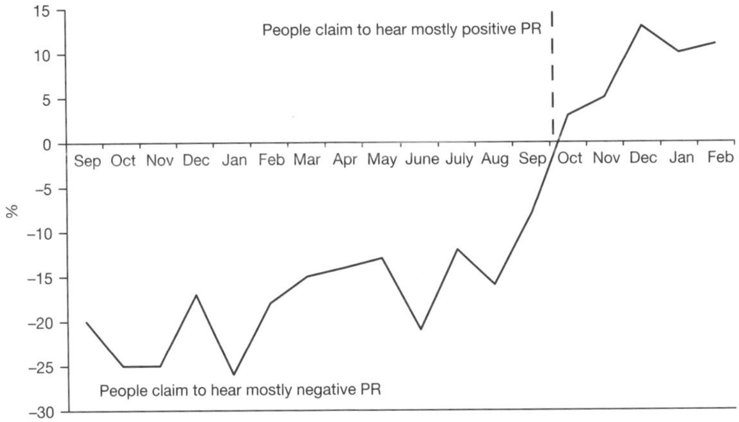
15
10
5
0
-5
-10
-15
-20
-25
-30
%
People claim to hear mostly positive PR
People claim to hear mostly negative PR
Sep
Oct
Nov
Dec
Jan
Feb
Mar
Apr
May
June
July
Aug
Sep
Oct
Nov
Dec
Jan
Feb

Source: Millward Brown Tracker, September 2004–February 2006; dotted line marks start of womenswear campaign
Base: 400 adults

**Figure 26:** *Red* magazine, November 2005

Key fashion journalists also endorsed the campaign and clothes (see Figure 26):

*They've cleaned up their act brilliantly, and given the confidence back to the consumer. A few years ago we weren't sure what M&S stood for, but now the advertising is fantastic.*

Jane Bruton, *Grazia*, April 2006

*Buoyed up the buzz created by a glossy ad campaign, the store's fashion directors put on a sizzling show. Critics are hailing the range as a bold and confident return to the high-street retailer's best.*

*Hello!*, Autumn 2005

### Brand image

Brand momentum is now at its highest point ever (see Figure 27) and M&S is increasingly seen as being 'one step ahead of the competition'. Moreover, perceptions of innovation are increasing across both food and clothing ranges (see Figure 28).

### Consideration

First choice/serious consideration has significantly increased in Food and Womenswear in line with campaign timings (see Figures 29–31).

### Footfall

Improvements in footfall have brought in an additional 18 million customer visits over the course of the year.[24] Footfall peaks in September and November as Womenswear and Christmas campaigns start (see Figure 32).

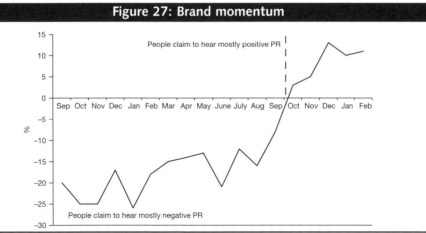

## Figure 27: Brand momentum

Source: Millward Brown. Based on claimed perceptions that M&S is 'On the way down' vs 'On the way up'. Base: 400 adults

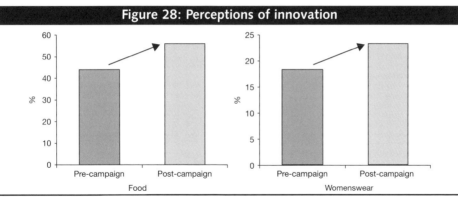

## Figure 28: Perceptions of innovation

Source: Millward Brown tracking, statistically significant shifts. Food is February/March 2005 vs February/March 2006, Womenswear is June/July 2005 vs February/March 2006. Base: 400 adults

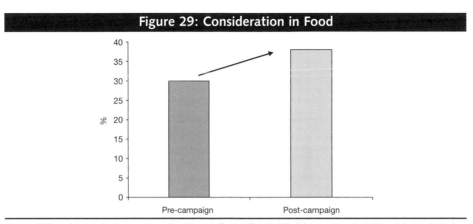

## Figure 29: Consideration in Food

Source: Millward Brown business unit tracker. Statistically significant shift. February/March 2005 vs February/March 2006. Base: 400 adults

## Figure 30: Consideration in Womenswear

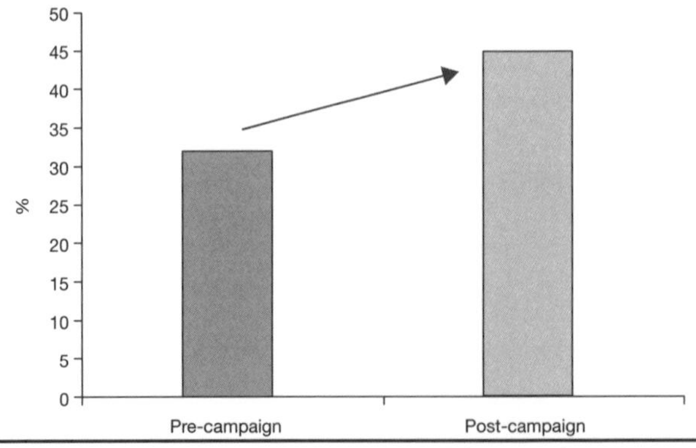

Source: Millward Brown business unit tracker. Statistically significant shift. June/July 2005 vs June/July 2006.
Base 400: adults

## Figure 31: Significantly more women 'love to wear' M&S

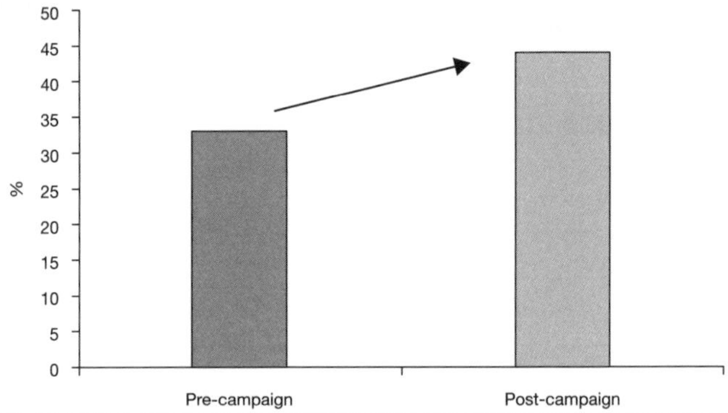

Source: Millward Brown business unit tracker. Statistically significant shift. June/July 2005 vs June/July 2006.
Base: 400 adults

## Figure 32: Footfall rises vs the market (removes seasonal effect)

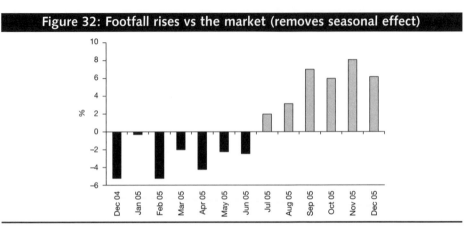

Source: Marks & Spencer

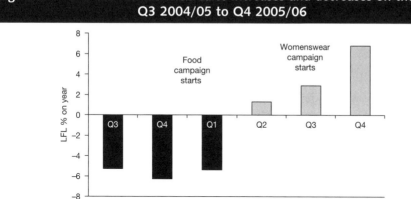

**Figure 33: Total like-for-like M&S sales increases and decreases on the year, Q3 2004/05 to Q4 2005/06**

Source: Marks & Spencer

## Sales

On 11 April 2006, M&S 'smashed expectations'[25] by announcing a fourth-quarter increase in UK sales of 9.1% on the year. Food sales were up 8.4%, whilst sales of general merchandise rose by 9.1% (see Figure 33).

Impressively, these results were achieved against a backdrop of mounting gloom on the high street, with March 2006 sales 1.4% lower than in 2005.[26] Recent like-for-like sales trends at rival Next show sales tumbling around 9% whilst Philip Green warned that operating profits at BHS were likely to be down 30% this year.[27]

On the back of these sales results Stuart Rose, gave initial profit guidance for the year ending April 2006 of between £745 and £755m.[28]

## Share price

At the time of writing, the M&S share price was 595.5p, vindicating the City's faith that M&S was worth much more than the Revival Acquisitions proposed 400p per share offer.

# The role of communications

A casual glance at Figures 27–33 shows a clear correlation between the turnaround in Marks & Spencer's fortunes and the timing of communications. However, given the changes at product level, without econometric modelling, disentangling the precise overall contribution of communications is impossible.

In proving beyond reasonable doubt that communications have contributed more than they have cost, we have therefore restricted ourselves to demonstrating that the key Womenswear and Food campaigns paid back at category level. In fact, this approach is likely to underestimate the communications effect because it does not account for the halo effect of people coming in to one department and then browsing in other departments on their way through the store.

In each instance we will show:

- what other factors must be taken into consideration
- that people saw the communications
- that people perceived the desired messages
- that communications were persuasive amongst occasional and lapsed shoppers
- that items featured in the advertising were runaway bestsellers.

Because just over 70% of M&S's shares are estimated to be in the hands of financial institutions,[29] in discussing the potential effect of communications on share price, we will look at the reaction of retail analysts, who are the key influencers of fund managers.

## The impact of marketing communications on clothing

### What other factors have changed?

The truth is that when it comes to M&S clothing much has changed. Opening prices are lower, the in-store environment is improving, there's a new staff service training programme, and clothes are becoming more stylish (see Figure 34). The importance of these changes should not be underestimated, and should take a large share of the credit for current incremental sales amongst existing customers.

### The impact of communications on clothing

Awareness of the campaign is now near universal (see Figure 35) and the campaign also communicates the correct message (see Figure 36).

### The campaign is persuasive

The campaign was persuasive across all media (see Figure 37).

**Figure 34: In-store improvements, September 2005**

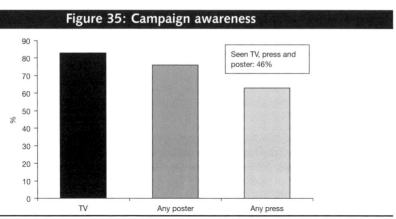

**Figure 35: Campaign awareness**

Source: Millward Brown advertising evaluation, March 2006. Base: 80 women (low sample size as these are initial results)

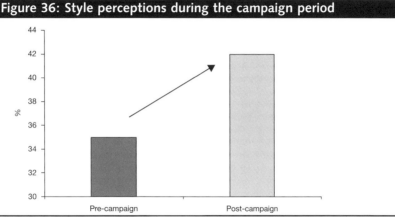

**Figure 36: Style perceptions during the campaign period**

Source: Millward Brown womenswear tracker. Statistically significant shift. July/August 2005 vs February/March 2006. Base: 400 adults

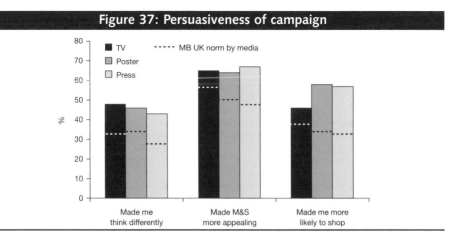

**Figure 37: Persuasiveness of campaign**

Source: Millward Brown advertising evaluation, February 2006. Base: TV 195, Poster 128, Press 157

*Items featured in adverts were runaway bestsellers*

A cream three-quarter-sleeved blouse worn by Twiggy in the February execution has sold more in one week than any other product in the history of M&S. Even the travel bags that the girls carry in the ad, which retail for £119, have had to be re-ordered to cope with demand. Sales of products from the first execution were equally impressive (see Table 2).

| Table 2: Weekly sales uplift peaks on hero featured items in first execution, September 2005 | | | | |
|---|---|---|---|---|
| **Twiggy** | *Crew Neck* | *Indigo Jean* | *Boots* | *Wrap Cardigan* |
| Uplift on week | 105% | 64% | 107% | 934% |
| **Erin** | *Military Jacket* | *Culottes* | *Wedge Boot* | *Black Cap* |
| Uplift on week | 115% | 110% | 128% | 317% |
| **Noemie** | *Green Skirt* | *Riding Boot* | *Fur Gilet* | *Polo Neck* |
| Uplift on week | 197% | 78% | 652% | 161% |
| **Laura** | *Grey Cardigan* | *Culottes* | *Boots* | *Silver Scarf* |
| Uplift on week | 721% | 458% | 60% | 291% |

*Lapsed shoppers re-engaged*

It could be argued that sales increases could be accounted for purely by existing customers spending more on better products. Research shows, however, that we have successfully re-engaged lapsed clothing customers (see Figure 38).

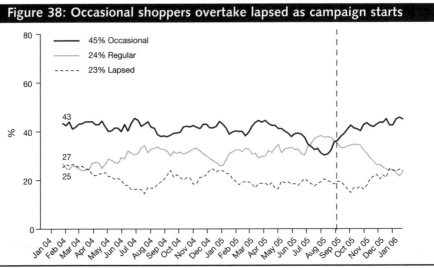

Figure 38: Occasional shoppers overtake lapsed as campaign starts

Source: Millward Brown womenswear tracker. Base: 400, 2004–2006

*Campaign creates a halo effect on general merchandise sales* (see Figure 39)

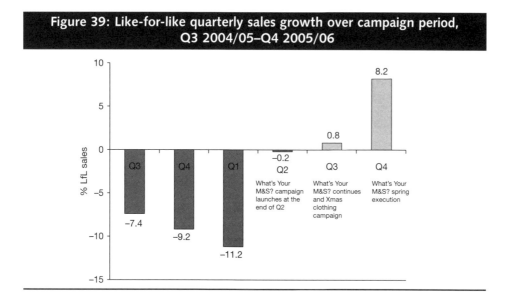

Figure 39: Like-for-like quarterly sales growth over campaign period, Q3 2004/05–Q4 2005/06

## The case for payback in clothing

Given the likely effect of improvements to product and price on existing customers, the fairest way to assess payback in clothing is to look only at the value of lapsed shoppers who re-engaged with M&S during campaign periods.

Fashion Trak data tells us that over the autumn 2005 period in which the 'What's Your M&S?' campaign aired, an additional 1.4 million people claim to have shopped for clothes at M&S.[30] Like most retailers, M&S does not disclose average basket size or customer frequency, so in order to assign a value to these customers we will have to make some educated estimations.

At the most conservative estimate, communications can only ever fully take the credit for people's first visit, as all subsequent visits will be influenced by their initial experience, so let's assume that each of these people came in only once.

Even Verdict does not have access to an average UK clothing retail basket size. However, Paul Mason, the chief executive of Matalan, went on record in 2002 to say that he wanted to raise the company's average basket size above £20.[31] So let's imagine that an M&S shopper's average basket size is the same as a Matalan shopper's was in 2002.

That would give us 1.4 million people coming in once, and each spending £20, which is the equivalent of £28m worth of incremental sales in autumn alone. Again, M&S does not disclose a clothing margin, but Deutsche Bank's model estimates it to be in the region of 53.3%.[32] This suggests that the extra customers would have generated an incremental £14.9m worth of profit over this autumn period alone.

Clothing media spend for this period was £5.7m,[33] suggesting an estimated ROI for the launch of the clothing campaigns of £2.61 per £1 spent on media.

During the autumn period (Q3 2005/06) like-for-like general merchandise sales (95% of which are clothing) were up 0.8% on the year. Over the Q4 period in which the second spring 'What's Your M&S?' execution appeared, like-for-like general merchandise sales were up 8.2%, suggesting that the campaign has built momentum, and that the ROI for this second phase would be significantly higher.

## The impact of communications on food

*People saw the communications*

Every execution in the 'Not Just Food, M&S Food' campaign has outperformed branding and recognition tracking norms (see Figure 40).

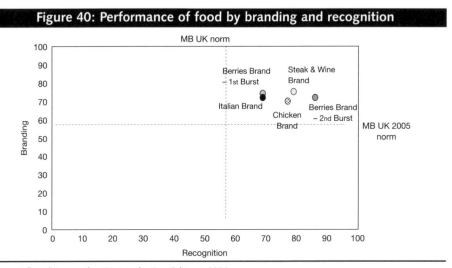

**Figure 40: Performance of food by branding and recognition**

Source: Millward Brown advertising evaluation, February 2006

*People took out the right messages*

Since the campaign launched, M&S has regained the lead from Tesco on the key measures of 'food you would be happy to serve your friends' and 'No 1 for special occasions'.[34] Advertising evaluation showed that people clearly took out the fact that M&S is passionate about quality in food (see Figure 41).

*The campaign is persuasive*

The launch execution achieved the highest ever persuasion score for any M&S ad. Subsequent executions have continued to drive increases in claimed likelihood of shopping at M&S. Importantly, the advertising has proved persuasive amongst occasional and lapsed shoppers as well as loyal customers (see Figures 42 and 43).

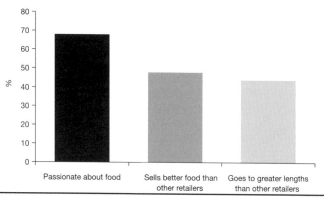

**Figure 41: Customer evaluations of M&S's passion for food**

Source: Millward Brown advertising evaluation, September 2005. Base: 201

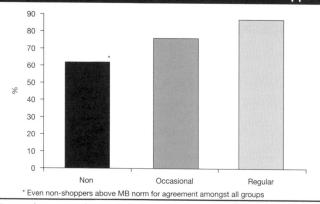

**Figure 42: Italian execution: 'made M&S seem more appealing'**

\* Even non-shoppers above MB norm for agreement amongst all groups

Source: Millward Brown advertising evaluation, September 2005. Base: 196

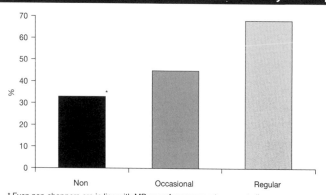

**Figure 43: Italian execution: 'made me more likely to shop'**

\* Even non-shoppers are in line with MB norm for agreement amongst all groups

Source: Millward Brown advertising evaluation, September 2005. Base: 196

*Featured products sell like hot cakes*

The launch execution caused a national stampede on hot chocolate puddings (see Figure 44). Other featured products have seen equally significant sales uplifts (see Table 3).

**Figure 44: In-store sold-out sign from time of launch advert, April 2005**

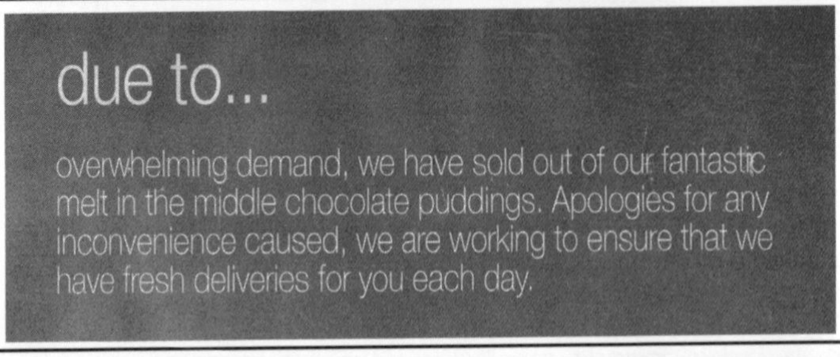

due to...
overwhelming demand, we have sold out of our fantastic melt in the middle chocolate puddings. Apologies for any inconvenience caused, we are working to ensure that we have fresh deliveries for you each day.

**Table 3: Weekly sales uplifts on the week prior to the campaign, April 2005 and June 2005**

| | | | | | |
|---|---|---|---|---|---|
| **1st advert** | *Roast potatoes* | *Tender stem broccoli* | *Channel Island cream* | *Chocolate pudding* | *Roast chicken* |
| Uplift on the week prior to campaign | 454% | 145% | 246% | 288% | 103% |
| **3rd advert** | *Reserve Parma ham* | *Pannacotta* | *Spinach ricotta ravioli* | *Basil pesto* | |
| Uplift on the week prior to campaign | 249% | 1207% | 301% | 367% | |

*Campaign creates a halo effect on total sales*

Communications campaigns coincide with step-changes in the overall performance of food sales (see Figure 45).

**Figure 45: Quarterly like-for-like sales growth, Q3 2004/05–Q4 2005/06**

% LfL sales
7
6
5
4
3
2
1
0
−1
−2
−3
−4
Q3
Q4
Q1
Q2
Q3
Q4
−2.5
−3.1
0.7
2.7
5.1
5.6
Not Just Food campaign starts

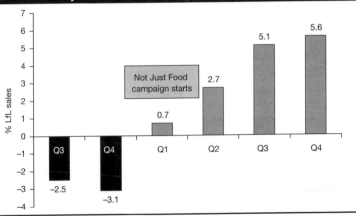

## The case for payback in food

At the time of writing, M&S had not yet published full-year revenue figures, but applying City forecasts to the percentage swings above we can estimate the value of incremental sales over the campaign period. If the Q4 2004/05 trend had continued into financial year 2005/06, like-for-like performance would have declined 3.1% rather than risen an estimated 3.6%. Like-for-like improvement using the estimated 6.7% swing from −3.1% to an estimated +3.6% implies a benefit of around £230m.[35]

M&S does not disclose a food margin, but Deutsche Bank's model estimates it to be in the region of 32%,[36] which gives us an estimated incremental profit figure for food of £73.6m. On a food media spend of £17.6m[37] we would have to assume only that communications have contributed 24% of incremental sales to pay back at a category level. We have seen that communications have been persuasive amongst lapsed, occasional and regular shoppers, and that since the launch of the campaign M&S has regained the high ground from the supermarkets on key quality measures. Given that the only other changes to have happened over the campaign period are the Cook! relaunch, repackaging of sandwiches, and the EAT WELL scheme, M&S is more than comfortable that communications contributed more than 24%:

> We are firmly of the opinion that communications contributed to considerably more than the increase in incremental sales required for them to pay back. Our confidence in the financial return of the campaign is reflected by our ongoing commitment to supporting it.

> Guy Farrent, M&S Director of Food

## The impact of communications on City analysts

City analysts are frequently reticent about attributing the financial success of the companies they monitor to marketing. A recent survey by the IPA found that only 5% of analysts felt that marketing was not at all 'a big black hole'[38] (see Figure 46).

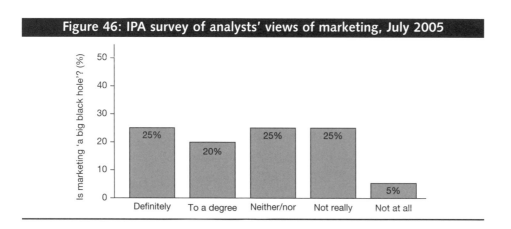

**Figure 46: IPA survey of analysts' views of marketing, July 2005**

By contrast, many leading retail analysts have cited communications as a significant factor in M&S's performance (see Table 4).

Some analysts have included pictures, whilst others reference advertising in their report titles (see Figure 47).

| Table 4: Quotations from leading retail analyst equity notes, from September 2005 to date | |
| --- | --- |
| **Merrill Lynch** | 'Sales of womenswear fuelled by Twiggy *et al.*' |
| **JPMorgan** | 'We believe that M&S is getting increasing traction with its high-profile advertising campaigns' |
| **Dresdner Kleinwort Wasserstein** | 'The well-judged advertising campaign is clearly benefiting footfall' |
| **citigroup** | 'Advertising and product innovations drove Food LfL of +5.1%' |
| **CAZENOVE** | 'Meanwhile food LfL sales saw a sequential step up – likely to be benefiting from the marketing message reinforcing the business's core credentials' |
| **Deutsche Bank** | 'The adverts have played a more important role than in the typical retail recovery story' |
| **CHEUVREUX** | 'The clothing, combined with an aggressive marketing campaign, has hit all the right notes with customers and the media' |
| **UBS** | 'The company believes that the bulk of trading improvements reflects product innovation and the willingness of customers to return to a brand less tarnished by past troubles … although the high-profile TV campaign was also a major contributing factor' |

### Figure 47: Extracts from City analysts' reports

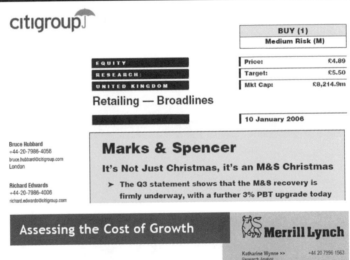

Some analysts explicitly relate confidence in future earnings to marketing:

*Food benefited from an increase in advertising, its campaign has now been in place for several months so it looks likely to drive respectable LfL growth for the rest of the year.*

Bruce Hubbard, Citigroup, January 2006

*The new adverts have been first class, they will deliver further benefits through increasing trust in the brand and thereby conversion, and through giving M&S the right to sell premium products at premium prices.*

Rod Whitehead, Deutsche Bank, March 2006

*We expect the M&S shares to still outperform the sector next year because:*

*Food which represents 50% of net UK retail sales is a relatively defensive area of retail ... and keeps footfall flowing through the stores, especially if the current advertising continues to support customer acquisition and sales growth.*

Phil Rudman, Chevreux, October 2005

Q2 sales results, which showed positive growth for the first time in over two years, were announced on 12 October 2005. Figure 48, however, clearly shows an accelerated increase in share price starting in September 2005 at the time of increased PR buzz around sales of clothes featured in the 'What's Your M&S?' campaign.

**Figure 48: M&S share price: accelerated increase coincides with the launch of 'What's Your M&S?'**

## An objective perspective on payback

Writing this paper, we will admit to a vested interest in arguing that communications paid back, so we advise you not to simply take our word for it. Here's what Rod Whitehead, Senior Retail Analyst at Deutsche Bank, has to say on the matter of payback at a total business level:[39]

*We estimate that M&S has spent an extra £15m (20%) on advertising over the last year. This has only taken advertising from 1% to 1.2% of sales, and will only have needed to generate an extra £35m of sales (0.5%) to pay for itself, which we believe it has comfortably done.*

Rod Whitehead, Deutsche Bank, April 2006

## Increasing shareholder value

In the absence of modelling it would be naïve to attempt to estimate communications' potential impact on share price. However, if you believe that the incremental sales and PR stemming from communications have played any role at all in raising share price, it is worth considering what this means in terms of shareholder value.

If, in a hypothetical world, shareholders had accepted Revival's proposed offer of 400p, and re-invested their money back in an averagely performing UK retail stock, those shares would now be worth 461.4p,[40] representing a growth on investment of 15.5%. By contrast, shares in Marks & Spencer are now worth 595.5p, representing a 48.9% increase on the proposed offer of 400p.

In addition to this growth, since July 2004 M&S shareholders have received dividends worth 16.9p per share.

## We rest our case ...

Looking back on where M&S was in April 2004 and at where it stands today, it is clear that communications have been key to changing the public face of the organisation. Furthermore, in the course of this paper we have proven the following:

- that communications helped turn a vicious PR circle into a virtuous one
- that communications combined with the associated PR changed the lens through which people see the M&S product, reminding everyone just how irresistible M&S Food is and making lapsed shoppers confident enough in the style credentials of M&S to be happy to shop there for clothes again
- that City retail analysts have taken marketing communications into account when assessing M&S's potential to deliver sustained growth.

If you agree with the above, it would seem *beyond reasonable doubt* that communications have played an indispensable role in helping M&S turn the corner towards growth. For as long as the product stays good, these re-engaged customers will continue to add value to M&S (see Figure 49).

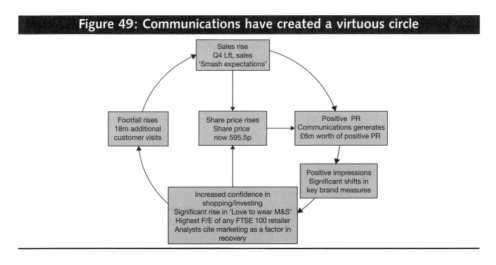

**Figure 49: Communications have created a virtuous circle**

# Notes

1. Source: British Retail Consortium.
2. An update on official trading results was submitted one week after the competition closing date, outlining the key figures included in the May 2006 Annual Review which could not be included earlier due to the regulations outlined in the Financial Services and Markets Act 2004. Total Group Sales for the year ending April 2006 were £7.8bn vs £7.5bn in 2005. Total Group Operating Profit for the year ending April 2006 was £855.8m vs £649.1m in 2005. Over the course of the year, customer visits increased by nearly 350,000 a week to just over 15 million (vs 14.7 last year). In the final quarter post-Christmas, which saw the continuation of the Food campaign and the second execution in Womenswear, customer visits rose by 4.7% – against an overall market decline of 7%.
3. Philip Green first made an attempted bid for M&S in 2000.
4. Source: Marks & Spencer press office.
5. Mary Portas, the *Telegraph*, 27 February 2006.
6. The single biggest institutional investor in M&S, who at the time of the bid had built up over a 12% stake in M&S.
7. Under Takeover Panel rules, Green was barred from making another offer for M&S for at least six months.
8. bbc.co.uk, 14 July 2004 – based on a survey of 200 shareholders outside the AGM.
9. This title is taken from a comment made by Barry Hyman at the 2004 AGM: 'I'd rather have a Marks & Spencer seen through Rose-tinted glasses, than one going Green around the gills.'
10. Stuart Rose, AGM, 14 July 2004.
11. Stuart Rose, AGM, 14 July 2004.
12. Stuart Rose, Land Securities Conference, 2004.
13. Stuart Rose, Speech, July 2004. Millward Brown research shows that spontaneous claimed shopping is higher amongst female clothing customers than any other category of shoppers. This is borne out by qualitative research. Womenswear was also where the City was most keen to see growth.
14. 'Bill Bernbach Said …', DDB 2002.
15. This includes Simply Foods.
16. Opening price points were lowered across clothing to be in line with the competition, and more stock was moved into the 'good' bracket of the retail categories 'good, better, best' increasing share of sales in this area.
17. In spring 2004 Tesco overtook M&S for the first time ever on the Millward Brown tracking measure 'No 1 for Special Occasion' and switching data showed that Waitrose was also a threat.
18. Kate Bostock, the new Director of Womenswear's internal buying mantra in 2005.
19. Flamingo Qualitative Research, 2003.
20. This was calculated by collating press coverage that mentioned the 'Your M&S' campaign, and equating the column inches to paid-for advertising space. Source: Walker Media.
21. Source: GSC.
22. This phrase was used in a TV guide to describe the production values of a television adaptation of *A Midsummer Night's Dream*.
23. The sketch went something along the lines of 'this is not just a potato … this is a priapic tuber' and ended with the priceless 'this is not just M&S Food … this is S&M Food'.
24. Source: Marks & Spencer.
25. Source: DrKW Equity Research, 11 April 2006.
26. Source: British Retail Consortium survey including both food and clothing retailers.
27. Source: *The Sunday Times* Rich List, April 2006.
28. This compares to profit before tax and exceptional charges of £560m for the financial year 2004/05. Source: Marks & Spencer.
29. Source: Marks & Spencer.
30. Fashion Trak, 12 weeks ending 11 December 2005.
31. The *Independent*, 24 October 2002.
32. Source: Deutsche Bank, April 2006.
33. Source: Walker Media.
34. Source Millward Brown – base 400 adults, pre measure is February/March 2005.
35. Due to the legal restrictions at the time of writing, our pay-back calculations in Food could be based only on analyst estimations of full-year revenue uplifts. We can now confirm that the actual uplift in like-for-like sales of M&S Food was 3.6% which was exactly in line with analyst expectations.
36. Source: Deutsche Bank, April 2006.
37. Source: Walker Media.
38. *How Analysts View Marketing*, the IPA, July 2005.
39. Rod Whitehead, one of London's leading retail analysts, Deutsche Bank, 'No Ordinary Recovery', March 2005.
40. Calculated using a market cap weighted virtual basket of UK retail stocks (Bloomberg code F3R ETG), between 8 July 2004 (the day Green's bid was rejected) and the time of writing (26.4.06).

## Chapter 7

# Naturella

## Mother Nature's gift: how communications drove one of the most successful launches in one of the most challenging marketplaces in the world

**By Gurdeep Puri, Leo Burnett, and Mark Stockdale, Wheelbarrow**

Feminine protection is big business, worth about $16bn a year worldwide. It is, however, also one of the most conservative, sensitive and deeply entrenched market sectors, with 75% of women staying with one brand of pad their entire life – as well as being a difficult topic for effective communications.

Despite these challenges, Procter & Gamble (P&G) decided to launch a new premium-price pad brand, Naturella, in a number of emerging markets. Brands such as Always, P&G's main product in more developed markets, were struggling in these countries, where cheaper, more basic pads attracted the loyalty of women. Market research showed that Naturella was seen as reflective of femininity and nature – rather than 'plasticky' and technological – and so the creative strategy broke from the rational, scientific norms of the category to create a subtle, feminine 'world of nature' that positioned menstruation as a positive and life-affirming part of what it means to be a woman.

By creating communications that women in these markets would want to see and act upon, the campaign was able to forge a genuine connection with its target audience, and thus easily surpassed all its original price and mass share targets. Tracking studies also showed that the TV ads were regarded as much more enjoyable than others in the category. Furthermore, econometric modelling demonstrated that communications played an integral role in establishing the Naturella brand, and also produced an estimated ROI ratio of at least 2:1.

## Introduction

Right now, roughly 10% of the world's women are menstruating. And they will do so, regularly, for 30–40 years of their life. 'Feminine care' (femcare) is thus big business – about US$16bn a year worldwide, of which roughly US$10bn is pads.[1]

But it is also an exceptionally challenging category in which to do business. Periods are a tricky topic, and not just for men. Cultural sensitivities are complex (for many this is a strict taboo) and poor product performance can have profoundly embarrassing consequences. Unsurprisingly, therefore, consumers tend to stick with brands they know and trust – three-quarters of women typically stick with the same pad brand their entire lives.

Procter & Gamble (P&G) markets the most successful femcare brand in the world: Always.[2] Worth US$2bn globally, in some countries its volume share exceeds 50%.[3]

So why develop another brand, especially if it meant targeting some of the most conservative consumers in the world? And given it was clear from the start that success was going to depend largely on our ability to produce unusually effective communications, wasn't that decision fairly risky?

This paper will show how communications[4] overcame formidable barriers-to-entry to change profoundly entrenched consumer behaviour. The key was to produce communications that women wanted to watch and wanted to act upon – just getting noticed wasn't enough. The result was one of the most rapid and profitable new product launches ever seen in this unique and difficult marketplace.

## Background

Always Ultra is a technologically advanced product: a thin pad consisting of a firm, super-absorbent top layer over an 'inner gel core', promising 'ultimate protection' (dramatised in advertising by the 'blue-goo test'). The brand dominates developed markets, but in emerging markets its premium positioning limits its potential. In these countries cheaper brands dominate the mass market with softer pads that rely simply on their thickness for absorption.

To compete with these brands, P&G needed a more keenly priced product. So, in 2002, it launched an inexpensive thick, soft pad, branded 'Always Classic'. However, despite testing well against the competition, it failed to achieve a substantial share, and a significant proportion of its volume came from within the Always portfolio. Clearly, just introducing an inexpensive, good-quality thick pad wasn't enough to persuade large numbers of loyal mass-market consumers to switch.

The decision was therefore taken to develop a new brand, to sit alongside Always. But launching a completely new mass-market brand presented formidable challenges: the competition was solid and firmly established, and consumers were, to say the least, hesitant about trying 'new and untested' brands.

Moreover, commercial analysis established a price floor below which P&G couldn't fall and an investment ceiling above which it couldn't rise. Fighting on price was clearly not an option – indeed, a premium was more likely – and to achieve even a reasonable price point, the scope for building in significant product advantage was limited by the need to contain costs.

It was clear, then, that success was going to be dependent largely on our ability to use communications to transform deeply ingrained patterns of behaviour.

## The new brand

Talking to consumers in emerging markets, we found that Always women were quite different from those loyal to mass-market brands – the former progressive in their attitudes, the latter traditional. The more traditional women were drawn to natural products across a range of categories:

*These are better for body and soul.*

And they saw Always as 'technologically plasticky'.

They also believed passionately in the importance of femininity – in part, being attractive to the opposite sex but also, more deeply, 'what it means to be a woman'. This has particular, yet paradoxical, relevance during menstruation: on the one hand, periods are central to 'womanhood' (being integral to the ability to give birth); but, on the other, the experience of menstruation can undermine any feeling of attractive femininity, especially in a social context. Yet brands weren't reflecting these emotional complexities.

Mass-market products were perceived to be both affordable and reliable – highly relevant because traditional women were very concerned about spending 'too much' of their limited household income on their own personal needs. However, talking to traditional women about these thicker pads also revealed two untapped strengths: first, their use of cotton in the top sheets conveyed tradition and naturalness; and, second, their softness conveyed femininity.

And so a positioning opportunity was identified, built around the latent strengths of soft pads, reflecting traditional women's preference for 'things natural' and 'things feminine'. It was summarised as 'Natural Feminine Care', a territory unique in the category, avoiding the existing rational battlegrounds of 'value and reliability' or 'technological protection'. And so Naturella was born (see Figure 1).

### Figure 1: Naturella pack

## Launch objectives

The objectives were ambitious.

1. Articulate the 'Natural Feminine Care' positioning compellingly enough to change deeply entrenched behaviour.
2. Build awareness of this positioning rapidly – targets for Year 1 were:
   - 70% (Latin America)
   - 80% (Central and Eastern Europe).

Thereby:

3. Achieve Year 1 critical mass – volume share targets were:
   - 7.4% (Mexico)
   - 7.4% (Venezuela)
   - 9.0% (Russia)
   - 8.0% (Poland).
4. Steal volume share from mass-market brands, whilst supporting a price premium.
5. Grow overall P&G volume share by minimising cannibalisation of Always:
   - less than 22% of volume to come from Always in any market.

## Creative strategy

The role for communications was twofold.

1. Be disruptive: shake conservatively minded consumers out of their long-established behaviours.
2. Be inviting: give them the confidence to try something new.

Given the strength of mass-market competitors, we knew this was a tough job. To change behaviour, shouting louder or just looking different wasn't enough; we had to make traditional women want to see our commercials and want to act on what they saw.

Despite their associating menstruation with fertility, the category was anything but natural and life affirming: advertising was invariably rational, generally portrayed periods as a problem, and products as 'technological', 'reliable' or 'affordable'. The more we considered this, the more inappropriate it seemed – after all, our emotionally intuitive audience does not choose products on the basis of cold, hard logic.

It also struck us that this functional approach demeans menstruation as just 'A.N. Other' bodily function. As one Russian lady put it:

*I'm ashamed in front of my husband because of these commercials.*

Our creative strategy was therefore built on four pillars.

1. Break from the coldly rational category norms.
2. Tap into the emotional, intuitive way traditional women choose.
3. Be delicate – avoid making them feel awkward, let alone ashamed.
4. Implicitly position menstruation as being positive, natural and life affirming.

## Creative executions

The key that unlocked the creative strategy was the insight that traditional women see menstruation as part of the 'gift of fertility'. Indeed, a common euphemism for periods was 'Mother Nature's gift' – an empowering thought evoking a uniquely matriarchal view of all things natural and life giving.

So we probed the idea of 'nature' in groups, and women talked about a timeless, sensual, beautiful place – an escape from the pressures of daily life. It struck us that this perception of nature was itself a powerful metaphor for protection – not a harsh and technological protection, but a natural, soft, feminine protection, 'good for body and soul'.

Our creative idea, then, was to create a 'Naturella world of nature' where women could feel protected, happy and liberated; where they could celebrate 'what it means to be a woman'.

The first executions featured a 'green door' through which the viewer passes as a voiceover announces 'Mother Nature has something to show you.' We enter a beautiful natural world, and see women happily at ease, enjoying themselves away from the pressures of day-to-day life.

Instead of technological claims and imagery, we use symbolism and language drawn from nature, describing the product subtly, almost sensually.

The collage of stills (see Figure 2) taken from the first two commercials conveys the style and tone of the campaign.

**Figure 2: Collage of stills from 'Mother Nature' and 'My World' TVCs**

## Communications plan

An integrated, multi-sensory communications plan was designed to bring Mother Nature's world to life as evocatively as possible, across a variety of communications channels.

In each market the core of the plan was TV supported by communications within the trade. This was because:

- the target audience are very heavy TV viewers, therefore we could build coverage rapidly
- TV is particularly effective at involving its audience emotionally
- special events ('Naturella Havens') and dramatic in-store displays evoked values of 'naturalness and femininity', and delivered brand experiences directly to the audience (see Figure 3).

**Figure 3: Examples of trade communications activities**

These core media were supplemented according to local habits, the strengths of local channels and their 'fit' with our creative strategy. Wherever possible the team worked with media owners to make the most of the local environment.

## How successful was the launch?

The launch exceeded all expectations.

### Naturella share

Initially the plan was to test Naturella in Mexico City for nine months. However, after only three months volume share reached a national equivalent of 8.2%,[5] 11% ahead of the first-year target. So rapid was this growth that the test was cancelled in favour of a full national roll-out. And within six months of going national, volume share reached almost 15%, twice the Mexican Year 1 target.

It soon became clear we had a runaway success on our hands, and the experience was repeated everywhere we launched – entrenched consumer behaviours were disrupted, and dramatic share growth followed. Consequently, all the first-year 'critical-mass' targets were beaten comfortably (see Table 1).

| Table 1: Naturella Year 1 volume share of pads | | | |
|---|---|---|---|
| | % volume share after Year 1 | Year 1 'critical mass' % volume share target | % difference over target |
| Mexico | 11.9 | 7.4 | 60.8 |
| Venezuela | 10.4 | 7.4 | 40.5 |
| Russia | 12.1 | 9.0 | 34.4 |
| Poland | 9.5 | 8.0 | 18.8 |

Note: Year 1 Mexican national figures are made up of six months of regional tests followed by six months of national distribution

However, the true scale of success is masked by the challenges of managing distribution in emerging markets. Supply issues in Russia, for example, limited effective distribution to only 60% after three months (well below plan); despite this, national volume share reached 7.4%, equivalent to 12% where distributed. How many other brands can claim a national volume share of 12% within three months of launch?

If we adjust for these distribution shortfalls, the shares achieved are even further ahead of target (see Table 2).

| Table 2: Naturella Year 1 adjusted volume share of pads (share per point of distribution) | | | |
|---|---|---|---|
| | % volume share after one year where distributed | Year 1 'critical mass' % volume share target | % difference over target |
| Mexico | 15.3 | 7.4 | 106.8 |
| Venezuela | 11.4 | 7.4 | 54.1 |
| Russia | 13.9 | 9.0 | 54.4 |
| Poland | 12.7 | 8.0 | 58.8 |

*P&G share*

In each market P&G's share increased significantly, achieving category leadership for the first time in both Mexico and Russia.

Indeed, if we combine the four markets to view them as one aggregated 'global emerging market',[6] the growth of P&G is nothing short of spectacular, volume share climbing from 24% before Naturella's launch to almost 40% by the end of 2005 – virtually doubling in just over three years (see Figure 4).

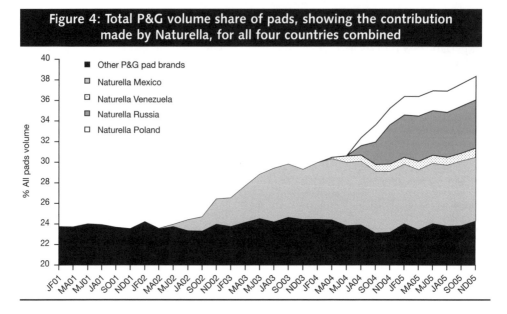

**Figure 4: Total P&G volume share of pads, showing the contribution made by Naturella, for all four countries combined**

- Other P&G pad brands
- Naturella Mexico
- Naturella Venezuela
- Naturella Russia
- Naturella Poland

The reason for P&G's huge growth is clear from Figure 4: not only did Naturella grow rapidly, it also brought in new business with little impact on P&G's existing pads volume. Indeed, analysis of Naturella buyers reveals that only 15% of brand-switching volume came from Always (see Table 3).

**Table 3: Naturella brand-switching analysis: Naturella buyers who came from Always**

|  | Weighted average of all countries (%) | Mexico (%) | Venezuela (%) | Russia (%) | Poland (%) |
|---|---|---|---|---|---|
| Always | 15.3 | 19.0 | 12.0 | 12.3 | 13.2 |
| Other brands | 84.3 | 81.0 | 88.0 | 81.3 | 86.6 |
| Total switching | 100.0 | 100.0 | 100.0 | 100.0 | 100.0 |

Not only is this 15% figure well below the 22% cannibalisation target, it's also less than would be predicted by Always' brand share (see Table 4).

## Table 4: Naturella brand-switching analysis: the contribution made by Always is lower than might be predicted

|  | Weighted average of all countries (%) | Mexico (%) | Venezuela (%) | Russia (%) | Poland (%) |
|---|---|---|---|---|---|
| % Naturella switches | 15.3 | 19.0 | 12.0 | 12.3 | 13.2 |
| Always % all pads[†] | 84.3 | 81.0 | 88.0 | 81.3 | 86.6 |
| Index[‡] | 100.0 | 100.0 | 100.0 | 100.0 | 100.0 |

[†] Always average volume share in the 12 months prior to Naturella launch in each country
[‡] Index of switches over share (100 = % share and % switching are the same)

## Table 5: Always volume share of pads, 2005 vs 2004, for all four countries combined

|  | 2004 (%) | 2005 (%) | Point change (%) |
|---|---|---|---|
| January–February | 20.2 | 20.8 | +0.6 |
| March–April | 20.0 | 20.3 | +0.3 |
| May–June | 19.8 | 20.7 | +0.9 |
| July–August | 20.1 | 20.6 | +0.5 |
| September–October | 19.6 | 20.9 | +1.3 |
| November–December | 19.9 | 21.2 | +1.3 |

## Table 6: Naturella brand-switching analysis: Naturella buyers who came from mass-market brands

|  | Weighted average of all countries (%) | Mexico (%) | Venezuela (%) | Russia (%) | Poland (%) |
|---|---|---|---|---|---|
| Mass-market thick brands | 79.6 | 70.9 | 85.2 | 71.3 | 84.4 |
| Other brands | 20.4 | 29.1 | 14.8 | 28.7 | 15.6 |
| Total switching | 100.0 | 100.0 | 100.0 | 100.0 | 100.0 |

Which is why Always has continued to grow, despite the rapid rise of Naturella, as indicated in Table 5.

### Source of business

By contrast, the mass-market brands have really lost out (see Table 6). Indeed, the non-P&G brands suffered immediately Naturella launched. Looking at the aggregated Global Emerging Market we can see the full extent of these competitive losses – from over 75% of all pads prior to Naturella's launch, to almost 60% just over three years later (see Figure 5).

### Sustaining a price premium

The price positions at launch are given in Table 7. In three countries Naturella was at a significant premium, and in Mexico it was at parity. Overall, Naturella had a 5.2% price premium against other non-P&G thick pads.

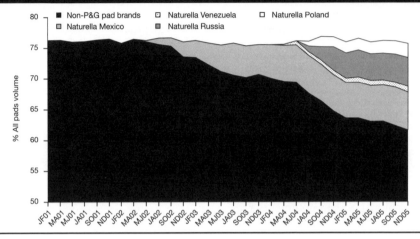

**Figure 5: Total non-P&G volume share of pads, showing the impact made by Naturella, for all countries combined**

| Table 7: Average pack prices in Year 1 of Naturella launch, in US$ | | | | | |
|---|---|---|---|---|---|
| | Weighted average of all countries | Mexico | Venezuela | Russia | Poland |
| Naturella | $1.01 [105] | $1.24 [100] | $1.40 [167] | $0.86 [112] | $0.93 [108] |
| Other non-P&G thick pads | $0.96 [100] | $1.24 [100] | $0.84 [100] | $0.77 [100] | $0.86 [100] |

Note: Figures in square brackets denote index of Naturella price over competitive price (100 = price parity)

Clearly, Naturella's rapid growth has been achieved whilst sustaining a price premium.

In summary, then, the launch was extraordinarily successful: deeply entrenched consumer behaviour was disrupted and so Naturella grew rapidly, despite a premium price, stealing heavily from competitors with minimal impact on Always, thereby virtually doubling P&G's volume share in just over three years. In short, Naturella didn't just meet its launch targets, it smashed them.

We'll now show that communications were largely responsible for this success, and that they've been the main driver of the brand's profitability. We shall provide three proofs.

1. An analysis demonstrating that the advertising and communications worked exactly as intended – traditional women wanted to see our commercials and wanted to act on what they saw.
2. Evidence that no other factors can explain Naturella's rapid growth.
3. Rigorous statistical analysis measuring directly the contribution made by advertising and communications.

## How did the advertising work?

*Breaking norms*

Research[7] showed the creative idea to be very impactful, Naturella ads generally scoring in the top fifth of results ever recorded by P&G (see Table 8).

| Table 8: TV ad testing: how engaging do viewers find the Naturella ads? | | | | |
|---|---|---|---|---|
| | Mexico (%) | Venezuela (%) | Russia (%) | Poland (%) |
| 'Mother Nature' | Top 20 | – | Top 20 | Top 20 |
| 'Nature Girls' | Top 20 | – | – | – |
| 'Discovery' | Top 20 | – | – | – |
| 'Balance' | Top 20 | Top 20 | Top 20 | Top 40 |
| 'Happy Skin' | – | Top 40 | – | – |

Typical respondent comments were:

*This advertising is like nothing else I see, it really stands out to capture my imagination.*

Poland

*It is most unusual for advertisements of products such as this to look as this does.*

Mexico

Once on-air, the advertising cut through the clutter of other commercials.[8] And not only were the executions more striking than the competition, but the strength of branding – and therefore correctly branded recall – was the highest in the category (see Table 9).[9]

| Table 9: Ad tracking: executional recognition, branded recall and strength of branding of pads advertising | | | |
|---|---|---|---|
| | Executional recognition (unbranded ad recognition) (%) | Correctly branded ad recall (%) | Correct brand attribution[†] (%) |
| **Russia**[†] | | | |
| Naturella | 81 | 61 | 75 |
| Always | 49 | 20 | 41 |
| Kotex | 77 | 42 | 55 |
| Bella | 18 | 2 | 11 |
| Carefree | 19 | 2 | 11 |
| Libresse | 60 | 18 | 30 |
| | | | |
| **Poland**[†] | | | |
| Naturella | 64 | 38 | 60 |
| Always | 52 | 15 | 29 |
| Bella | 22 | 4 | 18 |
| Subtelle | 20 | 4 | 20 |

[†] All data averaged for the first year of Naturella launch
[‡] The proportion of women who had recalled the executions who could then also correctly identify the brand being advertised (=2nd column divided by the 1st column)

## Table 10: Ad tracking: how much 'bang per buck' did each brand achieve?

|  | Share of voice (SOV) (%) | Execution recognition (unbranded ad recognition) (%) | Percentage points of recognition per percentage points of SOV[‡] | Correctly branded ad recall (%) | Percentage points of recall per percentage point of SOV |
|---|---|---|---|---|---|
| **Russia[†]** |  |  |  |  |  |
| Naturella | 14.7 | 81 | 5.51 | 61 | 4.15 |
| Always | 13.7 | 49 | 3.58 | 20 | 1.46 |
| Kotex | 18.5 | 77 | 4.16 | 42 | 2.27 |
| Bella | 5.4 | 18 | 3.33 | 2 | 0.37 |
| Carefree | 8.7 | 19 | 2.18 | 2 | 0.23 |
| Libresse | 14.3 | 60 | 4.20 | 18 | 1.26 |
| **Poland[†]** |  |  |  |  |  |
| Naturella | 12.6 | 64 | 5.08 | 38 | 3.02 |
| Always | 14.4 | 52 | 3.61 | 15 | 1.04 |
| Bella | 5.7 | 22 | 3.86 | 4 | 0.70 |
| Subtelle | 5.7 | 20 | 3.51 | 4 | 0.70 |

[†] All data averaged for the first year of Naturella launch
[‡] Amount of rcognition per amount of share of voice (= 2nd column divided by 1st column)
Each ad's score compared within its own country (= each ad divided by its country average, 100 = the country average)

However, this impact wasn't 'bought' with media weight, it was 'earned': by breaking from the norms of the category, per media dollar spent Naturella was more impactful, and generated the most branded recall, of any brand (i.e. we got more 'bang for our buck') (see Table 10).

Inevitably, then, brand awareness grew extremely quickly, becoming virtually universal by the end of Year 1 (see Figure 6). These awareness levels are well ahead of the launch targets (see Table 11).

## Figure 6: Brand tracking: total brand awareness of pad brands by the end of Year 1 of Naturella launch

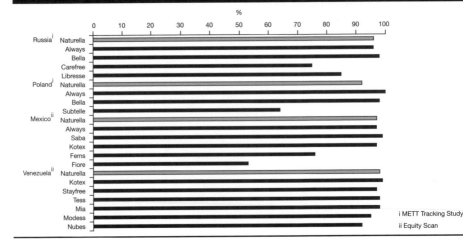

| | % total brand awareness after one year | Year 1 % total brand awareness target | % difference over target |
|---|---|---|---|
| **Table 11: Naturella's performance against brand awareness targets** | | | |
| Mexico | 96 | 70 | +37 |
| Venezuela | 98 | 70 | +40 |
| Russia | 96 | 80 | +20 |
| Poland | 92 | 80 | +15 |

### Wanting to watch

But breaking from the norms did more than just grab attention; it also won hearts:

*This commercial is beautiful – it combines natural beauty, harmony and life.*

Poland, ORS advertising pre-testing

*I want to be there – it is bright, clean, fresh and untouched, it is the world as it should be.*

Venezuela, ORS advertising pre-testing

*I love those advertisements with the girls in the hammocks – it is so beautiful, so peaceful.*

Mexico, in-market qual post-launch

*They are not city commercials – they talk about what is natural and good for you.*

Russia, in-market qual post-launch

Moreover, the association between femininity, fertility and nature (the 'Mother Nature' insight) was clearly understood:

*Nature is like a woman, women are of nature.*

Mexico, ORS advertising pre-testing

*It is very nice the ladies are in nature ... it expresses that the period is something natural.*

Venezuela, in-market qual post-launch

*Seeing womanhood in this way gave me positive feelings about being a woman.*

Poland, ORS advertising pre-testing

*It showed the beauty of nature and the beauty of women.*

Russia, ORS advertising pre-testing

And many women welcomed our more delicate approach:

*I can feel good watching it – this is the most attractive way I have seen of talking about this private, sensitive subject.*

Russia, ORS advertising pre-testing

*There was nothing unappetising about the ad, I can watch it with my family and still feel good about myself.*

Poland, in-market qual post-launch

| Table 12: Ad testing: how do viewers react to the Naturella ads? | | | | |
|---|---|---|---|---|
| | % favourable comments (% unfavourable comments) | | | |
| | Mexico | Venezuela | Russia | Poland |
| 'Mother Nature' | 82 (7) | – | 89 (39) | 91 (24) |
| 'Nature Girls' | 98 (12) | – | – | – |
| 'Discovery' | 87 (11) | – | – | – |
| 'Balance' | 95 (5) | 94 (8) | 79 (37) | 90 (22) |
| 'Happy Skin' | – | 95 (4) | – | – |

Because the advertising won hearts, traditional women wanted to watch it – indeed it prompted an exceptional number of favourable spontaneous comments (see Table 12).[10]

In-market tracking[11] showed the commercials to be the most 'watchable' in the category – if we compare Naturella to its respective country average, we're around 1.5 times 'more watchable' (see Table 13).

| Table 13: Ad tracking: did viewers enjoy watching the Naturella ads? | | |
|---|---|---|
| | Watchability[‡] (%) | Index vs rest of country |
| **Russia[†]** | | |
| Naturella | 56 | 151 |
| Always | 40 | 109 |
| Kotex | 45 | 123 |
| Bella | 23 | 62 |
| Carefree | 22 | 61 |
| Libresse | 35 | 94 |
| **Russian average** | **37** | **100** |
| | | |
| **Poland[†]** | | |
| Naturella | 84 | 149 |
| Always | 72 | 129 |
| Bella | 57 | 101 |
| Subtelle | 12 | 21 |
| **Polish average** | **56** | **100** |

[†] All data averaged for the first year of Naturella launch
[‡] Defined as % agreeing with statements 'I would like to see this ad this evening' or 'I would not mind seeing this ad this evening'
Each ad's score compared within its own country (= each ad divided by its country average, 100 = the country average)

## Wanting to act

The audience also clearly felt predisposed to acting on what we had to say to them:

*I remember seeing the commercials and thinking 'that is a product I must buy'!*

Mexico, in-market qual post-launch

*It made me want to try them.*

Russia, ORS advertising pre-testing

## Table 14: Ad testing: did viewers feel the Naturella ads were convincing?

|  | Mexico (%) | Venezuela (%) | Russia (%) | Poland (%) |
|---|---|---|---|---|
| 'Mother Nature' | Top 20 | – | Top 20 | Top 20 |
| 'Nature Girls' | Top 20 | – | – | – |
| 'Discovery' | Top 40 | – | – | – |
| 'Balance' | Top 20 | Top 40 | Top 20 | Top 20 |
| 'Happy Skin' | – | Top 40 | – | – |

Hence, the ads scored extremely highly on 'convincingness'[12] – the message being more likely to be accepted as true and relevant, compared to other ads (see Table 14). And the more women saw the ads, the more they considered purchasing Naturella (see Figures 7 and 8).[13]

## Figure 7: Ad tracking: what impact did the Naturella ads have on purchase intentions? (Poland)

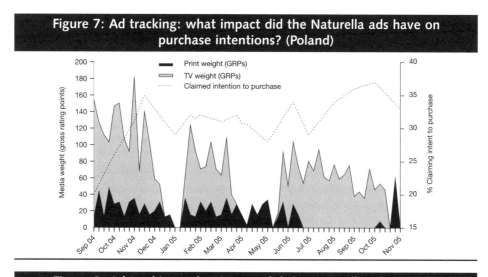

## Figure 8: Ad tracking: what impact did the Naturella ads have on purchase intentions? (Russia)

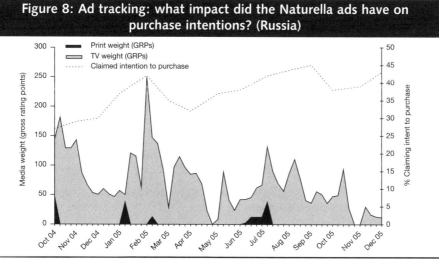

*Disruptive and inviting*

Viewers' emotional involvement in the advertising drove directly:

■ how much they wanted to see it, and
■ how much they wanted to act upon what they saw.

If we plot each brand's 'watchability score' against its 'bang per buck score', we can see a strong relationship (see Figure 9).

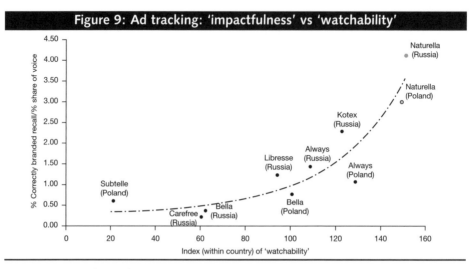

**Figure 9: Ad tracking: 'impactfulness' vs 'watchability'**

So emotional involvement (as measured by watchability) isn't just an end in itself: it drives campaign efficiency – Naturella's exceptional 'bang per media buck' is a function of having won the viewer's heart.

Moreover, there's an equally strong relationship between 'watchability' and purchase intention (see Figure 10).

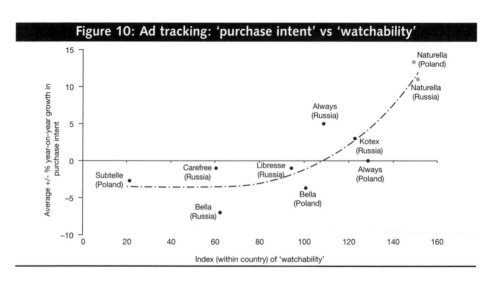

**Figure 10: Ad tracking: 'purchase intent' vs 'watchability'**

So winning hearts also increases campaign effectiveness because more people wanted to act upon what they saw.

In summary, the evidence is that Naturella's advertising worked as intended:

- it grabbed attention by breaking from category norms
- it was emotional, natural and empowering
- it was something traditional women wanted to see
- it was enjoyable and handled a difficult topic delicately
- it was something upon which traditional women wanted to act
- it tapped into the intuitive way they make choices.

In short, it was as inviting as it was disruptive.

## What other factors might have been responsible?

### Price

Naturella launched at a premium price versus the competition so its rapid share growth was not price driven.

### Distribution

Although distribution grew in each country,[14] we can remove its impact by looking at share per point of distribution (see Figure 11). Indeed, as noted earlier, Naturella's distribution build was slower than anticipated. So in reality the effect of distribution was to hamper, not fuel, Naturella's rapid growth.

### Media weight

Naturella's success wasn't 'bought' by outspending the competition. We've demonstrated already that the brand's communications worked harder per media dollar, being the most efficient and effective in the category.

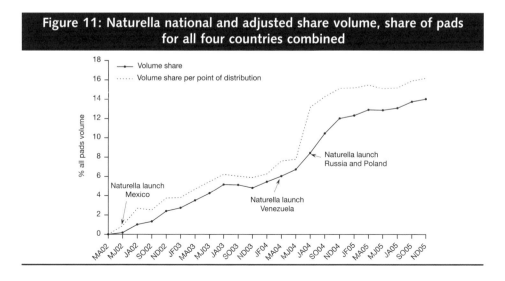

**Figure 11: Naturella national and adjusted share volume, share of pads for all four countries combined**

## Competition

It is highly unlikely that Naturella's success is due to changes in competitor activities. We launched in four countries, at three different times, so whilst it might be a plausible explanation of one market's success, to explain all four this way presents too many coincidences to be reasonable.

Indeed, rather than a weakening competitive environment, competition actually increased during Year 1 of Naturella's launch. For example, Kotex increased its media spend by 31% between 2002/03 and 2003/04, and as we shall discuss shortly, Naturella's success prompted competitive launches.

## Category

Did category level changes[15] drive Naturella's success? Again, this seems far-fetched (changes in four countries, each precisely when Naturella launched?). Besides, any category-level change would benefit all brands, not just one. That said, there have been no such category-level changes.

## Product

Although Naturella is a good product, at launch it was pretty similar to the competition – it's a pad, neither thicker nor softer. And as Always Classic demonstrated, simply launching a good-quality thick, soft pad at a mass-market price isn't enough to disrupt mass-market behaviour on the scale achieved by Naturella.[16]

At launch, however, the Naturella product did have one novel physical attribute: as part of bringing the 'natural feminine care' positioning to life, the pads contained camomile extract. However, the importance of this should not be exaggerated. Research[17] found that portraying camomile as an active (quasi-medicinal) ingredient is off-putting: women felt unsettled by the idea that it 'might be doing something down there' in such a delicate area – so claiming camomile actively *does something* might even harm sales.

We also know from ad testing[18] that over-emphasising camomile confuses communication. This is largely because, as noted earlier, traditional women are drawn to natural products, and camomile is known first and foremost for its calming properties[19] (think camomile tea), not as something to put in your knickers during your period!

So whilst it is true that, alongside 'natural fibres', camomile's an important reason-to-believe in the 'natural feminine care' positioning, as the sole selling point, it is not enough.

Competitive responses in Mexico support this: Kotex and Saba launched variants with camomile as the central proposition, but neither has enjoyed Naturella's extraordinary share growth (see Figure 12).[20]

Moreover, in their first years both Kotex Control and Saba Confort grew, under-cutting Naturella.[21] And each invested significantly in advertising – Kotex Control, in fact, outspending Naturella over this period (see Figure 13).

So, although Naturella is undoubtedly a good-quality product that provides reasons-to-believe in the positioning, its physical attributes alone cannot explain the brand's remarkable success.

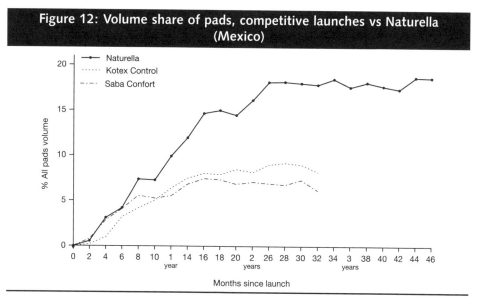

**Figure 12: Volume share of pads, competitive launches vs Naturella (Mexico)**

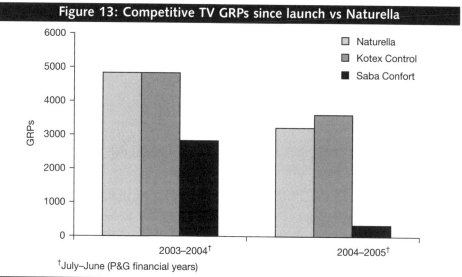

**Figure 13: Competitive TV GRPs since launch vs Naturella**

## Quantifying the contribution of communications

The truest possible estimate of the contribution made by communications requires a single econometric model to analyse globally the drivers of Naturella's volume growth.[22] Such a global approach presented some major technical difficulties, however the resulting model is nonetheless extremely robust.

The model provides a stark demonstration of just how important communications were to the launch: it predicts that, without TV advertising, Naturella wouldn't have achieved any sales at all.

## Figure 14: The predicted impact on volume sales of a 10% upweight of TV advertising

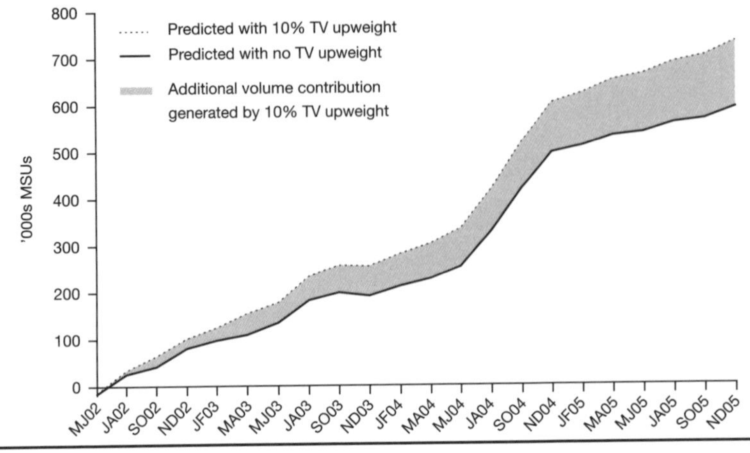

Although this may sound like an exaggerated claim, it is actually quite reasonable: as we have discussed, this is an unusually challenging category (deeply entrenched consumer behaviour, strong established brands, profound cultural sensitivities, etc.), and so to suggest that it would be possible, without any advertising, to switch consumers out of mass-market competitors is just not credible.[23]

The model shows clearly that increasing TV advertising increases growth. Indeed, the response elasticity for advertising is exceptionally large – at least 2.5 times typical advertising elasticities. For example, a 10% upweight in TV advertising would have delivered 26% more volume sales since launch (see Figure 14).

What's more, the upweight would have further improved profit margins (see Table 15).

The model estimates that TV advertising was far and away the most important driver of growth, accounting for an estimated 23% of Naturella volume since launch. TV advertising has therefore clearly paid back (see Table 16).

## Table 15: The predicted financial impact of a 10% upweight of TV advertising

|  | No TV upweight | 10% TV upweight | Change (%) |
|---|---|---|---|
| Predicted volume (MSUs) | 6,284,987 | 7,908,966 | +26 |
| Revenue (US$) | 170,769,520 | 214,894,698 | +26 |
| Media costs (US$) | 18,036,000 | 19,839,600 | +10 |
| Production costs (US$) | 1,761,000 | 1,761,000 | 0 |
| Net revenue less advertising costs (US$) | 150,972,520 | 193,294,098 | +28 |

Note: The media costs quoted here are for all media (including print and outdoor) – in other words, this slightly exaggerates the cost of a 10% upweight in TV alone

96

| Table 16: Payback analysis of Naturella TV advertising since launch | |
|---|---|
| | Naturella |
| Predicted volume (MSUs) | 6,284,987 |
| Revenue (US$) | 170,769,520 |
| Media costs[†] (US$) | 18,036,000 |
| Production costs (US$) | 1,761,000 |
| Contribution of TV advertising (US$) | 39,464,837 |
| Profitability of TV advertising (US$) | 19,667,837 |
| ROI of TV advertising[‡] | $2.00 |

[†] The media costs quoted here are for all media (including print and outdoor) – in other words, this slightly exaggerates the cost of TV alone and thus slightly depresses the profitability and ROI figures
[‡] For every $1 invested in TV advertising (in both media and production), $2 incremental profit will be generated (a ratio of 1:2)

However, this ROI estimate excludes trade communications,[24] which are estimated to account for a further 4% of Naturella's volume. And neither does it include any secondary media.[25]

Furthermore, given that TV advertising was shown to have been a necessary condition for growth, the true, full ROI figure is likely to be well in excess of the 2:1 return for every dollar invested in communications calculated here.

In short, Naturella's communications not only delivered rapid, massive growth, but they did so extremely profitably.

## Summary

There are few product categories where the typical consumer stays with one brand their entire life. Attacking established brands in a market such as this is like laying siege to a city of fortresses. To launch a new brand successfully is therefore pretty impressive. And to have done so at a price premium is remarkable.

But to have delivered growth at a scale and rapidity no one could have anticipated is quite simply staggering. As Naturella's CEE Brand Manager puts it:

> Compared to other launches I have worked on in femcare, Naturella has been
> extraordinary, over-delivering against all our expectations. This launch is best-in-class.
>
> Andy Lotter (P&G)

The impact this has had on the business is formidable. As P&G's Global Finance Manager for femcare comments:

> Naturella has contributed to both the top line and the bottom line in every market.
> It has delighted not only consumers, but the trade and our shareholders as well.
>
> Robert Bosley (P&G)

Communications have clearly been fundamental to this success. As both Naturella's Global Brand Manager and a director of TNS remark:

> Naturella's success is explained by having a great idea consistently communicated
> to consumers.
>
> Pedro Herane (P&G)

*This is for me the perfect example of how you should introduce a new brand. Naturella turned the market upside down, and focused on a new, strong idea, executing the entire brand-building process in a holistic, integrated manner.*

Andreas Schurek (TNS)

The strength of the campaign is its deep emotional connection with traditional women; as P&G observes:

*From the TV, print and other advertising media, through to the communications programme in-store, Naturella's communications have touched consumers and delighted them.*

Pedro Herane (P&G)

When P&G's chief executive, AG Lafley, took up his post in 2000 he said: 'We're going to serve the world's consumers', placing particular emphasis on the need to engage with emerging markets. It is a bold mission, and the company is completely focused on delivering it.

And whilst it's not a one-size-fits-all strategy, pan-regional brands like Naturella obviously have a major role to play, providing enormous economies of scale – not least the ability to share advertising production costs across markets, as is the case here.

But in any geography – be it a country or a region, the world or a continent – communications are most successful when they 'touch and delight' consumers; exceptional effectiveness is about creating communications people want to see and want to act upon.

This has been Naturella's real achievement: to create a campaign that traditional women in emerging markets wanted to see and that they wanted to act upon, thereby driving one of the most successful launches ever seen in one of the most challenging marketplaces in the world.

---

## Notes

1. P&G estimates & Euromonitor (2005).
2. Although Always is branded 'Always' throughout most of the world, it is known as 'Whisper' in Asia.
3. ETPD and Nielsen.
4. Developed by Leo Burnett and Amazon (a creative partnership partly owned by Leo Burnett).
5. Nielsen.
6. This pads market as defined had a total value of almost US$680m in 2005.
7. P&G proprietary global ORS quantitative advertising pre-testing system.
8. Equity Scan (data not available for Venezuela).
9. METT Tracking Study (available only for CEE markets).
10. ORS advertising pre-testing (to put these scores in context, 39% and 37% are the lowest-ever Russian unfavourable scores recorded by ORS, 78% favourable versus 39% unfavourable is average in Mexico, 88% favourable versus 16% is average in Venezuela, and 73% versus 50% in Poland).
11. METT Tracking Study (available only in CEE).
12. ORS advertising pre-testing.
13. METT Tracking Study (available only in CEE).
14. ETPD and Nielsen.
15. For example, regulatory changes, a sudden growth in number of menstruating women, a major shift in consumer attitudes in favour of pads, etc.
16. Technically speaking, Always Classic and Naturella are very alike – they're even designed around the same 'pad base'.
17. Concept development qual.

18. ORS advertising pre-testing.
19. Both calming emotions and calming digestion.
20. Nielsen (remember that Naturella's overall national share was depressed for the first six months as it was only in regional test).
21. Nielsen.
22. There are a number of reasons for this, not least that it would have been impossible to develop separate models for either Russia or Poland given that we have only nine data points for each of these markets. Constructing a global model, made up by aggregating the data from each of the four markets, therefore allowed us to include data from CEE as well as LA, and analyse directly Naturella's drivers of lifetime value.
23. That said, to go on to claim that all sales were down to the advertising would be a non-sequitur. Whilst it appears true that Naturella wouldn't have got off the ground without TV support, nonetheless, as the model shows, there were also other important drivers of sales (not least, distribution and trade communications activity). And to be clear, we will provide an estimate of the proportion of volume sales that can be attributed uniquely to TV advertising. What the model is telling us, then, is that TV advertising was a necessary, but not sufficient, condition for growth.
24. We are unable to get reliable figures for the cost of the trade communications activities, so unfortunately we are therefore not in a position to examine their payback.
25. Unfortunately no consistent, reliable data were available across countries to include secondary media in the model.

# Chapter 8

# O$_2$

## The best way to win new customers? Talk to the ones you already have

**By Sophie Maunder, Vallance Carruthers Coleman Priest, and Louise Cook, Holmes & Cook**

Contributing authors: Nadine Young, ZenithOptimedia Group; Bob Udale, Archibald Ingall Stretton; Nick Hough, Lambie-Nairn; and Andrew Cox, O$_2$ UK

---

At the start of 2005, all the major UK mobile airtime operators – including O$_2$ – were intensively soliciting new customers through advertising and incentives, while doing little to reward, or even talk to, the customers they already had. The market was reaching maturity, with few new entrants, leading to increased customer churn and little or no affinity with any particular brand.

In response to this, O$_2$ sought to challenge the advertising conventions of the market via communications aimed at its existing customers, with the intention of making them feel both wanted and rewarded for their loyalty. Its new campaign, 'A World That Revolves Around You', spoke directly to this audience via broadcast and personal media, from text messaging to TV and outdoor. It announced a shift in rewards for loyalty, not defection, and was supported by a new emphasis on improved customer service.

The campaign managed to reverse the rising trend in disconnections within six months, while the average revenue per user remained steady, showing that the offers of free airtime had led to incremental phone use, not a loss in revenue. Alongside short-term business results that were the best in the market, 'A World That Revolves Around You' also served to attract new customers, so that, by the end of 2005, O$_2$ had the largest UK user base. Brand affinity scores also improved across measures including bonding, consideration and recommendation, and econometric analysis estimated a medium-term ROI ratio of up to 80:1.

## Introduction

This is the story of how $O_2$ took a bold step that changed the rules of the UK mobile airtime market. As all brands were becoming entangled in an increasingly destructive spiral of directing their marketing efforts to attracting each other's customers, $O_2$ and its agencies realised that the customers themselves were experiencing this as neglect, and so becoming disaffected with all the brands.

The solution for $O_2$ was to put the customer firmly at the centre of everything the brand did: customer service, rewards programmes and, not least, communications. This was not without the risk of losing out, at least in the short term, in the scramble for acquisitions. But $O_2$ bet on the probability that the first brand to develop a better relationship with its customers would immediately offer something very appealing to all frustrated mobile users.

And so it proved. Talking to existing customers, with the right messages and in the right tone of voice, turned out to be a more effective acquisition strategy than the previous 'acquisition-driven' approach. After all, 'acquisition' and 'retention' are not really different things – the common imperative is *making the brand more attractive*. And to succeed in one without the other is no formula for business success.

## Background

$O_2$ is one of nine mobile operator brands providing mobile airtime services in the UK. $O_2$ was born in 2002, a relaunch of the former BT Cellnet. Despite initial stock market scepticism, the brand flourished, as detailed in an earlier IPA paper.[1] We take up the story again from the beginning of 2005.

$O_2$'s customers divide into four categories; we are chiefly interested here in the first two.

1. **Pre-pay customers.**[2] These buy airtime as 'top-ups' when needed. This appeals to people who like to feel in control, and dislike or cannot commit to regular payments. They account for two-thirds of personal mobile users in the UK, but are generally lighter users so only about one-third of the market by value.[3] (There is, however, an important group of high-value pre-pay users.) Without minimum contracts, pre-pay customers can switch between operators at will.

2. **Contract customers.** These have a minimum contract over a period where they pay a regular monthly amount for an airtime package. Retailers often provide handsets free or at reduced cost as part of the contract; these in turn are usually funded by operators' payments to the retailers. This can induce contract customers to switch when their contract expires.

3. **SMEs** (small and medium-sized enterprises). Small businesses have their own forms of contract.

4. **Corporate customers** (larger businesses). These, too, have their own forms of contract.

The business model for O$_2$ can be summarised as follows:

**profit = user base × average revenue per user − costs**

- **User base** fluctuates according to net gain or loss of connections, hence the importance of acquisition and retention. A key measure is 'churn', which is disconnections expressed as a proportion of the user base.
- **Average revenue per user** (ARPU) is created by levels of usage and price paid. The trend is for usage to go up while costs of calls and texts fall. ARPU can be stimulated by new, higher-priced services. It also reflects success in attracting and retaining higher-value users.
- Most **costs** of operating a network are fixed. The main variable costs are marketing: advertising, retailer payments, and incentives offered to acquire or retain customers.

These are the key metrics determining bottom-line growth: churn, net acquisitions, user base, ARPU and marketing costs.

## Market situation

By the end of 2004 the UK mobile telephony market was changing.

- With penetration levelling at around 74% (Europe's highest),[4] it was no longer possible to grow by attracting new category users.
- The number of brands in the market had increased. As well as five network operators – O$_2$, 3, Orange, T-Mobile and Vodafone – there were now four mobile virtual network operators (MVNOs):[5] Virgin, easyMobile, Tesco Mobile and fresh.[6]
- Functional variations between most networks, such as geographical coverage, once important, were now less significant. Competitive parameters had become price, service and brand affinity.
- One major factor for buyers was the appeal of a new handset. Both handset manufacturers and retailers were effectively rupturing the network–customer relationship by actively advertising handsets and repackaging airtime deals. This increased buyer power and forced operators to increase payments to retailers.[7]

Operators were driven into a spiral of advertising and promotional deals to acquire new customers, even though increasingly this was merely replacing those lost to competitors.

Mobile users found themselves rewarded, often significantly, for changing network, but not for loyalty. Unintentionally, the market was creating a system for eroding brand loyalty (see Figure 1). This was not good for the operators, and not even much liked by customers. While they could obtain discounts, this was at the cost and inconvenience of frequently reviewing complex offers and changing operator. Brand affinity research in 2004 showed that operators were seen as interchangeable, and none inspired very positive feelings in the customer. Customer satisfaction was sliding for all networks (see Figure 2).

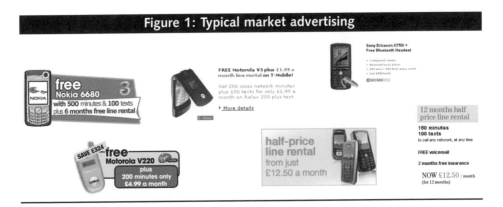

**Figure 1: Typical market advertising**

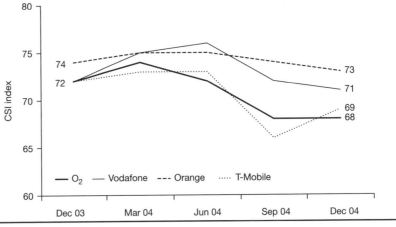

**Figure 2: Overall customer satisfaction scores by mobile network operator**

Source: TNS Prognostics

Meanwhile the operators were eroding their own margins, paying money to retailers that could have been invested in their own service.

All this led to increased churn and higher acquisition costs. During 2004, $O_2$'s churn rose from 30% to 35%,[8] a signal that the conventional market strategy was broken (see Figure 3).

The same factors affected all operators, not just $O_2$. But the market looked over-supplied, and some analysts regarded $O_2$ as the most vulnerable. Just before the new campaign broke, one offered the opinion:

> *If there is to be a casualty, I think it's very likely that it would be $O_2$. Even hiring 2000 new customer service staff and recognising the need for retention and superlative service in a supersaturated market is not going to be enough to save it if the market decides it doesn't need a fifth player.[9]*

Nine months later, as we shall see, the 'fifth player' would be the biggest and strongest brand in the UK market!

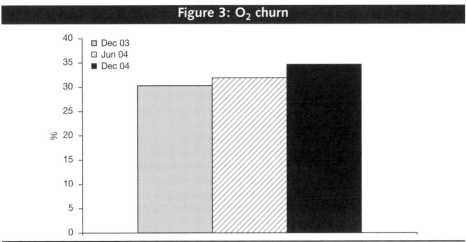

**Figure 3: O₂ churn**

Source: O₂ 12-month blended rolling churn

## The new strategy

But what was to be done? The pressure to attract new customers, even (or especially) if largely refilling a leaking bucket, was a difficult treadmill to step off. By simply cutting acquisition programmes and substituting 'loyalty' deals, a brand would risk losing share as other operators continued to offer 'jam today' rather than 'jam tomorrow'. To avoid this, it was necessary to address the issues that allowed the market to become so deal-driven in the first place.

Consumer research showed that the promotional wars were exacerbating one fundamental problem: people saw mobile operators as all the same, without positive emotional attachment to any. People believed operators were poor on service, and neglected their existing customers, offering deals only to new ones. They felt ignored, and were often happy to 'punish' operators by switching.

*I use the phone, they send me a bill.*

*You shouldn't have to threaten them before they offer you something.*

*Let me know they know I'm out there!*

The one positive insight, however, was that mobile users genuinely wanted a brand that they really could trust and stay with. If one existed.

*I want to be treated as a person not a number.*

*If I knew I was getting value for money I would just leave well alone.*

Source: brandaffinity

O₂ had made a good start in creating a relationship with its customers,[10] but the focus on acquisitions threatened to erode this. Failing to reward existing customers was important not just practically, but at a deeply symbolic level: it said 'we don't really care about you'. It was this underlying message that needed to be changed.

And if $O_2$ could be seen as the brand that really put its own customers first, should this not also be effective in attracting the alienated users of other operators?

The marketing programme for 2005 therefore started from a deep commitment by $O_2$ to its own customers, to be backed up by deeds as well as words. So there were three aspects to the strategy.

1. **Operational** improvements in service: these included hiring an extra 2000 customer service staff, new training programmes, improved systems, and re-aligning costs to areas customers would value. This decisively implemented programme made a noticeable difference in customers' experience during 2005, and internal surveys showed big improvements in staff attitudes and competences.[11]

2. A shift in **rewards** so that 'loyalty', not defection, was rewarded: breaking market convention by offering the same deals to existing customers as to new customers. Pre-pay customers were offered '10% of top-ups back every three months'. Contract customers were offered '50% extra airtime on your bundle for life' when renewing a contract exclusively through $O_2$.[12] (Later in the year another promotion, 'Treats', offered various extras such as free text bundles.) These were 'great value, no-catch offers' to the customer, but as long as they encouraged incremental usage represented no cost to $O_2$.

3. **Communicating** the new customer strategy and the rewards programmes: $O_2$ could not afford to wait for the marketplace to make sense of its new behaviour – it needed to communicate its new commitment to the customer quickly and openly, in a way that would earn results.

## The communications campaign

Since launch, $O_2$ had created a consistent and distinctive visual identity, a stylised universe based around blue and a stream of bubbles ($O_2$ is the chemical symbol for oxygen). This evokes freedom, clarity and fresh air; $O_2$ advertising feels calm and serene, the antithesis to clutter and chaos, a contrast to the often frenetic world around mobile phones ($O_2$ never shows hassled people talking on mobiles).

Emotional attachment to a brand is strongly enhanced by such non-rational, non-verbal communication (Heath, 2002). Orange had used a powerful visual identity in its launch years, but later lost this clarity and consistency. $O_2$ would not make this mistake. But it was necessary to refresh the identity, and make it different enough to carry a set of messages about the new rewards and positioning, now for the first time speaking directly to existing customers.

The creative solution from VCCP was '$O_2$: A World That Revolves Around You', visualising the customer both as the centre of their own, personal communications network, and as the centre of $O_2$'s concern and attention.

The idea of 'world' led to an image of planets in the evening sky, echoing the existing palette of bubbles and blueness, as created by Lambie-Nairn. Peaceful,

## Figure 4: Campaign phasing

### Campaign phasing '04 (main campaigns)

| April | May | June | July | Aug | Sept | Oct | Nov | Dec |

DMP

Business
Zones

Happy Hour (London)  Happy Hour (National)  Upgrades (London)

Friends    X-Range

### Campaign phasing '05 (main campaigns)

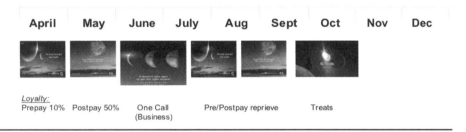

| April | May | June | July | Aug | Sept | Oct | Nov | Dec |

*Loyalty:*
Prepay 10%   Postpay 50%   One Call (Business)      Pre/Postpay reprieve      Treats

otherworldly music emphasised that $O_2$ had created a new kind of mobile phone world, one removed from the brash, deal-driven perceptions of the public.

Past $O_2$ advertising, while visually consistent, had always been planned as discrete campaigns lasting one to two months. Now, Zenith proposed a unified campaign that would run for six months on the same theme, while carrying specific promotional messages aimed at different target audiences: 10% of top-ups for Pay & Go customers, 50% extra for life for Contract, and with a service message (One Call Ownership) for SMEs (see Figure 4).

The message was presented with strong creative consistency, and broadcast media were designed to work together with individually targeted 'touchpoints', through Archibald Ingall Stretton, such as text messaging. MMS messages contained visuals from the TV campaign, offering the rewards as a 'present' to the customer rather than a 'sale'. To accept, they simply had to text a number back, thus establishing a reciprocal relationship. So $O_2$ spoke to its customers using its own devices as the media, and straight into their hands (see Figure 5).

At the same time, broadcast media were a highly cost-effective way of addressing 16 million existing $O_2$ customers. $O_2$'s new positioning had to become public, an open statement of commitment to all its customers, not just a few – and, not just incidentally, for customers of other networks to hear about too. Forty-second TV commercials on the 'loyalty' theme were 'topped and tailed' with reward messages, while heavy transport advertising, indexed highly against $O_2$ customers, created ubiquity[13] (see Figure 6).

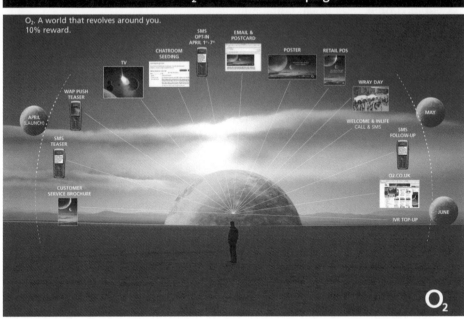

Figure 5: An example of the integrated touchpoints used for O₂'s '10% back' campaign

Through 2005, O₂'s share of voice continued, as in previous years, to be less than its share of market. The success of the campaign did not depend on outspending the competition (see Figure 7).

## Results

By December 2005, O₂, far from losing out on acquisitions, had the largest UK user base of any network – without any loss in average revenue. A range of brand measures also showed it had become the strongest brand.

*Short-term metrics: business results*

- **Immediate uptake:** responses through SMS were unprecedented – more than four million pre-pay customers, over 50%. SMS response began even before the outgoing SMS campaign started, but SMS and TV together multiplied the levels of response, which increased as TV coverage and frequency were built over the period of the campaign. More than 200,000 contract customers have already taken up 50% extra.[14]
- **Churn:** O₂'s churn fell, while increasing for all major competitors. By the end of 2005 O₂'s churn was the second lowest (see Figure 8). Churn was modelled separately for pre-pay and contract groups. The models show that, by December 2005, pre-pay churn had reduced by 15 percentage points (more than a third) with contract churn falling four percentage points (see Figure 9).[15]

## Figure 6: Examples of advertising in different media

TV

*Imagine a world where loyalty is rewarded*

*Where it's not just the new customer who gets the latest deal*

*Where it's you, the existing customer, who feels new and wanted*

*It's about time your loyalty was rewarded*

*O2. A world that revolves around you. See what you can do.*

**Launch 96 Sheet**

**Launch Escalator Panels**

**Promotional Day**

**Pre Pay 48 Sheet**

## Figure 6: Examples of advertising in different media (continued)

Pre Pay Bus Panel

Pre Pay Taxi Tip Up

Post Pay Press Ad

One Call 48 Sheet

Treats TV

Online

Below The Line

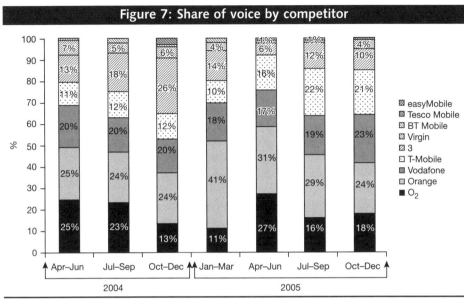

Figure 7: Share of voice by competitor

Source: NMR

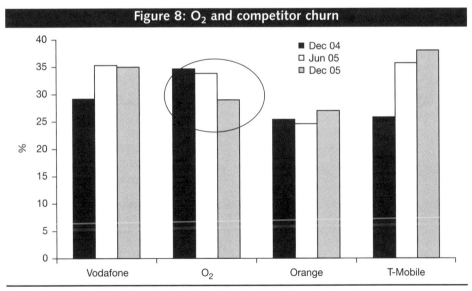

Figure 8: O₂ and competitor churn

Source: Company releases and O₂ estimates, 12-month blended rolling churn

In both groups, churn responded to pre-pay and contract messages equally (see Figure 10). High adstock carryover[16] suggests these effects should be long lasting.

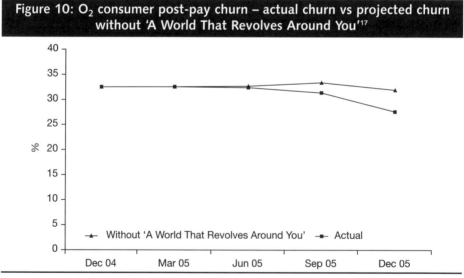

**Figure 9: O₂ pre-pay churn – actual churn vs projected churn without 'A World That Revolves Around You'**

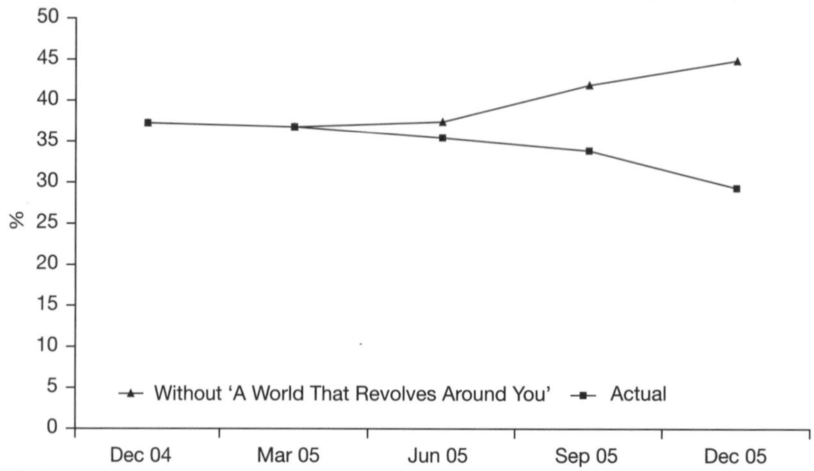

Source: Holmes & Cook econometrics (original models based on monthly data but only quarterly data is published)

**Figure 10: O₂ consumer post-pay churn – actual churn vs projected churn without 'A World That Revolves Around You'[17]**

Source: Holmes & Cook econometrics (original models based on monthly data but only quarterly data is published)

Figure 11 shows the results of using the models to simulate overall O2 churn without the new strategy.

■ **Net acquisitions:** despite switching the focus of communication away from acquisitions, $O_2$'s net acquisitions increased faster than competitors' (see

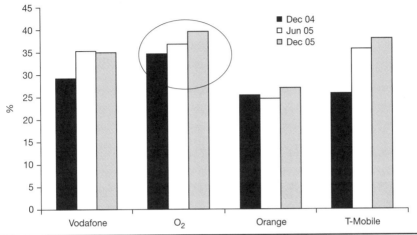

**Figure 11: Where $O_2$ churn would have been without the campaign: model simulation**

Source: $O_2$ internal estimates and company releases, Holmes & Cook econometric analysis, 12-month blended rolling churn

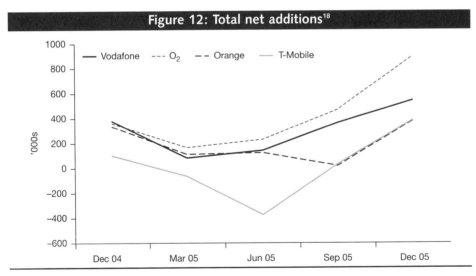

**Figure 12: Total net additions[18]**

Source: $O_2$ and company releases

Figure 12). By December 2005, $O_2$ had the largest UK user base by a considerable margin (see Figure 13).

■ **Gross connections:** while improved retention was a factor in determining *net* acquisitions,[19] acquisitions themselves performed very strongly. Acquisitions (gross connections) were modelled separately for pre-pay and contract groups (see Figures 14 and 15). Although addressing existing customers, the

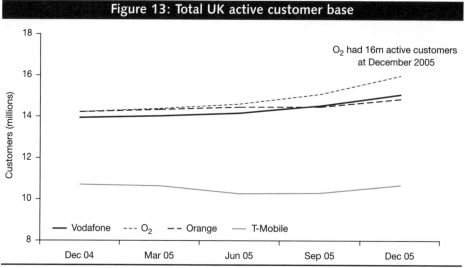

Figure 13: Total UK active customer base

Source: O$_2$ and company releases

campaign had as strong an effect on new pre-pay connections as most previous, acquisition-led advertising.[20] In the case of contract customers, the new campaign generated twice as many new connections per TVR as any previous O$_2$ advertising, an outstanding result.

■ **ARPU:** while all other operators' ARPU fell, O$_2$'s held up well, despite giving more value to the customer (see Figure 16). This suggests that the customer base retains a similar or enhanced proportion of high-value users, and shows

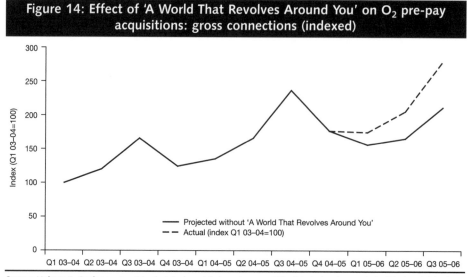

Figure 14: Effect of 'A World That Revolves Around You' on O$_2$ pre-pay acquisitions: gross connections (indexed)

Source: Holmes & Cook econometrics (original models based on monthly data but only quarterly data is published)

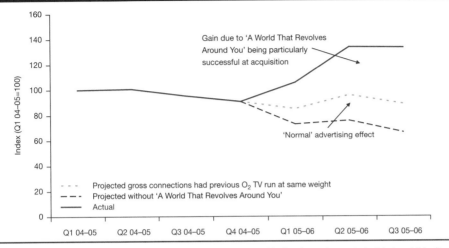

**Figure 15: The effect of 'A World That Revolves Around You' on O₂ contract acquisitions: gross connections indexed**

Gain due to 'A World That Revolves Around You' being particularly successful at acquisition

'Normal' advertising effect

- - - Projected gross connections had previous O₂ TV run at same weight
－ － Projected without 'A World That Revolves Around You'
——— Actual

Source: Holmes & Cook econometrics (original models based on monthly data but only quarterly data is published)

(as we also know from other data) that free airtime promotions led to incremental usage of the network, not reduced revenue.

In summary: in less than a year, O₂ has become the leading brand in the UK in terms of business results.

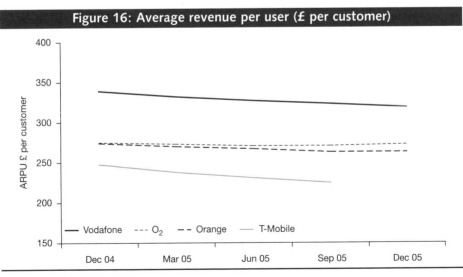

**Figure 16: Average revenue per user (£ per customer)**

——— Vodafone    --- O₂    — — Orange    ——— T-Mobile

Source: O₂ and company releases

*Longer-term indicators: brand affinity*

■ **Consideration:** By autumn 2005, $O_2$ was the operator most cited as the 'only brand' or 'one of a few brands' consumers would consider (see Figure 17).

**Figure 17: Consideration of leading mobile phone brands – top 2 boxes**

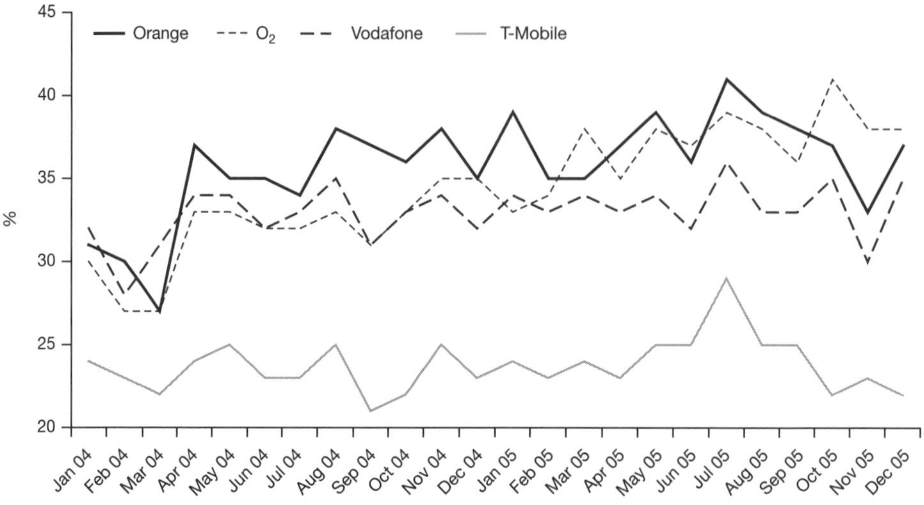

Source: Millward Brown – Consumers for which $O_2$ is the 'only' brand or 'one of a few' they would consider

■ **Awareness and image:** Millward Brown tracking shows $O_2$ as clearly the strongest brand in the market, taking a spread of ratings into account.

Table 1 summarises a mass of data. The four leading brands are rated by their own customers and by non-customers on five attributes. Prior to $O_2$'s campaign, Orange dominated the 'scoreboard', but post-campaign $O_2$ shows fastest growth on all scales and highest absolute figure on most. Orange, the biggest spender and historically strong, has lost its leading position (see Table 1).

Millward Brown also analysed brand perceptions using its BrandZ affinity pyramids. $O_2$ is on a positive trend and now has the strongest 'bonding' in the market. Conversion from 'presence' to 'bonding' is especially strong compared with Vodafone and Orange, brands with longer histories and larger spenders; consider also the gap between $O_2$ and T-Mobile, launched at the same time (see Figure 18).

An exceptional performance in the context of any market:

*Increasing consumers' true loyalty to a brand (as the bonding metric shows) is no easy task, and in doing so, $O_2$ should be commended for its work.*

Peter Walshe, Global Brands Director, Millward Brown

## Table 1: Four leading brands rated by customers and non-customers

| | Pre Highest absolute rating 8 wks to 3/4/05 | Post Highest absolute rating 8 wks to 22/1/06 | Pre → post and points gained Fastest growing[21] 3/4/05 to 22/1/06 | | | |
|---|---|---|---|---|---|---|
| **Ratings amongst own customers (% or % agreeing)** | | | | | | |
| Spontaneous brand awareness | Orange | $O_2$ | $O_2$ | 84 → 92 | +8 | |
| Recommendation | $O_2$ | $O_2$ | $O_2$ | 78 → 82 | +4 | |
| Have a higher opinion of | $O_2$ | $O_2$ | $O_2$ | 73 → 78 | +5 | |
| Brand you want to be seen with | Orange | $O_2$ | $O_2$ | 63 → 70 | +7 | |
| Setting standards for the future | Vodafone | $O_2$ | $O_2$ | 48 → 56 | +8 | |
| **Ratings amongst non-customers (% or % agreeing)** | | | | | | |
| Spontaneous brand awareness | Orange | Orange | $O_2$ | 53 → 60 | +7 | |
| Recommendation | Orange | $O_2$ | $O_2$ | 16 → 20 | +4 | |
| Have a higher opinion of than | Orange | Orange | $O_2$ | 15 → 20 | +5 | |
| Brand you want to be seen with | $O_2$ | $O_2$ | $O_2$ | 21 → 23 | +2 | |
| Setting standards for the future | Orange | Orange | $O_2$ | 16 → 20 | +4 | |

Source: Millward Brown, 8-week rolling data based on approx 200 customers and 700 non-customers for each brand. Periods of comparison are 8 wks to 3/4/05 (pre-campaign) vs 8 wks to 22/1/06 (post-campaign)

## Figure 18: Brand pyramids: Q4 2004 (Jan–Mar 2005)–Q3 2005 (Jan–Dec 2005)

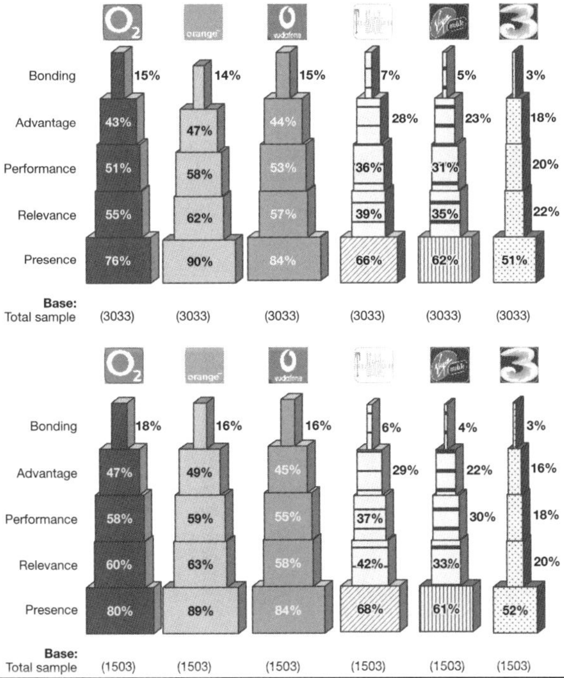

| | $O_2$ | orange | vodafone | T | Virgin | 3 |
|---|---|---|---|---|---|---|
| Bonding | 15% | 14% | 15% | 7% | 5% | 3% |
| Advantage | 43% | 47% | 44% | 28% | 23% | 18% |
| Performance | 51% | 58% | 53% | 36% | 31% | 20% |
| Relevance | 55% | 62% | 57% | 39% | 35% | 22% |
| Presence | 76% | 90% | 84% | 66% | 62% | 51% |
| **Base:** Total sample | (3033) | (3033) | (3033) | (3033) | (3033) | (3033) |

| | $O_2$ | orange | vodafone | T | Virgin | 3 |
|---|---|---|---|---|---|---|
| Bonding | 18% | 16% | 16% | 6% | 4% | 3% |
| Advantage | 47% | 49% | 45% | 29% | 22% | 16% |
| Performance | 58% | 59% | 55% | 37% | 30% | 18% |
| Relevance | 60% | 63% | 58% | 42% | 33% | 20% |
| Presence | 80% | 89% | 84% | 68% | 61% | 52% |
| **Base:** Total sample | (1503) | (1503) | (1503) | (1503) | (1503) | (1503) |

■ **Customer satisfaction:** Other surveys of $O_2$'s own customers show increased levels of satisfaction and expectation of remaining with $O_2$, especially the more volatile pre-pay sector (see Figures 19 and 20).

Qualitative research by Patrick Corr in January 2006 concluded that $O_2$ appears to be reaping the benefits of recent brand activity. In particular, existing customers appear more satisfied and more conscious of the company's efforts to look after them via proactive communication and good deals.

**Figure 19: Overall customer satisfaction scores by mobile network operator**

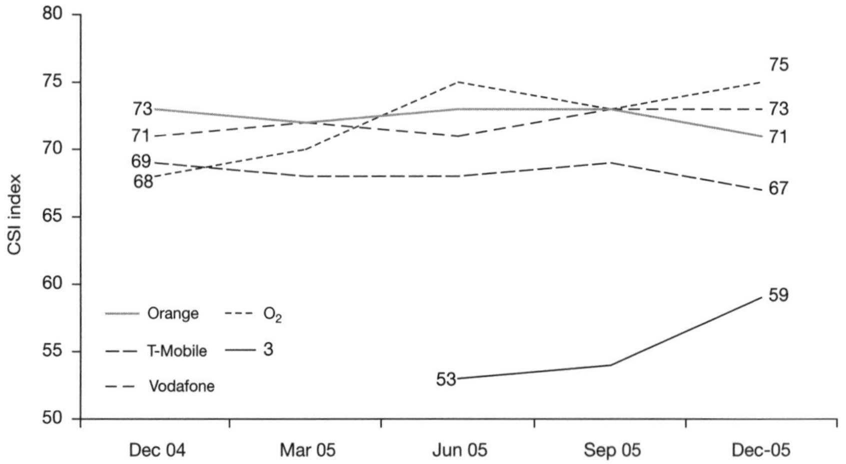

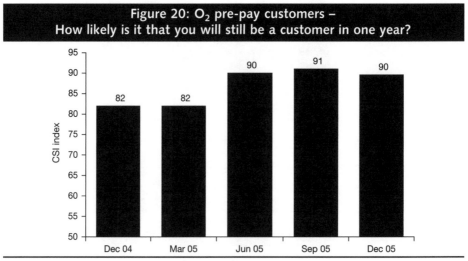

Source: TNS Prognostics (1-point movement required for statistical significance at the 90% level)

**Figure 20: $O_2$ pre-pay customers –**
**How likely is it that you will still be a customer in one year?**

Source: TNS Prognostics (2-point movement required for statistical significance at the 90% level)

Potential customers also appear more aware of $O_2$'s competitiveness and in their words, 'generosity':

*You get loads with $O_2$.*

People have a sense that the momentum is with $O_2$ compared with competitors:

*Loads of people I know are going over to $O_2$.*
*$O_2$ is clearly the one in the ascendancy.*

■ **Recommendation:** Reichheld (2003) says recommendation is the best predictor of brand affinity, and research suggests recommendation has become more important in this category recently.[22] It is therefore very positive that $O_2$ is the only brand to show a year-on-year increase in recommendation among both pre-pay and contract customers, and in pre-pay now has the highest brand score at 80% (see Figure 21).

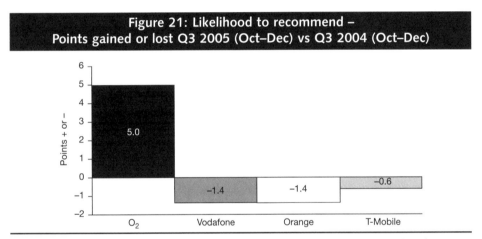

**Figure 21: Likelihood to recommend – Points gained or lost Q3 2005 (Oct–Dec) vs Q3 2004 (Oct–Dec)**

Source: TNS Prognostics (pre-pay and contract customers) (1-point movement required for statistical significance at the 90% level)

In summary: brand affinity tends to move slowly, but in less than a year $O_2$ has moved clearly into the lead on a whole range of brand measures – against competitors with longer histories and bigger budgets.

## How did it work? What was the role of communications?

During this campaign, $O_2$ became the UK's leading brand on both business and brand measures. But what were the decisive factors behind this?

The 2005 strategy had three components:

1. Operational improvements to service.
2. Changed reward structures.
3. Communications.

We believe all three elements were essential. We also believe it is pointless to try to factor out in any way the relative importance of any individual component: all were necessary, and were mutually supportive.

Brand affinity is created as people develop associations and feelings about a brand, based on all the signals they receive about it. In this sense, all the brand's actions are forms of communication.

People make sense of a brand taking into account (largely subconsciously) such signals as:

- the brand's **behaviours** – e.g. service, efficiency, rewards
- the brand's **verbal or cognitive messages** – e.g. claims, messages about rewards
- the brand's **non-verbal or emotional messages** – e.g. tone of voice (in ads or on the phone), images, music.

If these signals are all consistent, they develop a particular relationship at both a cognitive and an emotional level.

Research at the start of 2005 showed most people's relationships with their operators was distant. This was caused by a host of signals that said 'we don't care about you' – e.g. emphasis on deals, failure to reward existing customers, perceived lack of touchpoints other than the bill. Failure to communicate is in itself a powerful form of communication, like ignoring a friend in the street. Operators were in effect blanking out their own customers.

$O_2$'s strategy in 2005 changed this by making the customer the centre. It needed to do this through actions, through symbolic patterns of interaction and reward, but it also needed to *talk* to the customer, and to do so in the right tone of voice. Without this overall framing of the new relationship the actions and rewards could easily have been ignored or misunderstood.

$O_2$'s rewards in themselves were not the most motivating in the market. Their power came from being framed within an overall campaign that gave them symbolic value, as evidence that $O_2$ cared for its customers (see Figure 22).

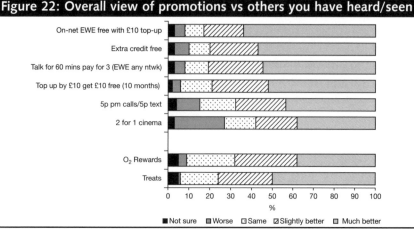

**Figure 22: Overall view of promotions vs others you have heard/seen**

Source: Sweeney Pinedo. Base: 300 $O_2$ customers not taking up rewards
EWE = evening/weekend. On-net = own network

The cognitive messages – 'O$_2$: A World That Revolves Around You', '50% extra for life' – were mutually supportive, but were further supported by the way they were communicated. People appreciated the clear and informative nature of O$_2$'s advertising in a confusing market, and believed it gave a better impression of the network (see Figure 23).

### Figure 23: O$_2$ customers' impressions of O$_2$'s above-the-line advertising

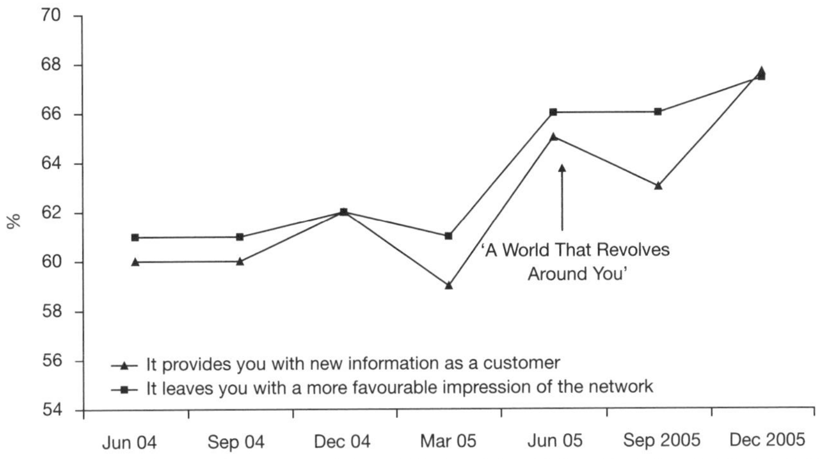

Source: TNS Prognostics (1-point move required for statistical significance at the 90% level)

The peaceful and consistent visual images and music also sent distinctive emotional signals.[23] Millward Brown research on perceptions of the TV ads shows very high scores above the norm on the 'passive positive' quadrant – 'Pleasant', 'Soothing' and 'Gentle'. In the frenetic mobile market these were exactly what O$_2$ wanted (see Table 2).

For the first time, customers felt a mobile operator was talking directly to them, not somebody else. But as well as being heard by customers, this conversation was also *overheard* by non-customers! Evidence of how O$_2$ customers were treated proved a more attractive inducement to join than any direct sales pitch.

### Table 2: Millward Brown passive positive engagement scores – O$_2$ executions vs study norm

| % agreeing | Orbit | 10% Back | 50% Extra | Treats | Study norm | Average by which O$_2$ exceeds norm |
|---|---|---|---|---|---|---|
| Pleasant | 48 | 43 | 50 | 48 | 35 | +12 |
| Soothing | 43 | 35 | 45 | 41 | 12 | +29 |
| Gentle | 59 | 54 | 66 | 52 | 32 | +26 |
| Base: total sample | 813 | 308 | 247 | 187 | 37 ads | |

We also know from econometrics that pre-pay customers responded to messages that were aimed at contract customers and vice versa; all messages were consistent signals about $O_2$'s caring approach.

$O_2$'s communications made the rewards simple, accessible and credible. In contrast, a week after the launch of '10% top-ups back', Orange responded with a superficially stronger offer – 50% of top-ups back! However, it was hedged with conditions, and was interpreted as yet another deal, not quite to be trusted. In isolation, this seems not to have changed perceptions of Orange.

Finally, more satisfied customers created more positive word of mouth for $O_2$ – an increasingly important factor in choosing a network.

In all these ways, building a better relationship with $O_2$'s existing customers not only improved retention, but also proved, beyond expectations, to be the most effective and efficient way of attracting new customers from other brands (see Figure 24).

## Figure 24: Effects on the business

| Net increase in user base to *largest* in the market | x | ARPU (which holds up well) | – | Costs (payments to retailers *stabilise*) | = | Highest growth in EBITDA in category |
|---|---|---|---|---|---|---|

By strengthening brand affinity and successfully exiting the battle for acquisitions, $O_2$ could pay less to retailers relative to its competitors, investing instead in service and rewards that benefit its own brand (see Table 3).

All this has immediately shown up in the bottom line. EBIDTA outperformed the market in 2005 (see Table 4).

## Table 3: Rank out of top four network operators in terms of third-party retail commission payments

| Rank | Dec 2004 | Dec 2005 |
|---|---|---|
| $O_2$ pre-pay | 2 | 3 |
| $O_2$ contract | 2 | 3 |

Source: $O_2$ best estimate
Note: rank 1 spends most

## Table 4: Average of quarterly EBITDA growth rates vs previous year[24]

| | $O_2$ | Vodafone (Q1 and Q2 only) | T-Mobile | Market avg (Q1 and Q2 only) |
|---|---|---|---|---|
| Year-on-year growth (average of growth rates in first 3 quarters of FY05/06) | +5 | −4 | −6 | −3 |

Note: information from Q1 FY2005/06 (April–June) to Q3 FY2005/06 (October–December)

## Payback on the media budget

One million disconnections were prevented by this campaign between April and December 2005.[25] The additional margin resulting just to December 2005 covered 95% of the £36m media expenditure (NMR).[26] If those retained customers stay for just one further year they will contribute sufficient additional margin to repay the media budget 3.8 times.

But this is the tip of the iceberg. The models suggest fairly slow adstock decay, meaning future disconnections should also be prevented. Over the next three to four years, reduced disconnections should repay the media budget 17 times.

But the acquisition effects are the most important. Those new customers joining O$_2$ from April to December 2005 as a result of the campaign will, over their expected lifetime,[27] generate sufficient additional margin to repay the media budget 18 times.[28] But, as with disconnections, adstock decay rates are slow, so that over the next three to four years the total additional margin is expected to repay the media budget 63 times.

Bringing together retention and acquisition effects produces a payback of 80:1 – even greater than the 62:1 reported in the 2004 Grand Prix paper!

## Effects on the value of the business

The future benefits of this campaign are shown in the gradual improvement in the brand's affinity relative to competitors.

As a business, O$_2$ now looks highly rated. Share price grew throughout 2005 (see Figure 25) and in November, after several other approaches, O$_2$'s board accepted Telefonica's offer to buy the company for £18bn.

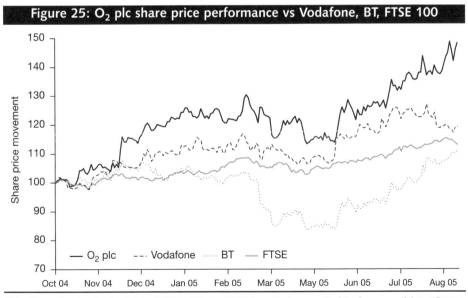

**Figure 25: O$_2$ plc share price performance vs Vodafone, BT, FTSE 100**

Note: Share prices baselined 1 October 2004 to 100; April 2005 is omitted as a result of the frequency of data collection.

*The brand O₂ reflects the whole aspirations of the sector, they have the name which is recognised as a symbol of quality, of innovation, of service and a future.*

César Alierta, CEO, Telefonica

*O₂ came out of the blocks from BT four years ago, with nobody giving it a chance of survival. I think this is the end of chapter one and the beginning of chapter two. I think under Telefonica now and with their scale, we can make the next journey even more exciting and I think we may well look back in four years' time and say in 2005 we'd only just begun.*

Peter Erskine, CEO, O₂ Group

If there is to be a 'casualty' in this market, it seems unlikely to be O₂!

## References

Heath, Robert (2002), *The Hidden Power of Advertising*, Henley-on-Thames: WARC.
Reichheld, Frederick F. (2003), 'The One Number You Need to Grow', *Harvard Business Review*, Dec, Vol. 81, Issue 12.

---

## Notes

1. 'It only works when it all works', IPA Effectiveness Awards Grand Prix Winner 2004 – *Advertising Works 13*.
2. O₂'s pre-pay scheme is called Pay & Go™.
3. Source: O₂, Ofcom.
4. Source: O₂ internal and external market research estimates.
5. MVNOs pay to use the five network operators' networks, e.g. Virgin uses the T-Mobile network, Tesco uses the O₂ network. (N.B. all figures in this paper are for O₂ only and do not include Tesco's use of the O₂ network.)
6. From Carphone Warehouse.
7. For example, a package at Carphone Warehouse might offer a Nokia handset and a Vodafone contract, with other operators excluded.
8. This is 12-month blended rolling churn — the standard industry reporting measure. It is a 12-month rolling average over all consumer types.
9. Sara Harris of Strategy Analytics, quoted in *Marketing Week*, 31 March 2005.
10. See previous IPA entry from 2004.
11. Staff feel more confident about explaining O₂'s aims (4-point movement from 67 in Oct 2004 to 71 in Oct 2005) and see O₂ as more successfully adapting to market changes and delivering customers' needs and expectations (10-point move from 60% in Oct 2004 to 70% in Oct 2005). Source: Internal staff survey. Base: 7800. 1-point move required for statistical significance.
12. 'For life' means while you remain on the relevant tariff, with customers required to sign a new 18-month minimum term to get the benefit of this offer.
13. Econometric analysis carried out by Ninah Consulting in summer 2005 showed that the April–June outdoor activity delivered 16% more spontaneous brand awareness per £ than any previous outdoor activity.
14. For existing customers this normally occurs at contract renewal stage.
15. All else remaining equal.
16. Adstock carryover rates were generally 95% month to month. Source: Holmes & Cook.
17. We see underlying churn (i.e. churn without communication) decreasing on this chart as a result of the operational improvements implemented by O₂.
18. Although market penetration was increasing only minimally, there is still some market growth as a result of multiple phone ownership (e.g. some consumers have a business mobile phone and a personal one). This has, however, generally diluted ARPU, as consumers split their calls between two phones.
19. Net acquisitions equate to gross connections – disconnections.
20. Pay & Go Wild, the most successful acquisition campaign to date, had particularly marked effects in 2002.
21. These are large image movements to occur in a short period of time. Many of these measures had shown little in the way of trend movement in the previous year.
22. Source: holden pearmain – research into reasons for consumer churn. Sept 2004, March 2005, July 2005.
23. See Robert Heath's monograph, *The Hidden Power of Advertising*, for a fuller explanation of the mental processes involved.

24. Orange's profits not reported.
25. Source: Holmes & Cook econometric models.
26. We do not wish to reveal actual spend media, and by implication buying costs, but this figure is sufficient to include both actual spend and production costs.
27. This average lifetime has been assumed to be as at April 2005, i.e. at peak churn levels. (Average lifetime is calculated as one divided by the percentage churn rate, i.e. a churn rate of 30% would give an average lifetime of 3.33 years.) This will almost certainly lead to an understatement of final payback as churn rates are now much lower.
28. By December 2005 new customers had already generated sufficient additional margin to repay the media budget 1.6 times.

## Chapter 9

# TV Licensing

50 pints or a TV Licence? How an integrated campaign made student TV Licences 'the norm' over evasion on campus

**By Adrian Hoole, Proximity London**
Contributing authors: Debi Bester, Kate Harding, Paul Sturniolo and Arabel Thomson, Proximity London, and Peter Kirk, BBC TV Licensing
Media agency: PHD

Persuading students to buy a TV Licence is one of the toughest 'sells' on campus – but this case study details how TV Licensing overcame the old 'norm' of on-campus evasion and encouraged record numbers of students to fork out £126.50 for a TV Licence, despite all the other temptations.

Over the course of three years, more than 30 different media channels were used, from the traditional, such as TV and PR, to the more unusual, such as aerial sockets and personalised posters. Using 'anti-humour' and other communications methods intended to appeal directly to its target audience, this approach repeatedly produced record sales of TV Licences to students during this period.

The campaign was based on a truly integrated strategy from both the creative and media perspective, and also sought to account for the contribution of each different channel used to communicate the message. The results were assessed using a unique 'brick' analysis, based on the analogy that 'the more bricks you throw, the more impact you will make'. One 'brick' equated to the sales attributable to broadcast activity (such as TV, PR, mass mailings and inserts) alone. Two 'bricks' added targeted direct mail into the mix. Three 'bricks' also incorporated targeted student TV. Finally, four 'bricks' detailed the impact of all 30 touchpoints, revealing that, overall, the campaign achieved almost double the sales than could be expected by the use of broadcast alone. This innovative approach will also help guide the cost-effective deployment of future campaigns and hence increase value for money for the BBC.

## Background

Students are an important acquisition target for TV Licensing. The law states that each separately occupied dwelling in the UK where TV is being watched needs to be covered by a licence – and that includes a room in a hall of residence. The consequences of watching TV without one can involve prosecution, a court appearance and a £1,000 fine. And students are by no means exempt.

This may come as a surprise to some of you reading this. It certainly comes as a surprise to many students leaving home for the first time and entering such an exciting stage of life. Clearly the average new student has many priorities, temptations and concerns to occupy them over and above the need for a TV Licence.

A typical 'hierarchy of student needs' is unlikely to feature a TV Licence (see Figure 1)!

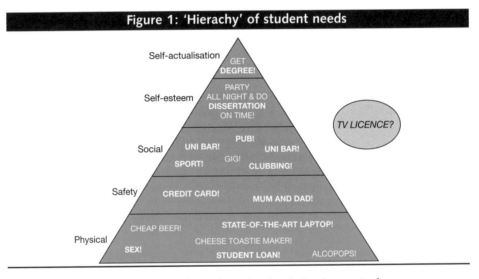

**Figure 1: 'Hierachy' of student needs**

According to HESA (the Higher Education Statistics Agency), there are approx. 317,000 on-campus student rooms. Our research shows that 45% of students on campus take a TV to university.[1] With a TV Licence costing £126.50,[2] this means a maximum on-campus opportunity of approximately £18m licence fee income potentially at risk from a mixture of ignorance, apathy or perhaps even bravado.

As in any market, long-term purchase habits are also undoubtedly instilled by early experience. In the case of a TV Licence, if students buy a licence as soon as they need one, they are more likely to take the habit with them into the wider world. The converse is also undoubtedly true.

Historically (and maybe understandably) evasion on campus has been the norm. If you are under 30 and bought your own TV Licence for your room in halls, you are almost certainly in a minority! Efforts to tackle high on-campus evasion go back some years. However, in 2002, when Proximity London took over the business, the BBC made the decision to address the issue with increased investment.

This case study thus covers the three subsequent campaign periods – 2003/04, 2004/05 and 2005/06 – for which compatible data are available.

## The challenge

Given the other exciting priorities they face, how could we get uninterested students to fork out £126.50 for a TV Licence? And, ultimately, how could we make TV Licence purchase the norm on campus, in place of evasion?

## The communications strategy

Over the course of the last three years, qualitative research and a 'test and learn' approach have informed the development of an integrated campaign to encourage students to purchase a TV Licence.

Essentially, the overall communication objectives haven't changed over that period:

- to educate students about the need and ways to pay for a TV Licence
- to inform them of the consequences of not having one
- to convince them of the reality that they will get caught if they evade.

The campaign aims to maximise TV Licensing's visibility and presence at as many 'touchpoints' as possible along the metaphorical 'journey' from parents' home, through arrival at hall of residence and on into term-time. Multi-channel delivery (including TV, DM, PR and ambient) has therefore been a key feature of the approach.

The campaign itself has become increasingly sophisticated over the three years, with progressively greater focus on:

- optimising and expanding the media mix
- increasing creative consistency and effectiveness
- rigour and clarity of evaluation.

## Multi-channel delivery

TV Licensing has valuable access to BBC airtime to promote its message. TV and radio 'trails' developed in-house by the BBC have thus provided an important broadcast 'backbone' to the campaign. However, TVRs on the BBC are a scarce resource, and using TV advertising to target such a niche audience is inevitably inefficient. 'Broadcast' messaging is therefore increasingly delivered through PR, direct mail and inserts (for example, in UCAS mailings).

The need to maximise visibility and accuracy of targeting on campus has also led to increased focus away from broadcast advertising to activity 'on the ground'.

TV Licensing would much rather students bought a licence than have to enforce the law against them. So, at universities with the highest hall of residence populations, we unleash our multi-channel, integrated communications. This involves a 'blitz' of innovative ambient activity designed to create a noticeable presence on campus and spur into action those students who have yet to buy a licence.

For example, on 'drop-off days' – when students arrive at university (often with their parents) – we ensure TV Licensing's message is highly visible. This involves targeting posters and leaflets around the campus, and placing application forms in rooms and other unexpected locations such as libraries. We continue presence into Freshers' Week with themed Fresher Fair stands, and beyond into term-time, with activity ranging from sponsored student TV in the unions to additional PR and enforcement visits; and a range of online and digital initiatives including text messaging, banner advertising, content on union websites and targeted emails.

This is backed up by an ongoing targeted mailing programme driven by the TV Licensing database to unlicensed students, escalating the 'consequences' message as term-time unfolds. Mailings are coordinated with enforcement officers, who visit unlicensed addresses as promised in the mailings (see Figure 2).

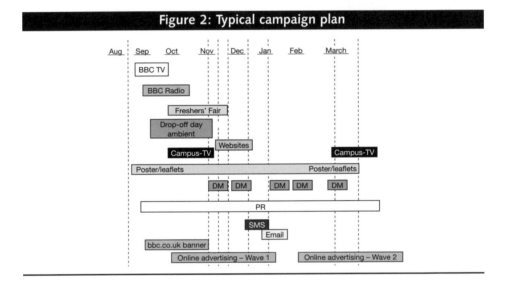

**Figure 2: Typical campaign plan**

## An effective and successful campaign

An increasingly sophisticated approach has also delivered improved results over the period. Taking 2003–2004 as base we've seen sales increase by 8% in 2004–2005 and by a massive 24% in 2005–2006, with an ROI of 12:1, 10% up on the previous year (see Figure 3).

## Reducing evasion on campus

The student campaign is targeted primarily at students in halls of residence. These addresses are flagged on the TV Licensing database as students. Their 'licensable status' enables us to calculate how many students have bought a licence.

Focusing specifically on on-campus addresses, the number of students in halls of residence has remained fairly constant over recent years – an important factor to eliminate when looking at growth in sales (see Figure 4).

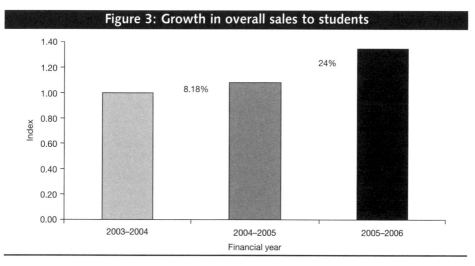

Figure 3: Growth in overall sales to students

Over the last three years the number of students taking TVs to university has also remained constant at 45%,[3] so the number of on-campus 'licensable premises' has not changed significantly. The constraints of commercial confidentiality prevent TV Licensing from publishing actual current evasion rates. However, a crucial 'tipping point' was reached three years ago when licence penetration exceeded 50% for the first time.

With large year-on-year sales increases over the last three years, it is clear that the vast majority of students on campus now buy a licence rather than evade.

Figure 5 shows the increasingly steep sales curve over the last three campaign periods, illustrating how the latest campaign produced more sales in the first four months than in the whole of the previous year.

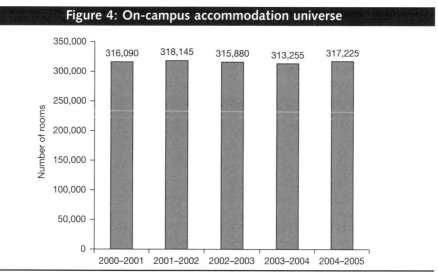

Figure 4: On-campus accommodation universe

Source: Higher Education Statistics Agency

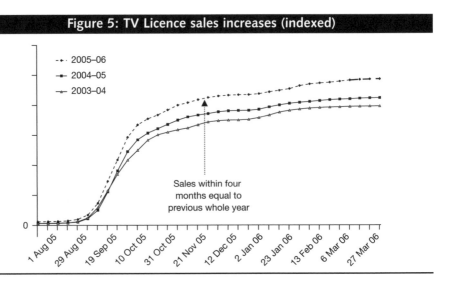

Figure 5: TV Licence sales increases (indexed)

## Creative's contribution to increased effectiveness

*2003–2004: 'Beans'*

In 2002–2003, Proximity London developed its first campaign, 'Beans', to complement trails being run on the BBC. Creative set out to dramatise the impact of being fined £1,000 as a student. A series of executions, designed to look like the kind of thing you'd typically find on a union noticeboard, formed the basis of the on-campus work, which included posters, leaflets in halls of residence and stands at Freshers' Fairs (see Figure 6). Direct mail was also used, targeting new students in

Figure 6: 'Beans' – on-campus poster execution

their parents' homes before they left for university and then on into term-time in halls.

The campaign produced good results, with overall sales exceeding target by 6% and on-campus sales penetrating over 50% for the first time. This meant that we'd reached our major goal – it was now more likely that students would be licence holders than evaders. However, evasion remained high and there were clearly opportunities for further improvement.

### 2004–2005: 'Work It Out For Yourself'

In 2004, we carried out qualitative research, revealing some seminal insights that were to improve the effectiveness of the campaign.

Students told us how they hate being 'marketed to'; how 'clever' advertising annoys them. They are an intelligent audience and it's important to treat them as such. They hate being 'hoodwinked', particularly so in the case of serious brands like TV Licensing. They basically just wanted the facts, presented to them in a clear and 'no frills' way.

Whilst the previous campaign had clearly struck a chord, there was some indication that it was perhaps trying a bit too hard to come down to the students' level in its presentation, and that our key message – watching TV without a licence is against the law – was in danger of being obscured by 'clever' execution.

Another important and actionable insight emerging from the research was the fact that students value each other's opinions far more than those of advertisers. Word of mouth in this market is incredibly powerful and if you can get students on your side, they will spread the message for you.

The research also identified a number of myths about TV Licensing prevalent amongst students – a long list, in fact, that included commonly held beliefs such as:

- you don't need one as your parents' licence covers you
- nothing ever happens anyway if you don't have one, the consequences aren't real
- they don't let enforcement officers on campus so you'll never get caught
- TV detector vans don't work, they just stick a coat hanger on top of a Transit van to scare you.

The creative brief focused on dispelling the myths and encouraging students to 'spread the word' on our behalf. In particular, the brief stressed the importance of delivering straight facts without being too 'gimmicky'. Thus the 'Work It Out For Yourself' (or 'WIOFY') campaign was born (see Figure 7).

In addition to the enhanced creative, the media plan was refined to maximise on-campus activities, in particular, exploiting the key touchpoints around arrival days, Freshers' Fairs and first-day lectures. Innovative ambient executions were introduced at these points to complement the core programme, including specially designed stickers to go over aerial sockets in rooms; door signs; 'Reserved Parking' TV Licensing signs in car parks; and even messages projected onto lecture theatre screens.

Increased emphasis on ambient was particularly important since allocated TVRs on BBC had been reduced from 373 the previous year to 234. A new trail was nevertheless developed, which was aired on BBC channels at the start of the

**Figure 7: Examples of 'Work It Out For Yourself' on-campus posters**

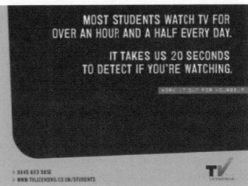

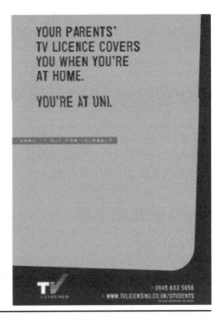

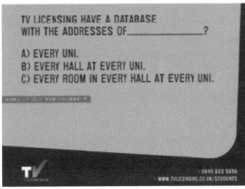

campaign. Creative, tying in with the 'WIOFY' theme, dramatised the contrasting summers enjoyed by one carefree student, with another working in a carwash to pay off his £1,000 fine (see Figure 8).

'WIOFY' was a huge success. Not only did overall student sales increase by 8%, and evasion on campus reduce still further, but 'WIOFY' was inundated with a series of industry accolades for both strategy and creativity. It was named 'Campaign of the Year' at the Marketing Week Effectiveness Awards, also taking Gold in the Business, Services & Utilities category; it swept the board at the Precision Marketing Awards, taking overall 'Grand Prix' winner as well as Gold – Best Utilities & Public Services and Gold – Best Integrated Campaign; it also won Gold, Silver and Bronze DMAs (Direct Marketing Association Awards) and even a John Caples Bronze.

**Figure 8: Stills from 'Work It Out For Yourself' TV trail**

*2005–2006: 'It's Not Funny'*

How do you follow that?! With such a strongly performing campaign, we could have done worse than simply roll it out for a second year. However, evasion on campus was still unacceptably high and there was a need to drive performance still further.

The situation was neatly summed up by one of Proximity's account managers:

*If you do what you've always done, you'll get what you always got.*

Intent on raising the bar by 'doing something different', we revisited the previous year's research to see if there were any further insights that could take the campaign to the next level.

The 'WIOFY' campaign was clearly effective in getting its message across with its straight delivery. But how could we increase overall standout? How could we make the campaign more involving?

The agency team had started to focus on a previously overlooked, yet evidently powerful, insight: the TV Licence is a serious subject, but students won't take it seriously if they don't believe they need one, don't believe the consequences of not having one, and don't believe they will get caught. In fact, students can see TV licensing as a 'bit of a joke'. It was this very observation that directly inspired a new creative idea – 'anti-humour'.

'Anti-humour' is particularly popular on student websites. It is a type of indirect humour that involves the joke teller raising expectations but then delivering something that is deliberately not funny or lacking in intrinsic meaning. The most common example of anti-humour joke is the classic:

Q: 'Why did the chicken cross the road?'
A: 'To get to the other side.'

The joke has become too much of a cliché to be funny, but it illustrates how punchlines in anti-jokes can achieve their effect by being mundane.

Another example:

Q: 'What do you get when you cross a muffin with chocolate chips?'
A: 'A chocolate chip muffin'.

Not laughing yet? Well that's the point! For TV Licensing, 'anti-humour' provides a unique creative platform from which to communicate a 'serious' message, by involving students with what looks like a series of appealing jokes about the TV Licence. Except that the punchline isn't funny – it is deadly serious. In fact, as the audience quickly realises: 'It's not funny watching TV without a licence.'

Rather than simply telling students to get a licence, the 'It's Not Funny' campaign involves them, allows them to 'get it' for themselves, then encourages immediate action via the TV Licensing website or phone number (see Figure 9).

The 'involvement' element of the campaign also went significantly further. Most brands make ads for their consumers. We used consumers to make our ads! We got students to spread the word for us with their own programming content on Sub TV, the on-campus TV channel. The 'anti-humour' theme – already taking shape in posters and mailings across campus – was now being broadcast on TV.

Student TV crews filmed fellow students in 16 universities telling their 'most unfunny joke', edited with branded voiceovers and specially themed ads. The package provided a uniquely powerful way to get a serious, strongly branded, local message across in a light-hearted, engaging way.

Another innovative 'involvement' element was used to attract students to our stands at Freshers' Fairs and spread the message around campus. You've heard of personalised direct mail, well how about personalised posters? Our cartoonist caricatured new students in the style of the campaign, scowling under our campaign headline – 'It's not funny watching TV without a licence'. After what amounted to a full five-minute engagement with the brand (one student even commented that they'd just been persuaded to watch our ad campaign taking shape before their very eyes), we sent them the full-colour version as a permanent reminder for their wall. Some students even asked us to send a copy to their parents!

Because the concept was such a departure from the previous and highly successful approach, verification research was carried out before committing to roll-out.[4] The research was positive, showing that – as we had hoped – the new campaign

### Figure 9: 'It's Not Funny' main on-campus campaign posters

What do you call a first-year student
watching TV without a licence?

A first-time offender.

It's not funny watching TV without a licence. In fact, it's a serious
offence for which you can be prosecuted and fined up to £1,000.

Seriously, get a TV Licence.
Go to www.tvlicensing.co.uk/students or call 0845 603 5656

What do you get if you cross an Enforcement
Officer with an electronic detector?

Caught.

Watching TV without a licence isn't funny. Neither is the fact that
our detection equipment can pick up a signal from your TV within 20 seconds
of you switching it on.

Seriously, get a TV Licence.
Go to www.tvlicensing.co.uk/students or call 0845 603 5656

was more likely to stand out and appeal to students and, furthermore, that it was more appropriate in tone, less patronising and more helpful (see Table 1).

Sales results were to bear out these advance findings and prove the efficacy of the anti-humour route. Sales in 2005–2006 to the end of March are 24% up on the previous year (as shown in Figure 3). In fact, we sold more licences in the first four

### Table 1: 'Work It Out for Yourself' vs 'It's Not Funny' – online concept tests

Scores rated on scale of 1–5, where 1 = Disagree strongly, 5 = Agree strongly

|  | WIOFY | INF |
|---|---|---|
| **INF is less likely to be ignored ...** <br> *I tend to ignore it* | 3.71 | 3.66 |
| **INF is more appropriate in tone ...** <br> *Tone is appropriate* | 3.46 | 3.66 |
| **It's less patronising ...** <br> *It is patronising* | 3.38 | 2.89 |
| **More helpful ...** <br> *It's designed to be helpful* | 2.97 | 3.25 |
| **And is perceived as making it easier to get a licence** <br> *It makes it easier to get a licence* | 2.73 | 2.98 |

Source: TVL Opinion Panel student research, April 2005

months than in the whole of the previous year (as shown in Figure 5)! The ROI delivered by the campaign overall was 12:1, a 10% increase on the previous year.

It is now substantially more likely that students on campus will have a TV Licence than not – evasion on campus really is no longer the norm.

## The campaign contribution: eliminating other factors

It is relatively simple in the case of a TV Licence to eliminate factors that might contribute to sales over and above the campaign activity. We saw earlier that 'market growth' is not responsible for increased sales, as on-campus accommodation – hence the licensable universe – has remained constant (Figure 4).

In addition, our 'marketplace' is unique. Unlike a traditional marketing task, the full set of the '4P's' are not available to us.

- **Product:** The product has no variables, extras, add-ons, features, functions or benefits other than the generic – it's the law.
- **Pricing:** A licence costs the same whoever you are, wherever and however you buy it – student or not. There are no discounts or variations in price (short of the yearly increase decided by Government).
- **Place:** Again, distribution does not vary regionally, and there are multiple purchase channels to maximise accessibility of purchase. Students all have an equal opportunity to buy a licence over the phone, internet, PayPoint outlet, Post Office or post. They can pay by cash, cheque, credit card or direct debit.
- **Promotion:** Advertising (in its broadest sense) is the only variable available in the mix to stimulate sales amongst students. Compelling communication – ensuring students are aware of the need for a TV Licence, the consequences of not having one, where and how to get one and how much a licence costs – is therefore the one key determinant of success. Effective communication is entirely the difference between a student buying a licence or acquiring the status of 'evader' – either wilfully, or through ignorance or inertia.

## So exactly how did the campaign work?

It was highly visible. Tracking study results[5] show that in 2005–2006, 94% of students recalled the new campaign by month one, with posters and mailings generating the greatest impact (see Figure 10).This is further confirmed through prompted recall of the individual campaign elements. Note the significance of the internet element of the campaign to students (see Figure 11).

## We changed attitudes, knowledge and understanding

There is a close correlation between awareness of the campaign and attitudes towards the myths that 'Parents are responsible' or that 'Students are exempt' (see Figure 12).

Knowledge of the licence fee also increased in line with awareness of the campaign – for example, in increasing awareness of the cost of the TV Licence and the fine (see Table 2).

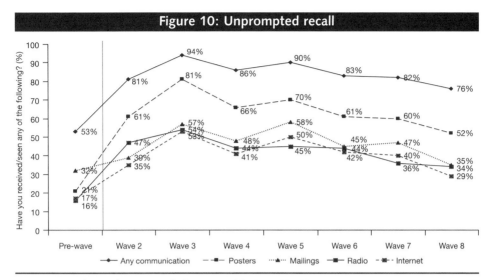

Figure 10: Unprompted recall

Source: TVL Tracking Study, test research, Opinion Panel/Spring 2005–2006

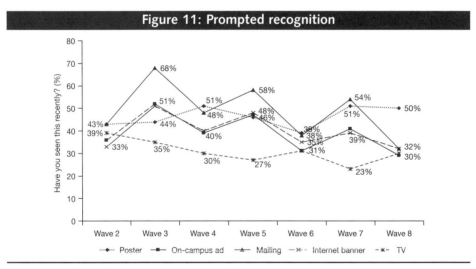

Figure 11: Prompted recognition

Source: TVL Tracking Study, test research, Opinion Panel/Spring 2005–2006

We also increased the perception amongst students that TV Licensing was more active on campus as the campaign progressed, particularly amongst first year students (see Figure 13).

Finally, the campaign achieves positive shifts in other myths: that enforcement officers aren't allowed on campus, that students can get away without paying, and that nothing happens if you get caught anyway (see Figures 14 and 15).

## Figure 12: Addressing the myths about TV Licensing

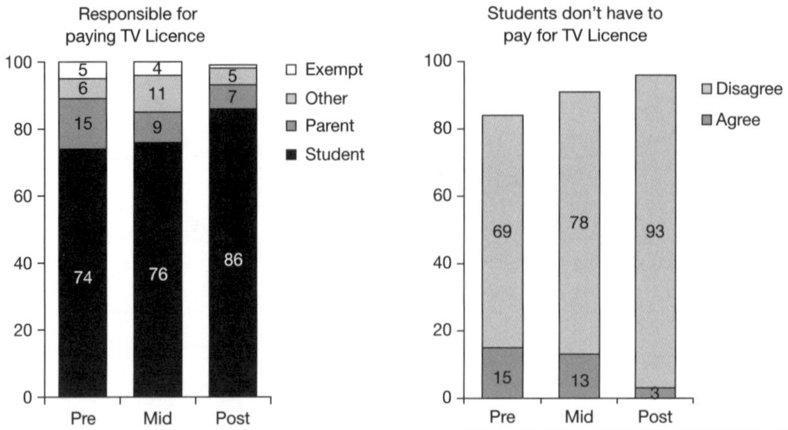

Responsible for paying TV Licence

| | Pre | Mid | Post |
|---|---|---|---|
| Exempt □ | 5 | 4 | 5 |
| Other □ | 6 | 11 | 7 |
| Parent ▨ | 15 | 9 | |
| Student ■ | 74 | 76 | 86 |

Students don't have to pay for TV Licence

| | Pre | Mid | Post |
|---|---|---|---|
| Disagree ▨ | 69 | 78 | 93 |
| Agree ■ | 15 | 13 | 3 |

Source: TVL Tracking Study, test research, Opinion Panel/Spring 2005–2006

## Table 2: Increasing knowledge

**How much do you think a TV Licence costs a student/year?**

| | £120–£130 | | | Don't know | |
|---|---|---|---|---|---|
| pre | mid | post | pre | mid | post |
| 30 | 46 | 53 | 35 | 21 | 19 |

**The fine amount if you get prosecuted?**

| | £1,000 | | | Don't know | |
|---|---|---|---|---|---|
| pre | mid | post | pre | mid | post |
| 44 | 66 | 71 | 36 | 23 | 19 |

Source: TVL Tracking Study, test research, Opinion Panel/Spring 2005–2006

## Figure 13: Increased awareness of TV Licensing activity on campus

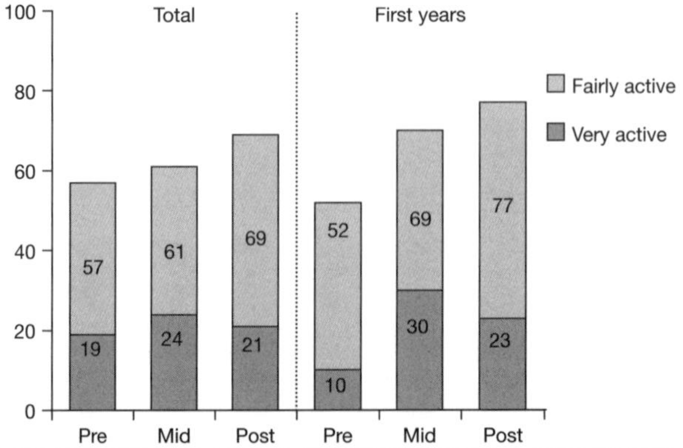

Total

| | Pre | Mid | Post |
|---|---|---|---|
| Fairly active □ | 57 | 61 | 69 |
| Very active ▨ | 19 | 24 | 21 |

First years

| | Pre | Mid | Post |
|---|---|---|---|
| Fairly active □ | 52 | 69 | 77 |
| Very active ▨ | 10 | 30 | 23 |

Source: TVL Tracking Study, test research, Opinion Panel/Spring 2005–2006

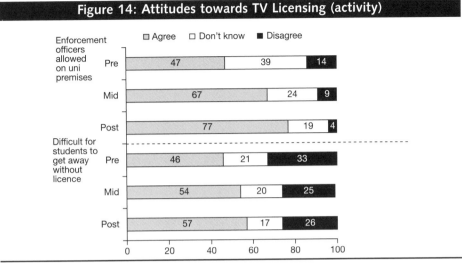

Source: TVL Tracking Study, test research, Opinion Panel/Spring 2005–2006

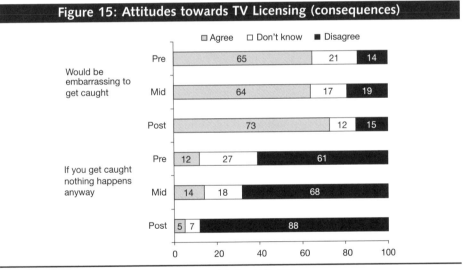

Source: TVL Tracking Study, test research, Opinion Panel/Spring 2005–2006

## Proving the commercial value of integration (the really interesting bit!)

As anyone who has tried it will testify, isolating the individual media contribution within an integrated framework can be very difficult. This campaign is no different. Everyone has their own pet interest – for example, 'How many licences did the aerial sockets sell?' However, not all universities receive all activities, for the simple reason that contact opportunities vary massively by site. For example, student TV covers only the bigger universities, some campuses are not accessible for ambient advertising and/or direct mail. In short, 'Not all "aerial socket" sites receive the same level of support!'

To make sense of these issues, we developed an innovative evaluation methodology: the 'brick analysis'. This groups activity into four broad categories, designated 'bricks' (the theory being that the more 'bricks' thrown, the greater the impact!):

One brick – 'background'-level broadcast activity reaching students at all sites (UCAS mailings, online ads, PR and trails on the BBC)

Two bricks – as one brick plus direct mail targeted to specific sites on campus

Three bricks – as two bricks plus extra student union presence at Freshers' Fairs and programming on student TV

Four bricks – as three bricks plus additional on-campus targeted activity including increased field presence – the full multi-channel campaign.

We hoped to correlate sales directly to the number of 'bricks' deployed at each university site. If the campaign was working as it should, then sales should increase in line with the number of 'bricks'. An analysis of comparative purchase rates could not have revealed a more rewarding picture (see Figure 16).

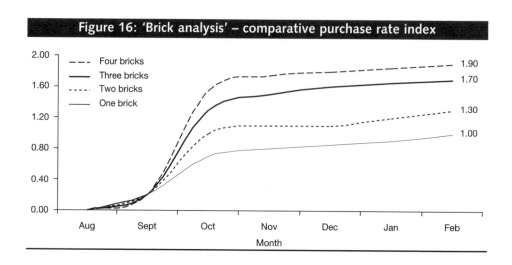

**Figure 16: 'Brick analysis' – comparative purchase rate index**

It is clear that the full 'four brick' integrated campaign is nearly twice as effective as the 'one brick' broadcast activity and 50% more effective than broadcast plus DM ('two bricks').

These four combinations account for 64% of activity. Other combinations also exist, revealing the effect of different integrated mixes in delivering different objectives:

- the 'cheapest' sales were achieved in the broadcast + student union combination
- the 'most expensive' sales were achieved in the broadcast + one element of student union + field focus combination
- broadcast + both elements of student union + field focus delivered the highest sales rate
- sub TV uplifted DM sales by 30%.

Using data from the 'brick analysis', a model has been developed to predict sales and costs for future activity, allowing us to identify the result of different media combinations and roll-out scenarios to optimise both sales volume and ROI (taking practical account of the fact that not all sites are accessible for all combinations). The optimum mix is likely to be a blend of the activity with the best ROI vs the activity that maximises purchase rate, all of which can now be identified.

## Conclusion

This is a textbook example of an effective integrated campaign in action. The campaign as a whole has delivered an impressive and progressively improving integrated performance, in both execution and results.

Incremental, measurable sales have been generated as a direct result of the campaign, which has convinced the vast majority of students in halls of residence who need a licence to buy one. The campaign is highly profitable, currently delivering an overall ROI of 12:1, a year-on-year improvement of 10%.

Our 'brick analysis' has brought rare clarity to the contribution of the component parts of such a complex, integrated campaign, providing clear guidance to optimise future performance.

Persuading students to buy a TV Licence is one of the toughest 'sells' on campus – but thanks to the impact of this truly integrated campaign, evasion is no longer the established 'norm'.

Without this campaign, it is certain that the opposite would be the case.

---

## Notes

1. TV Licensing Tracking Study, test research 2004–2005, 2005–2006.
2. The statutory cost of a TV Licence between April 2005 and March 2006.
3. TV Licensing Qualitative Research amongst evaders (MOSAIC Group 'Urban Intelligence'), 2004.
4. TVL Opinion Panel student research, April 2005.
5. TVL Tracking Study, test research, Opinion Panel/Spring 2005/06.

## Chapter 10

# Vehicle Crime Prevention

Crime doesn't pay ... but advertising to stop it does: how communications empowered the nation to protect themselves from vehicle crime

**By Emily James, RKCR/Y&R**
Contributing author: Louise Cook, Holmes & Cook

England and Wales have one of the highest rates of vehicle crime in the world, with an average of 8,000 incidents every day. The vast majority of vehicle crime is opportunistic, so the best way to set about reducing it was to encourage the public to take preventative measures, and thus effectively remove these opportunities.

Past campaigns tackling the issue had sought to 'demonise' the criminal. Given a sense of increasing 'crime paranoia', however, it was felt that another similar campaign would simply fuel people's sense of powerlessness and lack of control. Rather, the new advertising strategy chose to 'humanise' the criminals and give the audience an insight into their minds, restoring people's sense of confidence and their ability to challenge vehicle crime personally.

An integrated campaign using a wide variety of media sought both to motivate and remind people about vehicle crime, with the aim of changing their attitudes, arming them with preventative measures and warning them of the immediate risks at vulnerable moments. Over the period assessed, vehicle crime decreased by 37%. Tracking studies demonstrated that there was a significant attitudinal shift in line with the campaign's core messages, and econometric analysis estimated that communications were responsible for half this figure. Based on Government estimates of the cost of crime, the campaign is also said to have delivered an ROI ratio of 28:1 on an investment of £21.4m during its first four years – with a greater payback predicted in the long term.

## Introduction

Driving to the cinema one night you notice you're low on petrol. Time is short, but you pull into the next petrol station to fill up. You go through the usual motions: turn off the engine; get out of the car; wait for the register to be put back to zero; then wait patiently as the tank fills. You close the petrol cap, lock the car and run into the shop to pay. A minute or so later, you return to the car to continue your journey.

Nothing unusual about this, is there? Well, six years ago the scenario might have been different. A small but significant detail. You might not have thought to lock the car before going to pay.

This is a paper about vehicle crime. It describes how communications led to long-term behavioural change that substantially reduced vehicle crime in England and Wales.

Campaigns tackling vehicle crime in the past had chosen to 'demonise' criminals (see Figure 1). In light of unprecedented public anxiety fuelled by media portrayal of crime, it was felt that continuing with a similar approach would simply close people down and increase the sense of the inevitability surrounding vehicle crime.

We chose instead to 'humanise' criminals by giving the audience an insight into their motivations.[1] Through this we were able to reduce anxiety about vehicle crime and reinstate people's sense of control in challenging it. In summary we demonstrated that the vehicle criminal is someone to outwit rather than fear.

During the campaign, vehicle crime reduced more than 37%. While a variety of factors influenced the overall reduction, compelling evidence suggests that communications made a significant contribution. Rigorous econometric analysis estimates that investment in the campaign gave a return of 1:28.

The campaign was deemed to be so successful at changing consumer attitudes and behaviour towards vehicle crime that the communications task has since been broadened to include robbery and burglary.

**Figure 1: The 'Hyenas' campaign ran from 1992–1996**

## Vehicle crime in England and Wales

England and Wales have a higher rate of vehicle crime than any other country monitored on the International Crime Victims Survey.[2] In 1999 there were more than three million incidents of vehicle crime, at a cost of £2.7bn.[3]

After peaking in the mid-90s, vehicle crime rates had fallen steadily. However, by 1999, the decline had started to level off and a new impetus to reduce the problem was required.

In 1999 the Government launched its new Crime Reduction Strategy. With vehicle crime accounting for more than one in five incidents of crime,[4] an ambitious target of a 30% reduction over five years was set.[5]

The strategy comprised a range of initiatives to reduce both theft from and theft of vehicles.[6] But, with an average of 8,000 incidents of vehicle crime occurring every day, it was felt that these initiatives alone would not be sufficient to meet the target.

To make a significant impact on crime of such scale the active cooperation of the public was required and a communications campaign was central to the strategy for achieving this.

> *The biggest thing you can do to cut vehicle crime is to get people to remove things from their cars – remove the opportunity for crime.*
>
> Nick Ross, *Crimewatch UK*, telephone interview, 24 February 2000

## A campaign to tackle vehicle crime

*Understanding the communications task*

The brief for communications was to give the public a shared sense of responsibility in fighting vehicle crime, and empower them to take preventative action to protect their belongings.

To help lay the foundations for strategic development, we commissioned qualitative research to gain a better understanding of people's attitudes towards crime in general and to ascertain why people were leaving themselves vulnerable to vehicle crime.[7]

In today's society, crime sells. Television crime dramas draw viewers in their millions. Lurid newspaper headlines compete for readers. More than two-thirds of new film releases feature crime as a central theme.[8] While not new, the media's obsession with crime has become more pronounced in recent years[9] (see Figure 2).

Our research revealed the alarming impact that this portrayal of crime has on people's attitudes towards fighting it.

Vehicle crime was viewed as an inevitability of life. People saw little point in fighting it. It was 'something to be expected and tolerated, like bad weather'.[10] What was an ever-present backdrop to the media had become an ever-present backdrop to everyday life – in the face of what people perceived to be an ever-mounting threat, they felt powerless to challenge it.

From this, a clear role for communications emerged. We needed to disassociate vehicle crime from the mass portrayal of crime in the media and empower people to take preventative action.

Figure 2: Portrayal of crime in the media

To add to the complexity of the task, research showed we were dealing with a sensitive issue. In the eyes of the public, responsibility for reducing crime rested firmly with the criminal justice system.[11] To suggest that people themselves play a role in fighting vehicle crime ran the risk of being seen to be side-stepping the real issue. Therefore, striking the right tone in communications would be critical to success.

### Reality of vehicle crime

The reality of vehicle crime is a far cry from the intimidating, predatory picture painted in the media. The vast majority of incidents are opportunistic and vehicle thieves are, in the main, young men or boys who, by virtue of their youth as much as economic or social circumstances, have a relatively small stake in society. Consequently, because they believe they have little to lose, even loose change under the handbrake can be as much an invitation to break in as a suitcase left on the back seat.

We needed to convey the message that vehicle crime was something that people could fight successfully themselves, by adopting common-sense preventative measures. But we needed to find an emotional trigger to give that message impact.

### Getting inside the criminal mind

We conducted a series of depth interviews with ten recently convicted offenders of assorted theft-related crime.[12]

Although all the respondents had been caught committing crime ('the occupational hazard'), none showed remorse for what they had done. If anything, they were proud of their skills.

*I'm free and independent, not a wage-slave.*

Male, 17, history of car crime, Liverpool

Each constructed their own morality to justify their actions:

*Why should they have all this when I have nothing?*

Male, 16, history of car crime, car theft and burglary, Liverpool

*It's all insured anyway.*

Male, early thirties, wide range of offences including robbery, Radlett area

While we were gaining an insight into the motivations and attitudes of vehicle criminals on one side of the viewing glass, we were also witnessing an intense reaction on the other side.

Most people viewing the groups had experienced vehicle crime. Seeing what little remorse vehicle criminals showed for their actions incensed those who had themselves been victims. Hearing of personal possessions discarded without a thought – a £200 stereo sold for just £10 or a vehicle taken on the justification that it was insured – in the eyes of the victims such criminals were loathsome.

From these observations emerged a strategy to portray the criminal not as someone violent or dangerous, but as a 'chancer' with too small a stake in society to think twice when temptation is put in his way.

In short, someone to be outwitted rather than feared.

The emotional response we wanted to elicit from our audience was one of indignation. We wanted to induce a determination to stop the vehicle criminal getting away with it.

## Model for communications

The model for communications, including key evaluation criteria, is shown in Table 1.

| Table 1: Model for communications including key evaluation criteria | | | |
|---|---|---|---|
| | **Now** | **Future** | **Evaluation** |
| **Attitude** | Vehicle crime is predatory | Vehicle crime is opportunistic | *'Most vehicle crime is opportunistic'* |
| | Vehicle crime is inevitable | Vehicle crime is avoidable | *'There are things you can do to reduce risks'* |
| | | | Increase in perception of ease of avoidance (TNS Tracking) |
| **Response** | Block it out and hope for the best | Vehicle thief is someone to outwit | *'People have responsibility to prevent vehicle crime'* |
| | – 'not my responsibility' | – shared responsibility | *Shift from 'police' to 'public/ individual' responsibility* |
| | 'RESIGNATION' | 'INDIGNATION' | (TNS Tracking) |
| **Behaviour** | Do nothing | Take preventative action | Claimed and actual behaviour (TNS Tracking and Crime Statistics) |

*Creative idea*

The primary roles for communication were:

■ to make people see that most vehicle crime is opportunistic
■ to show them how they could avoid it happening to them.

By communicating these messages we wanted people to see that they had an ability to prevent vehicle crime.

The creative proposition was: **'It's easy to outsmart the vehicle criminal.'** This was supported by the preventative measures people can take to avoid becoming a victim of vehicle crime. For example:

■ don't leave anything on show in your car. A bag or even loose change is an invitation to break in
■ don't leave the car unlocked even for a moment, e.g. while buying petrol.

Messages were weighted in favour of avoiding theft from vehicles as they represent 85% of all vehicle crime incidents.[13]

The creative idea was to see things from the criminal's point of view. This had the effect of 'humanising' the criminal, thereby making him less threatening. At the same time it reinforced the audience's indignation by showing the disregard with which he treated other people's belongings. The audience sees how easy it is to avoid becoming a victim and is determined to prevent the criminal getting away with it.

The campaign line was: **'Don't give them an easy ride.'** The overall objective of this approach was to instil a sense of shared responsibility to prevent vehicle crime. However, we were careful not to state this directly in communications. Given the sensitivities around the issue of responsibility, we needed to avoid being seen to be lecturing.

*An integrated media approach*

Taking a new strategic approach to tackling vehicle crime required a new approach to media.

Changing people's attitudes towards vehicle crime in order to provoke a reaction would form the basis of success. But to ensure attitudinal change was translated into long-term behavioural change, it was crucial to remind them of our message as close to the point of leaving their car as possible. To achieve this, a dual media strategy consisting of 'motivation' and 'reminder' activity was developed (see Table 2).

The most efficient way to deliver 'motivation' was through TV, supported by outdoor and radio. The 'reminder' activity followed an 'optimum moments' strategy – targeting people at those moments they were most likely to leave their vehicle vulnerable to thieves. Media properties were utilised in a range of 'optimum moment' environments such as car park posters and petrol pump nozzles.

As more 'optimum moments' were identified, increasingly innovative ways to deliver messages were found. As a result of this campaign two fresh media properties were developed.[14]

Local councils were approached with a proposal to run sticker messages on parking meters and the backs of 'pay and display' tickets as well as the issuing

| | 'Motivation' | 'Reminder' |
|---|---|---|
| **Role** | Change attitudes towards vehicle crime and provoke a reaction, while providing solutions to avoid becoming a victim | Drive habitual behavioural change |
| **Media** | TV, outdoor, radio, press, online | Media formats in 'optimum moment' environments – car park posters and barrier arms, pay and display ticket backs, petrol pump nozzles in garage forecourts, washroom posters in service stations |
| **Message** | Don't give them an easy ride + solutions | Reminders to take action against the immediate risk |

**Table 2: Dual media strategy**

machines.[15] By February 2003 over 11 thousand machines ran the campaign in 74 towns.

With 22% of all vehicle crime taking place in car parks,[16] these were a focus for ambient media formats and car park barrier arms were used for the first time to remind people of the risk as they entered the car park.

Far from being an 'add-on' to the campaign, the 'reminder' activity was a crucial part of the strategy, meriting significant investment.

As the campaign progressed over a four-year period, the balance between 'motivation' and 'reminder' activity was adjusted to reflect the gradual shift from awareness building to maintenance (see Figure 3).

*Media targeting*

Incidence of vehicle crime is closely linked to population density and to areas where households with different socio-economic profiles live in close proximity to each other. A fusion analysis of British Crime Survey data, ACORN and TGI data

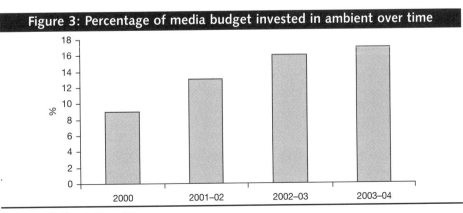

**Figure 3: Percentage of media budget invested in ambient over time**

Source: Mediaedge:cia/Home Office

151

## Figure 4: The vehicle crime risk pyramid

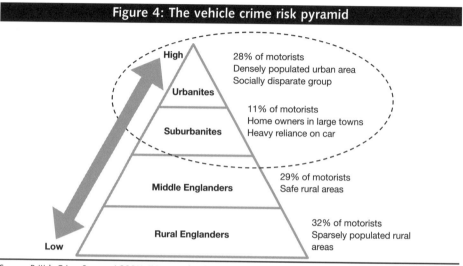

**High**

**Urbanites**
28% of motorists
Densely populated urban area
Socially disparate group

**Suburbanites**
11% of motorists
Home owners in large towns
Heavy reliance on car

**Middle Englanders**
29% of motorists
Safe rural areas

**Rural Englanders**
32% of motorists
Sparsely populated rural areas

**Low**

Source: British Crime Survey, ACORN, TGI – Mediaedge:cia

identified the audiences and areas at highest risk, and regional media were weighted accordingly (see Figure 4).

Vehicle crime is higher in the winter months when the days are shorter. To accommodate this seasonality, the campaign ran from October to March each year.

### Creative work

Examples of the creative work are provided in Figures 5–9.

## Figure 5: Car park barrier advertising

## Figure 6: TV storyboards

| Advertiser: | COI Home Office Crime Prevention | Product: | Crime Prevention |
|---|---|---|---|
| Title: | Dishonest Mistake | | |
| Agency: | Rainey Kelly Campbell Roalfe Y&R | Duration: | 30" |
| Date: | 7/01 | | |

(THIEF): This is a great place. It's really handy. Anything you want within easy reach, if you keep your eyes open.

Always something on special offer. Hello.

What's this rubbish?
(MVO): They might think it's worth something. Never leave anything on show.
(THIEF): Never mind, there's plenty more.
(MVO): Don't give them an easy ride.

## Figure 7: Posters in motorway service stations and NCP car parks

**Figure 8: Washroom activity in service stations**

**Figure 9: Petrol pump nozzle**

## Results – vehicle crime reduction

The target of a 30% reduction in vehicle crime over a five-year period was surpassed. By 2004–2005 vehicle crime had reduced 37.3% and the Government targets had been surpassed every year[17] (see Figures 10 and 11). This is one of those few occasions when it's better to see the bars on the charts getting smaller!

The reduction in vehicle crime was evident for both theft from and theft of vehicles (see Figures 12 and 13).

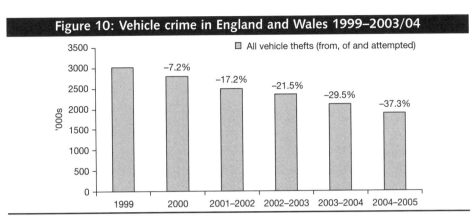

Figure 10: Vehicle crime in England and Wales 1999–2003/04

Source: BCS 1999–2004/05[18]

Figure 11: Performance against target – % reduction in vehicle crime from baseline of 1999

Source: BCS 1999–2004/05

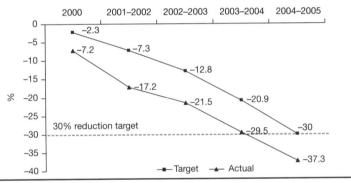

Figure 12: Incidents of theft from vehicles 1999–2004/05

Source: BCS 1999–2004/05

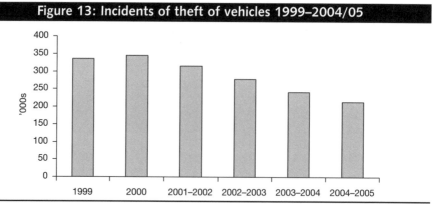

Figure 13: Incidents of theft of vehicles 1999–2004/05

Source: BCS 1999–2004/05

We have chosen to present the results using British Crime Survey data. However, the target of a 30% reduction over five years was also met when analysed through Recorded Crime data.

Crime statistics are subject to influence from many factors. Communication is just one of these. However, compelling evidence demonstrates that communications was responsible for a substantial incremental reduction in vehicle crime, helping to ensure Home Office targets were met.

The next section will show, through tracking data, that communications worked exactly as intended. Then we will present the econometric analysis, which isolates the significant contribution advertising made to reducing vehicle crime.

## Evidence that communication worked as intended

### Strong cut-through and recognition

Over the four-year campaign period, spontaneous awareness of advertising relating to vehicle crime increased from 23% to 42%, with each burst building on the effect of the previous one.[19] By the end of the campaign, prompted recall of advertising was 90%, with 64% of respondents recognising the line 'Don't give them an easy ride' (see Figure 14).

'Reminder' activity also achieved high levels of recognition, reaching 53% by the end of the campaign. This increased in accordance with greater investment in ambient formats (see Figure 15). At the start of the campaign in 2000–2001 'reminder' media accounted for just 9% of the total budget. By 2002–2003 this had risen to 16%.

Recognition was significantly more pronounced among car drivers, who were the intended audience (see Figure 16).

### Message communication was as intended

As stated earlier, the primary roles for communication were:

■ to make people see that most vehicle crime is opportunistic
■ to show them how they could avoid it happening to them.

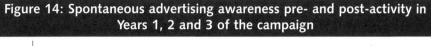

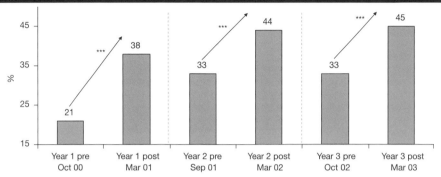

Figure 14: Spontaneous advertising awareness pre- and post-activity in Years 1, 2 and 3 of the campaign

Q: Have you seen or heard any advertising related to vehicle crime recently?
Source: TNS October 2000 to March 2003. Base: All respondents
***Each increase is statistically significant at 99% confidence

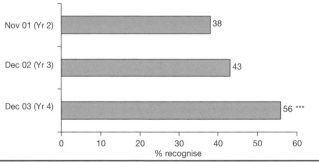

Figure 15: Recognition of ambient media for Years 2, 3 and 4 of the campaign

Source: TNS Tracking. Base: All respondents
*** Statistically significant increase from November 2001 at 99% confidence

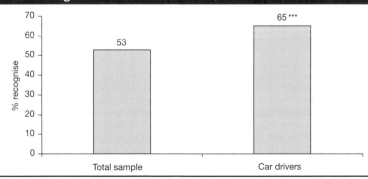

Figure 16: Recognition of ambient media, car drivers versus total sample

Source: TNS, March 2004. Total sample 791, car drivers 457
*** Statistically significant versus total sample at 99% confidence

## Figure 17: Message communication relating to vehicle crime being opportunistic

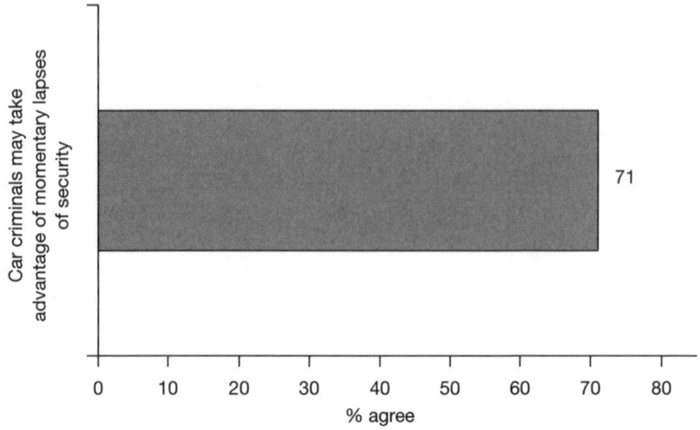

Source: TNS March 2004

## Figure 18: Message communication relating to ways to avoid becoming a victim

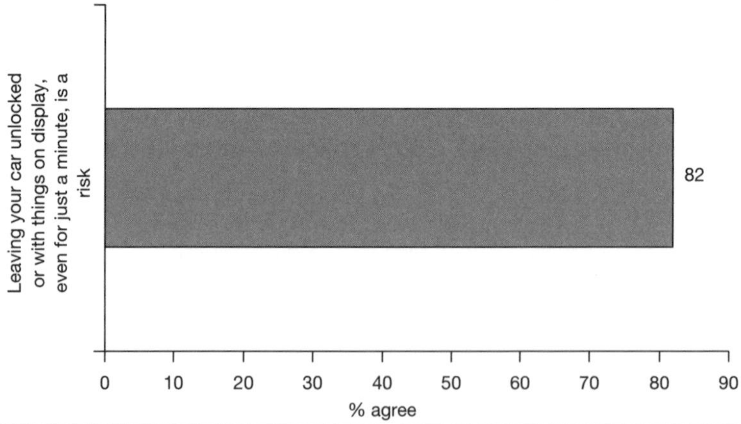

Source: TNS March 2004

These were the two top-performing impressions given by the advertising about vehicle crime (see Figures 17 and 18).

### Substantial shifts in attitudes towards vehicle crime

The two key messages conveyed in the communication translated directly into a substantial attitudinal shift (see Figure 19).

Perceptions of how easy vehicle crime is to avoid increased significantly. For those who were advertising-aware the increase is even more marked (see Figure 20).

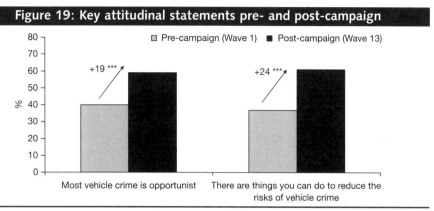

**Figure 19: Key attitudinal statements pre- and post-campaign**

□ Pre-campaign (Wave 1)  ■ Post-campaign (Wave 13)

Source: TNS – Wave 13 (end of campaign March 2004) versus Wave 1 (pre-campaign August 2000)
*** Statistically significant at 99% confidence

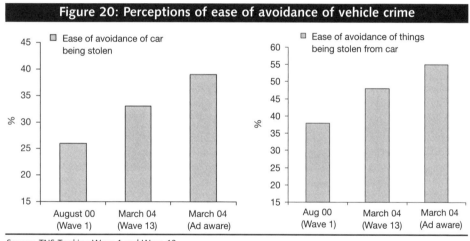

**Figure 20: Perceptions of ease of avoidance of vehicle crime**

Source: TNS Tracking Wave 1 and Wave 13

## Increase in shared responsibility to tackle vehicle crime

People also accepted a greater sense of shared responsibility in tackling vehicle crime, which was the intended take-out of the campaign. Agreement with the statement 'People have a responsibility to prevent vehicle crime' increased 15 percentage points (see Figure 21).

People agreeing that prevention of crime in the local area is the responsibility of the police reduced four percentage points, while those agreeing it is the responsibility of the public and individuals increased eight percentage points (see Figure 22).

## Impact on future behaviour

By November 2001, just one year after launch, 80% of people agreed that the campaign had prompted them to think about what they could do to reduce vehicle crime (see Figure 23).

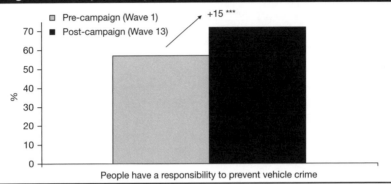

**Figure 21: Responsibility for preventing vehicle crime (tracking)**

Source: TNS August 2000 to March 2004
\*\*\* Statistically significant at 99% confidence

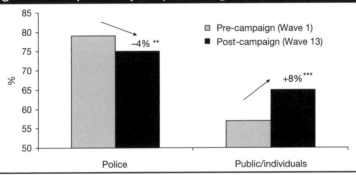

**Figure 22: Responsibility for preventing crime in the local area**

Q: Who's responsible for reducing crime in your area?
Base: all respondents W1 = 924, W13 = 791
Source: TNS Tracking Wave 13, March 2004
\*\* Statistically significant at 95% confidence, \*\*\* Statistically significant at 99% confidence

**Figure 23: Anticipated effect on future behaviour**

Source: TNS Tracking Wave 7, November 2001
Base: all respondents (791)

*Summary of tracking measures against communications model*
Tracking results are shown in Table 3.

| Table 3: Tracking results | | |
|---|---|---|
| **Now** | **Future** | **Evaluation** |
| **Attitude** Vehicle crime is predatory | Vehicle crime is opportunistic | *'Most vehicle crime is opportunistic'* +19 percentage points |
| Vehicle crime is inevitable | Vehicle crime is avoidable | *'There are things you can do to reduce risks'* +24 percentage points |
| | | Increase in perception of ease of avoidance +13 percentage points (theft of) +17 percentage points (theft from) (TNS Tracking) |
| **Response** Block it out and hope for the best | Vehicle thief is someone to outwit | *'People have responsibility to prevent vehicle crime'* +15 percentage points |
| – 'not my responsibility' | – shared responsibility | *Shift from 'police' to 'public/ individual' responsibility* |
| 'RESIGNATION' | 'INDIGNATION' | Police −4 percentage points Public/individual: +8 percentage points (TNS Tracking) |
| **Behaviour** Do nothing | Take preventative action | Claimed behaviour • 80% agree campaign made them think about how to reduce vehicle crime |
| | | Actual behaviour (TNS Tracking and Crime Statistics) |

Note: Tracking results are August 2000 to March 2004. Ease of avoidance shows scores for ad-aware.
Econometrics estimates that half of the total reduction in vehicle crime over the first three years of the campaign was attributable to advertising; no econometric analysis was carried out in the fourth year

## Isolating the effect of communications

As shown in the results section, vehicle crime fell 37.3% over the campaign period. Many factors will have contributed to this reduction, so to evaluate what part communications played we needed to find a way to isolate its effect.

*Developing a methodology*

Isolating the effect of communication in this context is not straightforward. Factors influencing crime levels are far-reaching and many are reported infrequently or prove difficult to quantify.

Many approaches were investigated by econometricians Holmes & Cook before the final methodology was selected. Louise Cook described the task as 'the most complex and challenging project we have ever worked on'.[20]

The selected methodology worked on the basic premise of comparing vehicle crime reduction in regions that received high-level advertising spend, with vehicle crime reduction in regions that had received low-level advertising spend. If the campaign had been effective, one would expect the region with a higher spend to have seen a bigger reduction in vehicle crime than the region with a lower spend.

This approach had a distinct advantage over other methodologies because it enabled us to discount the effect of any factors that would impact on all regions equally. For example, any change to the proportion of young males in the population, shown to influence crime levels,[21] would impact both regions equally and could not therefore account for the variation in crime reduction between the two.

However, simply comparing high-spend regions with low-spend regions would not be a robust analysis, because factors other than communication could have influenced the crime levels in one or other of the regions. For example, if the region with higher advertising spend also had a greater proportion of newer cars on the road, a greater relative decrease in crime could be a result of superior car security rather than communications. Therefore to isolate the effect of communications from other influencing factors, we needed to ensure that the regions we compared shared similar characteristics. In other words, we needed to make sure we were comparing like with like.

The process of matching regions was complex. It started with the 43 police regions in England and Wales. Each region was classified on the range of dimensions shown in Table 4.

Through this process a proportion of regions were eliminated from the analysis. The remaining regions were paired, then analysed to assess the impact of communications.

Four media models were tested in order to isolate the effect of TV, the effect of ambient media, and the effect of TV and ambient media together. In total 37 pairs of regions were analysed across the four models. The approach is summarised in Figure 24.

| Table 4: How regions were classified for analysis | |
| --- | --- |
| Recorded Crime statistics | Data from each region had to be consistent in order to be comparable.[22] |
| Crime profile | The police force groups regions according to the prevalence and nature of crime and their approach to tackling it.<br>*Note: there were no major changes to policing on a national level over the campaign period and this grouping would account for any variation at a regional level.* |
| Average vehicle age | Newer vehicles are less likely to be stolen because they have superior security. Therefore when matching regions it was key that they had a comparable profile of vehicles. |
| Correlation with TV regions | In order to establish whether a police region had received high- or low-weight media spend, we needed to overlay TV regions and eliminate any police regions that bridged more than one TV region. |

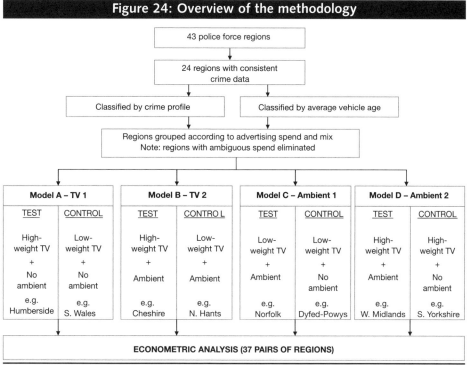

**Figure 24: Overview of the methodology**

Source: Holmes & Cook

The National Consumer Council recently reviewed the evaluation of a range of Government communication campaigns and cited the vehicle crime analysis as 'exemplary'.[23]

## Quantifying the effects of advertising on vehicle crime

On the basis of 37 models (pairs of regions) there is compelling evidence that communications made a substantial contribution to the reduction in vehicle crime over the period.

When evaluating the advertising, both the initial impact on crime levels and the longer-term change resulting from it can be measured, for both TV and ambient media. There was a high level of consistency across the regions both in terms of the scale of the initial reductions in crime and the lengths of time over which communication effects persisted.

## Quantifying the TV effect

The modelling states that every 100 TVRs (30-second adult) led to an initial reduction in theft from vehicles of around 1%–2%, and a 0.5%–1.5% reduction in theft of vehicles.[24]

To put this in context, a reduction of 1% in theft from vehicles over the first year of the campaign (when over 1000 TVRs were delivered) would be in the region of 180,000 fewer incidents.

But TV advertising was found to have long-lasting effects. The modelling shows that the reduction in crime levels persisted long after the advertising was aired, indicative of long-term behavioural change. For every 1% initial reduction, crime levels were still 0.77% lower 18 months later (all else remaining equal). The persistent effect then continued but at a declining rate.

The models predict that the impact of advertising on vehicle crime would still be evident up to 20 years after airing, indicative of habitual change (see Figures 25 and Table 5). Long-term behavioural change of this nature is rarely witnessed in advertising communications.

Figure 25: TV effect – initial % reduction in vehicle crime (theft of and theft from) per 100 TVRs (low and high estimates)

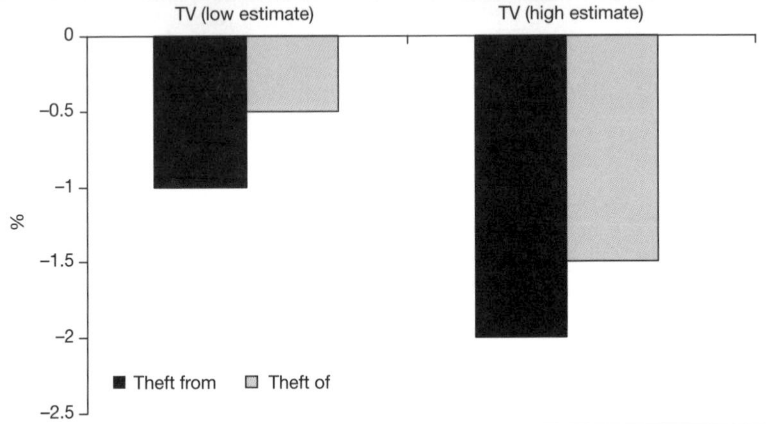

Source: Holmes & Cook

### Table 5: Crime reduction pattern over time for TV advertising aired in Q1 (effect continues declining similarly after the period shown)

|  | Q1 | Q2 | Q3 | Q4 | Q5 | Q6 |
|---|---|---|---|---|---|---|
| % reduction in vehicle crime | −1.0 | −0.95 | −0.90 | −0.86 | −0.81 | −0.77 |

Source: Holmes & Cook

### Quantifying the ambient effect

Ambient media produced marked short-term reductions in crime, typically lasting up to six months. The initial reduction for both types of crime was in the range of 3.5% to 5.7% for every £380,000 spent (this is the approximate cost of 100 TVRs to enable comparison with TV) (see Figure 26).

The lowest TV responses were typically in regions where there was no ambient media, suggesting there could have been a multiplier effect where TV and ambient were aired together, although it was not possible to establish this conclusively.

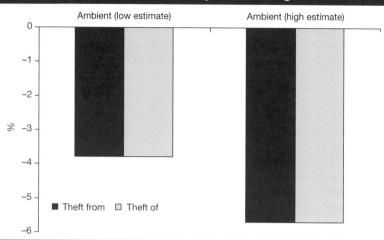

**Figure 26: Ambient effect – initial % reduction in vehicle crime (theft of and theft from) for ambient activity (low and high estimates)**

Source: Holmes & Cook

## Quantifying the effect of the campaign as a whole

Holmes & Cook concluded (based on taking the lower band of all the effects quoted above) that for every £1m spent, in line with prior media allocations, vehicle crime declined by 2.4% over the first year after airtime. This effect then persisted but at a declining rate over time.

Obviously it is not appropriate to multiply this figure by the total media budget, as activity was spread over several years and part of the budgets post-Year 1 would be maintaining the reductions already generated, as well as producing some further reduction.

Given this, looking at the campaign as a whole, Holmes & Cook estimates that communication was responsible for up to half of the reduction in vehicle crime over the campaign period.

*Summarising results against the communications model*

A summary of the results is shown in Table 6.

## Return on investment

The Home Office estimates the cost of individual crimes based on a number of key measures including policing, insurance costs, Criminal Justice System time and loss to individuals.[25] The theft of a vehicle costs an average of £4,138 per incident, whilst theft from a vehicle costs on average £858 per incident.

Media investment in the campaign totalled £21.4m over four years. Based on communications delivering an estimated half of the reduction in vehicle crime over this time the total saving as a result of the campaign was just over £590m.[26] This gives a return on investment ratio over the campaign period of 28:1.

| Table 6: Summary of results | | |
|---|---|---|
| | **Now** | **Future** | **Evaluation** |
| **Attitude** | Vehicle crime is predatory | Vehicle crime is opportunistic | *'Most vehicle crime is opportunistic'* +19 percentage points |
| | Vehicle crime is inevitable | Vehicle crime is avoidable | *'There are things you can do to reduce risks'* +24 percentage points |
| | | | Increase in perception of ease of avoidance +13 percentage points (theft of) +17 percentage points (theft from) (TNS Tracking) |
| **Response** | Block it out and hope for the best | Vehicle thief is someone to outwit | *'People have responsibility to prevent vehicle crime'* +15 percentage points |
| | – 'not my responsibility' | – shared responsibility | *Shift from 'police' to 'public/ individual' responsibility* |
| | 'RESIGNATION' | 'INDIGNATION' | Police −4 percentage points Public/individual: +8 percentage points (TNS Tracking) |
| **Behaviour** | Do nothing | Take preventative action | Claimed behaviour • 80% agree campaign made them think about how to reduce vehicle crime |
| | | | Actual behaviour • Vehicle crime reduced 37.3% over advertising period • Communications estimated to have contributed **half** of the reduction (TNS Tracking and Crime Statistics) |

Note: Tracking results are August 2000 to March 2004. Ease of avoidance shows scores for ad-aware.
Econometrics bases half reduction on data from three out of four years of campaign

When taking into consideration the long-term change in behaviour generated by the campaign, advertising was still delivering a return on investment ten years after the airtime. Holmes & Cook calculates the savings resulting from the campaign over a ten-year period to be more than £1.5bn. This delivers a ROI ratio of 71:1.

## Summary

This campaign was successful in ending the culture of inevitability surrounding vehicle crime.

'Humanising' the criminal was the key to convincing people that vehicle crime was not something to be tolerated but something they could fight. Showing the disregard with which the criminal viewed his victims fuelled the indignation that was required to make people take action.

By employing a dual media strategy of 'motivation' and 'reminder' activity in 'optimum moments', we were able to fundamentally change attitudes towards vehicle crime and effect a long-term change in behaviour.

Communication was estimated by Holmes & Cook to have contributed up to half of the reduction in vehicle crime between 1999 and 2003–2004. This resulted in an estimated total saving of £590m over the campaign period and investment in media paid for itself 28 times over.

Our strategic approach, challenging the acceptance of crime as an inevitability of today's society, has now been applied to the broader remit of acquisitive crime, including vehicle theft, robbery and burglary, and early results across all three categories look promising.

## Notes

1. Throughout the paper the term 'we' refers to the Home Office, RKCR/Y&R and Mediaedge:cia (and Holmes & Cook when relating to econometric analysis).
2. This was true in each successive survey (1988, 1991 and 1995). In 1995, *The International Crime Victims Survey* included 35 countries.
3. BCS 2000 and *The Economic and Social Cost of Crime*, Home Office, 2000. Cost of crime includes those costs incurred in anticipation of crime (e.g. insurance administration), as a consequence of crime (e.g. property costs, lost output) and in response to crime (e.g. criminal justice system and police time).
4. Vehicle crime accounted for 21% of all crime incidents in 1998–1999 – Police Recorded Crime.
5. The target end date was 31 March 2004. The reduction would be measured through two sources: Police Recorded Statistics and the British Crime Survey data (interviews in 2004–2005 – which relate to incidents in the previous 12 months).
6. These included a drive for increased car security, tighter controls to curb the trade in stolen cars, and improved security in car parks.
7. Ten representative qualitative groups were conducted by Cragg Ross Dawson.
8. 'Changing Media Images of Crime', Robert Reiner, LSE, November 1997.
9. For example, crime content in *The Times* has tripled since the late 1940s. Robert Reiner, LSE, November 1997.
10. Cragg Ross Dawson, February 2000.
11. Including the police and court system.
12. Research conducted by Cragg Ross Dawson, 2000.
13. British Crime Survey, 2000.
14. New media properties were secured by Mediaedge:cia and Home Office poster specialist Portland.
15. Car park pay and display ticket backs had been used in the past but not council roadside machines.
16. Government Crime Reduction Strategy, 1999.
17. Although the campaign finished in March 2004 it is necessary to look at BCS data from 04/05 because the survey addresses crime levels from the previous year.
18. Data from 2001–2002 cannot be wholly compared with data from 2000 because of changes to the way the data were collected. To eliminate any risks of over-reporting, we have included only half the actual reduction witnessed in the above graph.
19. Initial awareness is at 23% due to attribution of ongoing local activity by police or local authorities and some recall of historical advertising. There was no other significant activity relating to vehicle crime over the campaign period.
20. This was a complex piece of analysis and there is not space within the body of the paper to discuss it in anything but the most cursory detail. The analysis was carried out by Holmes & Cook and was discussed at all key stages with the Home Office. It is based on data from the first three years of the campaign.
21. Young men make up a large proportion of vehicle theft offenders and crime levels are shown to be directly related to the proportion of young men in the population at the time.

22. Changes in recording methodology (introduction of NCRS) meant that data from some forces were not consistent over time and these were dropped from the analysis.
23. Tim Jennings, National Consumer Council.
24. The relative scale of effects is in line with expectations.
25. *Economic and Social Cost of Crime against Individuals and Households*, 2003/04.
26. Actual saving was £590,384,779, of which £292,956,352 was theft from vehicles and £297,428,427 was theft of vehicles – Holmes & Cook.

## Chapter 11

# Volkswagen Golf
## 30 years in the making

**By Daniel Hauck, DDB London, and Tristram Harrison, DDB Matrix**
Contributing authors: Les Binet, DDB Matrix, Sarah Carter, DDB London, and
Luke Bozeat, MediaCom

This case study tells the life story of the Volkswagen Golf, and examines how, from its introduction into the UK market in 1974, communications have helped to establish it as an enduring and financially valuable brand as other trends, fashions and marques have come and gone.

It identifies three specific eras of Golf communications: 'The Early Years', from 1974–1994, when communications moved from a position based on mechanical reliability to emotional reliability; 'Becoming an Adult', from 1995–2001, when new thinking about the car-buying process led to a new, dual strategy; and 'The Mature Years', from 2002–2005, when a number of different channels were used in combination.

As well as charting some of the brand's best-known ads – from 'Casino' and 'Changes' in the 80s to 2005's 'Singin' in the Rain' – the case study also offers a snapshot of the broad changes that have taken place both in communications strategy and society as a whole during that time. Ultimately, however, it documents how Volkswagen deployed various communications strategies over time that allowed the Golf to remain fresh and relevant over a number of decades. Analysis also shows how communications added £334.5m in profit to Volkswagen, and how the Golf has consistently built its share over the course of 30 years, to become the third biggest-selling car in UK history.

## Introduction

We're going to take you on a journey through time, charting the growth of a brand that, while being a much-loved and enduring icon, has also become the third biggest-selling car in UK history.

Thirty years ago, a small car called Golf was born. This car arrived into the era of punk and the three-day week, and has grown up through Thatcherism, cool Britannia and the new millennium.

This paper is its life story; how communications have helped create, nourish and nurture the genuinely loved and financially valuable brand Golf is today. We think it's one of the most interesting stories you can tell about communications, holding up a mirror to changes both in communications and society as a whole.

There are some of the UK's most famous ads – from 'Casino' and 'Changes' in the 80s, to 'Singing in the Rain' in 2005 – but this is not just about them. It's about how Golf communications have become increasingly sophisticated, based on continually evolving thinking about the car-buying process, and the role of communications within it.

The results – more than 1.2 million sold, at a value over £12.5bn – have been staggering. This says nothing of the genuine affection the Golf has inspired: four dedicated magazines, over 30 enthusiast websites and countless driving clubs are all testament to this. There is no other car quite like the Golf.

We'll explain the three eras of Golf communications: 'The early years' (1974–1994), 'Becoming an adult' (1995–2001) and 'The mature years' (2002–2005). Obviously we can't recount everything, but we can remind you of the highlights.

So, first, cast your mind back to the 70s.

## The early years: 1974–1994

Our story begins when car communications were, quite frankly, dull. The arrival of the Mark I[1] changed this – dropping (quite literally) into people's lives with the help of a slightly odd Japanese man (see Figure 1).

**Figure 1: 'Japanese Drop' TV, 1974**

Golf. Still No.1 imported car in Japan.

So began the long-running association of Golf with superior build quality and reliability – exploiting the widespread perception associating German cars with these attributes.

By the 80s, people's relationships with their cars were changing. Many previously unable to afford cars now could, giving them a new sense of freedom, and a more emotional relationship with their car. Golf, as a relatively affordable and dependable small car, was ideally placed to capitalise on this.

So our new strategy moved on from *mechanical* reliability, to *emotional* reliability (especially smart since mechanical reliability was becoming a less competitive claim). Communications sought to create a new, more emotional bond between owner and car, by focusing on the relationship between them. It may seem obvious now, but no car had done this before (see Figure 2).

### Figure 2: The change in emphasis

| Golf is reliable | → | You can rely on Golf |
| --- | --- | --- |

From this seemingly small strategy shift came a series of now classic TV campaigns, starting with the famous 'Casino' and 'Changes'.

A powerful brand idea began – *that whatever else happens in life, you can always rely on your Volkswagen Golf.* This was inextricably linked to a rational truth but, more importantly, was the foundation for the unique and valuable brand values that endure today. A distinctive Golf 'tone of voice' was also firmly established, which would go on to unify all future Golf communications.

'Casino', for the new Mark II Golf, came first (see Figure 3).

### Figure 3: 'Casino' TV, 1985

Then 'Changes', one of the UK's favourite ads (see Figure 4).

### Figure 4: 'Changes' TV, 1987

And 'Squeak' (with the squeaky earring) – another clever Golf take on the message of reliability (see Figure 5).

### Figure 5: 'Squeak' TV, 1990

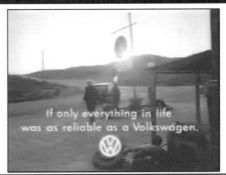

They touched a powerful emotional nerve with the public, becoming defining images of their times. 'Changes' and 'Casino' perfectly captured the materialism of the 80s, whilst 'Divorce', launching the Mark III Golf, reflected changing attitudes towards divorce (see Figure 6).

### Figure 6: 'Divorce' TV, 1993

By featuring highly aspirational men and women (even if some had lost their money), these ads positioned Golf as desirable and premium, as we will see, helping Golf to establish and defend a valuable price premium over its rivals.

The result – Golf was *the* must-have car of the time, a fact reflected in the extraordinary sales figures we will see later.

## Becoming an adult: 1995–2002

As Golf evolved, so did the communications. This was based on new under-standing about how people buy cars – outlined in an award-winning IPA paper in 1998, so explained only briefly here.

We identified two phases for car communications, and devoted separate channels to each (see Table 1).

| Table 1: The passive/active distinction | |
| --- | --- |
| **Passive phase** | Create desirability for Golf, ensuring it gets onto mental shortlist. Broadcast channels (TV, outdoor, press, radio) serve this purpose best. |
| **Active phase** | Provide rational product information, pushing those already considering a Golf towards purchase. Direct marketing, targeted press communications and digital most suited for this task. |

For the 'passive' phase task, a number of powerful ads were produced between 1995 and 2002.

There was no single product story over this period. A variety of messages were communicated – from design to price – all held together by the understated but intelligent Golf 'tone of voice' established by earlier communications.

'UFO' (with the strange American couple) was an engaging way of advertising something previously seen as boring: diesel engines. It also used a new (and hugely imitated since) format of spoof reportage (see Figure 7).

### Figure 7: 'UFO' TV, 1996

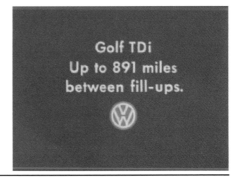

Golf TDi
Up to 891 miles
between fill-ups.

The 'Labels' TV ad, launching the Mark IV Golf, also seemed to catch the mood of the time. As people left behind the image-consciousness of the 80s and 90s, we dramatised the Golf as a truly democratic car (see Figure 8).

**Figure 8: 'Labels' TV, 1999**

The 'Cry' campaign emphasised the classic design of the Golf by gently poking fun at the growing army of Golf 'modifiers' (see Figures 9 and 10).

**Figure 9: 'Cry' TV, 2000**

**Figure 10: 'Cry' poster**

And 'Forever' showed how Golf has journeyed through all the eras – and the dodgy fashion choices – that we all have (see Figures 11 and 12).

**Figure 11: 'Forever' TV, 2001**

**Figure 12: 'Forever' poster**

The 'Don't Forget it's a Diesel' campaign helped Golf become the biggest-selling diesel car in the UK (see Figures 13 and 14).

**Figure 13: 'Don't Forget it's a Diesel' TV, 2002**

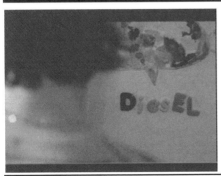

### Figure 14: 'Don't Forget it's a Diesel' press

The new 150 bhp Golf GTI. Don't forget it's a diesel. (VW)

Even for something as normally uninspiring as price advertising, Golf managed to find an interesting and distinctive way to do it (see Figure 15).

### Figure 15: 'Surprisingly Ordinary Prices' campaign

**'Piano' TV**

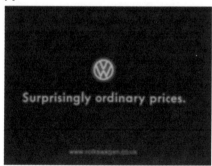

**'Dentist' TV**

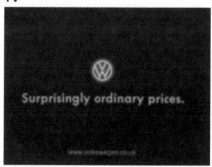

This creativity was maintained in the 'active' phase communications, helping to convert brand goodwill to huge numbers of sales during this period. Ads in motoring magazines gave specific Golf product details (see Figure 16).

**Figure 16: 'ABS' press**

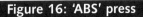

**Figure 16: 'ABS' press**

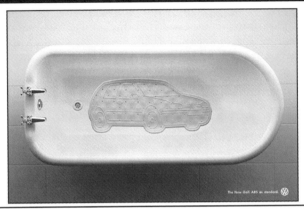

Direct marketing targeted potential Golf customers at two points: prior to 'active' phase to get Golf shortlisted, and during 'active' phase to direct them towards purchase (see Figure 17).

**Figure 17: 'Match' DM pack**

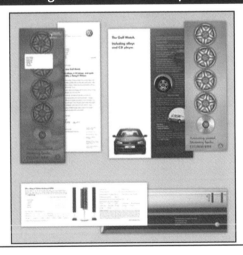

And as penetration of the internet hit 47% by 1999,[2] it became an increasingly important information-gathering tool. As early as 1997, Golf communications started directing people to an information-rich Golf website.

## The mature years: 2003–2005

As Golf matured, and we entered a new millennium, our communications became ever more sophisticated. As you will see, for the Golf Mark V and GTI launches below, we moved from simple channel *co-existence* to channel *integration*.

*Golf V launch 2004*

This launch needed to be a high-profile showcase for the long-waited fifth-generation Golf. The campaign idea was that this car was '30 Years in the Making'.

TV dramatised the development of the car through the eyes of an ever-present German designer (see Figure 18).

### Figure 18: '30 Years in the Making' TV

Motoring enthusiasts were targeted to spread the word about the upcoming launch. One edition of *Autocar* magazine was devoted entirely to Golf (see Figure 19).[3] Direct mail packs showed the progression from Marks I to V (see Figure 20).

### Figure 19: *Autocar* **Golf special**

1974 was a milestone in motoring history. The launch of the first-ever hatchback. Our very own Volkswagen Golf. And with the launch of the new Mark V, we wanted to show you just how far it has come in its 30 year life with a look back through our 'scrap book', if you like. You may not have been there at the beginning. But you can be now.

### Figure 20: '30 Years in the Making' DM pack

We then moved to broaden interest out into the general public. A Golf Icons film season was created, following the careers of film stars over 30 years of their lives (the first season was Robert De Niro). A competition ran alongside this, giving away Golfs to people born on the same day as Golf (see Figure 21).

### Figure 21: '30 on the 30th' email

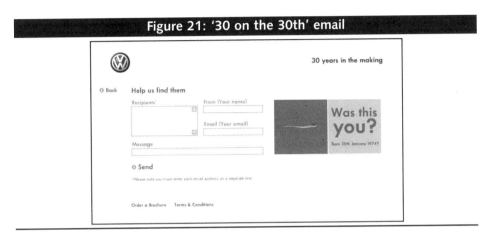

People were asked to vote online for their favourite Golf ads, promoted through a heavyweight pre-launch poster campaign. It's hard to think of another car brand with a history of communications compelling enough to motivate people to vote for their favourite ad.

But vote they did. By the time the car launched, and the TV commercial aired, thousands of votes had been cast.[4] Awareness of the launch peaked just in time for a special ad break showing the most popular Golf ads in a series, culminating in the first showing of the '30 Years in the Making' ad.

So an interesting mix of channels was used to create launch awareness, each maximising the impact of others, and of the overall campaign message.

It also gave us an excuse to watch lots of Robert De Niro films.

### Golf GTI launch 2005

This thinking was taken a stage further with the launch of the Mark V Golf GTI in 2005.

Golf GTI – the high-performance version of the Golf – has an army of dedicated enthusiasts. Talking to this audience first could nudge them the short distance towards purchasing the car and generate healthy pre-launch sales. They would then spread the word to non-enthusiasts about the Golf's imminent arrival – in other words, get some nice free advertising.

A groundbreaking online GTI configurator was created, on which people could build their GTI and then place their early order (see Figure 22). Enthusiasts were alerted to this via a direct mail campaign (see Figure 23).

The broader campaign thought was that this car had the classic GTI elements, but updated with the latest technology: 'The Original, Updated'. So, in the 'Singing in the Rain' TV ad, we saw Gene Kelly updated with modern music and dance (see

## Figure 22: GTI configurator

## Figure 23: 'Be the First to Own' DM pack

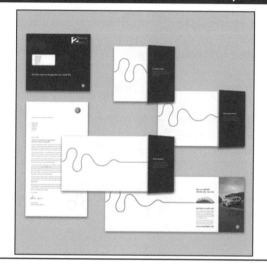

## Figure 24: 'Singing in the Rain' TV

Figure 24). The music was also designed to create interest, entering the singles chart at number 20 (although it didn't get us invited to *Top of the Pops*!).

A groundbreaking interactive TV element was also created – a medium typically used by other brands just to provide product information. This was designed to give people the chance to *genuinely interact* with the product (see Figure 25).

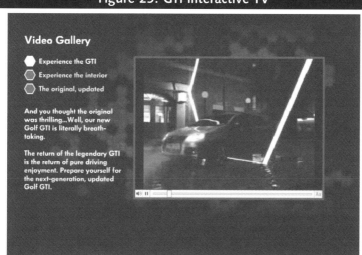

**Figure 25: GTI interactive TV**

So, the Golf V and GTI launches together demonstrate an evolving under-standing about how different channels, new and old, can work together. The channels were *integrated* in that they shared one campaign message, but also went a stage further, to *cooperative integration* – each channel also maximising the impact and effectiveness of other channels.

That was the life story of an icon. We have outlined how Golf grew up and matured over 30 years, supported by famous and increasingly sophisticated communications, resulting in the unique phenomenon it is today: a car as loved as it is successful. Now we can show you how it all worked.

## Sales performance: 1974–2005

*The contribution of Golf to Volkswagen*

The introduction of Golf in 1974 transformed the fortunes of Volkswagen in the UK, kick-starting an upward sales trajectory that took Volkswagen from niche manufacturer with 2% share, to third in the UK market[5] (see Figure 26).

Over this period, Volkswagen has steadily expanded its portfolio – from five models in 1980, to 12 models now (see Figure 27). Remarkably, Golf's share of Volkswagen sales over this period has actually increased (see Figure 28). Golf is more important to Volkswagen now than it has ever been.

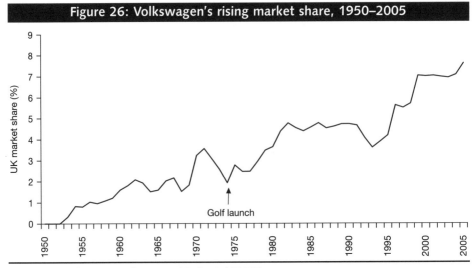

Figure 26: Volkswagen's rising market share, 1950–2005

Source: Society of Motor Manufacturers and Traders Ltd (SMMT)

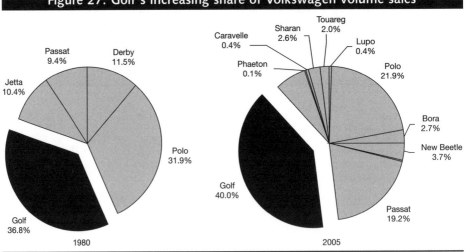

Figure 27: Golf's increasing share of Volkswagen volume sales

*Golf's unique sales curve*

Golf's importance to VW is clear from its sales – over 1.2 million models in the UK[6] – and more in 2005 than any previous year. Over this time, Golf's annual volume has grown from 18,516 units in 1980 to a massive 74,191 in 2005.

As a result, Golf's market share has consistently increased over its lifetime, and continues to do so.[7]

This kind of sales curve is unique. When we look at other long-available models in the UK over the last 30 years, sales and share consistently fall away over their lifespan (see Figure 29).

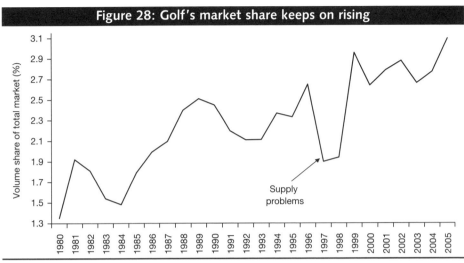

Figure 28: Golf's market share keeps on rising

Source: VW

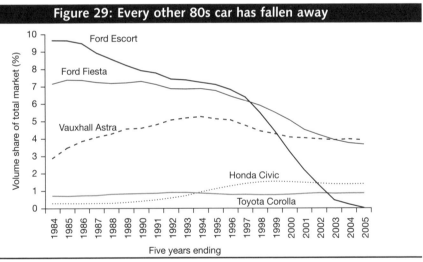

Figure 29: Every other 80s car has fallen away

Source: VW

Golf sits in the 'lower medium' sector – broadly comprising all mid-range cars, and the biggest sector in the UK market. Looking at more recent models in this sector, they too have shown a similar pattern of decline (see Figure 30).

The Golf has also enjoyed an unusually high loyalty rate – each sale generating proportionately more revenue in the long run. Figure 31 shows that the number of people citing 'always buy the same model' as a reason for buying Golf is higher than the sector average (see Figure 31). This loyalty has enabled Golf to command a higher price than average in its sector (see Figure 32).

Golf's performance relative to other long-available models is more remarkable given that price has increased relative to them over this period (see Figure 33).

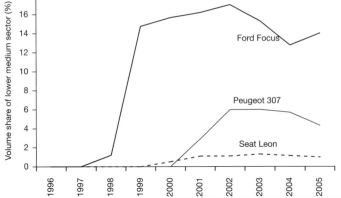

Figure 30: Recent launches already showing signs of decline

Source: VW

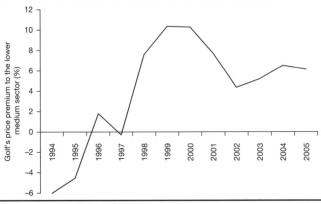

Figure 31: Golf has better than average loyalty

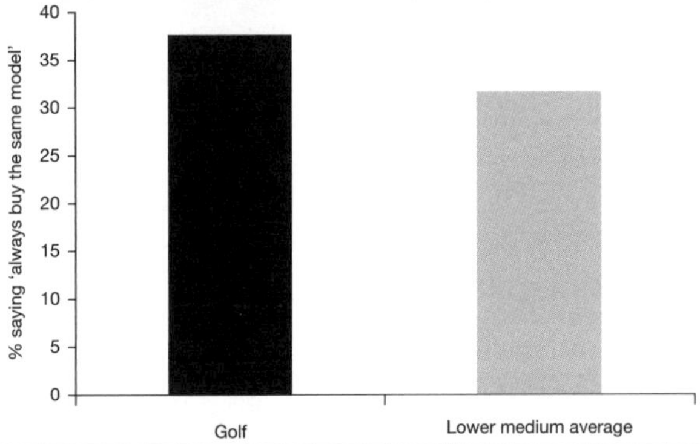

Source: New Car Buyers Survey (NCBS)

Figure 32: Golf has become more premium relative to the market

Source: New Car Buyers Survey (NCBS)

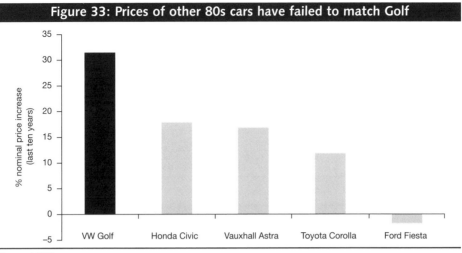

Figure 33: Prices of other 80s cars have failed to match Golf

Source: NCBS

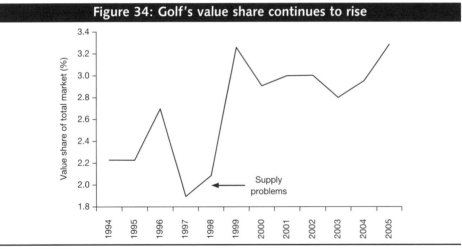

Figure 34: Golf's value share continues to rise

Source: VW, NCBS

As a result, Golf's value share growth over time has been even more impressive than its volume share growth, with a total value of over £12.5bn for the period 1990–2005 (see Figure 34).

## Performance of communications: 1974–2005

### Universal popularity of broadcast communications

Golf communications have set new standards for car advertising. They are loved by the public. In a Channel 4 programme in 2004, the public voted 'Changes' as one of the 100 greatest commercials ever. In qualitative research, Golf communications are consistently well received. Table 2 presents a brief snapshot of what people have said.

### Table 2: Quotes from qualitative research, 1990–2005

| | |
|---|---|
| Casino | 'I remember it, I think it's wonderful.' |
| Changes | 'It's just on a completely different plane.' |
| UFO | 'Something out of the ordinary.' |
| Surprisingly Ordinary People | 'I find a lot of advertising quite patronising. With these ads there's always a bit to get, so I don't feel they're talking down to me.' |
| Forever | 'What better way to tell the story of the car's heritage than showing a man on his way to buy a vintage Golf in his new one?' |
| Life in a Day | 'The idea of 30 years of evolution is spot on, that's exactly what it is.' |
| Singing in the Rain | 'Probably one of the best adverts for a car I've seen.' |

Source: Firefish, Richard Shaw, BMP DDB qual

### Figure 35: Golf broadcast communication awareness, 1999–2005

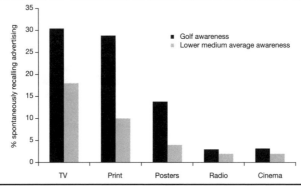

Source: Millward Brown. Base: Lower medium owners/considerers

Golf advertising has been very memorable (see Figure 35). Golf TV communications have consistently scored above the industry average in all tracking measures (see Figure 36). And press communications have performed similarly strongly (see Figure 37).

### Figure 36: Golf TV tracking, 1999–2005

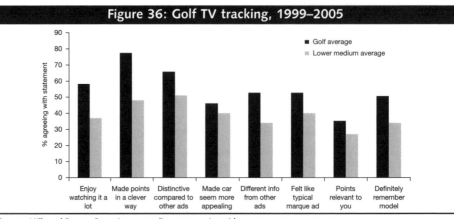

Source: Millward Brown. Base: Lower medium owners/considerers

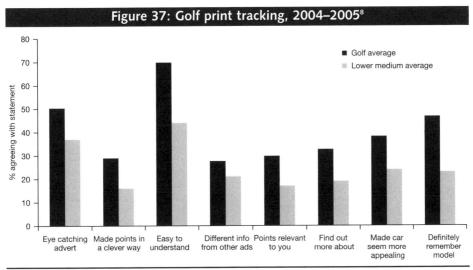

Figure 37: Golf print tracking, 2004–2005[8]

Source: Millward Brown. Base: Lower medium owners/considerers

The advertising industry has recognised the creativity of Golf communications, making Golf the most awarded car in the UK for the last 30 years. Table 3 lists a selection of the awards Golf has won.

## Table 3: Awards for Golf advertising, 1974–2005

| Awards body | Awards won |
|---|---|
| BTV | 2 Silver, 1 Bronze |
| Creative Circle | 1 Platinum, 5 Gold, 12 Silver, 11 Bronze |
| Cannes | 1 Gold, 3 Silver, 4 Bronze, 12 Shortlist |
| Art Directors Club | 1 Silver, 1 Merit |
| Kinsale | 4 Gold, 2 Silver, 1 Bronze, 1 Diploma |
| British Television Awards | 1 Gold, 5 Silver, 7 Bronze, 4 Diploma |
| Eurobest | 2 Gold, 2 Shortlist |
| Campaign press | 1 Gold, 3 Silver, 1 Bronze, 2 Finalist |
| D&AD | 2 Silver, 14 Accepted |
| Clio | 1 Gold, 2 Silver, 3 Bronze |
| Epica | 1 Silver, 1 Bronze |
| APA | Hall of Fame for last 25 years |

## Other channels maintaining the high standard

This performance has been carried through to all other channels. Non-broadcast communications have been extremely memorable (see Figure 38).

Direct mail communications have consistently achieved better than average response rates. For example, the mailing packs for the Mark V launch achieved overall response rates of 10% – and 29% for certain segments – far exceeding the industry norm of 7%.[9]

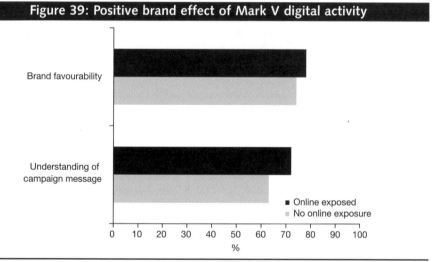

**Figure 38: Golf non-broadcast communication awareness, 2004–2005**

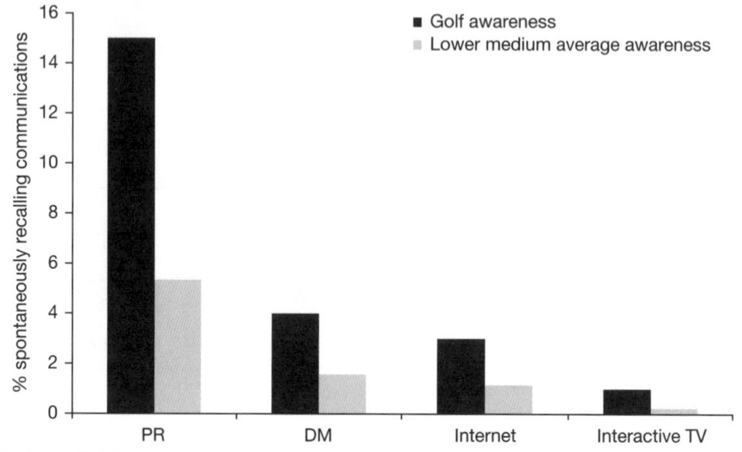

Source: Millward Brown. Base: Lower medium owners/considerers

**Figure 39: Positive brand effect of Mark V digital activity**

Source: Dynamic Logic Research

Digital has been equally effective. The Mark V activity showed remarkable results, generating 9,200,000 impressions, 69,000 clicks and 30,000 leads.[10] As we can see above, people exposed to these communications understood the overall campaign message better, and felt more favourable towards the brand (see Figure 39).

The online GTI configurator generated staggering results. Over 19,000 people configured and saved cars on the website, and of these 9% went on to order their car. This meant that 2,300 cars – many costing in excess of £20,000 – were ordered without the car ever being seen.[11]

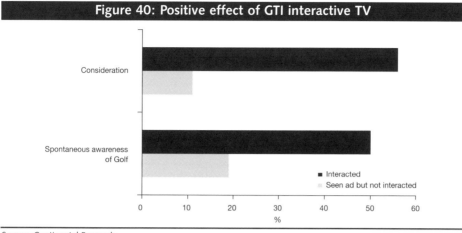

Figure 40: Positive effect of GTI interactive TV

Source: Continental Research

PR has worked well. The competition surrounding the launch of the Golf Mark V generated 1,225 entries from a possible 1,800 eligible to enter. For the GTI launch, PR to the value of £480,000 was generated from a budget of £53,000.[12]

Finally, interactive TV was successful. Figure 40 shows the positive impact on awareness and consideration for those that interacted.

From TV to interactive, Golf communications have set new standards over the last 30 years.

## An iconic brand

These communications have helped to build and sustain an icon.

Spontaneous awareness[13] of the Golf has risen over time, far exceeding the industry average. This shows that Golf has consistently been at the top of people's minds (see Figure 41).

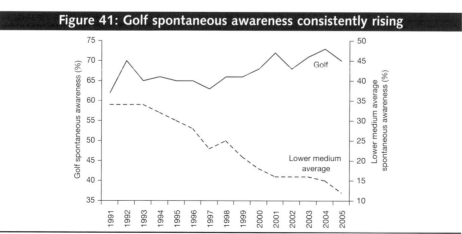

Figure 41: Golf spontaneous awareness consistently rising

Source: Image and Awareness Check

**Figure 42: Golf above average in all image measures, 2004–2005**

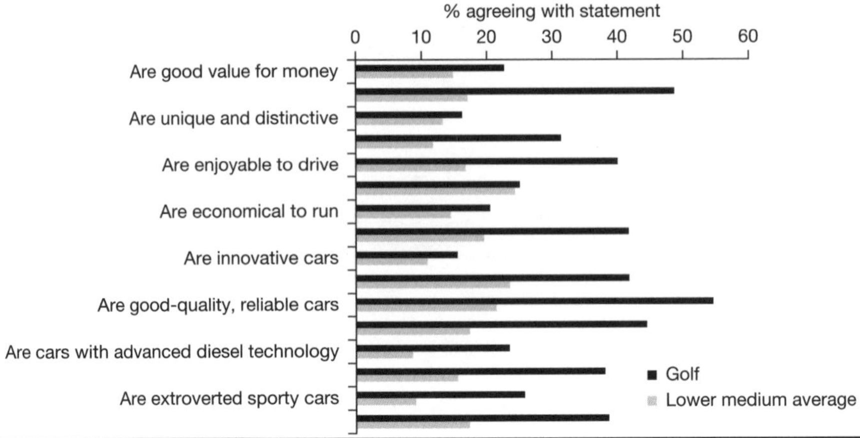

% agreeing with statement

Are good value for money
Are unique and distinctive
Are enjoyable to drive
Are economical to run
Are innovative cars
Are good-quality, reliable cars
Are cars with advanced diesel technology
Are extroverted sporty cars

■ Golf
■ Lower medium average

Source: Millward Brown. Base: Lower medium owners/considerers

People also think very highly of it. Golf out-performs its rivals on every single image measure. Golf scores particularly well in terms of reliability (see Figure 42). We will see the value of this to the brand a little later. This is supported by responses in qualitative research. Here's a sample of what people have said (see Table 4).

**Table 4: Quotes from qualitative research, 1990–2005**

'You're proud to be seen in it.'

'It's stylish and fashionable. It's seen as the classic car within a cetain price bracket.'

'Nearly everyone has a favourable impression of Golf.'

'It's a design classic.'

'It just doesn't date. It's like certain clothes you buy.'

'It's trendy even though it is old.'

'It's got class and style ... staying power.'

'Been around through three decades and still going strong.'

Source: Firefish qualitative research, BMP qualitative research

You would expect that Golf is very desirable. And it is. The number of people saying they would consider buying a Golf is way above average (see Figure 43).

## Proving the effect of communications

We can demonstrate the contribution of communications to this unique icon in two ways:

1. The correlation between sales and communication spend.
2. By comparing UK Golf performance with the rest of Europe.

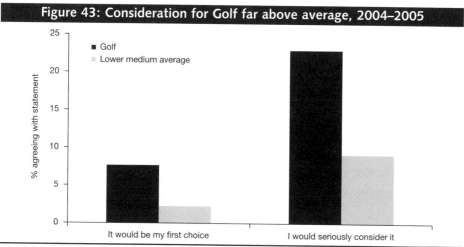

**Figure 43: Consideration for Golf far above average, 2004–2005**

Source: Millward Brown. Base: Lower medium owners/considerers

## Sales moving in line with communications

There is a clear correlation between sales performance and communication spend, with Golf's share of market moving closely in line with share of voice (see Figure 44).

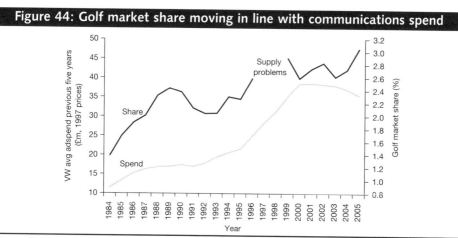

**Figure 44: Golf market share moving in line with communications spend**

Source: SMMT, Register-MEAL, MMS. NMR Association

## European comparison

We can isolate the effect of communications by comparing performance of Golf in the UK with other countries in Europe. The same Golf product, at approximately the same price level, has sold across the five main markets in Europe: UK, Germany, Italy, France and Spain. So, any differences in sales between these countries are likely to be the result of differing communications.

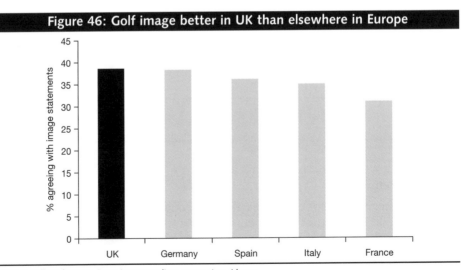

**Figure 45: Golf has experienced declining share in all other European markets[14]**

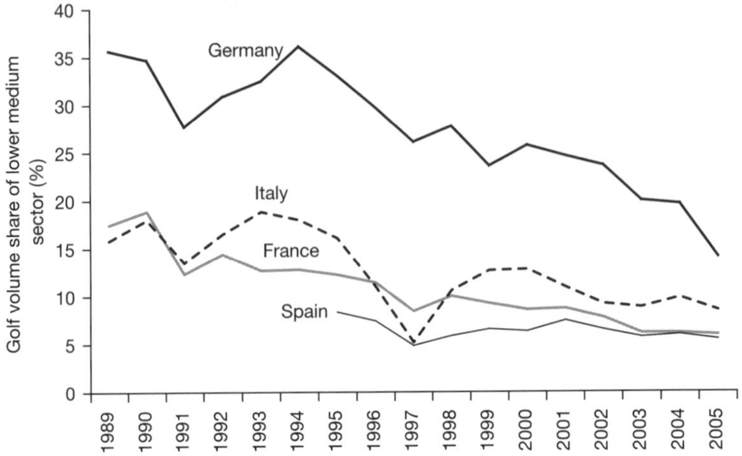

Golf volume share of lower medium sector (%)

Germany

Italy

France

Spain

Source: VW

It is clear that the Golf has been unusually successful in the UK in terms of sales, as Figure 45 shows. Golf market share outside the UK declines in much the same way as the other 80s cars we discussed earlier. Golf's performance in the UK is unmatched – by other UK models, or by the same model in other countries.

The *image* of Golf is also stronger in the UK (see Figure 46). Note that Golf has a stronger image in the UK than in Germany – impressive given that cars, which are often a source of patriotism, tend to be better regarded in their home market than elsewhere.

**Figure 46: Golf image better in UK than elsewhere in Europe**

% agreeing with image statements

UK    Germany    Spain    Italy    France

Source: Millward Brown. Base: Lower medium owners/considerers

So we have demonstrated the contribution of communications by showing the correlation between sales and communications, and the superior performance of Golf in the UK.

## Eliminating the product

To conclusively isolate the effect of communications, we need to prove that Golf's success has not *just* been because it is such a great product. We have gone some way towards doing this in the European comparison, by showing an equivalent product across Europe but extraordinary sales in the UK.

We can completely eliminate the product contribution, though, by two further pieces of evidence.

### *What experts and buyers think of the product*

The Mark I Golf was undoubtedly a fantastic car, and one that changed the face of the motor industry. But every version of the Golf since, including the recent Mark V, has received mixed reactions on arrival. Table 5 presents a selection of comments from motoring journalists.

| Table 5: Journalistic reactions to Marks II–V | |
| --- | --- |
| Mark II | 'A feeling of disappointment almost clouds our judgement on the new Golf: disappointment that the new model breaks little new ground, simply reinforcing existing strengths.'<br>*What Car?*, 1984 |
| Marks III and IV | 'Anybody who knew anything about motors agreed that the Mk III and later Mk IV had comprehensively missed their mark.'<br>*Sunday Mirror*, 2004 |
| Mark V | 'The bigger, heavier, better-equipped, vastly sensible Golf Mark V just isn't special any more – and it certainly isn't sexy.'<br>*Independent on Sunday*, 2004 |

Consumers have echoed this, expressing disappointment at how the Golf has progressed. Table 6 presents some typical comments.

| Table 6: Quotes from qualitative research, 1990–2005 |
| --- |
| 'The one thing that made the Mk I and Mk II popular was the handling and they lost a lot of that by building in comfort.' |
| 'When they first brought the Golf out, it was a driver's car, then they altered it, made it bigger, and it just lost something along the way.' |
| 'It now looks a lot like other cars.' |

Source: Firefish, BMP, DDB, Richard Shaw qualitative research

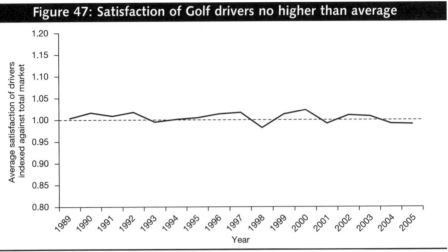

Figure 47: Satisfaction of Golf drivers no higher than average

Source: NCBS

Indeed, Golf drivers have not been any more satisfied with their cars than average (see Figure 47).

There have clearly been some issues with the product over the years, suggesting that its success may be down to more than just a great product.

### A 'blind taste test' for the Golf

We can eliminate the product effect altogether, by applying a well-known technique to cars for the first time – the 'blind taste test'.

Blind taste tests are often used to demonstrate the effect of brands on perceptions of taste. For example, the PG Tips IPA paper in 1990 showed that PG Tips scored better in branded than blind taste tests, proving the positive effect of the brand.

This is harder for durable products – you can't gauge product views as easily. But we have found a completely new way of proving that Golf product perceptions do not match reality.

In car production, there is a technique known as 'platform sharing', where a number of models share components. Typically, the components that cannot be seen are shared (chassis, engine, etc.), whilst those that can are tailored to individual models (interior design, etc.). This allows engineering and manufacturing costs to be spread over a number of vehicles.

Volkswagen is generally recognised as a pioneer of this technique. The Golf shares a platform with both the Seat Leon and Skoda Octavia. Whilst these cars look different, they share up to 70% of the same components. These models are therefore invaluable points of comparison for the Golf.

### Overall perception

The *objective* ratings of these three cars (road-test ratings from independent motoring publications) are very similar (see Table 7).

| Table 7: Road-test ratings for Golf, Leon and Octavia | | | | |
|---|---|---|---|---|
| | *What Car?* | *Autocar* | *Top Gear* | **Average** |
| **Golf** | 60% | 80% | 55% | 65% |
| **Leon** | 80% | 60% | 50% | 63% |
| **Octavia** | 80% | 80% | 55% | 72% |

However, the public's *perceptions* of these cars are quite different. Golf out-performs the other two models on every single image measure (see Figure 48).

**Figure 48: Golf out-performs Leon and Octavia on all image measures**

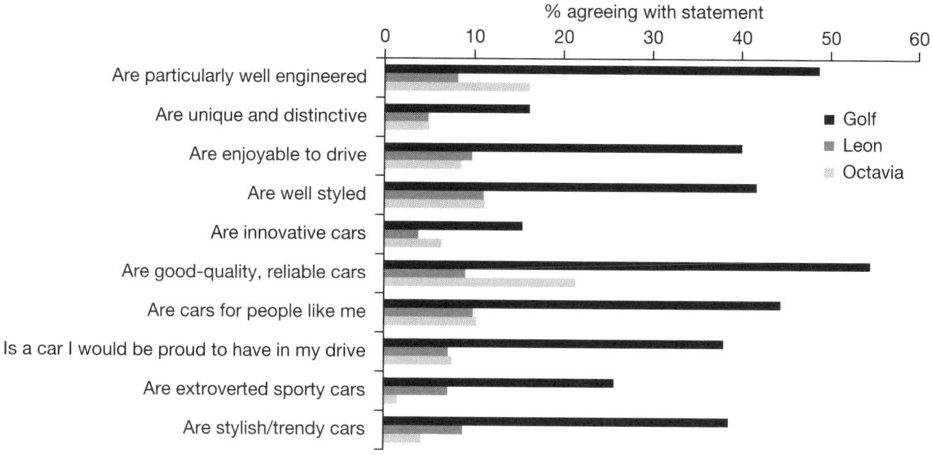

Source: Millward Brown. Base: Lower medium owners/considerers

## Perception of reliability

Figure 48 shows that Golf scores especially well in terms of reliability. Table 8 presents a small sample of the things people routinely say.

**Table 8: Quotes from qualitative research, 1990–2005**

'It's not going to die on you, stranding you on the side of the motorway.'

'Universally acknowledged to be a reliable car.'

'It is one less worry in a hectic life. It is always there, it will never let you down.'

Source: Firefish qualitative research, BMP qualitative research

And reliability is a key driver for purchase of the Golf – more so than for the other cars (see Figure 49). But, when we compare Golf with the other 'control' models, we can see that the perception of reliability for Golf far exceeds the reality (see Figure 50).

What accounts for this difference? Well, Golf communications have particularly focused on reliability over the years. This disconnect between perceived and real

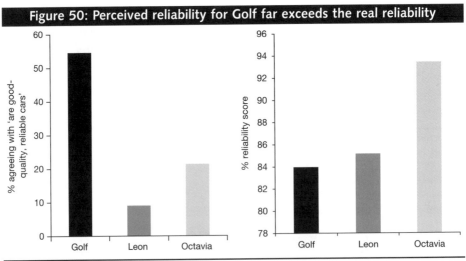

Figure 49: Reliability is a key driver for purchase for Golf

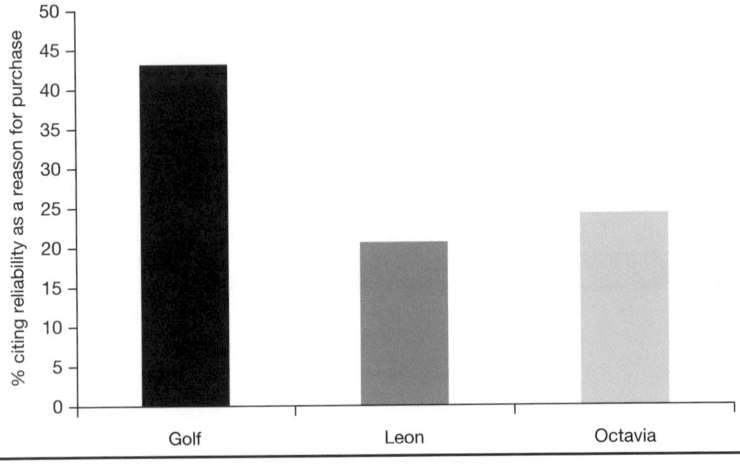

Source: NCBS

Figure 50: Perceived reliability for Golf far exceeds the real reliability

Source: Millward Brown                    Source: 2006 Driver Power Survey

reliability can only be a result of communications. By emphasising reliability, the communications have created a hugely powerful brand property that far exceeds the reality of the product.

The implications of this are very significant. It has enabled Golf to command a higher price than the Leon and Octavia (see Figure 51).

### Perception of residual values

The perception of reliability is the major factor determining the perception of residual value (i.e. the belief that a car will hold its value well). We can see the strong correlation between the two in Figure 52.

## Figure 51: Golf sells at a price premium to other cars built on same platform

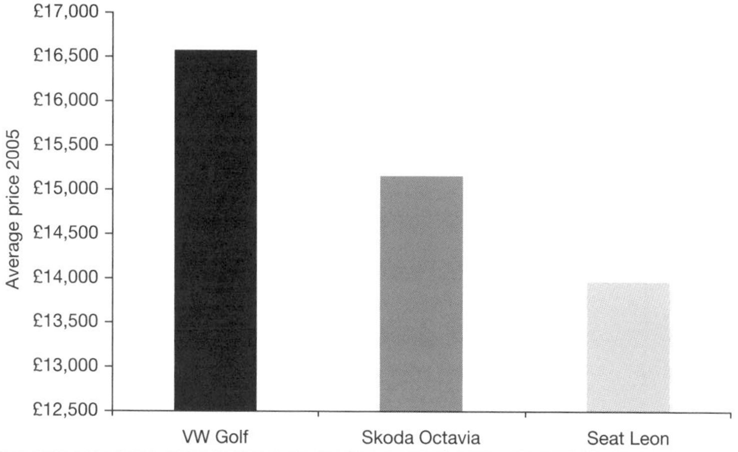

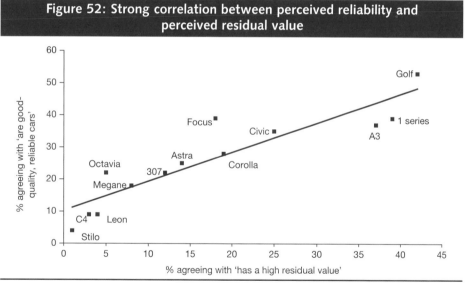

Source: NCBS

## Figure 52: Strong correlation between perceived reliability and perceived residual value

Source: Millward Brown. Base: Lower medium owners/considerers

Note that Golf is highest in the sector for both perceived reliability and perceived residual value.

For Golf, high residual value is one of the key motivations for purchase, far more so than for the other models (see Figure 53).

Again, when we compare perceived and real residual values, we see that whilst Golf is seen to have a far better residual value than both the Leon and the Octavia, the actual residual values for the three cars are very similar (see Figure 54).

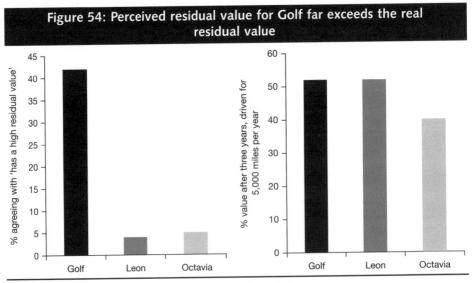

**Figure 53: High residual value is a key driver for purchase for Golf**

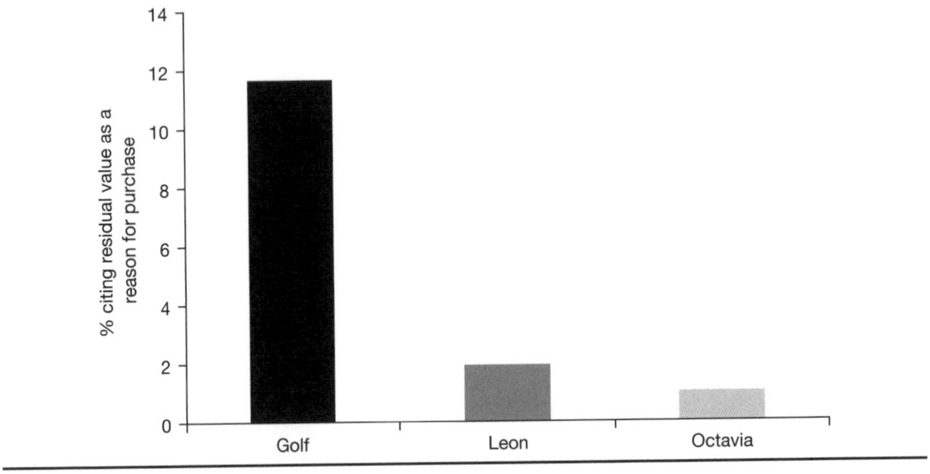

14
12
10
8
6
4
2
0
% citing residual value as a reason for purchase
Golf
Leon
Octavia

Source: NCBS

**Figure 54: Perceived residual value for Golf far exceeds the real residual value**

45
40
35
30
25
20
15
10
5
0
% agreeing with 'has a high residual value'
Golf
Leon
Octavia
60
50
40
30
20
10
0
% value after three years, driven for 5,000 miles per year
Golf
Leon
Octavia

Source: Image and Awareness Check

Source: AA

This analysis shows the powerful transforming effect of the Golf brand on perceptions of the car, and constitutes an entirely new piece of thinking in evaluating the effects of brand communications for durable products.

This conclusively shows that Golf's performance in the UK has been to a large extent a function of powerful and enduring brand values – built by the equally powerful communications over the last 30 years.

## Eliminating the other factors

Is there anything else that could be responsible for Golf's success?

### Distribution

Volkswagen's distributor network has consistently shrunk over the last 30 years (see Figure 55).

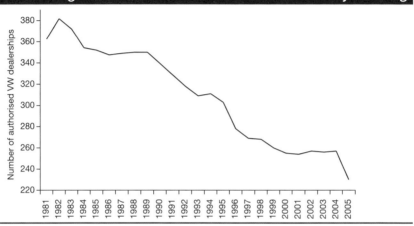

**Figure 55: Volkswagen's distributor network has been consistently shrinking**

Source: VW

### Dealer incentives

The number of incentives used by Volkswagen dealers has actually fallen over time. Figure 56 shows increasing numbers of buyers saying they received no additional incentives when purchasing their car.

**Figure 56: Customers received fewer incentives**

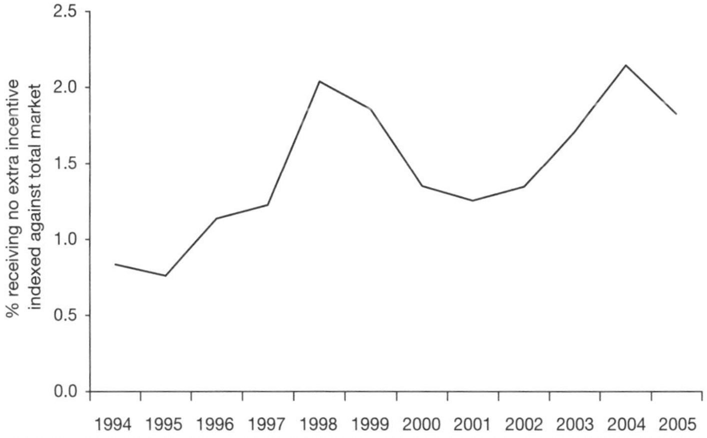

Source: NCBS

199

*Pricing*

We have already shown that the price of Golf has been consistently above the market average and has *increased* relative to the market.

## The financial contribution of communications

To work out the financial contribution of our increasingly sophisticated UK communications, we need to know what would have happened without them. Once again, we can use the European data to help us.

Other European countries have had exactly the same products, at the same prices, with similar media spends, yet Golf's market share on the continent fell. The only significant difference was the way Golf was advertised. One must therefore conclude that, without our communications, Golf's market share would have fallen rather than risen (as indeed it did for all the other 80s cars we looked at earlier) (see Figure 57).

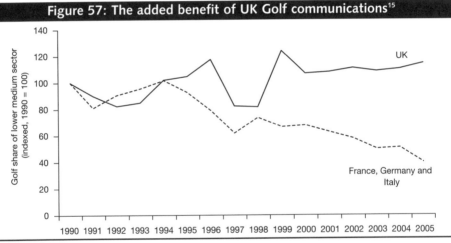

**Figure 57: The added benefit of UK Golf communications[15]**

Source: Jato

Figure 57 shows what would have happened if market share had fallen at the same rate as it did on the continent. This indicates that, since 1990, our communications have sold an extra 260,000 cars, which equates to an incredible £3.9bn in revenue. And this is an underestimate of the total effect, since we have data for only the last 15 years.

Based on an average 8.6% profit margin, this represents an extra £335.4m in added profit for Volkswagen as a result of communications. Given that this figure represents only the last 15 years of Golf sales, it does not nearly represent the true value of Golf communications. It is impressive nonetheless.

Media spend for 1990–2005 was £134.3m. This means that every £1 spent on communications produced £2.5 in added profit. Golf communications have been incredibly effective, generating vast amounts of profit for Volkswagen over a long period.

## Conclusion

So, we have completed our journey through time, charting the growth of an extraordinary brand and proving the vital contribution of three decades of pioneering communication to this business success. What wider lessons can we draw from this story?

> *icon; used, particularly in modern popular culture, in the general sense of symbol … readily recognised as having some well-known significance or embodying certain qualities.*
>
> *Source: Wikipedia*

We, in the communications world, probably use 'icon' too freely. But few would dispute Golf's entitlement to it.

What is remarkable is that Golf has *maintained* this iconic status for more than three decades. Why hasn't it gone the way of other iconic 'brands' of its early days: Farrah Fawcett Major, the Filofax, Wham!, the Yuppie?

How can some brands remain perennially relevant, never getting locked in time?

We believe that communications have been central to this brand's extraordinary staying power.

- The communications have never lost sight of the product. It's easy to get carried away with the design and imagery aspects of icons. But Volkswagen has consistently invested in evolving the Golf, and this evolving product story has never been forgotten by communications.
- Golf has never lost its sense of self. Over the years, communications have focused on price, engines, diesel or design, but all the time keeping true to the inimitable Golf tone of voice.
- How have we achieved this enduring sense of Golf? Ironically, because client and agency have never defined the brand too rigidly. There has been no one creative idea, no single end-line, no brand onions or pyramids. Instead, communications have been unusually free – able to reflect the times, without ever getting trapped in any one time.

This journey is now over. Golf's remarkable journey is still going strong.

## Notes

1. 'Mark' is the name given to each version of the Golf that has been produced. In total, there have been five 'marks' over the last 30 years.
2. Source: TGI 1999.
3. Along with the *Autocar* website.
4. 'Changes' was the most popular, with 'UFO' in second.
5. With a 700% increase in volume sales during the period.
6. This makes Golf the third best-selling car in UK history. Unfortunately, we only have Golf-specific sales data going back to 1980. As such, Golf total volume and value sales will be considerably higher than the figures quoted in this paper.

7. Volkswagen experienced significant supply problems in 1997 and 1998 with the new Mark IV Golf. This was due to Volkswagen Europe heavily prioritising right-hand drive versions of the new model, and experiencing severe delays in both the development and production of the right-hand versions of the car, suitable for sale in the UK. This resulted in the UK sales dip that we see 1997 and 1998.

8. Press communications have been measured specifically only since 2004.

9. Source: Royal Mail.

10. Source: DDB Tribal.

11. Source: DDB Tribal. For more detail on these remarkable results see the 2006 IPA paper entitled 'The New Golf GTI Mk V: A Launch Without a Car'.

12. Giving £9 of PR value for every £1 spent. Source: Freud Communications.

13. People mentioning the Golf without being prompted.

14. We do not have Spanish share data prior to 1995.

15. Spain is excluded from the European share figure as we only have data going back to 1995. Spain has the lowest Golf volumes of the five main European markets.

# SECTION 5

# Silver winners

## Chapter 12

# Actimel

## From Hampstead to Hartlepool: turning living bacteria into popular culture – how a drinking challenge helped take probiotic drinks to the people

**By Rebecca Moody, RKCR/Y&R**
Contributing author: Joseph Heath, RKCR/Y&R

Yoghurt first became popular in Britain during the 60s, but it remained a minority concern until the late 90s, when a discernible trend emerged in the direction of improved nutrition and healthy eating. In response, a number of yoghurt manufacturers introduced 'friendly bacteria' drinks, but by 1999 even the leading brands made it into just 1% of the nation's fridges.

Danone's entry into the market, with Actimel, a probiotic drink containing bacteria that helped to boost the body's natural immunity, originally looked set to achieve equally disappointing results. A drastic change in communications strategy followed, focusing on the emotional benefits of drinking Actimel. The 'Feel Good Challenge' was born, promising that if consumers didn't feel the benefits of drinking Actimel after just two weeks, they could get their money back.

During the campaign period from 2003–2005, brand penetration increased from 7.3% to 22.1%, meaning that some 13 million people had taken the challenge and tried Actimel. Repeat purchasing also more than doubled from 1.5 million homes to four million homes, while volume sales increased by some 426%. The probiotic drinks sector also almost tripled in value, from £62.3m in 2002 to £178.6m at the end of 2005, of which Actimel took a 62% share. Overall, its brand value increased by 359%, as Danone enjoyed £90.8m in incremental sales and £36.3m gross profit.

## Introduction

Yoghurt is one of the most magical foodstuffs known to man. In its natural state, it is a powerful probiotic, full of billions of microscopic, live bacteria, with a millennia-old reputation.

So why did the Brits shun yoghurt's livelier properties? Why, by the end of the second millennium, had the leading probiotic drink scarcely made it into 1% of the nation's fridges? And, subsequently, how did a national drinking challenge succeed in building a £112m probiotic drink brand now drunk in one in four British homes?

This paper tells how communications successfully overcame the mung bean image of probiotics and helped Danone take Actimel's health properties from Hampstead to Hartlepool to the tune of an estimated £90.8m incremental sales and £36.3m profit.

## Background

Yoghurt first came to prominence in Britain during the counterculture of the 60s, as the wacky choice of *Good Life*-style suburbanites.

The popular imagination was initially captured by Ski's 70s 'full of fitness food' campaign, depicting 'wildly continental, deeply aspirational' families, and Shape's low-fat, 'Jane Fonda body' promise.

Over the next two decades, while the category grew exponentially, it increasingly yielded to the treat values of Müller.

By the late 90s, yoghurt had moved away from hair-shirt health, into a better-for-you-dessert positioning, where it found mass appeal as 'permissive indulgence' to the staggering tune of £1.16bn turnover per annum.

However, at this time, a powerful interest in 'good for me' nutrition manifested itself in response to food scares. Yoghurt makers spotted the opportunity of returning the original 'functional food' to its roots and in flooded a host of new brands.

Yet the health pioneers quickly encountered mainstream resistance. By 1999, Yakult, the probiotic trailblazer, had barely reached 1% UK household penetration and claimed 1.7% share of total chilled yoghurts and desserts (CYD) after three years on-shelf.

Who could crack the mainstream code and democratise yoghurt health?

## Enter Danone

In 1919, Isaac Carasso, a Catalan businessman, set up Danone. His vision was to bring the health magic of yoghurt to the masses (in this case impoverished Barcelona street kids with digestive problems). Nearly 100 years later, Danone is the world number one in yoghurts, embracing a variety of sub-brands built on functional benefits.

In 1999, Danone set its sights on the UK, seeing the opportunity to resurrect yoghurt's roots as an accessible superfood where others were failing. The company objectives were as follows:

- re-engineer the UK yoghurt sector
- accelerate the democratisation of yoghurt health
- position Danone as the yoghurt health missionary.

Actimel was chosen by Danone as lead foot soldier – a probiotic yoghurt drink in a one-dose bottle (à la Yakult), containing the unique live culture, *Lactobacillus Casei Imunitass* – bacteria that helps support the body's natural defences. The brand had already enjoyed storming popularity in France.

The communications challenge was to drive UK probiotic drinks growth with the lion's share of market. Top-performing Euro copy was plucked for TV launch in 2001, focusing on a functional, common-sense approach to drinking Actimel every day.

By the start of 2002, Actimel had drawn level with Yeo Valley and marginally ahead of Yakult. Sales stood at £29m. However, this was achieved at cost to Actimel (outspending at £1.71 for every Yakult media spend of £1).

We had set out to crack the mainstream, but only 23% of the UK population had actually heard of probiotics, and only 15% knew Actimel was one. Furthermore, Probiotics still accounted for only 4.6% of total CYD. And of the new people we had attracted, the consumer profile showed yet more middle-aged, Hampstead trendies (see Figure 1).

## Figure 1: Actimel demographics 2002

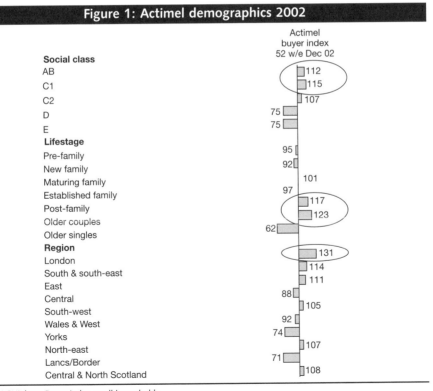

Source: ACNielsen. Buyer index vs all households

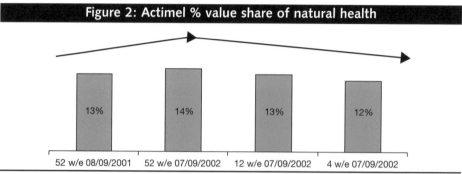

Figure 2: Actimel % value share of natural health

Source: ACNielsen/Grocery multiples. Four weeks ending 7 September 2002

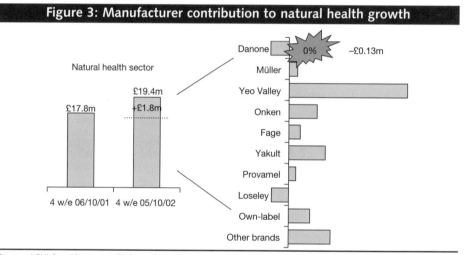

Figure 3: Manufacturer contribution to natural health growth

Source: ACNielsen/Grocery multiples. Value – four weeks ending 5 October 2002

This 'go slow' was frustrating enough for Danone, but more worrying indicators were coming to light: new autumn figures indicated a downturn in Actimel performance (see Figure 2).

Danone's contribution to natural health was in negative equity despite the category being in growth (see Figure 3).

## Why had Actimel failed to reach targets?

Communications research around the original launch copy illustrated a lack of branded visibility and cut-through. Actimel had only 39% total awareness among the UK population versus 56% for Yakult. People also questioned: 'How's it different from Yakult?' Actimel's emerging image was at parity.

Research reported our communications approach was 'lost on non-users', and dissection of the communication to date revealed that 40% of Actimel's advertising audience simply didn't know what the product was, or why they should use it, holding a highly sceptical view as to its benefit:

*Most [respondents] steadfastly refused to commit to trying Actimel until they knew more about it.*

Crea8tive.Net Research, June 2002

Three key criteria were in negative equity against mainstream Müller – 'tastes good', 'good for the whole family' and 'worth the price you pay' – essentially the criteria any value-conscious mum applies to her yoghurts.

The communications, it appeared, had confirmed the market suspicions about probiotics. As one non-user put it, 'It makes me think of medicine.'

Like competitors before us, we had over-estimated the UK market's desire for little drinks containing live cultures, and failed to crack the communications code that would unlock widespread demand for good bacteria.

## Towards a popular strategy

If we wanted to break probiotics out of their niche appeal, we needed to:

- demystify Actimel, making its usage and benefits clear
- position it in an approachable and appealing light (i.e. a tasty brand 'for me')
- justify our price premium versus other yoghurts.

The obvious solution, functionality, wasn't viable.

Consumer research had indicated that a direct expression of Actimel's functional claim – 'Actimel's unique culture L.Casei Imunitass works to balance the body's intestinal flora, thereby strengthening the body's natural defences' – had the potential to generate reappraisal and trial.

However, the Broadcast Advertising Clearance Centre did not accept Danone's scientific evidence supporting its natural defences claim. How could we build penetration, and justify a relative price premium among sceptics without telling them what the product does?

We conducted a strategic hothouse in summer 2002, to unearth a strong, emotive brand benefit to justify our relative price. This process revealed the importance of the 'feel-good factor' (see Figure 4).

### Figure 4: The feel-good factor

'Immune system' is the 'catch-all' term encompassing the body's natural defences to disease

⇩

The logic that consumers most easily understand as to how Actimel subsequently works is:
- Actimel contains friendly live bacteria called L.C. Imunitass
- L.C. Imunitass is involved with the immune system
- a strong, resistant immune system means 'feeling healthy'

⇩

The 'feeling healthy' hot button is best pressed when represented as 'freedom from fatigue', and resistance to catching coughs and colds

⇩

The emotional benefit Actimel was therefore found to fulfil was: 'health insurance'

⇩

The resulting self-expressive benefit territory our consumers helped us define was:

⇩

Felling invulnerable and carefree: the feel-good factor

This territory subsequently formed the basis of our new brand idea.

But Brits are inherently cynical, and we suspected they might give up on Actimel if they felt no immediate 'feel-good' benefit. Communications would also therefore need to answer: 'When and how often do you need to drink Actimel for it to be effective?', giving people a framework in which they could judge its efficacy. We knew from clinical work the magic time period was two weeks.

However, people were still resistant: *Will it really work, will I like it?*

So entered the idea of Actimel challenging its consumers to judge the positive effect of the product themselves, with the promise of their money back if dissatisfied:

> *Try the Actimel Challenge: just one delicious drink of Actimel every day for two weeks and find out for yourself how much better you feel. Or your money back.*

## The creative solution

The campaign moved through two creative phases.

### Phase 1: Crazy Ladies 2003–2004

Showcasing women, who had obviously sampled 'the difference', cunningly trying to claim their money back at their local supermarket despite having been filmed doing wild, feel-good stuff, like playing air guitar on zebra crossings.

### Phase 2: Jake 2005

A new brand property to help consolidate market leadership and elicit greater family involvement. Enter 'Jake', the boy who's crushingly embarrassed by his parent's exuberant, jaunty transformation on drinking Actimel.

These creative solutions did three things:

1. They showed the invulnerable, carefree 'feel-good factor'.
2. They implied an adversary in the weather or busy lifestyles (against which one needs strong immunity and health insurance).
3. They laid down the Actimel Challenge.

A total of £21.8m was spent on communications over the period January 2003 to October 2005. The predominant TV spend was supported by a range of media and marketing initiatives during that time.

## The communications effect: a nation feeling the Actimel difference

There is substantial evidence to suggest that the 'Feel the Difference' Challenge elicited a turnaround in Actimel's sales fortunes, and here we outline the relevant advertising and brand responses underpinning success.

*The advertising response*

## The Challenge achieved high awareness and cut-through (see Table 1).

| Actimel summary | 2002 | 2003 | 2004 | 2005 |
|---|---|---|---|---|
| | % | % | % | % |
| Total brand communications awareness | n/a | 36 | 73 | 77 |
| TV advertising awareness | 2 | 33 | 65 | 69 |

*Table 1: Actimel awareness and cut-through*

Source: Millward Brown

## People enjoyed the campaign

*The Actimel one is quite catchy. Even my son sings that.*

*She goes back to the supermarket saying she doesn't feel better. That's funny that one.*

*I liked the boy in it, children are always embarrassed by their parents if they do something new.*

*Entertaining, light-hearted and amusing.*

Source: Crea8tive.Net Research, 2003, and Millward Brown, 2004

## The campaign imparted news (see Figure 5)

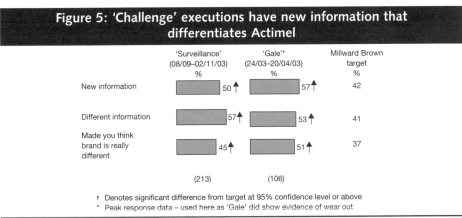

**Figure 5: 'Challenge' executions have new information that differentiates Actimel**

† Denotes significant difference from target at 95% confidence level or above
* Peak response data – used here as 'Gale' did show evidence of wear out

Source: Millward Brown, ATS, December 2004

## News was in line with 'feel good' (see Table 2)

*Encourages people to try the Actimel Challenge themselves, so they can notice the difference.*

*The woman was astonishing people with her vitality.*

*Boy's mother has a new lease of life after drinking Actimel.*

*They didn't half have a lot of energy after drinking it.*

Source: Crea8tive.Net Research, 2003, and Millward Brown, 2004

## Table 2: 'Challenge' successful in communicating more than the typical yoghurt 'health' message

Q: The advertising strongly suggests Actimel ...

| | 'Surveillance' spontaneous recall % | | 'Surveillance' prompted recall % |
|---|---|---|---|
| Gives you energy | 33 | Keeps you healthy | 52 |
| Healthy/good for you | 28 | Helps you feel better | 50 |
| Makes you feel better | 22 | Really does what it claims | 45 |
| Nice | 11 | Reinforces your body's natural defences | 43 |
| Helps your immune system | 6 | Contains unique LCI cultures | 27 |
| Base: Proven recallers | (36) | Base: Recognise ad | (213) |

Source: Millward Brown, ATS, December 2004

Weather cues inferred that Actimel helped you feel good by supporting the body's immune system. As Crea8ive.Net summarised in 2003:

> Respondents also noted that the ads intended to communicate both feeling better and defence against colds and flu ... The link, and the action of Actimel, was understood and credible.

### Actimel gained much needed credibility

> They've got proof that it works and it gets the point across.

> Get your money back ... They must be confident in their product to promise that.

> It will do something in two weeks or your money back if you don't feel better.

Source: Crea8ive.Net Research, 2003

*Brand response*

### Actimel's saliency grew (see Figure 6)

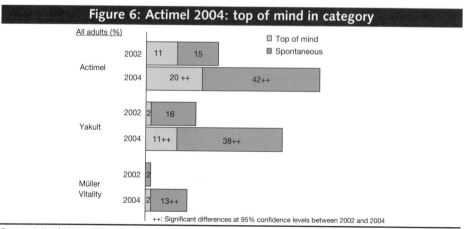

## Figure 6: Actimel 2004: top of mind in category

All adults (%)

Actimel — 2002: 11 | 15
Actimel — 2004: 20 ++ | 42++

Yakult — 2002: 2 | 16
Yakult — 2004: 11++ | 38++

Müller Vitality — 2002: 2
Müller Vitality — 2004: 2 | 13++

☐ Top of mind
▨ Spontaneous

++: Significant differences at 95% confidence levels between 2002 and 2004

Source: Actimel U&A, NFO 2004. Base: total 12–70 (441)

**Brand image shifted in line with our strategy** (see Figure 7)

### Figure 7: Actimel achieved positive image differentiation from the category

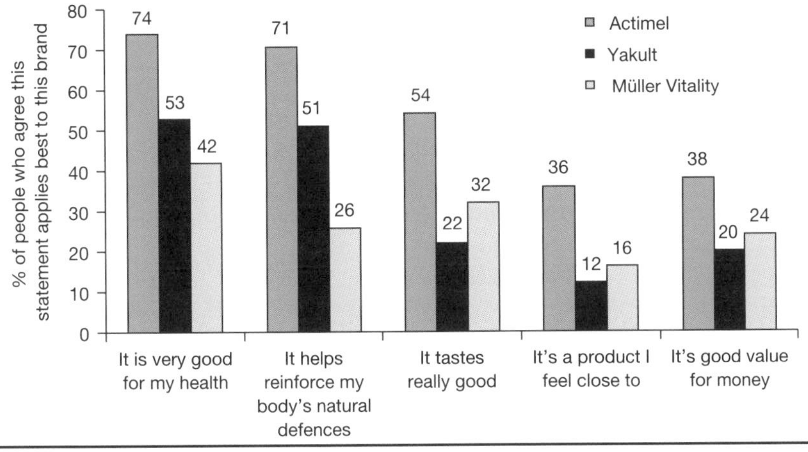

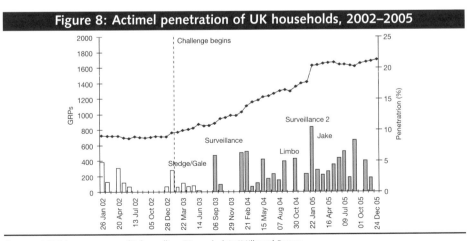

Source: Actimel U&A, NFO 2004. Base: all brand aware

### Actimel's appeal grew successively warmer and broader

By 2005, 'Jake' was driving significant shifts in brand appeal (+11% over UK advertising norms). Suitability as a drink 'for the family' rose from 23% to 52%.

### Consideration rose

Actimel has consistently enjoyed higher consideration (24%) than its arch-probiotic peer, Yakult (13%).

### The 'Feel the Difference' Challenge was adopted by the masses

Penetration tripled from 7.3% in 2002 to 22.1% in 2005, in line with campaign bursts, indicating that 13 million Brits have now tried Actimel (see Figure 8).

### Figure 8: Actimel penetration of UK households, 2002–2005

Sources: ACNielsen grocery multiples, rolling 52-week data/Millward Brown

## Trial has been a positive experience

A subsequent study among triallists indicated 71% would now recommend it. Only 24 people ever asked for their cash back.

## People now buy more Actimel

Repeat purchasing more than doubled during the Challenge campaign period, from 1.5 million homes buying again in January 2003, to four million by December 2005. Average weight of purchase rose from 5.51 kg to 8.04 kg at the close of 2005.

## Live bacteria has finally entered popular culture

Who are the people driving Actimel's success? Normal Brits. The Challenge achieved what it set out to do: introduce younger, more mass-market families to probiotics (see Figure 9).

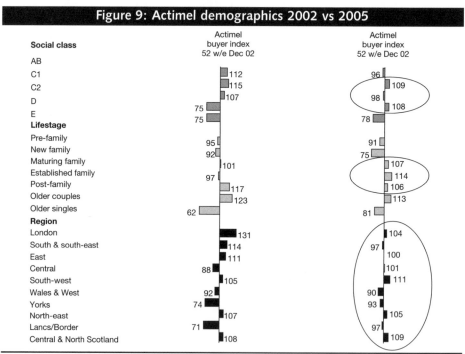

**Figure 9: Actimel demographics 2002 vs 2005**

Source: ACNielsen. Buyer index vs all households

## Britain is feeling good on Actimel

*Taking Actimel has now become like a habit, it's something I buy on a weekly basis ... you'd feel odd not to drink it.*

*I think you just feel genuinely better in yourself, you notice when you haven't taken it ... you feel sluggish.*

*I'm religious about this, I have to have it every day ... because I feel it keeps me healthy, something every day that does me good.*

Source: Stephen Wells & Company, March 2006

## The business results

To the end of 2005, Actimel 52-week volume sales rose +426% on 2002 (see Figure 10). Value also grew +359% to December 2005 (see Figure 11). The effect of such growth has been to engineer a whole new yoghurt sector – active health drinks – that now competes alongside the original, natural health, and within which probiotic drinks lead the way, having tripled in value from £62.3m in 2002 to £178.6m by the end of 2005.

In 2005, Actimel claimed the lion's 62% share of probiotic drinks, in the face of a rising competitive onslaught. It is now worth £111.5m – nearly quadruple the amount it was worth in 2002 (see Figure 12).

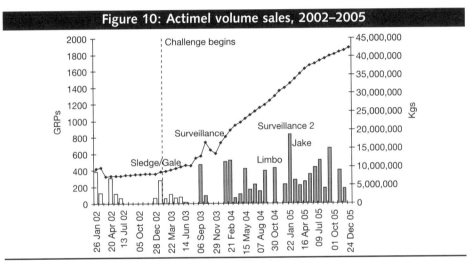

Source: ACNielsen grocery multiples, rolling 52-week data/Millward Brown

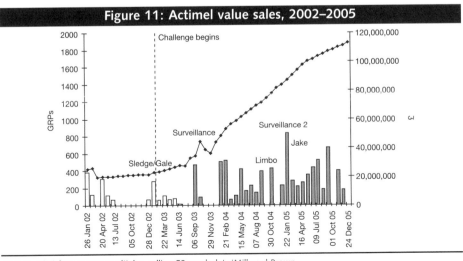

Source: ACNielsen grocery multiples, rolling 52-week data/Millward Brown

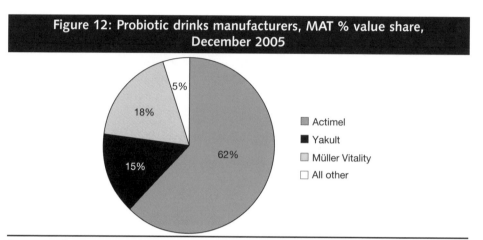

Figure 12: Probiotic drinks manufacturers, MAT % value share, December 2005

- Actimel
- Yakult
- Müller Vitality
- All other

Source: ACNielsen, grocery multiples, 52 weeks ending 24 December 2005

Nielsen singles out Actimel as the powerhouse behind probiotic growth, contributing 66.1% of total sector value to year-end February 2006. Probiotic drinks now claim a 10.3% share of the total CYD market.

In turn, total CYD continues to grow. The probiotics sector has welcomed new competitors like Müller Vitality and own-label, all looking for a slice of the lucrative action set up by Actimel. Actimel and its communications have helped boost their sales, a pertinent example being Müller Vitality – a brand to which Actimel TV contributed approximately 5,200 incremental tonnes over the period January 2003 to October 2005, roughly 15% of its total sales.

## Econometrics confirm substantial communications contribution

### The pure TV effect

Econometric analysis is able to isolate the sales and profit return of the 'Feel the Difference' Challenge campaign. Modelling from January 2003 to October 2005 estimates that TV advertising alone returned some 34,000 tonnes of incremental Actimel sales volume during that period on its £21.8m spend.

This compares to 4900 tonnes over the two-year pre-Challenge era on a £8.45m budget, indicating that the Challenge was nearly three times more efficient at driving volume.

### The estimated TV payback

Due to confidentiality, we are unable to publish the gross profit return this volume uplift represents. However, at an average industry-reported RSP of £2.67 per kg of Actimel sold, we estimate that the TV communications returned £90.8m incremental sales between 2003 and 2005. Based on an estimated average gross profit margin of 40% of RSP for fmcg/dairy products, we might therefore surmise that the Challenge delivered in the region of £36.3m profit, an effective ROI of £1.67 per £1 spent on media.

## Things are looking lively for Danone in the UK

The success of Actimel has helped strengthen Danone's stature in the UK as a recognised masterbrand, against the 'big daddy' Müller (see Figure 13).

**Figure 13: Danone's masterbrand strengthened considerably after 2002**

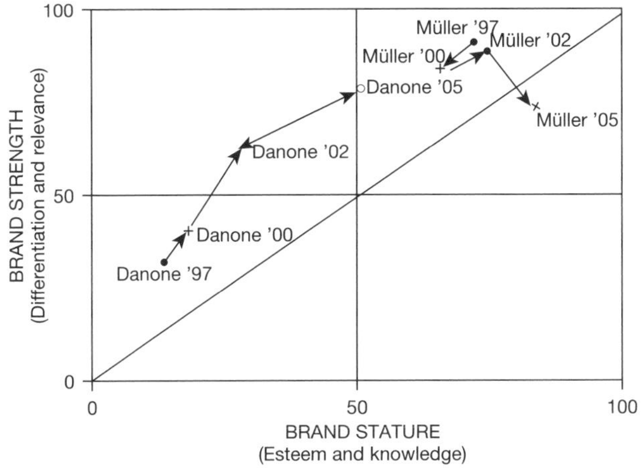

POWER GRID 'summarises a brand's position in the market, and its growth prospect.'
BAV™: UK 1997–2005 (primary shoppers)

Danone value sales were worth £209.6m to January 2006, a rise of 82% since January 2003, the start of the Challenge, making it the fastest-growing yoghurt brand in the UK.

Actimel is not the only success story. Since 2002, Danone has consistently worked to re-engineer the yoghurt sector in favour of health. For example, Activia, another 'popular culture' story, now competing in bio yoghurts, has successfully adopted its own challenge, with brilliant results.

As a result, Danone is fast closing the gap on Müller's 20-year hold on the CYD market.

## Summary

From a less than convincing start, we took an age-old functional food and positioned it on an emotive communications platform that opened the doors of one in four British fridges.

Since the advent of the 'Feel the Difference' Challenge in 2003, Actimel's success has in turn ignited the mass re-engineering of the CYD category in increasing favour of 'good for you' yoghurt, and those live bacteria benefits the people resisted for so long.

## Chapter 13

# Bakers Complete

Because dogs don't do the shopping: how consistent advertising helped make Bakers the pet food phenomenon of the last decade

**By Susan Poole, Burkitt DDB**
Contributing author: David Bassett, DDB Matrix

In 1994, Bakers – a complete dry dog food brand – held only a 0.6% share of the dog food market. Despite two advertising campaigns and a free sampling programme, it was found that advertising enjoyed little awareness, and just 20% of dog owners were even aware of the brand.

Convinced about the quality of the product, brand owner Edward Baker Petfoods looked for a new strategy that would go beyond the conventions of the category to help it stand out in a market of well established competitors, and also overcome the barriers facing dry dog foods. A new campaign was developed around the idea that 'real dogs would choose Bakers if they could', providing a fresh and novel way of speaking to dog owners, and one that appealed to the image most had of their dogs.

This approach has been used consistently since 1995, and during that time the brand has grown by an average of 32% year-on-year, taking it from £3.3m sales to almost £65m by the end of 2005. Market share has also increased 16-fold, as Bakers has grown into the country's second-biggest dog food brand. Econometric modelling estimates that advertising has contributed at least £75m in incremental revenue during the campaign period, while other benefits include an improved in-store presence and the successful relaunch of other products under the Bakers banner.

## Introduction

This paper is the story of an amazing brand success helped by a single, long-term advertising campaign.

Back in 1994, Bakers was a virtually unknown dog food brand with a less than 1% share of the UK market.

Today, in 2006, Bakers has increased market share 16-fold, becoming the country's second-biggest dog food brand. And even after a decade of growth Bakers is still the fastest-growing brand of dog food in the UK.

## The story of growth

Back in late 1994 (see Figure 1) Bakers was a tiny player in the world of dog food, owned by a small family business, Edward Baker Petfoods, and one of a small number of complete dry dog food brands. Just 20% of dog owners were even aware of the brand.

Since then the brand has grown by an average 32% year-on-year, taking it from £3.3m to almost £65m sales by the end of 2005 (see Figure 2).

It is worth pointing out that this growth has had to come at the expense of other established brands, with the total number of dogs in the UK actually dropping by 8% over the period.

The success of Bakers is reflected in a shift from wet to dry as the preferred format in the market. Between 1994 and 2005, the dry food sector approximately doubled in value, whilst Bakers grew its sales by a factor of 20. It is clearly more appropriate to think of Bakers driving this change in tastes, than benefiting from it (see Figure 3).

In the process, Bakers has become number two dog food brand overall in the UK. Not bad for a brand that once had a mere 0.6% share (see Figure 4).

**And Bakers hasn't stopped yet.**

### Figure 1: Bakers accounted for only 0.6% of dog food value sales in 1994

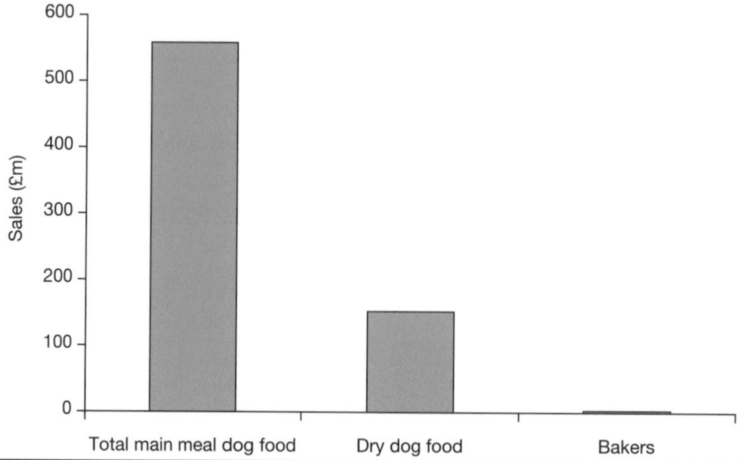

Source: PFMA/NPPC

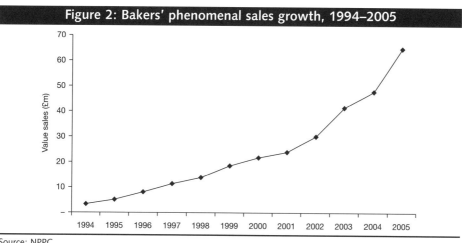

Figure 2: Bakers' phenomenal sales growth, 1994–2005

Source: NPPC

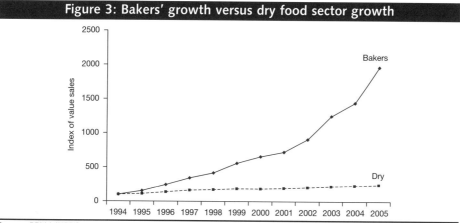

Figure 3: Bakers' growth versus dry food sector growth

Source: PFMA/NPPC

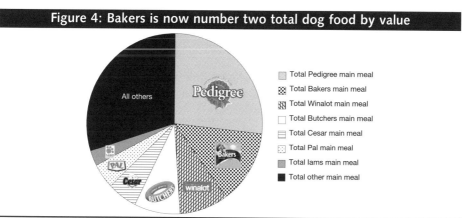

Figure 4: Bakers is now number two total dog food by value

Source: IRI. Value sales 52 weeks to 25 March 2006

Bakers is still the fastest-growing dog food brand in the UK, gaining a full percentage point of share in the last year.

## How the right advertising unlocked this growth

### Was it just a great product?

The Bakers product was intended to resemble the perfect doggy meal of 'meat and two veg', with moist meaty chunks and a number of shaped and coloured crunchy 'kibbles'. Technical palatability tests in 2000 confirmed what Bakers had always believed – that it did indeed have a product popular with dogs.

Unfortunately, dogs don't do the shopping! And in spite of high palatability and supposed benefits to owners, people just weren't willing to try it.

### Why the previous advertising hadn't worked

The previous advertising could best be described as conventional, with the traditional concentration on 'posh dogs'.

### Getting the advertising right

Research revealed that owners were judging Bakers from a human perspective, and to their eyes dry food simply wasn't as appealing as wet food. Typically, an owner's perspective on dry food would be as follows.

- Surely wet is much nicer than dry? Just like a buttered crumpet is nicer than a dry cracker?
- Dogs look like they struggle to eat it.
- Tins equal 'meat' whereas dry food is 'only biscuits'.
- Feel guilt about feeding a family member something they don't like.

Advertising clearly needed to address these concerns in a credible way, and various creative routes to deliver a message of enjoyment by the dogs were researched.

We realised that a key strength of the winning route was that the action took place in a 'real' dog-only world, where in fact the dogs behaved almost like humans. This went completely against the conventional, idealised dogs we are all so used to seeing in dog food advertising, and clearly tapped into how owners secretly liked to imagine their dogs: having a sophisticated and happy life that mimicked human existence.

The personality of the dogs gave us permission to get across the all-important product enjoyment points, and so the proposition became:

*Real dogs would choose Bakers if they could*

The campaign idea was developed according to the following findings.

- We featured a scruffy 'spokesdog' and a range of his normal dog mates.
- All dogs were located in recognisable or everyday environments.
- The advertising was set in a dog-only world where the dogs choose their own food and go to increasingly great lengths to get their paws on it.

- The palatability of the product was reinforced through presentation.
- Key product look and sound cues were adhered to.

The campaign launched with the execution 'Shopping' in which real dogs, quite literally, go shopping for Bakers.

### Launch media

Bakers launched its new campaign in 1995 with a £1m spend on TV, which gave a 4.4% total SOV.

### The next ten years

From 1995 to 2004 Bakers used solely TV. It spent £1–2m a year in two or three bursts, averaging about 9% SOV. In 2004 a cinema campaign was added, using the same executions as on TV, and in 2005 some print media was also tested.

### Executions 1995–2005

There have now been ten executions in the campaign (see Table 1).

| Table 1: Bakers TV executions, 1995–2005 | | | |
|---|---|---|---|
| **Execution** | **Product** | **Length** | **Date** |
| Shopping | Range | 30'/ 20' | 1995–2000 |
| Health Farm | Light | 30'/10' | 1996–1998 |
| Fish | Fish | 10' | 1998 |
| Pool | Range | 30' | 1998–1999 |
| Sensitive | Sensitive | 10' | 2001 |
| Usual Suspects | Range | 30' | 2000–2001 |
| TV Dinners | Range | 30'/ 20' | 2001–2003 |
| Wag-o-meter | Promotion | 10' | 2003 |
| Heist | Range | 40'/ 30'/ 20' | 2004–2006 |
| Meaty Treats | Treats | 20' | 2005–2006 |

### Getting the message across

Quotes from dog owners who had seen the advertising show that we had managed to make them see the brand as a tasty food:

> *The dogs put food in the bowl like a chef. That's if they would serve it themselves, they really love it.*

> *Any dog will go for them [Bakers].*

Verbatims from Millward Brown tracking

## The contribution of other elements of the marketing mix

### Was Bakers just cheaper?

Bakers has been priced competitively to the rest of the dry food sector throughout the period, and this has obviously been a contributing factor to sales growth. We give this price differential due weight in the econometric model.

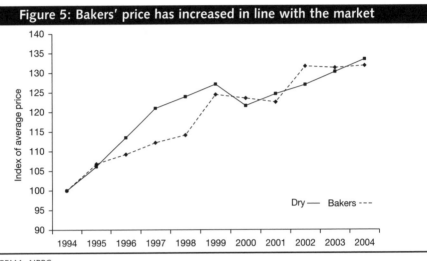

Figure 5: Bakers' price has increased in line with the market

Source: PFMA, NPPC

Figure 5 shows how price increases have generally been in line with, or slightly above, those of the rest of the market.

### Did we promote our way to the top?

Bakers has run just one national and three regional money-back guarantee promotions in the last ten years. Again, these are factored into the model.

### Did we outspend the competition?

Bakers has been fortunate to have reasonable advertising budgets, but these were certainly not exceptional within the market. Across the period, Bakers averages about 9% SOV (see Figure 6).

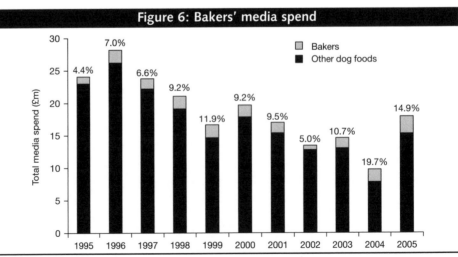

Figure 6: Bakers' media spend

Source: Nielsen Media Research

## Was the packaging preferred?

Bakers deliberately kept its 1.5 kg boxes instead of switching its whole range to bags as competitors had done.

We imagine this may have been a small contributor to sales growth, although we have no evidence beyond the merely anecdotal. In any case, this effect is most notable after pack redesign in 2001 to include the advertising property. As such we would claim this as a further benefit of the successful advertising campaign.

## Did we have greater distribution?

Increases in distribution have clearly been an important factor in Bakers' growth. We do not have distribution data prior to 2001, which is one of the major reasons why our econometric model covers only the last four years.

In estimating the return on advertising over the *full* period of the campaign since it began in 1995, we have chosen (in the absence of robust data) to assume that distribution gains were as important in the early years as in the later years. As we know that the most important distribution gains have occurred since 2002, since the ownership by Nestlé, we can be confident that our estimates of the advertising contribution over the full campaign period are decidedly conservative.

# Isolating and quantifying the effect of advertising

We will now demonstrate the relationship between the success of this advertising, and the success of the brand. We have four major pieces of evidence.

## The advertising was noticed in the market, and 'on message'

Frustratingly, we don't have continuous tracking of ad awareness since 1995, with various changes not only in methodology, but also research institutes. However, post-burst ad awareness has consistently been between 30% and 40%, and indeed peaked at over 50%.

Full tracking diagnostics have only recently been undertaken on a regular basis, but the results confirm that the campaign is seen as particularly distinctive, involving and interesting (see Figure 7).

The advertising was effective at making the brand stand out in the sector as a different and appealing alternative (see Figure 8).

## Regional analysis

Whilst product, packaging, pricing and distribution changes were national, advertising varied by weight regionally. Figure 9 clearly shows that those regions that were advertised at higher weights showed faster growth.

## Increasing advertising weight led to increased sales growth: the example of Scotland

Whilst Scotland's advertising was downweighted in 2002, its share growth was also slower than the Bakers national average. When Scotland's advertising was then upweighted above the national average in 2003, its share growth also shot up above the national average (see Figure 10).

## Figure 7: 'Heist' outperforms Millward Brown ATP norms

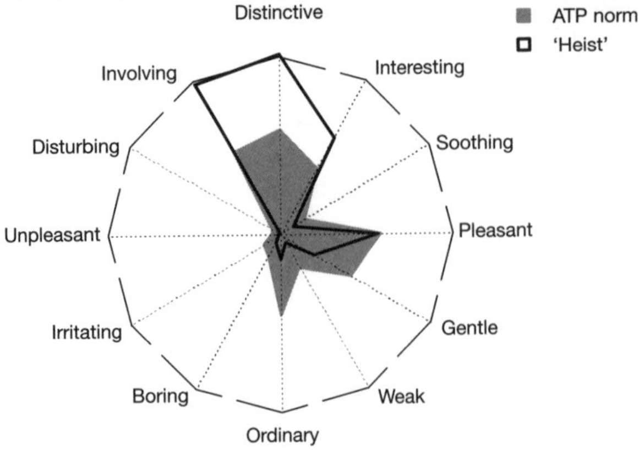

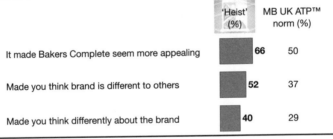

Source: Millward Brown, October 2004

## Figure 8: The ads are very effective at making Bakers seem appealing

| | 'Heist' (%) | MB UK ATP™ norm (%) |
|---|---|---|
| It made Bakers Complete seem more appealing | 66 | 50 |
| Made you think brand is different to others | 52 | 37 |
| Made you think differently about the brand | 40 | 29 |

Source: Millward Brown

## Figure 9: Upweighted regions show faster growth

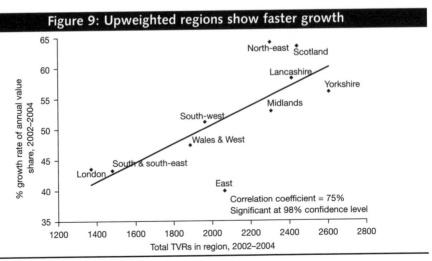

Correlation coefficient = 75%
Significant at 98% confidence level

Sources: Nielsen, BARB

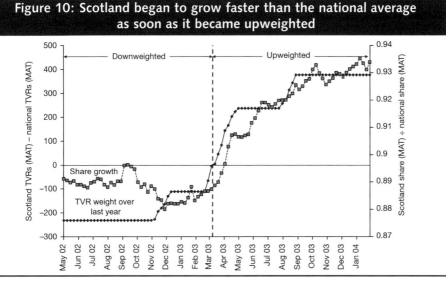

**Figure 10: Scotland began to grow faster than the national average as soon as it became upweighted**

Sources: Nielsen, BARB

Considering that the only variable change unique to Scotland during this period was the increase in advertising weight, it would be fair to suggest that advertising accounted for this share increase.

## The econometric model

In 2004 DDB Matrix was commissioned to build an econometric model of the brand's sales. The model covers the period from March 2001 to December 2005 as this is, unfortunately, as far back as sufficient data is available. The model incorporates all aspects affecting the brand, including advertising, pricing, promotions, distribution, competitor activity, market changes and seasonality.

### Evaluating the contribution of advertising

Using the econometric model it was found that advertising run between 2001 and 2005 directly resulted in £35m in incremental revenue, on an £8.4m media spend. Nestlé Purina PetCare is understandably unwilling to disclose margin data, but it can be confirmed that the additional volume generated has been highly profitable (see Figure 11).

### Payback

Using the model, we can estimate the contribution of the campaign to sales. As we have said earlier, we have decided to suppose that distribution increases have been as important throughout the period as over the last few years.

As such our estimate is conservative, particularly when one considers that the successful advertising campaign has no doubt played a role itself in gaining additional distribution. In total, the model suggests an additional £75m of revenue over the period, on a media spend of £18.8m (see Figure 12).

## Figure 11: Advertising contributed £35m incremental revenue 2001–2005 on a spend of £8.4m

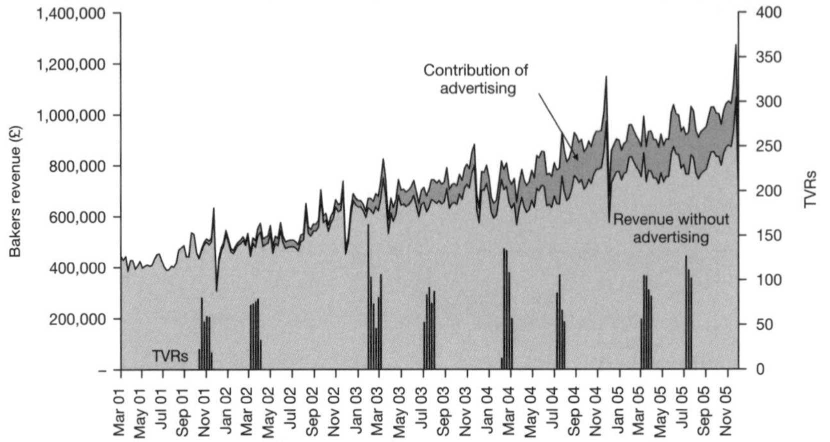

Sources: Nielsen, DDB Matrix econometrics model

## Figure 12: Advertising has contributed £75m incremental revenue since 1995 on a spend of £18.8m

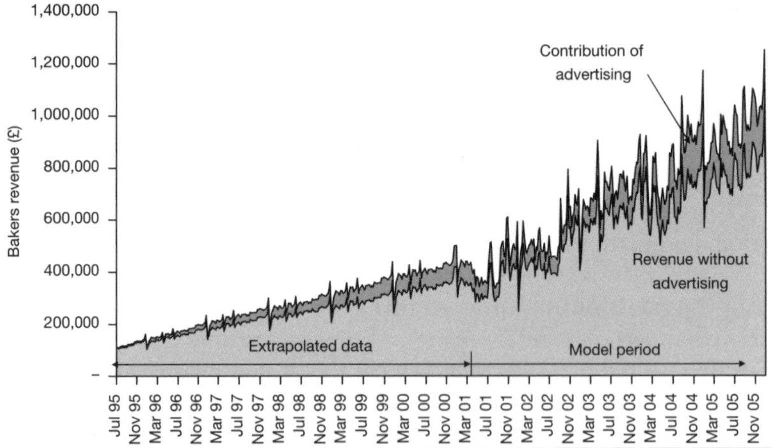

Sources: Nielsen, DDB Matrix econometrics model

The model shows that, in 2005, approximately 17% of total brand sales can be attributed to advertising effect.

### Further benefits of a successful advertising campaign

As we have said, the advertising created a very well-recognised brand 'spokesdog', who became the focus of the packaging in 1998. This is seen by the trade as a strong force behind Bakers' growth.

It is also a testimony to the strength of the brand property that in 2005 Nestlé decided to take a number of poor-performing treats from two brands (Purina and Winalot) and relaunch the same SKUs under a new Bakers 'Meaty Treats' brand, supported by advertising within the existing campaign.

This has led to a greater brand presence and consistency and has, in turn, led to significant improvements in sales terms. The same products relaunched under Bakers with advertising support have almost doubled in value share in just under a year. Annual sales have increased by 188%, from £3.2m to £6.1m, under the new range.

## Conclusions

- The campaign has been a key factor in driving Bakers from a £3.3m to a £65m brand in just over 11 years, making a huge impact on the nature of the dog food market in its wake.
- So far the campaign has delivered an estimated £75m in incremental revenue, and shows no signs of slowing down – the brand remains the UK's fastest-growing dog food.
- The campaign has established a valuable advertising property, which has improved in-store presence and facilitated the successful relaunch of other products under the Bakers banner.

There's life in the old dog yet.

## Chapter 14

# Branston Baked Beans

How going head to head with the brand leader created a world where Beanz also Meanz Branston, in just three months

**By Lisa Conway, Delaney Lund Knox Warren & Partners**
Contributing authors: Steven Gregory, Central Focus; Steve Marinker, Citigate Dewe Rogerson; Rhona Hurcombe, Phipps Public Relations, and Barbara Holgate, The Big Kick Company

In July 2005, Premier Foods lost the licence to make HP Beans, meaning a potential annual revenue shortfall of £15m. In an attempt to reverse the impact of this situation, Premier decided to launch a new brand of baked beans into a market effectively dominated by two key players – Heinz and own-label.

The short-term targets set for this new brand were to reach half the monthly sales of HP beans within six months and then, within a year, to match or better its predicted monthly performance. In an effort to change consumer behaviour and achieve these targets, the product would have to both taste better than the competition and match Heinz's price premium. To help reach these objectives, it was also decided that the new product would be supported by a brand from the Premier Foods stable – Branston.

The creative idea developed for the new Branston Beans was 'The Great British Bean Poll', which was designed to challenge people to compare Branston Baked Beans with Heinz for themselves, and was communicated via the national press, radio, sampling and PR. Some 750,000 people voted in the Bean Poll, and 76% chose Branston Beans as their favourite. Within three months of the start of the campaign, 86% of the HP business had been recreated. All commercial targets were also beaten (by an average of 70%), making Branston the number-two baked beans brand, with a value in excess of £14m – all set against a communications spend of £3.5m.

## Introduction

Premier Foods had just three months to make a success of the Branston Baked Beans launch or face an annual revenue shortfall of £15m.

This paper will prove how bravery in battle reaps rewards. In just three months we had created a new baked bean brand worth in excess of £14m, and on course to be worth £30m by the end of the year. No mean feat in a world where Beanz supposedly Meanz Heinz.

## Background

Premier Foods had been making HP Beans, under licence from Danone, for ten years. In July 2005, Danone announced the sale of the HP brand to Heinz. The transfer would come into effect in March 2006. As the buyer was Heinz, Premier Foods knew that its licence to make HP Beans would not be renewed. This meant that from March 2006 there would be no more HP Beans leaving the Premier factory gates, and no more annual sales of £15m coming in. In short, the sale of the HP brand left Premier with a significant revenue shortfall.

*No one knows more than Premier how difficult a task this is*

In the last 50 years only two mainstream brands had launched into this category, with limited success: HP Beans launched in 1955 and Crosse & Blackwell in 2003. Premier Foods is responsible for both brands.

There are three reasons why this is such a difficult sector in which to launch a new brand.

1. There is a dominant brand leader. Heinz has 65% market share, the love of a nation and the perception of being the gold standard in beans.
2. Own-label accounts for 25% of the market. Its quality has improved significantly over the years, while its cost relative to Heinz has gone down. In fact, Premier already supplies 95% of this market.
3. There are ingrained consumer habits. Baked beans are purchased on auto-pilot.

## The business objectives

The main business objective for the new brand was that it had to match, or better, HP's predicted monthly performance for March 2006 and beyond.

Premier Foods obviously could not wait until March to evaluate the success of its new brand. An internal deadline of 31 December was therefore set. By then, the new brand needed half the monthly sales of HP Beans (see Table 1).

## The strategy

If we were to meet our December objectives we had just one chance to get people to switch (the purchase cycle on beans is six weeks); there was only one way to change people's auto-pilot behaviour this quickly: we had to go head to head with Heinz.

| Table 1: Brand targets | | |
|---|---|---|
| | Projected HP performance for March | New brand targets for December |
| Value sales | £809,215 | £404,607 |
| Volume sales | 1,144 tonnes | 572 tonnes |
| Volume market share | 7.7% | 3.8% |
| Value market share | 6.6% | 3.3% |

Source: IRI

The strategy was straightforward: develop a product that was better than Heinz, with the strongest brand name available.

Premier developed a new baked bean with a richer, thicker, 'tomato-ier' sauce. Meanwhile a brand from the Premier Foods' stable, with a reputation for a big taste and a big personality, was chosen to support it: Branston.

To be a genuine challenger to Heinz, Branston Beans would have the same premium price.

### The weapon of communications

From initial taste tests we knew that the way to convert people to Branston was simply by getting them to try our beans versus Heinz. We needed a communications idea that could act as surrogate sampling and get the nation trying the two brands side by side for themselves.

## The campaign idea

The Great British Bean Poll was born. All people had to do was try Branston Beans versus their regular choice and vote for their favourite. Figure 1 shows the planned promotional activity in various media.

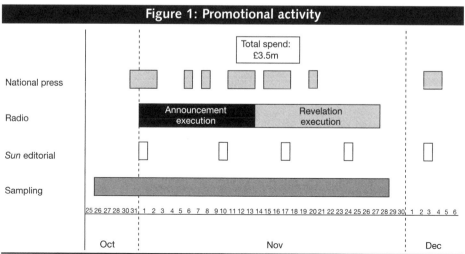

Figure 1: Promotional activity

Source: Central Focus

233

There were five key elements to the campaign.

*Advertising*

National press and radio were used to encourage people to do their own taste tests at home, to communicate the Branston difference and to get people voting. As an extra incentive to vote, every vote received an entry into a £10,000 prize draw.

The press activity was split into four stages to reflect an election campaign. Similarly, the radio activity was broken into two phases: an announcement phase followed by a revelation phase that captured the moment of conversion to Branston.

*Editorial*

Central Focus and ZenithOptimedia, responsible for planning and buying the media respectively, also secured the support of the *Sun*. Over the course of the campaign the *Sun* ran paid-for editorial championing the cause of Branston Beans.

*Sampling*

The sampling agency, The Big Kick, set up polling stations in 38% of supermarkets across Britain, where people blind taste-tested Branston Beans vs Heinz and registered their vote. At the end of the taste challenge people were given a 20p coupon towards a 420g can to further incentivise purchase in store.

*PR*

Throughout the campaign, the PR agencies, Citigate Dewe Rogerson and Phipps PR, generated an editorial voice to the Bean Poll by encouraging the media to do their own taste tests.

*Internal communications*

The idea was also used to galvanise staff at Premier. Tickertape machines, installed in head office reception and on the factory floor, showed the daily results of the poll as they came in.

## The results

*The results of the Great British Bean Poll*

The most important result first: 750,000 people voted in the Great British Bean Poll and 76% voted Branston Beans their favourite.

*Generated PR coverage that had a tangible effect on sales*

The campaign generated PR coverage worth £185,000. Importantly, the media did exactly what we wanted them to do: they conducted their own independent taste tests. Branston was victorious over Heinz 100% of the time.

The highlight was a five-minute feature on *Richard & Judy*, when they conducted a taste test among baked bean 'experts' – students, truckers and school kids.

Not only did this single piece of coverage constitute £80,000 worth of unpaid-for media, it also had a tangible effect on sales: the day after it aired, sales went up 153% in Tesco and 118% in Asda.

## The commercial results

■ We exceeded all our commercial targets by an average of 70% (see Table 2).

Rather than replacing 50% of HP's value and volume sales, we had replaced over 86%.

### Table 2: Commercial results

|  | Target | Actual | Difference |
|---|---|---|---|
| Value sales | £404,607 | £745,477 | + £340,870 |
| Volume sales | 572 tonnes | 982 tonnes | + 410 tonnes |
| Volume market share | 3.8% | 6.2% | + 2.4% |
| Value market share | 3.3% | 5.1% | + 1.8% |

Source: IRI

The campaign worked fast, even faster than expected. By December we had replaced 92% of HP's value sales and 86% of its volume (see Figures 2 and 3).

### Figure 2: Branston monthly value sales vs targets

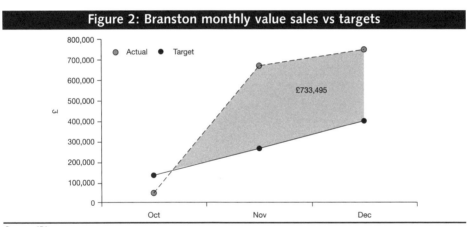

Source: IRI

### Figure 3: Branston monthly volume sales vs targets

Source: IRI

■ In three months we had become the number two brand ...

By December we had secured volume market share of 6.2% and value market share of 5.1% (see Figure 4).

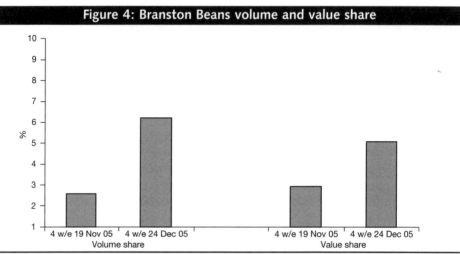

Figure 4: Branston Beans volume and value share

Source: IRI

■ ... gained retailer respect ...

We became the number two brand in beans overnight without devaluing the category. Market value actually rose to its highest point since 2003 during our Bean Poll Campaign (see Figure 5).

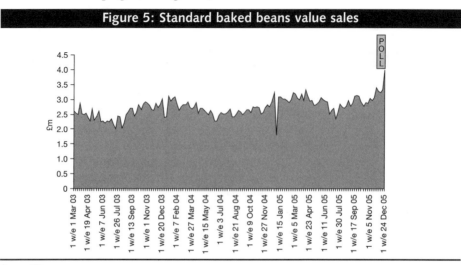

Figure 5: Standard baked beans value sales

Source: IRI

The criterion for success was simple: we had to match HP's rate of sale. By week three of the campaign Branston Beans' ROS was up 36% on HP's. By week six of the campaign it was up 210%.

The poll's success secured extra facings. At the end of the campaign, Morrisons reversed its decision to stock only one of the three SKUs for beans and Sainsbury's agreed to stock two more. On 6 April, the first official opportunity to review shelf space since the launch, Tesco increased Branston Beans' shelf space by 20%.

■ … and gained the respect of the City

Both the speed and the success of the Branston Beans' launch were a powerful demonstration to the City of Premier Food's capabilities.

*The way Premier handled the issue of losing the HP licence proved to the City what it could do: act in a fast and decisive manner.*

> Gwyn Tiley, Investor Relations Manager, Premier Foods

*The company has done a brilliant job with Branston Beans.*

> Baring Asset Management

The launch also strengthened the Branston brand in the eyes of the City by securing a new user base. Tesco's data showed that 83% of purchasers were not buyers of Branston pickle. If this ratio was reflected in other supermarkets, we had brought 1.4 million new customers to the Branston brand.

## Communications were integral to this success

We have three kinds of proof that the campaign was integral to the success of Branston Beans.

1. Campaign tracking.
2. What would have happened if there were no communications.
3. The elimination of other possible factors that could have influenced sales.

### Campaign tracking

During the campaign, awareness of Branston Beans increased from the base level of 7% to over a quarter of the population (see Figure 6).

We know that the campaign was responsible for this increase in awareness as over a quarter of the population recognised the radio and press executions, and 28% claimed to have read/heard/seen something about Branston Beans (see Figure 6).

Not only did the campaign cut through, but it also communicated the right messages; 69% of those who recognised the press or the radio took out a 'better taste'/'more flavour' message about Branston Beans.

### What would have happened if there were no communications?

In November 2003 Premier launched Crosse & Blackwell Baked Beans with no support other than an in-store promotion. Crosse & Blackwell is an excellent predictor of Branston Beans' performance without support, for four reasons.

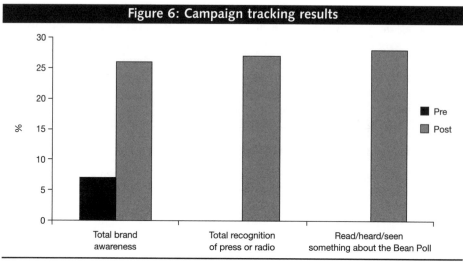

Source: Hall & Partners tracking, December 2005. Base: total sample (230)

1. Crosse & Blackwell is a brand that is perceived to make products of a high quality that you can trust.
2. It had no previous presence in the baked bean market.
3. Crosse & Blackwell launched with virtually the same range as Branston at the same price.
4. The market conditions in 2003 were virtually the same.

Branston was on trend to match Crosse & Blackwell until our communications broke. Six weeks later, Branston's ROS was five times higher than Crosse & Blackwell for the same period (see Figure 7).

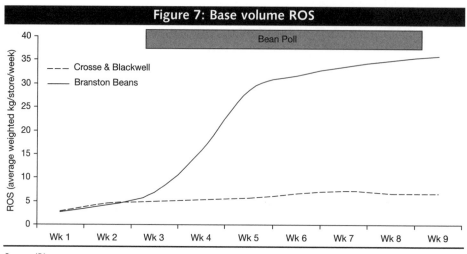

Source: IRI

*Eliminating other possible factors that could have influenced sales*

The other major factors that could have influenced sales were:

- in-store promotions
- the 20p-off coupon distributed at polling stations
- the £10,000 on-pack competition.

This section will prove how none of the above could have been solely responsible for the sales uplift that occurred.

### In-store promotions

Overall, there were three in-store promotions, two held in Asda during the campaign and one held in Tesco directly afterwards (see Figure 8).

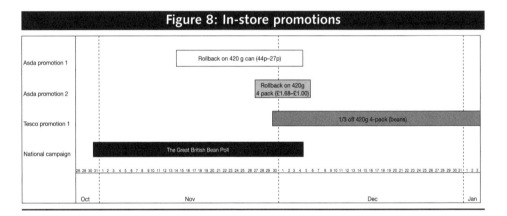

**Figure 8: In-store promotions**

During the launch period the Asda rollback promotion on the 420g can contributed to just 1.6% of total sales, and the rollback promotion on the 420g four-pack contributed even less: only 1.1% of total sales.

In Tesco, because the promotion on the four-packs ran over the Christmas period, a bad time for baked bean sales, daily sales were actually lower during the promotion period than in the weeks before. However, even if this promotion accounted for all sales of the four-pack during this period, this accounts for only 2.7% of total sales, and 4.4% of total Tesco sales. Therefore 96% of Tesco sales were not driven by a promotion.

### The 20p-off coupon

The 20p-off coupon, handed out at our polling stations, accounts for 1.7% of total sales.

### The £10,000 on-pack competition

Between 1 October and 31 December 2005, 18,655 people entered the on-pack competition. If we assume that every one of these people bought Branston Beans only because of the competition, this accounts for only 0.8% of total unit sales.

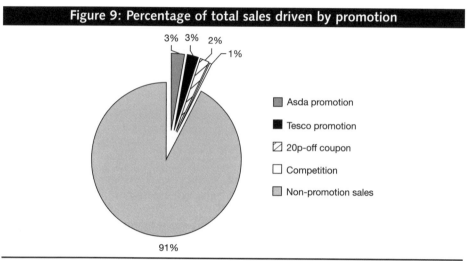

**Figure 9: Percentage of total sales driven by promotion**

3% 3% 2%
1%

- Asda promotion
- Tesco promotion
- 20p-off coupon
- Competition
- Non-promotion sales

91%

Source: EPOS sales. Competition entry figures and retailer redemptions supplied by The Big Kick

*Therefore 91% of sales were not accounted for by a promotion* (see Figure 9).

## The payback from the communications

When it comes to calculating payback, we will look at the contribution that Branston Beans has made to:

- the Premier Foods' P&L
- the Premier Foods' balance sheet.

### The Premier Foods' P&L

We have established that Branston Beans' market share value was 5.1% by 31 December. This equates to an annualised revenue of £12.75m, assuming the worst-case scenario of no further growth. The cost of achieving this was £3.5m. We are unable, for reasons of commercial confidentiality, to reveal the margins on Branston Beans, but can categorically state, especially with our 'best in class' repeat purchase levels, that it will more than pay back over a 12-month period.

### The Premier Foods' balance sheet

Premier Foods currently trades at a P/E ratio of 8.24 and has a market capitalisation of £694m, with operating profits of £108m and sales of £790m. Even if we assume that Branston Beans has a margin absolutely in line with the rest of Premier Foods (13.7%), and an annualised market share of 5%, we can assume a profit contribution of £1.75m, and given the P/E multiple of 8.24, a brand value for Branston Beans of £14.4m. In reality, the margin is much higher for Branston Beans, which leads, in turn, to an even higher brand value and a greater level of payback from the communications.

## Conclusion

Tackling the brand leader head on changed consumer behaviour in this market, and quickly. Within three months we had replaced 86% of the HP business, creating a new brand of baked beans worth in excess of £14m.

The Great British Bean Poll captured the imagination of the nation and the media, and got people to think about which corner they were in: the Heinz corner or the Branston corner?

## Chapter 15

# British Heart Foundation – Anti Smoking

How advertising helped the British Heart Foundation get 'Under the Skin' of hardened smokers

**By Gorse Jeffries and Tim Postle, Lowe**
Contributing authors: David Bratt and Claire Marker, Manning Gottlieb OMD

The challenge to reduce the number of smokers in the UK is constant, complex and multifaceted. Multiple organisations and advertisers, including the Government and a number of related charities, work towards minimising the number of people who start and maximising the number of people who successfully stop.

The British Heart Foundation (BHF) was part of the group behind the highly effective 'Fatty Cigarette' campaign, which dramatically displayed the harm that smoking can do. In an attempt to build on this success, the BHF sought to find a new approach that would persuade hardened smokers to quit, and also to turn to the organisation for help and support. The new campaign became centred round the song 'I've Got You Under My Skin', with visuals showing that blood clots can cause any smoker to have a heart attack at any time, anywhere – thus moving away from the category norm of shocking the audience, and making the cigarette the enemy, while avoiding being so negative as to induce the opposite response to that intended.

The campaign ran from October to November 2005, with a media spend of just under £3m. It encompassed a targeted but varied media mix, including everything from TV, outdoor and press to beer mats, with the intention of reaching smokers at every point of consumption. Results showed that 225,000 people contacted the BHF for help during this period, with 17% of those who saw the communications giving up smoking. In all, the campaign paid for itself 600 times over, saving over 5,000 lives in the process.

## Introduction: The war on smoking

The challenge to reduce the number of people in the UK who smoke is constant and multi-faceted. The combined forces of the Government, the British Heart Foundation (BHF) and all other related charities, work constantly towards minimising the number of people who start, and maximising the number of people who successfully stop.

2004's Gold-winning IPA Effectiveness Awards paper documents how the efforts of multiple advertisers produced a powerful combined effect, helping to reduce the number of smokers by over a million. The BHF's part in this was the now infamous 'Fatty Cigarette' campaign.

This case will demonstrate how the BHF was able to build on its track record, by finding a new and unexpected way to increase the determination of the hardened smoker to successfully quit, and position the organisation as a friend of the smoker.

'Fatty Cigarette' used the iconic imagery of fat dripping from the cigarette to create a visceral response of revulsion in the smoker, and successfully pushed many of its target over the tipping point to quitting. But those who resisted its message were now sufficiently de-sensitised to suggest its impact was abating. The law of diminishing returns had kicked in.

The responsibility towards those very smokers it was trying to help, combined with the fact that the campaign was to be funded by the Department of Health – taxpayers' money – pushed it to seek a new approach.

Picture a war cabinet where cigarettes are the enemy, and the people we were trying to help are the hardened multi-quitters from lower socio-economic groups.

Our mission was to use all the weapons at our disposal to give these people the ammunition they need to stop, break down all the false excuses that smoking puts in their way and, most importantly, make them feel like there is someone out there who wants to help.

We had a core target of what are termed 'multi-quitters': hardened smokers, aged 30–50, C1C2D, who have tried, but failed, to give up three times or more. They are open to cessation communication. They hear all these messages, but don't necessarily listen. We had to help them to listen.

Our secondary target would be influencers and medical professionals, and beyond that the rest of the smoking population.

In order to put together the strategic battle plan, we needed to understand the mindset of our core target, what they were expecting and how we could catch them unawares.

- They are expecting to be lectured and made to feel like socially unacceptable outcasts.
- They are expecting scary statistics, most of which they know already.
- They are expecting to be made to feel like pariahs, when in fact the cigarette is the real enemy.
- They have an amazing capacity to defer the effects of smoking into the future on the basis that they'll stop 'tomorrow', or convince themselves that the worst-case scenario won't happen to them.

## The strategic battle plan

We deployed outstanding creativity to increase smokers' determination to stop by removing their excuses for not quitting, whilst directing them to the BHF for help (see Figure 1). We eschewed traditional shock tactics and, before they even knew it, people were engaged in the campaign.

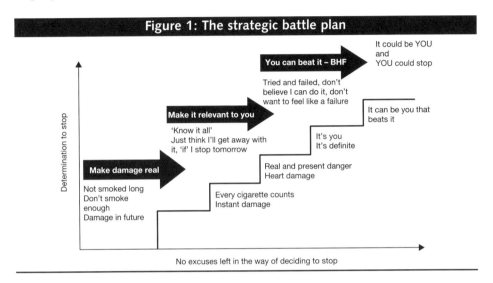

Figure 1: The strategic battle plan

## The creative arsenal

We took a feel-good, popular song about love and longing, and twisted it to refer to heart damage.

*I've got you under my skin.*

*I've got you deep in the heart of me. So deep in my heart, that you're really a part of me. I've got you under my skin. I'd sacrifice anything come what might. For the sake of having you near. In spite of a warning voice that comes in the night. And repeats, repeats in my ear. Don't you know, you fool, you never can win. Use your mentality, wake up to reality. But each time I do, just the thought of you. Makes me stop before I begin.*

*'Cause I've got you under my skin.*

The campaign did not portray someone on their death bed, but instead just regular people, seemingly healthy (beautiful even), in regular everyday smoking scenarios. It is the cigarette that is vilified, as the smoker is seen to be unaware of the clot that moves under their skin, moving ever nearer to the heart ... and a heart attack.

The creative focuses on communicating the ever present danger of breakaway blood clots that can cause a heart attack anytime, anywhere. The statistic 'A blood clot kills another smoker every 35 minutes' was a perfect fit.

Through making the cigarette the enemy, not the smoker, and by adopting a tone of helpful ally rather than disdainful judge, the BHF gave people hope.

## Deployment: the media strategy

Our strategy recognised that our audience are the most set in their ways of the smoking population. It acknowledged the anti-social aspect to smoking, which forces smokers to do so outside. To cut through an increasing volume of anti-smoking messages and engage with our core target we would need to disrupt their habitual behaviours. We focused on environments where people were already smoking, thinking about smoking and in key habitual 'media moments' (see Figure 2).

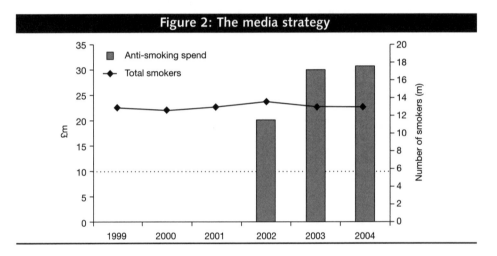

**Figure 2: The media strategy**

TV launched the campaign with a 60-second message, which was further developed through national press and outdoor executions. We employed radio to catch people first thing in the morning, when they are lighting up.

Underground posters showed the sinister ripple moving through arteries as people travelled up and down the escalators. Beer mats caught people who had a pint in one hand and a fag in the other. The online strategy reached smokers at work. Here they could examine in more detail what they had heard or seen in other media the same day, while the initial message was still fresh.

Tactical use of the outdoor creative on mobile transport formats (advans) allowed us to support cessation centres the breadth of the country. We encircled people, reaching them at the moment of consumption at home, work and during their leisure time. TV was the conductor of a catch-all choir.

## The aftermath: the results

Did the campaign actually make people more determined to quit? Did it improve the standing of the BHF? Did it assist the BHF in befriending smokers? Did it result in more people quitting smoking? Yes, yes, yes and yes.

*We shocked the unshockable by getting past their defences*

- 63% of our core target strongly engaged with the TV, with a third 'completely drawn into it'.
- The campaign was reported in detail, and at length, in most of the major national daily, and weekly, newspapers.
- More than four out of five of our core targets saw some element of the campaign. The tightly targeted media strategy did its job.
- Over half our target saw three or more parts of it. This compares to one in ten for the 'Fatty Cigarette' campaign.
- People who saw three or more channels were 70% more likely to set a date to quit than those who had seen just one. Setting a date is recognised by experts to be a serious step towards quitting; 18% of our target that saw three or more channels actually gave up, versus 16% that saw just the single channel.
- Influencers such as GPs liked what the campaign said, and how it said it:

  *It takes a more personal approach, showing the risks that are inherent.*
  
  Hall & Partners campaign evaluation

- As did smoking cessation centres, which reported having an increased number of people come to them following the campaign:

  *It had triggered them to finally do something.*
  
  Hall & Partners campaign evaluation

*The 'Under My Skin' campaign moved people to quit smoking*

- **17% of our core target who saw the campaign stopped smoking.** Of our core target that missed the campaign, only 11% stopped smoking. Yes, there were other ads and campaigns out there, and yes, people who noticed our campaign are more likely to be those who saw other campaigns too, but the difference is large enough to assert that our campaign didn't just make people more determined to quit, it nudged them over the quit line.
- **The figure rose to 20% for people who strongly agreed that the ad told them 'smoking causes blood clots'.** Yes, these people could lapse; they had in the past. However, the average smoker takes six attempts at quitting before they finally make it. At the very least this was one more step towards the final, successful, attempt.

*The campaign reaffirmed the role of the British Heart Foundation as a friend and ally*

- The BHF received 225,000 responses over the period of the campaign: two-and-a-half times more than the 'Fatty Cigarette' campaign.
- Nearly 10% of our entire core target physically responded to the campaign.
- Over two-thirds of our target who saw the campaign said they would be more willing to donate to the BHF after seeing it. A nice side-effect.
- Awareness of the BHF as an organisation that can help people give up went up by 50%.

- The campaign altered smokers' perceptions of the BHF. It cast the BHF more as 'the smoker's friend', as well as believable, efficient and pioneering.

## Return on investment

We invested £3m of taxpayers' money, but it paid back 600 times over. We've established that the campaign worked against its objectives in conventional advertising terms.

- It got past people's defences by circumventing their de-sensitisation to shocking messages built up by previous campaigns.
- It increased their determination to quit by making the damage real and relevant to each smoker in the here and now, not at some distant point in the future.
- Crucially for the BHF, it strengthened their perceived role as the friend of the smoker.
- People responded to it. Smokers actively sought help to quit from the BHF.
- It moved people to quit smoking.

## The ultimate objective

The campaign's grand purpose was ultimately to improve the health, and therefore life expectancy, of the people we targeted.

If we measure the campaign against the value of a life, it needs to save nine lives to warrant its £3m investment. In these terms the campaign massively over-exceeded its objectives by contributing towards saving over 5,400 lives.

For every £1 invested, £600 of value was retained within the economy.

## Home by Christmas: a happy ending

The property of the song will live on beyond the campaign. People who saw the campaign will hear it again and again, and it will continue to remind these people not of falling in love, but of blood clots heading to the heart. Betty McBride, Policy and Communications Director at the BHF, summed it up perfectly:

> *Thanks to Sinatra, every time they hear that song the smoker will bring to mind the unseen damage.*

Chapter 16

# Daz

## From dull to dazzling: how Daz harnessed the power of entertainment to break out of the soap wars

By Becky Barry, Gurdeep Puri and Mike Treharne, Leo Burnett
Contributing author: Maggie Merklin, Analytic Partners
Media agency: ZenithOptimedia

Since its launch in 1953, Daz has promised to provide high-quality whites at a low price. From 1993–1996, the Daz 'Doorstep Challenge' allowed it to stay ahead of the competition, but changes in both the marketplace and consumers' attitudes towards laundry meant that the campaign was becoming somewhat outdated, with the consequence that the brand was losing share.

While the product's core proposition remained highly relevant, a new campaign was needed to connect with Daz's target audience – family households doing a large amount of washing, but with a limited budget – in a more relevant and effective way. By getting deep into the lives of Daz buyers, it was discovered that television, and especially the sort of TV drama epitomised by soap operas, exerted a particularly powerful effect on their viewers. Based on this simple idea, Daz created a soap opera of its own: 'Cleaner Close'. The TV commercials were supported by magazines, online, radio and PR.

The campaign had an almost instant impact, with brand growth exceeding the short- and long-term sales targets, and advertising awareness rising to the second highest in the market, behind only Persil, but with a much smaller budget. This was all achieved without resorting to price cutting, a tool often used to boost the sales of laundry products, meaning Daz was able to reap even further rewards on its initial investment. ROI increased from £1.21 in 2001–2002 to £2.19 in 2004–2005, with predictions of further improving figures in the long term.

## Introduction

*Is TV advertising dead?*

Tom Woodnutt/Fiona Jack, *Admap*, 2004

In this paper we challenge this perception, by demonstrating how we used TV as the hub of a holistic media strategy that enabled us to reinvigorate Daz, from being an ailing giant of yesteryear to the favourite brand of British working-class mothers. By challenging some of the accepted conventions of laundry advertising, and armed with an in-depth understanding of our target market, we created an idea that blurred the divide between advertising and programming.

We will show how this new thinking achieved an impressive return on investment in a fiercely competitive category, and re-engaged consumers with the core equities of Daz in an innovative and motivating way.

## Episode 1: Background

Daz is a major brand in the £1bn UK laundry market, currently with a 10% share. It competes in the fiercely competitive value segment of the market, where its main competitor is Surf (5% market share). Brand owners Procter & Gamble (P&G) and Unilever have been fighting a soap war for years, relying heavily on price promotions.

The core target for both of these brands, as well as private label (20% share), is young mothers who have high volumes of laundry. Value for money rather than lowest price is their key purchase criterion – they must believe they are getting a product that delivers its functional promise, at a fair price. For Daz, that promise is 'no nonsense cleaning for whites you can be proud of'.

Daz brand awareness and share shot up following the launch of its 'Doorstep Challenge' campaign in 1993. Daz's value share increased 38% in four years, whilst Surf declined by 48%.

However, growth started to falter in 1996, and brand share declined from 12.3% to just 7.5% in 2002 (see Figure 1). After much soul searching, we realised that the Doorstep Challenge had lost touch with its core target audience.

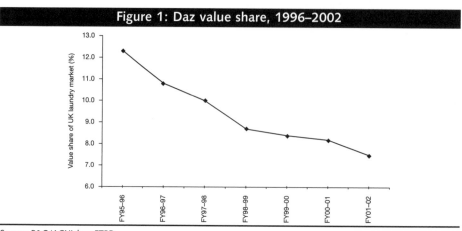

Figure 1: Daz value share, 1996–2002

Source: P&G/ACNielsen ETPD

This perception was supported by facts – the Daz consumer profile had become the oldest in the laundry category, indexing 127 for housewives over 65. We were in danger of being washed away.

## Episode 2: The business objective

The main business objective was to reverse Daz's long-term decline, achieving 8% value share by June 2004, with a longer-term objective of 8.5% share by June 2006.

### The communications objectives

- Encourage reappraisal of Daz from competitor brand users.
- Increase affinity and penetration among core target of C2DE housewives with children.
- Improve brand image by increasing 'leading brand' perceptions.
- Maintain strength in core equity of 'whiteness'.

## Episode 3: Our approach

There were two key stages to our approach.

1. Analysis of the rules of engagement.
2. Understanding the motivations of our target market.

### Rules of engagement

We began by laying out all of our potential constraints, regardless of whether they were client standards, brand guidelines or category conventions.

**Rules we couldn't break**
- In a highly innovative and dynamic market, product and commercial innovations (and the convincing communication thereof) were essential to a brand's success.
- Daz was one of several laundry brands in P&G's portfolio, and must avoid cannibalising from other P&G brands.

**Rules we could break**
- Talking to our consumers as *mums or housewives*. Laundry brands assumed that keeping her family looking its best was the centre of her universe.
- Announcement style, functional advertising.

Historically, laundry advertising has been typified by a well-branded campaign vehicle with familiar icons, such as Surf's *Birds of a Feather* actresses and our own 'Doorstep Challenge' celebrities. These branded icons then delivered new product news in individual TV spots, which meant that the news was linked to the brand via a third party, the icon. We wanted the brand itself rather than a celebrity to be the icon (see Figure 2).

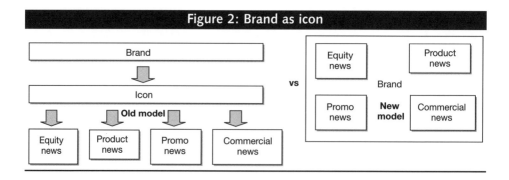

Figure 2: Brand as icon

*Understanding our core target's motivations*

> Core target: 'Working-class mums'
>
> (C2DE housewives with kids, accounting for 40% of UK laundry spend)
>
> Source: TNS HH panel data, 2002

Historically, all we had done was reflect the laundress in the housewife. We hadn't come close to revealing the individual. It's not to say that, as a mother, she didn't care about how her family looks – she did, enormously, but it wasn't her be-all and end-all. There were other important parts of her life: spending time with friends, being up with the latest gossip, being fashionable and having a giggle.

When we spoke specifically about how she relaxed, TV was cited more than any other medium. It was entertaining, her friends and family were watching the same things so she could share her experience, it was instant and it was pure escapism.

As we searched through different genres of programming, there was one that leapt out at us, and it couldn't have been more apt for our brand – soaps.

> 83% of women in our core target choose to regularly watch at least one soap
> (indexing 114 over women in general)
>
> Source: TGI, April 2002

Qualitative research revealed why soaps are held so close to the hearts of our target market: they provide 'me time', familiarity and an escape from their daily routine.

## Episode 4: Our strategy

Looking back into the history of laundry advertising, we could see an opportunity to take Daz back to its roots. So we created 'Cleaner Close', a spoof soap opera set within a small, urban community.

*Our strategic proposition*

- **Overall benefit**: Daz is the people's brand, delivering brilliant whites at a great price.
- **Campaign idea**: even in the unreal world of 'Cleaner Close', you can still rely on the benefits of Daz.
- **Campaign line**: 'Daz. The Soap You Can Believe In'.

## Episode 5: Our campaign

We had established that TV played a major part in the lifestyles of our consumer, and had the ability to deliver the emotional connection that we needed. It was also the only medium with enough cost-effective reach to turn this into a talked-about campaign.

ZenithOptimedia took off its media-buying hat, and acted as though it was a TV programmer – this wasn't simply a frequency breadth and depth exercise, there were considerations like episode continuity, repetition avoidance, character formation and familiarity to consider.

The 'Cleaner Close' campaign was launched with a completely reshaped schedule. Episode 1, 'Grubby Affair', was first aired on 19 March 2003. For two months we relied on TV to build awareness and affinity for the stories and characters, and then extended the campaign to other media in order to exploit the initial interest, as shown in Figure 3.

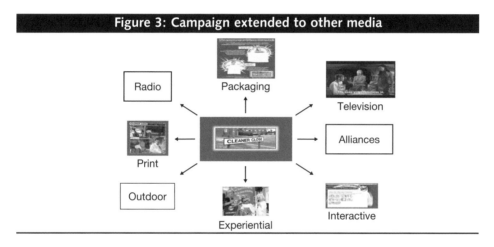

**Figure 3: Campaign extended to other media**

- **Print:** adverts and advertorials were placed in selected magazines from May, with the aim of creating further intrigue around the storylines developing on TV.
- **Online:** a brand new Daz website (www.dazwhite.co.uk) was launched in January 2003, specifically to enable consumers to interact more with the 'Cleaner Close' characters, and also to view episodes again, or see those they had missed.
- **Packaging:** as well as featuring the website URL, the reverse side of Daz's packaging featured a potted storyline of 'Cleaner Close', engaging consumers even when in 'laundry mode'.
- **Experiential:** to broaden our engagement strategy, we launched a roadshow in June 2003, in which thousands of consumers across the UK were auditioned to star in an episode of 'Cleaner Close'.
- **New news:** we were able to incorporate news into the 'Cleaner Close' campaign, including the Citrus Blast launch, Quick Wash upgrade and Vince's Millions promotion.

## Episode 6: Results

The overall business objective was to achieve a value share for Daz of 8% by June 2004 and 8.5% by June 2006. The launch of 'Cleaner Close' not only stemmed the share decline of Daz, but reversed it to the extent that not only did we pass the share target for 2004, but shot past the 2006 target as well (see Figure 4).

Importantly, in a value sector of the category, this share gain was achieved without resorting to price promotions, and therefore generated some genuine value in the category. Even when Surf attempted to reverse its declining share with a buy-one-get-one-free offer (BOGOF) in April 2005, and Daz was forced to respond, there was far more damage done to Surf in the counter-challenge than to Daz in the original promotion (see Figure 5).

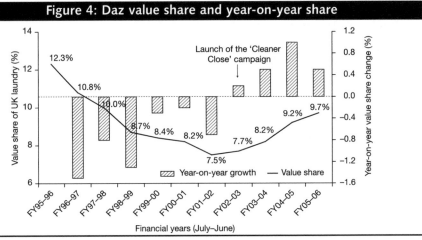

**Figure 4: Daz value share and year-on-year share**

Sources: P&G/ACNielsen ETPD

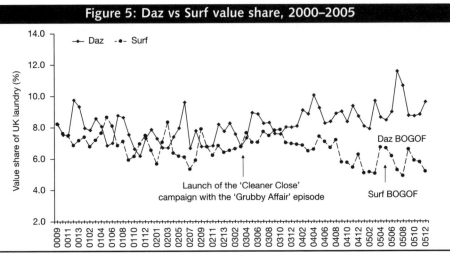

**Figure 5: Daz vs Surf value share, 2000–2005**

Sources: P&G/ACNielsen ETPD

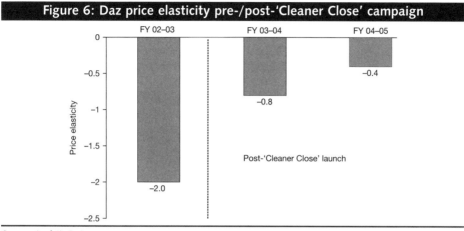

Figure 6: Daz price elasticity pre-/post-'Cleaner Close' campaign

Source: Analytic Partners

Importantly, it was our main competitor, Surf, that we were stealing share from, rather than other Procter & Gamble brands.

The fact that Daz has moved the market away from a reliance on price alone is further demonstrated by the price sensitivity of Daz, which has declined significantly since 'Cleaner Close' launched (see Figure 6).

Such a turnaround in Daz's fortunes was underpinned by us meeting or exceeding each of our four communications objectives.

## Encourage reappraisal of Daz from competitor brand users

Daz achieved the highest branded cut-through in the market (12% to Persil's 11% and Surf's 1%), with 100% correct brand attribution, proving consumers were successfully associating Daz with the advertising content. The scale of this achievement, given Daz's media budget, can be seen in Figure 7.

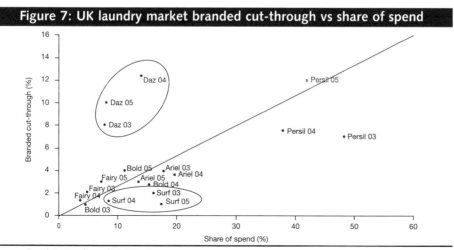

Figure 7: UK laundry market branded cut-through vs share of spend

Sources: ZenithOptimedia and P&G Equityscan

## Figure 8: Daz source of business (consumer spend) in Year 1 of 'Cleaner Close' campaign

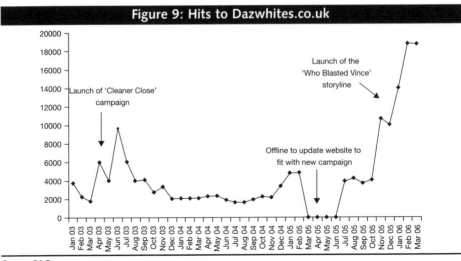

£('000s)

- Pre-existing Daz buyers buying more
- New buyers switching entirely to Daz
- New buyers adding Daz to their repertoires
- New buyers coming into the market

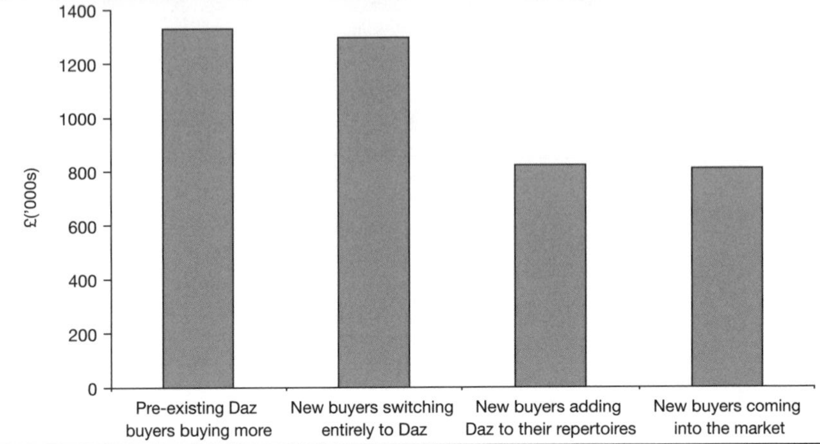

Source: TNS Switching analysis

TNS switching data showed that we had successfully increased volumes among both our existing consumers and other brand users (see Figure 8).

We also achieved a significant increase in hits to the Daz website, particularly following the 'Who Blasted Vince' episode in January 2006 (see Figure 9).

### Increase affinity and penetration among core target of C2DE housewives with children

'Cleaner Close' led to an increase in affinity and penetration among our core target of working-class mothers (see Figures 10 and 11), and we now count a higher share of young housewives among our loyal consumers – index 104 vs 64 previously.

## Figure 9: Hits to Dazwhites.co.uk

Launch of 'Cleaner Close' campaign

Launch of the 'Who Blasted Vince' storyline

Offline to update website to fit with new campaign

Source: P&G

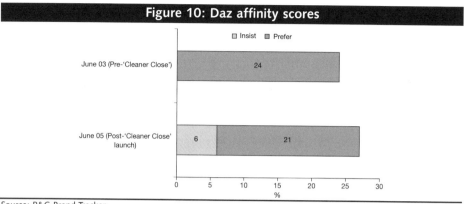

Figure 10: Daz affinity scores

Source: P&G Brand Tracker

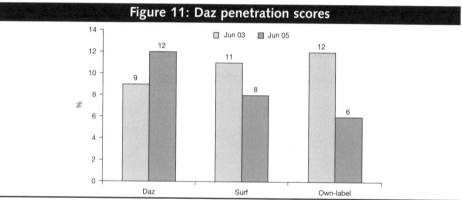

Figure 11: Daz penetration scores

Source: P&G Brand Tracker

## Improve brand image by increasing 'leading brand' perceptions

Daz showed a substantial increase on the statement 'will be a leading brand in the future', as well as on other related statements (see Figure 12).

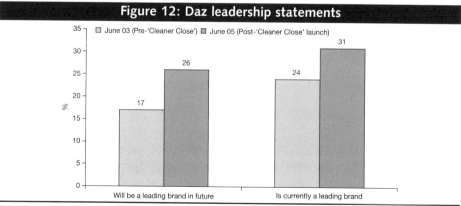

Figure 12: Daz leadership statements

Source: P&G Brand Tracker

257

*Maintain strength in core equity of 'whiteness'*

As well as reversing the negative brand imagery associated with Daz, we also moved further ahead on the core equity benefit of whiteness (see Figure 13).

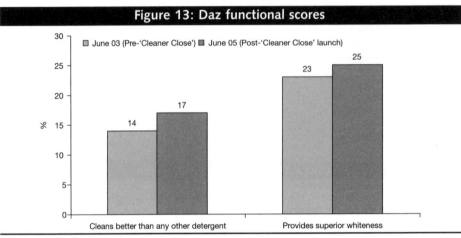

Figure 13: Daz functional scores

Source: P&G Brand Tracker

*Unexpected effects*

### Increase in all positive image statements

The increase in perceptions of Daz as a leading brand appeared to have a halo effect on other brand attributes (see Figure 14).

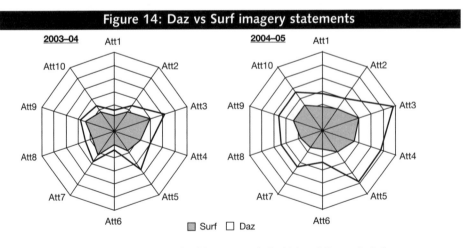

Figure 14: Daz vs Surf imagery statements

Att1 = Makes the laundry process more enjoyable
Att2 = Helps me feel like I'm taking care of my family
Att3 = Is currently a leading brand
Att4 = Will be a leading brand in the future
Att5 = Provides superior whiteness

Att6 = Makes clothes easier to iron
Att7 = Removes stains better than other brands
Att8 = Cleans better than other brands
Att9 = Is good for all the laundry I do
Att10 = Is an authority on taking care of fabrics

Source: P&G Brand Tracker

### Free PR that exceeded expectations

This included an article in the *Wall Street Journal Europe*, which recognised a departure from P&G's more typical advertising approach.

## Episode 7: Discounting other factors

We can discount other factors that might have contributed to the level of growth seen by Daz.

- **Price:** Daz's price at the launch of the 'Cleaner Close' campaign was actually higher than the previous year (£15.02/accounting unit in 2003 vs £14.8 in 2002). Daz's price over time (apart from the BOGOF in 2005) has remained within a constant band (see Figure 15). In relation to its main competitors in the value sector, Daz's price is actually higher (see Figure 16).

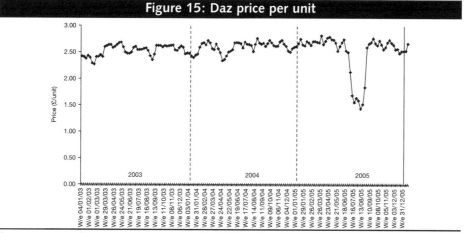

**Figure 15: Daz price per unit**

Sources: P&G/ACNielsen ETPD

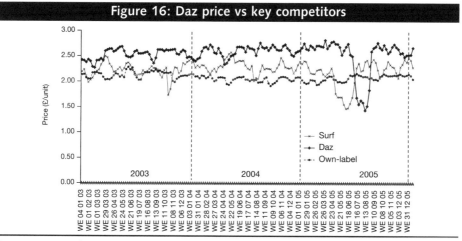

**Figure 16: Daz price vs key competitors**

Sources: P&G/ACNielsen ETPD

- **Product:** there were no product upgrades concurrent with the product launch of 'Cleaner Close' in March 2003. Subsequently Daz has introduced re-stages and line extensions, but these have been in line with innovation from the previous seven years.
- **Distribution:** distribution did not change throughout 2003–2005 (see Figure 17).
- **Birth rates and size of family:** birth rates were declining and there was no increase in the number of people per household.
- **Media spend:** Daz's media spend has been in decline since FY2002/03 (see Figure 18). Share of voice has not increased either (see Table 1).

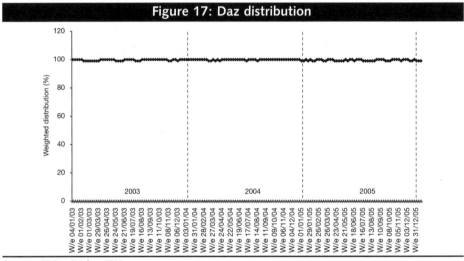

**Figure 17: Daz distribution**

Sources : P&G/ACNielsen ETPD

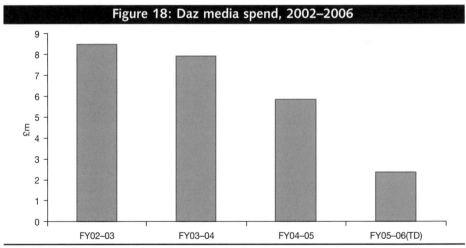

**Figure 18: Daz media spend, 2002–2006**

Source: ZenithOptimedia

| Table 1: UK laundry market share of voice (%) | | | | |
|---|---|---|---|---|
| | FY2002/03 | FY2003/04 | FY2004/05 | FY2005/06* |
| Daz | 12.9 | 11.9 | 9.9 | 7.6 |
| Surf | 13.1 | 14.4 | 11.0 | 16.4 |
| Persil | 22.1 | 40.4 | 43.6 | 27.6 |
| Bold | 10.8 | 8.3 | 14.9 | 25.9 |
| Ariel | 22.4 | 20.2 | 15.1 | 16.6 |

*2005–2006 to date
Source: ZenithOptimedia, 2006

## Episode 8: Econometric analysis

Procter & Gamble conducts econometric analysis on an ongoing basis to evaluate communication and media investment on its campaigns. Figure 19 shows actual sales vs the model prediction.

The 'Cleaner Close' television campaign, from launch to March 2005, has accounted for 13% of total Daz sales. Figure 20 demonstrates the contribution of television to overall sales.

As our data sources report only 50% of total Daz shipments in the UK, the revenue generated by the campaign is estimated to be £18.4m. The cost of the campaign (media and production) is £14.5m. Clearly the campaign has paid for itself; even if one includes the cost of the other communications media, we still see a positive contribution. This revenue figure excludes the effects of print, outdoor and PR, and the associated viral effect, which we expect to be substantial.

We also show return on investment (ROI) figures for this campaign. Since the launch of 'Cleaner Close', the Daz ROI has substantially increased, from £1.21 pre-campaign to £2.19 for FY2004/05 (see Figure 21).

The Daz 'Cleaner Close' campaign has the highest ROI in the P&G portfolio (see Figure 22).

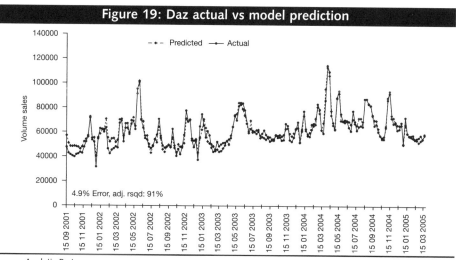

Figure 19: Daz actual vs model prediction

4.9% Error, adj. rsqd: 91%

Source: Analytic Partners

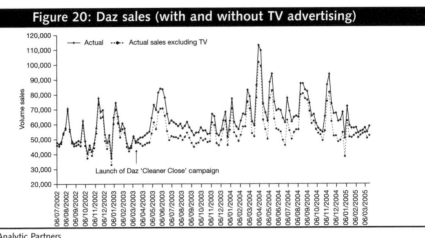

Figure 20: Daz sales (with and without TV advertising)

Source: Analytic Partners

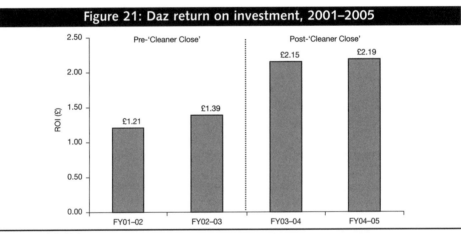

Figure 21: Daz return on investment, 2001–2005

Source: Analytic Partners

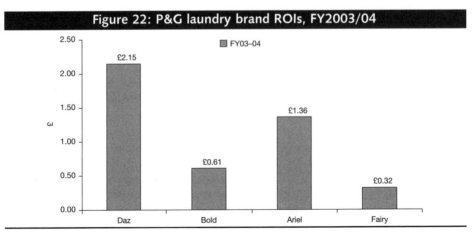

Figure 22: P&G laundry brand ROIs, FY2003/04

Source: Analytic Partners

Finally, Analytic Partners have estimated a long-term ROI figure of £3.29. This is a fairly conservative estimate, as looking at evidence from other studies within P&G, it's believed that the real ROI could be as high as £5.00.

## Conclusion

Having spent several years struggling to connect with its consumers, Daz has found the right formula again.

By tapping into the value of TV as entertainment rather than a sales vehicle, we emerged with an idea that was very different to that which conventional thinking would have produced. And, whilst we employed a multi-media strategy, TV was the hub that linked the different media.

All of which goes to show that, for one brand at least, to borrow from Mark Twain, reports of TV's death have been greatly exaggerated.

## Chapter 17

# Dero

Powder to the people ('Pudra pentru popor'):
how knowing when a global brand should
reaffirm local roots proved highly profitable
for Unilever

**By Ben Jenkins, Bartle Bogle Hegarty**
Contributing author: Gabriel Predescu, Unilever plc

Under Romania's Communist regime, Dero, short for 'Detergent Romania', was one of only two near-identical detergents that each controlled half the market. By the early 90s, however, a number of western brands had moved into the country and the old Romanian brands – now seen as unglamorous – were forgotten, meaning that Dero lost half its volume share, surviving only thanks to its low-price positioning.

By 2003, however, even this position had come under threat by the dual pressures of premium-priced western brands and a stream of budget imports that were flooding the market. In response to this, Dero's owners, Unilever, decided that defending volume leadership was critical, but that this should not be achieved by merely cutting price, which would jeopardise profitability. Rather, a campaign was needed that would improve perceptions of the brand by creating an emotional engagement with consumers in what was normally a low-interest area.

While the resulting '99 stains' had been a success in western Europe, it was decided that, rather than adopting it wholesale, its premise should be adapted to ensure that it resonated directly with consumers by tapping in to the unique humour and heritage of Romania. The ultimate success of the campaign led to Dero recapturing volume leadership and increasing its overall penetration, resulting in an estimated ROI of 3:1. The fact that West isn't always best could also prove a very valuable lesson for brands operating in similar markets in the future.

## Introduction

Europe's second poorest country might not seem like the most fertile territory for an IPA Effectiveness Awards paper. Traditionally, the focus is on more developed and especially western European economies. But this is a story about breaking with tradition.

It reveals how a marketing team realised nearly 300% profit on their investment by ignoring the wisdom of 'West is best' and tapping into the dormant local equity of a former state-owned commodity.

This is not just a story about Romania, and it's not merely a story about detergent wars. The lessons have resonance for other global companies moving into vastly bigger developing markets such as China and India, which have considerably larger populations than Romania. In little more than a generation from now, the consumer purchasing power of the seven largest developing nations will exceed that of the current G7 by 75%.

Furthermore, much of this purchasing power will be held by the majority of consumers, who are unwilling (or unable) to pay the premiums associated with western brands. These are nations where 75% of the population live on less than $10 a day.

This paper examines a successful approach to winning over these consumers without slashing profits. It is an approach that may increasingly become the norm.

## Market background

Imagine a world in which the expression 'shop around' means nothing. One in which you'd acquire your state-subsidised staples from a designated collection point – most branded only with your country's name. Consider a world without choice anxiety, conspicuous consumption or retail therapy. Then imagine all this changing, almost overnight.

This is what happened after the fall of Ceauşescu in Romania. Global brands bombarded eager consumers with promises of unprecedented quality and new ways of announcing status. State-owned brands suddenly looked decidedly unglamorous and were abandoned without a thought. It was within this climate of rapid change that Dero would relaunch.

Communist Romania had two detergent factories, producing near identical products (Dero and Perlan), and supplying half the market each.

In the mid-90s, Procter & Gamble (P&G) bought one factory and Unilever the other. P&G made the decision to import its global brand, Ariel, and to change the name of its local acquisition. During the land-grab that ensued, Ariel's premium offering gained leadership with a 20% value share.

Meanwhile, Unilever chose to relaunch Dero under the Surf positioning of 'relevant affordable quality' to appeal to the vast majority of low-income Romanians. Dero and Ariel took command of the market, securing nearly half of it between them.

### Tough decisions for Dero

Until 2002, Dero's low price strategy served it well, and might have continued to do so in a more stable market. Romania, however, was still very much a developing market.

By the end of 2003, dozens of super price-fighters flooded the market – threatening it with commoditisation due to being priced at 50% of the market norm (Dero was at between 65% and 70%). Dero was now caught between two stools, with neither the premium (or western) status to compete with Ariel, nor a low enough price to fend off the new imports.

## Business objectives

This new competitive environment raised fundamental questions for Dero: should it enhance its offering and compete directly with Ariel in the premium sector? No, Dero recognised that defending *volume* leadership was critical for two key reasons.

First, sheer volume through retailers would secure good relations with them – and retailers could be key allies in the fight against the multiplying competition.

Second, as detergent choice is largely inherited from parents, volume leadership would also secure future generations who might be able to pay more. This would also include the generation moving into washing machines for the first time.

Should it, therefore, buy its volume? Aggressive pricing would have been an easy way to secure short-term volume leadership. However, Dero's view was that, in a such a volatile market, it was imperative to maximise short-term profitability. In addition to setting up long-term success, the strategy would have to deliver immediately in terms of profits, not just volume.

Very simply, Dero's three commercial goals were:

1. To re-establish and widen volume leadership (without just cutting price).
2. To do so profitably.
3. To do this by driving penetration.

The communications objectives were set as follows:

- grow value perceptions of the Dero brand (relevant, affordable quality);
- by strengthening Dero's performance credentials; and
- by adding emotional engagement.

These objectives, however, presented three linked challenges:

1. Laundry is a low interest category and Dero would have to work hard to engage consumers with purely functional messages.
2. Lack of interest was intensified because, in Romania, 'value' was primarily understood as meaning 'low price'. The growth of the super-cheap imports was testament to the fact that consumers were not engaging deeply with anything beyond cost.
3. Romanian brands were the last place you'd look for quality; Romanians knew this better than anyone else.

## Communications solution

The Surf brand – which had operated in Europe for 50 years – provided part of the solution. The 'Removes 99 stains' platform was a tried and tested approach for communicating good performance at an affordable price, and had featured in campaigns and on-pack in the UK and France. It had been proven to be a more credible alternative to the 'best ever whiteness' claims that accompanied the higher prices of other brands – and one that was unique to and ownable by Surf. So in 2004 the '99 stains' promise was featured on the Romanian pack and formed the core of the client's brief.

Given the received wisdom about the appeal of all things international ('West is best'), the obvious temptation would have been simply to import the European advertising wholesale. After all, international brands instantly connoted 'quality'.

Some timely research findings caused us to take a different approach. While we were relatively happy that the '99 stains' idea could successfully communicate performance, we were less sure how we would make it more *emotionally* relevant for Romanians.

Engaging low-income consumers with a low-interest product was always going to be tough. We'd need to do more than a few focus groups if we were to cut through. We used a range of ethnographic approaches, combining domestic visits and cultural immersion in films, books, news and programmes.

What we learned confirmed what we'd started to glean from qualitative research. It boiled down to two crucial insights.

### 1. A yearning for the past

Despite Romanians initially welcoming closer links with the West, nostalgia for old Romania was resurgent. We realised that Dero's perceived weakness – its Romanian heritage – might in fact be the key to adding emotional value to the brand.

> *We didn't like Romanian things before, but now there's none left it's a bit sad really.*
>
> Source: Consumer home visit, January 2004

### 2. A strong sense of Romanian humour

Second, we uncovered a nation with an extremely sophisticated sense of humour. A review of Romania's best-loved ads, favourite TV programmes and films revealed a strong comic heritage.

Not only did we have licence to write amusing ads, humour would be imperative if we were to engage cash-strapped consumers within such a low-interest category.

In summary, the challenge would be to re-interpret '99 stains' in an engaging, entertaining and, above all, *Romanian* way.

The creative proposition had 'Romania' at its core:

*Dero removes 99 of Romania's most common stains*

The creative leap was to dramatise the unexpected arrival of stains. The idea being that if it removes the least expected stains it will remove anything.

Creative idea: *Dero removes 99 stains – including those you least expect*

## Media

The media strategy was two-fold: to create fame and emotional engagement. Although we used a variety of media to answer this we didn't simply replicate our approach from other Surf markets. Whereas in most western markets Unilever tends to invest increasingly in non-TV media, in Romania, TV advertising was much more critical as it was demonstrative of quality, and was much more efficient. GRPs, for instance, are around 40 times cheaper than in the UK.

The creative idea of 'unexpectedness' provided excellent opportunities for other ATL channels, activation and PR to engage consumers with the '99 stains' proposition beyond TV. The TV was supported by a light burst of outdoor at launch to make the '99 stains' concept famous.

The entire campaign represented a step-change in the way a detergent brand spoke to consumers. Nowhere else was this more apparent than in the TV executions, which not only contrast strongly with previous Dero work, but also with the category leader, Ariel.

## Campaign results

Dero achieved its business objectives.

### Volume leadership was re-established

In the period immediately after the campaign ran, volume leadership was re-established, with an increased lead over Ariel, and to the detriment of the cheap import, Fax (see Figure 1).

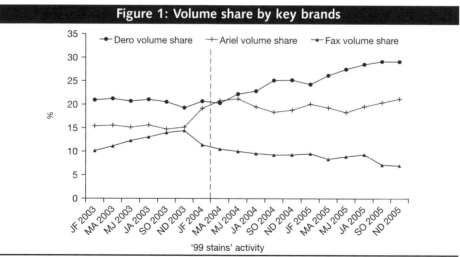

**Figure 1: Volume share by key brands**

Source: ACNielsen, 2006

### Volume leadership was achieved profitably

In less than a year after the activity launched, it had paid for itself, as will be shown in the payback section. Value share increased (see Figure 2).

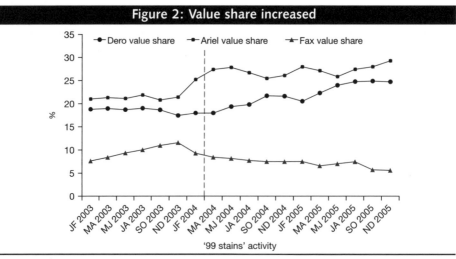

Figure 2: Value share increased

Source: ACNielsen, 2006

## Penetration increased

Dero already had a healthy level of penetration. However, following the launch of the '99 stains' campaign, this grew by 10% (see Figure 3). By the end of 2005, nearly three-quarters of the population were using Dero.

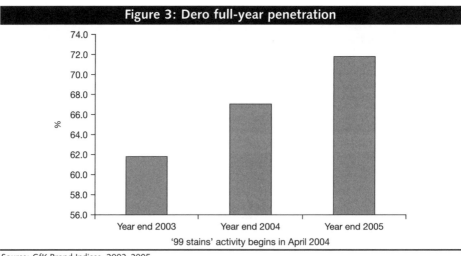

Figure 3: Dero full-year penetration

Source: GfK Brand Indices, 2003–2005

## Role of advertising

There are three main strands of proof that, together, comprise compelling evidence of the central role that advertising played in the performance of Dero in 2004 and 2005.

1. Advertising worked according to plan.
2. Nothing else can explain this impressive performance.
3. Econometrics have been used to identify and quantify the contribution of advertising.

## Advertising worked according to plan

### The advertising was memorable

Immediately after the launch, top-of-mind awareness of Dero advertising doubled and other ad awareness measures grew significantly (see Figure 4).

### The advertising shifted perceptions of value

Given the impending threat of commoditisation, the most important task for advertising was to grow value perceptions – and it did (see Figure 5).

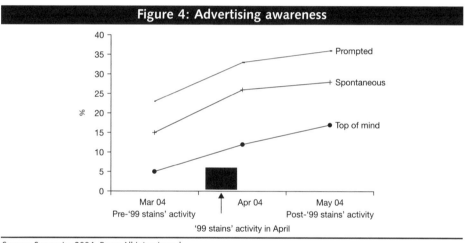

**Figure 4: Advertising awareness**

Source: Synovate, 2004. Base: All interviewed

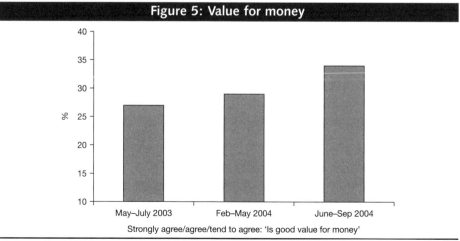

**Figure 5: Value for money**

Source: Synovate, 2004

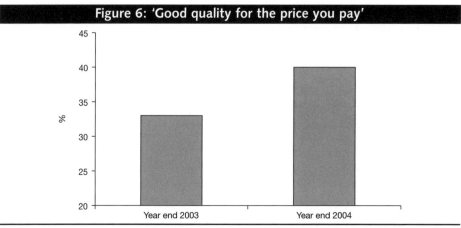

Figure 6: 'Good quality for the price you pay'

Source: Synovate, 2004. Base: All interviewed

Figure 7: 'Better value for the price you pay'

Source: Millward Brown, 2005. Base: All respondents

'Good quality for the price you pay' grew by 18% year-on-year (see Figure 6).

In 2005, the new Millward Brown tracking study continued to see dramatic rises in Dero's value perceptions, with Dero overtaking Ariel as 'the best value' (see Figure 7).

### Advertising shifted performance perceptions

Following the advertising, Dero was seen to wash cleaner, whiter and be tougher on stains (see Figure 8).

### Emotional engagement was reinforced

The campaign certainly spoke directly to the Romanian people (see Figure 9).

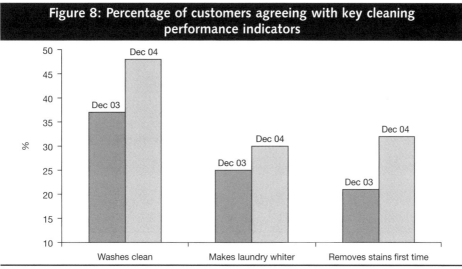

Figure 8: Percentage of customers agreeing with key cleaning performance indicators

Source: Synovate, 2004. Base: All respondents

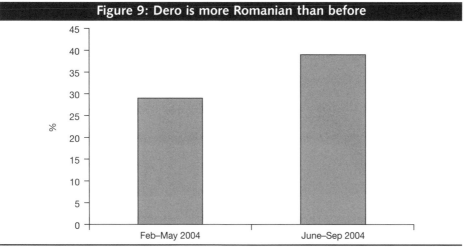

Figure 9: Dero is more Romanian than before

Source: Synovate, 2004

Consumers increasingly saw the brand as offering something distinctive – critical in a commoditising category (see Figure 10).

Consumers found the ads twice as original, fun, lively and involving as the average Romanian ad (see Figure 11).

## The campaign created cultural impact

Dero became more culturally relevant, with top-of-mind brand awareness growing by over 70%, quite an achievement for a budget Romanian brand within a low-interest category (see Figure 12).

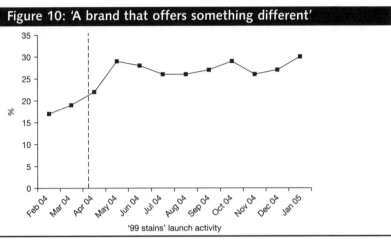

## Figure 10: 'A brand that offers something different'

35
30
25
20
15
10
5
0
%
Feb 04
Mar 04
Apr 04
May 04
Jun 04
Jul 04
Aug 04
Sep 04
Oct 04
Nov 04
Dec 04
Jan 05
'99 stains' launch activity

Source: Synovate, 2004. Base: All respondents

## Figure 11: 'How would you describe the brand in these ads?'

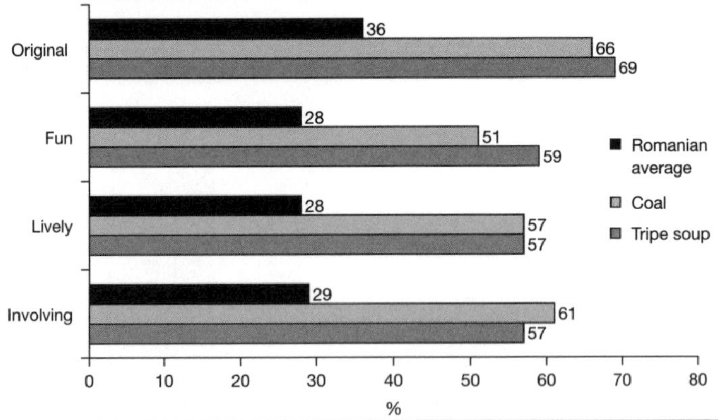

Original
36
66
69
Fun
28
51
59
Lively
28
57
57
Involving
29
61
57
Romanian average
Coal
Tripe soup
0
10
20
30
40
50
60
70
80
%

Source: Millward Brown PreView test. April 2004. Base: All respondents

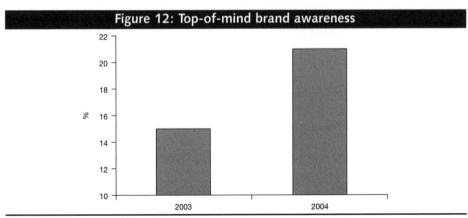

## Figure 12: Top-of-mind brand awareness

22
20
18
16
14
12
10
%
2003
2004

Source: Synovate, 2004

### The advertising reignited a sense of Romanian pride
Dero was applauded by the media for having reawakened a latent sense of Romanian pride.

The '99 most common stains' line was borrowed elsewhere in Romanian culture – most notably by the media, who used it as their slogan for a corruption scandal in the Liberal Party.

### Nothing else can explain this performance
Econometric analysis has been carried out on Dero sales from 2002 to 2005 in order to identify and quantify the contribution of advertising. The fit of the model is strong, indicating that all variation in sales has been successfully accounted for. We have used this to eliminate certain factors below.

### Dero's marketing mix
*Did we buy the volume through price cuts?*
Dero's price went up although relative price declined slightly. This has been accounted for in the model.

Dero did have a 1.7% greater share of voice during the launch period. However, in 2002, share had been even higher, but Dero had not experienced any significant volume share growth. Furthermore, the model accounts for media spends.

*Could growth have come from promotional activity?*
The '99 stains' idea was brought to life through in-store activity, promotions and activation. This undoubtedly had a positive effect on sales, especially in such a price-sensitive market. However, it is unlikely that less than 5% of the marketing spend would have explained all the growth. In addition, promotions are explicitly accounted for in the model.

*Could new products in the Dero portfolio have caused this level of growth?*
This is a category that thrives on innovation. Indeed, a 2-in-1 product had been launched in 2000, and growth had come from this when it was supported. However, there had been no further growth on the 2-in-1 until the '99 stains' activity. The '99 stains' campaign was designed to benefit all Dero products, and thus it could be argued that it actually 'turbo charged' the renewed growth seen in 2-in-1, not the other way around.

*Was increased distribution a factor?*
Before '99 stains', Dero's distribution was already very high. During the period of the campaign and in the immediate aftermath it remained constant, with a mean of 88%. Thus, distribution could have had no significant effect on the rapid growth in Dero volume and market share. Furthermore, rate of sale increased.

### Competitor and market factors
*Did the overall market grow?*
The detergent market did grow during the period. However, Dero showed absolute share growth within the market, so this cannot explain Dero's success.

Market growth would have been influenced by the following factors, so these were also analysed in order to identify whether they might have benefited Dero unduly:

- increased personal wealth and ownership of credit cards
- growth in washing machine ownership
- a shift from informal retailers to large supermarkets
- western-influenced trends in cleaning
- growth in dirty nappies
- legislative changes in the move towards EU enlargement – which would benefit international investors.

None of these was found to have any greater positive effect on Dero than on the competition.

### Quantifying the effect of advertising

Figure 13 shows the modelled paths for volume sales with and without the '99 stains' advertising, demonstrating the incremental volume up to the end of the advertising period.

It is clear that advertising has generated incremental volume for Dero (see Figure 14). The increase in sales was nearly four times greater than it would have been without advertising. This equates to two million extra packs.

## Calculating payback

In order to calculate the point at which the campaign pays back we have used the model to project forward the contribution of advertising. This assumes an adstock of 80%, which demonstrates the best fit with the model.

Modelling suggests incremental volume, generated between April 2004 and December 2008, of 11,256,000 kilograms.

It's not possible to disclose Unilever's profit margins here. We calculate that Dero received a 300% return on advertising investment.

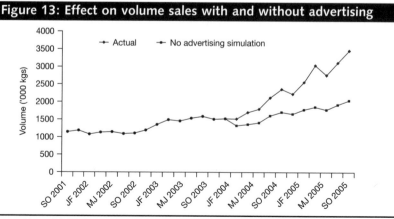

**Figure 13: Effect on volume sales with and without advertising**

Source: Econometric model, 2006

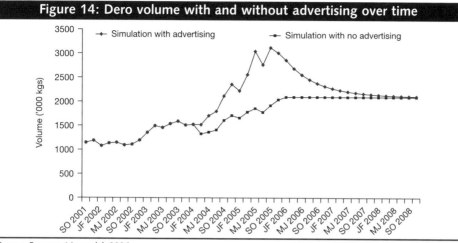

Figure 14: Dero volume with and without advertising over time

Source: Econometric model, 2006

## Summary

Before the '99 stains' campaign, Dero was under pressure from premium brands at the top end and cheaper competitors flooding the market at the bottom, a low-interest product in a low-interest category in a low-income market.

The '99 stains' campaign generated substantial incremental revenues for Unilever, and it did so profitably. More significantly, the campaign created a profound emotional bond with Romanians that places Dero in a strong position for the longer term. Today, Dero is a credible, value-added (and not merely competitively priced) washing powder brand.

## Conclusions

*To each according to his needs.*

Karl Marx

Unilever's '99 stains' campaign was a proven winner in numerous markets across Europe. On arrival in Romania, the logical action for Unilever would have been to rest on its laurels, deploy its existing communication assets, and wait for the powder to fly off the shelves. It did not. Instead, Unilever realised that it could reposition Dero as a Romanian brand that was re-connecting with Romanians.

The learnings from this case extend well beyond Romania. Developing markets from China to India, from Russia to Brazil, tend to be volatile economic environments, overwhelmingly populated by people with low disposable incomes. Working successfully with and within the local culture, and calculating when it's best to revive local assets, demands both strong consumer insight and a brave marketing team.

The last point is important, because in many ways it's the major lesson we've learned from the '99 stains' campaign in Romania. West isn't necessarily best. Identifying where and when that's the case can help change perceptions, build equity and, ultimately, transform business fortunes.

## Chapter 18

# Felix

## Continuity saved the cat

**By Georgia Challis and Barry Lustig, DDB London, and
Julia Wood, DDB Matrix**
Contributing authors: Les Binet, DDB Matrix, and Sarah Carter, DDB London

This case study is about the power of continuity in advertising, an approach that has come under increasing pressure from the 'disruption' culture that pervades current communications thinking. A sales decline in 2000–2001 threatened the long-standing campaign for Felix cat food, and Purina, the owner of the brand, faced the choice of either changing its approach or persisting in the face of this sudden difficulty.

Upon its inception in 1989, the Felix campaign constituted a radically different approach to selling cat food; since then, however, the market had changed significantly, and a decision had to be made as to whether current communications could reflect the new climate. While conditions had changed, however, the basic driver of the Felix brand – the relationship between cat and owner – had not and, as such, the decision was made to stick with the existing campaign.

Felix emerged stronger and more effective as a result. Over the course of 16 years, it was transformed from a brand on the verge of being delisted into one with sales of over £138m a year – all with an average annual communications spend of just £2.5m. Furthermore, the launch of a new single-serve pouch within the existing advertising platform allowed Felix to overtake the leader in the sector, despite the fact its own offering reached the market much later, and offered no distinct product or price advantage. As a result, a premium variant was then also successfully introduced.

## Introduction

This paper turns the spotlight on an endangered species: the long-running campaign. Once the stalwart of our TV screens, now most are extinct. We estimate that only ten campaigns have been running for more than 15 years in the UK.

Here, we examine the power of continuity. The long-standing Felix campaign came under pressure when sales slumped in 2000–2001. Most managers would have abandoned the campaign at the first sign of trouble. But, for Purina, the gutsy choice was to resist the temptation to change and to reap the hard benefits of continuity. In direct contrast to Whiskas, Felix's flip-flopping competitor, Felix dug in its claws through tough times to emerge stronger than its better-funded rival.

This paper will also illustrate some broader lessons for clients and agencies alike, namely:

- there is a particular role for long-running campaigns for brands that form the 'glue' in *enduring relationships* like that between a pet and an owner
- contrary to popular wisdom, long-running campaigns *can* be used effectively to introduce new news *and* to introduce products into a different market sector
- when things are not going well, the answer is not always to change the advertising.

## Felix vs Whiskas 1989–1999: the growth years

Until the 80s, Whiskas dominated the UK cat food market. Its strength was supported by a hefty £11m annual advertising investment. By 1988, Whiskas' 53% market share left its six remaining competitors scrambling for the leftovers.

Whiskas created a formula that set the norms for cat food advertising: perfect housewife, perfect cat, a scientist explaining the nutritional value of the product. It was all very rational and focused around the cat as an animal rather than a friend or pet. For over a decade, this proved a successful approach.

By contrast, in 1988, Felix was an undifferentiated brand with 5% market share, facing delisting. So Felix was relaunched with an extended range of flavours, new packaging and, for the first time in the brand's history, a £250,000 budget for advertising.

After winning the Felix brief, our research uncovered a useful insight: the perfect cats represented in Whiskas ads were unrecognisable to many cat owners. Their cats were naughty, cheeky and demanding. They loved their cats because they had fun-loving and mischievous personalities.

The black and white animated cat called Felix was born. He was scruffy and designed to remind owners of their cat at home. If the animated Felix liked Felix cat food, then the chances were their cat would, too. Indeed, 'Cats like Felix [would] like Felix.'

There were no clichéd lines about meatiness, nutrients and goodness. The ads disrupted every established rule of cat food advertising.

It worked. Even though Whiskas spent the equivalent of Felix's entire annual budget every eight days, Felix's market share began to rise. By 1992, Felix was the

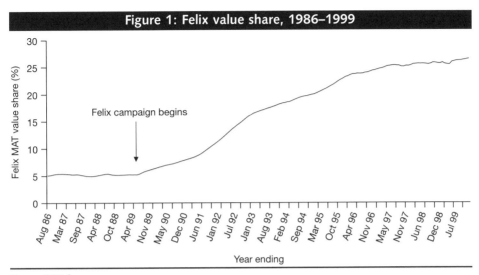

Figure 1: Felix value share, 1986–1999

Source: ACNielsen

second fastest-growing brand in any grocery category and the second biggest brand in the market (see Figure 1).

We'd found a winning formula by tapping into people's real relationships with their cats. As Felix expanded overseas, the campaign went too. By 1999, Felix was tussling with Whiskas for market leadership (see Figure 2).

Whiskas repackaged, lost the men in white coats and rolled out a succession of new campaigns. Try as they might, Whiskas' ever-changing advertising campaigns failed to engage cat owners. Their market share kept slipping away (see Figure 3).

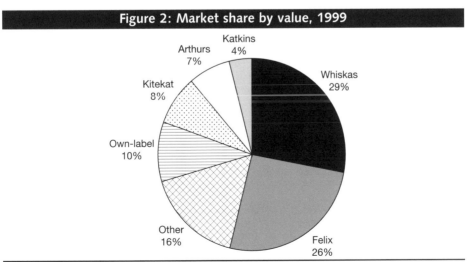

Figure 2: Market share by value, 1999

Source: ACNielsen

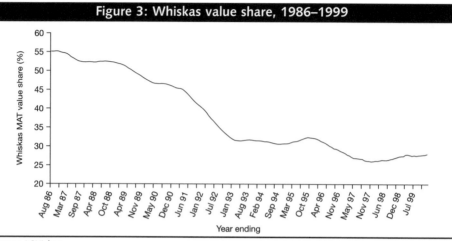

**Figure 3: Whiskas value share, 1986–1999**

Year ending

Source: ACNielsen

## The wobble and the crisis: 2000–2001

*What Whiskas did next*

At last, Whiskas hit upon a winner. In 1997 it launched a 100 g single-serve foil pouch, with just enough food for one meal. Single serve formats offer benefits over the standard 400 g 'multiserve' cans.

- For the cat, the main benefit is taste. Cats don't like food that has been hanging around for the best part of a day. Individual portions mean fresh food every time as well as a greater variety of flavours throughout the day.
- For owners, there are no half-eaten cans of cat food stinking out the kitchen or the fridge. There is less waste and single-serve products tend to be easier to open than cans.

Single-serve portions did exist before Whiskas, but only from upmarket, niche brands like Sheba and Gourmet, and appealing only to people who lavished money and attention on their cats. Until this point, it was thought that only these cat enthusiasts would pay a premium for single-serve cat food.

Whiskas' success came from opening up single serve to a broader market. Its foil pouch served as a mid-point between mainstream cat food and these more expensive 'luxury' brands. This widened the appeal of single serve – mainly to 'empty nesters'. They were generally women, with a bit more money to spend on a new easy-to-use cat food, without being total cat obsessives.

Yet another creative idea supported Whiskas' new pouch. Whiskas' share started to rise again at Felix's expense.

*What Felix did*

Felix did have single-serve products: a tray and a small can. But consumers wanted the pouch. While a pouch was developed, the brand team started to wobble and the classic symptoms of a brand in trouble started to appear:

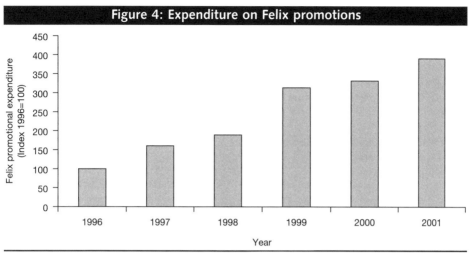

Figure 4: Expenditure on Felix promotions

Source: Friskies

- adspend was cut back and transferred to increased spend on tactical promotions to boost volume (see Figure 4)
- questions were raised about the campaign and its role in the share decline.

But the promotions didn't work. Felix kept losing market share. Whiskas kept growing at Felix's expense (see Figure 5).

In May 2002, Felix was finally ready to launch its own new pouch. In product, packaging and price it went head to head with Whiskas.

Now we had to decide the best way to launch into a new market segment. The choices were neither easy nor clear.

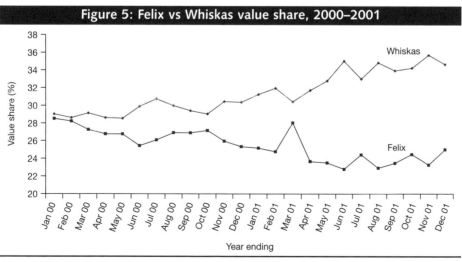

Figure 5: Felix vs Whiskas value share, 2000–2001

Source: ACNielsen

*The threat to the black and white cat ...*

The pouch was new territory for the Felix brand.

Sales, as we have seen, were flagging. We had a long-running campaign that had not carried such important product news before. And we were conscious of the conventional wisdom that well-established campaigns can overwhelm new product stories. Our research was telling us the same thing – adding to the momentum for change.

> *A new campaign is most likely to cause the disruption necessary to get consumers to reassess the brand offer.*
>
> Source: Added Value Brand Consultants

New concepts were created featuring a different version of Felix. He stood on two legs and was dressed as a posh waiter who served posh new Felix food from a pouch.

Qualitative research on the new concepts quickly brought us to our senses:

> *He's not my Felix.*
>
> *It's quite cute, but it's not the Felix I know.*
>
> *Please don't change it, no, no.*
>
> *Oh no, no, they mustn't change it ... I love that cat.*
>
> *It doesn't feel right.*
>
> *I'm going to lose my cat soon ... if they've still got the adverts it's like I've still got my cat.*
>
> Source: Added Value, and DDB qualitative research

Felix buyers were unhappy at the threat posed to their long-time friend. Their enduring relationship with the Felix cat in our ads mirrored the relationship they had with their own cats. We had failed to realise the power of this long-term relationship.

We decided that the long-running campaign could and should be adapted to launch the pouch and other new products. So we kept good old Felix but changed the focus of the advertising. We linked Felix the cat with insights about why the new pouch was appealing.

There was one other significant benefit to keeping the Felix of old. Our research revealed that although families were by far the biggest sector of cat food buyers, they still perceived pouches as extravagant and not for people like them. Felix could change this.

What we had thought was our weakness was, in fact, our greatest strength. Although the Felix pouch was the same price as Whiskas', when introduced via our well-loved, familiar and down-to-earth campaign it suddenly felt much more accessible to mainstream cat owners.

So the campaign was saved – a brave and unusual decision given the circumstances.

## Felix vs Whiskas, 2001–2005: the return to growth

### Launch of Felix pouch

Once persuaded of the new direction, the brand team reallocated the budget from price promotions back to advertising. The Felix pouch launched in May 2002, supported by media targeted at cat food-buying families.

Felix sponsored *You've Been Framed*, a family-orientated TV comedy show that matched Felix's target and perfectly complemented the brand's personality.

Buying the same amount of airtime in the form of advertising around the programme would have cost on average three times more than the sponsorship.

### Next phase: launching more premium products

In 2004, Felix added another new product to its range, called 'As Good As It Looks'. Priced at 38p above the standard pouch, it was for people prepared to spend a bit more on their cats.

This new premium pouch was supported by outdoor and TV advertising that targeted more affluent cat owners.

Even with a higher-end premium product in a new price category, Felix's advertising proved elastic enough to accommodate the launch.

### What about Whiskas?

While Felix stuck with its long-running campaign, adapting to accommodate new products, Whiskas succumbed to the temptation of continual disruption.

Year after year the Whiskas campaign chopped and changed. It had:

■ dancing, animated mice
■ a charity appeal for cats who are fed tinned food
■ ads to attract the attention of cats
■ grannies enticing cats away with pouches
■ 90% of cats prefer Whiskas in pouches
■ a trendy young urbanite in his New York apartment
■ a purring cat in a family home.

Whiskas was one crazy, mixed-up cat.

It is likely that Whiskas' confused communications strategy inadvertently reinforced the enduring relationship between the Felix cat and cat owners.

As we will see, the introduction of new products and their inclusion in our existing campaign helped Felix quickly recapture lost share.

## Results

### Single serve

In 2002, with its new pouch and renewed investment in advertising, the Felix brand saw an immediate uplift in sales in the single-serve category. By 2004 Felix surpassed Whiskas in both single-serve volume and value (see Figure 6).

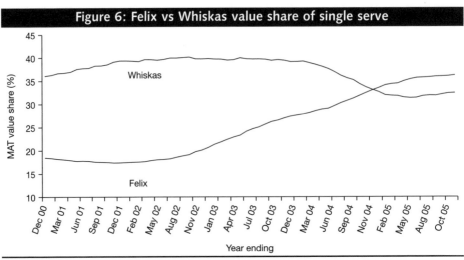

Figure 6: Felix vs Whiskas value share of single serve

Source: ACNielsen

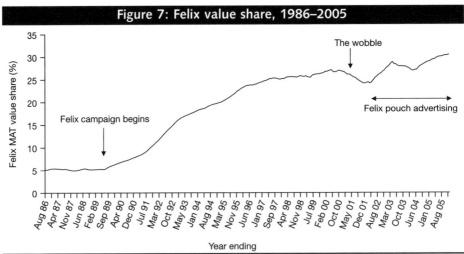

Figure 7: Felix value share, 1986–2005

Source: ACNielsen

*The Felix brand*

More importantly, the new products and their advertising managed to reverse the fortunes of the Felix brand (see Figure 7).

This brought the brand's market share almost back to parity with Whiskas, competing for top position in the market again (see Figure 8).

## Proving the effectiveness of Felix advertising

We've shown how the Felix brand bounced back after the 'wobble'. New products played a critical role. However, new products alone are not enough to account for the success of the brand. Advertising's contribution can be proved in several ways:

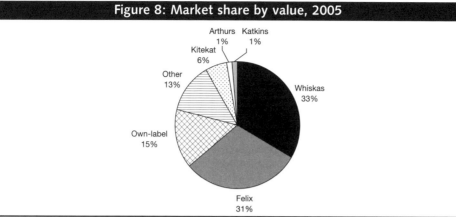

Figure 8: Market share by value, 2005

Source: ACNielsen

1. The timing of the campaign.
2. Regional variations in sales and advertising.
3. Econometric analysis.
4. Eliminating the contribution of other variables.

*Timing*

There is a clear correlation between market share and adspend over time (see Figure 9).

*Regionality*

Even if this relationship seems to be closely correlated, this alone does not prove causality. We can strip out the effects of the new product launches using regional analysis. Felix's new products have been introduced nationwide with no regional

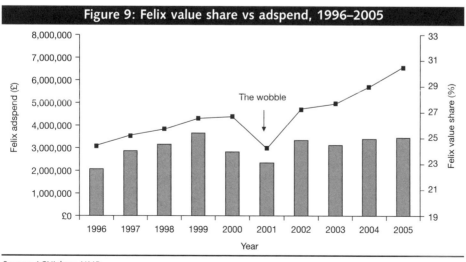

Figure 9: Felix value share vs adspend, 1996–2005

Source: ACNielsen, NMR

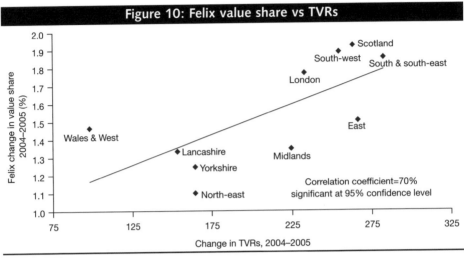

Figure 10: Felix value share vs TVRs

Source: ACNielsen

differences in price, distribution, public relations, below-the-line activity or promotion. However, there have been regional differences in Felix's TVRs. Some regions got more advertising than others. Those regions with more advertising grew faster than regions that had less (see Figure 10).

We can do a similar thing with European countries. Different countries got the same products at similar prices, supported by the same advertising. However, there are variations in the relative spend in different countries, which prove useful in isolating the effects of advertising from the effects of new products themselves. Countries with a larger growth in share of voice also saw enhanced growth in value sales (see Figure 11).

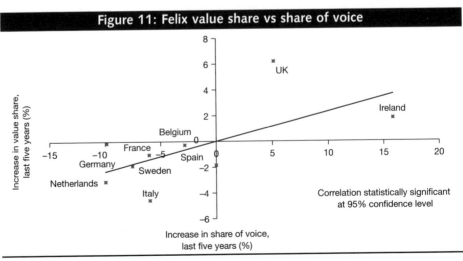

Figure 11: Felix value share vs share of voice

Sources: ACNielsen, local media agencies

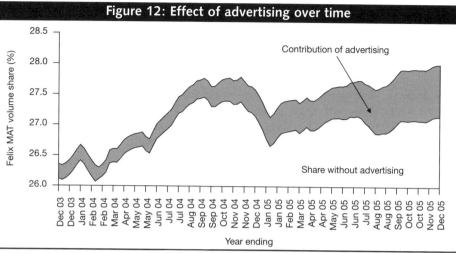

Figure 12: Effect of advertising over time

Sources: ACNielsen, DDB Matrix

## Econometrics

In 2005, Purina commissioned an econometric analysis to help measure and optimise the effects of its marketing. Its model shows that, while new products are crucial to growth, advertising played a pivotal role in driving sales. Advertising was responsible for 67% of the brand's growth over the last three years, and currently generates a return of £1.38 for every £1 spent (see Figure 12).

## What about other factors?

Can we be absolutely sure nothing else generated these results?

### The market?

Felix's growth cannot be due to an increase in the market overall as Felix increased its share of the market.

### Better distribution?

Distribution of the Felix brand did not increase over the period.

### More variants in-store?

- The number of in-store variants did increase, but only slightly, and only after market share had begun to rise. Later we will show that this in itself may be an advertising effect.
- The number of variants in-store was the same throughout the UK, so they can't account for the regional variations in share.
- Econometrics takes the effects of distribution and numbers of variants in store into account.

### The nature of the new products

- Different countries and regions all had the same products, but those with more advertising grew more.

- The econometrics shows that new products alone can't explain all the growth.

### Price

- Felix didn't grow by cutting prices. In fact, our price relative to the market *increased*. We are now the most expensive mainstream brand in the market.
- Felix's prices do not vary regionally, so price cannot account for the regional discrepancy in sales share.
- The econometric model takes price effects into account.

### Promotions

- Promotional spend has been fairly static since 2002.
- All promotions are national, so cannot account for the way regional growth rates correlate with advertising.
- Purina's econometric model shows that their contribution to growth over the last few years has been minor.

### Reduced competitor activity?

Felix was consistently outspent by its key competitor. Between 2003 and 2005 the gap between the Whiskas and Felix spends widened.

Supermarket own-label products were also launching new, premium products and gaining market share.

## How it worked: the virtue of consistency

We will now explain how the advertising worked.

*People remembered the ads* (see Figure 13)

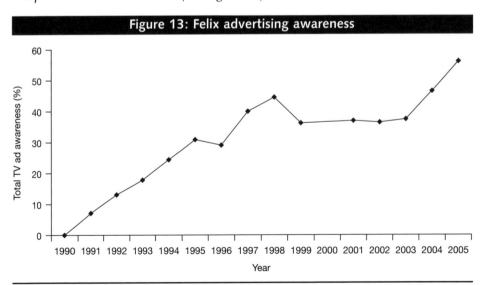

**Figure 13: Felix advertising awareness**

Source: Millward Brown

## Brand image improved (see Figure 14 and Table 1)

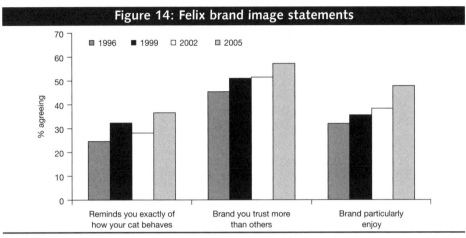

**Figure 14: Felix brand image statements**

Source: Millward Brown

### Table 1: Key Millward Brown image statements

| Image statement | Felix | Whiskas |
|---|---|---|
| Reminds you of how your cat behaves | +9% | −6% |
| Understands your relationship with your cat | +15% | −6% |
| Brand you trust more than others | +6% | −7% |
| Brand cats particularly enjoy | +10% | 0% |
| Cats find irresistible | +1% | −20% |
| Better quality than other products | +9% | −7% |
| Always coming up with new ideas | +12% | −12% |
| Wide range | +15% | −8% |

Source: Millward Brown. Pre = March 2003. Post = Dec 2005

## Penetration increased (see Figure 15)

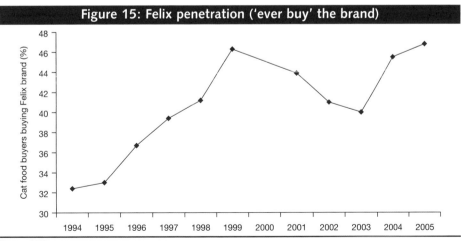

**Figure 15: Felix penetration ('ever buy' the brand)**

Source: TGI

*Loyalty improved* (see Figure 16)

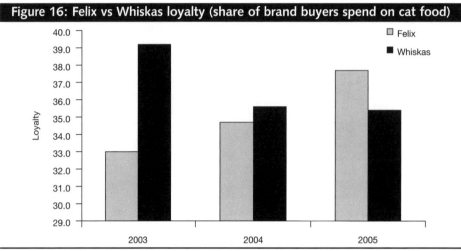

**Figure 16: Felix vs Whiskas loyalty (share of brand buyers spend on cat food)**

Source: NPPC

## Price elasticity fell

Felix customers became less price sensitive. Since the early 90s, price elasticity for Felix has fallen by 20%.

*This enabled the price to rise* (see Figure 17)

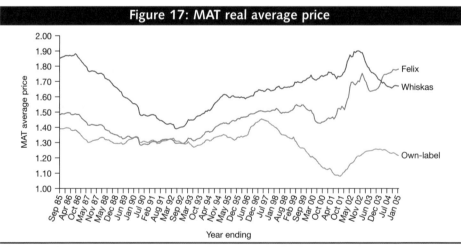

**Figure 17: MAT real average price**

Source: ACNielsen

## Increases in the rate of sale drove aggregate distribution gains

Aggregate distribution gains lagged behind sales increases (see Figure 18). This seems to be, because we had managed to increase trial and loyalty, the rate at which Felix sold through supermarkets increased. As the rate of sale increased, and

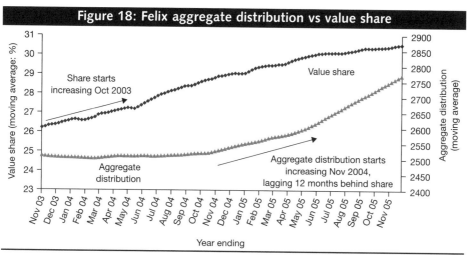

Figure 18: Felix aggregate distribution vs value share

Source: ACNielsen

Felix was commanding a higher selling price, it became increasingly attractive to retailers. So it was stocked in more stores.

This suggests that 'demand pull' from advertising is forcing the trade to stock more of our variants. This in turn increases sales further. In this way, advertising has an additional long-term effect on sales (see Figure 19).

Figure 19: Advertising drives distribution by increasing rate of sale

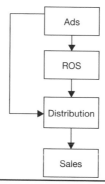

## Continuity and efficiency

All this has been achieved in the face of Whiskas consistently outspending us by an average factor of 2:1. In every way, we became more efficient and effective than Whiskas (see Figure 20). This enabled Felix to have a lower advertising to sales ratio than Whiskas (see Figure 21). As the long-running campaign has worn in over time, Felix's AIs have grown steadily (see Figure 22). This enabled Felix's advertising to sales ratio to fall, making it increasingly efficient over time (see Figure 23).

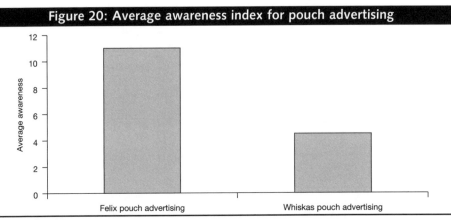

Source: Millward Brown

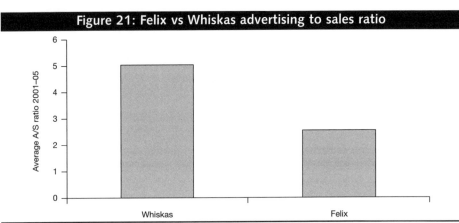

Source: NMR

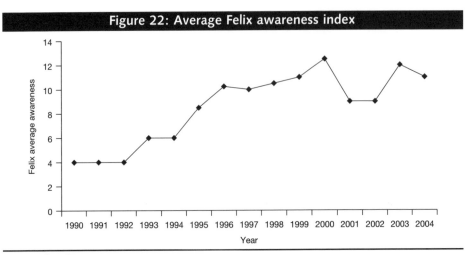

Source: Millward Brown

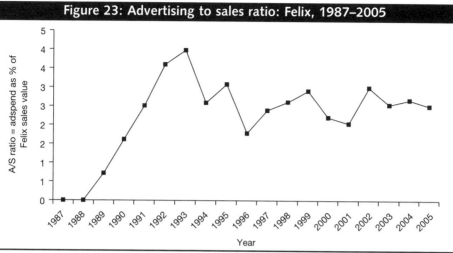

Figure 23: Advertising to sales ratio: Felix, 1987–2005

Sources: ACNielsen, NMR

The fact that the efficiency of Felix advertising has increased over time provides strong support for the idea that continuity drove the efficiency.

## Conclusion

For Felix, the decision to stick with its campaign through a time of wobble paid off handsomely. With a spend of a mere £2.5m per year over 16 years, the Felix campaign transformed a minor brand on the verge of delisting into a mainstream brand with sales of over £138m a year.

Felix has challenged many tenets of current thinking on long-running campaigns.

### Long-running campaigns need changing when market dynamics change

The wet cat food market has changed significantly since the Felix campaign began. But the basic driver for the Felix brand – the relationship between cat and owner – has not. If the insight at the heart of the campaign remains relevant, market changes do not necessitate campaign changes.

### Long-running campaigns can't introduce news

Pouch sales soared in response to their announcement in Felix advertising. And the same campaign also successfully launched a premium variant – 'As Good As It Looks' – to a different sector.

### Long-running campaigns wear out

We have shown how this long-running campaign has become more cost effective and efficient over time. Meanwhile, the constant changing of Whiskas communications means that its media spend needs to be twice as high to maintain just a 2% differential in market share.

*Disruption is good*

Yes, but not always. Back in 1989 Felix built its brand success on a radically different approach. Disruption at its best. But the great skill in marketing is knowing when change is good and when it isn't. Felix has been smart enough to not succumb to change for change's sake.

We work in an industry that celebrates change and the new. We believe this paper is important because it celebrates the opposite. Continuity saved Felix the cat. It may well save your brand, too.

Chapter 19

# Kwik-Fit

Back in the fast lane: how Kwik-Fit broke the rules and reaped the rewards

By Rachel Lawlan, DDB London; David Bassett, DDB Matrix; Clare Newman, MediaCom, and Doug McKenzie, Kwik-Fit
Contributing author: Rachel Congdon, MediaCom

As the market leader in its category, Kwik-Fit was a very well-known brand, enjoying spontaneous awareness of 69% – a figure over 45% higher than its closest competitors. Despite this, sales were in decline, and little had been invested in marketing for some time: indeed, Kwik-Fit was best remembered for a TV campaign last shown in the 80s.

A campaign was needed to revitalise the brand, drive growth, and increase margins, market share and profitability. Initially, communications focused on price, but while an uplift in sales did result, this improvement could not be sustained in the long term. Further research revealed that a high proportion of customers were more concerned with quality, and receiving an honest, reliable service, than price – and that recommendations were powerful influences in the decision making process.

Breaking with industry convention in both creative style and content helped Kwik-Fit overcome 'negative truths' about the industry, and communicate with these consumers, most especially with women, who were often neglected in campaigns for the sector. By adopting a tactical approach, and emphasising softer values rather than focusing exclusively on price, brand communications helped to produce a highly profitable outcome. In the first instance, the 'Recommendations' campaign, with a total spend of £17m, contributed to what was a record-breaking year for Kwik-Fit in 2005. The company was also sold by CVC to PAI in the same year for £800m – a profit of nearly £$\frac{1}{2}$bn on the £330m CVC had paid for it less than three years previously.

## Introduction

This is the story of a retailer that turned market convention on its head.

As market leader, Kwik-Fit was extremely well known. But sales were in decline, little had been invested in marketing for some time, and it was best remembered for a TV campaign last aired in the 80s.

Brand revitalisation was essential. Initially, communications concentrated on price messages, according to received wisdom about the category. Although this led to an uplift in sales, growth proved to be unsustainable.

Research uncovered an entirely different audience and a strategy never tried in this market. Benefits were immediate, showing that brand advertising can work tactically in the short term as well as building equity in the longer term.

In less than three years, this helped to dramatically reverse the fortunes of the company, culminating in a sale netting a staggering £½bn profit.

## The challenge

Kwik-Fit revolutionised the UK aftercare market with the introduction of 'fast fits', offering while-you-wait car part replacements and repairs. The majority of sales have always been tyres and exhausts (>90%) with a smaller contribution from brakes (<10%).

In August 2002, Kwik-Fit was sold to CVC Capital Partners for £330m. CVC had bought an established and famous brand, but there were problems:

- more than half of the market admitted that although they might consider Kwik-Fit, it wouldn't be the first place they'd go
- there was no longer anything to differentiate Kwik-Fit from its competitors
- it had started to feel a bit 'past it', being most famous for the 'You can't get better than a Kwik-Fit fitter' TV campaign last aired more than 15 years ago.

With the growth of the UK car parc (the total number of cars within the country) slowing down, and with technological advances resulting in higher-quality, longer-lasting parts, the market itself was no longer growing (see Figure 1).

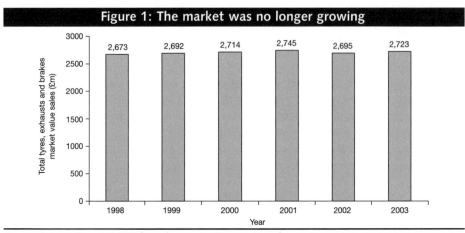

**Figure 1: The market was no longer growing**

Sources: Datamonitor report, ONS for exchange rates (Datamonitor values are in euros)

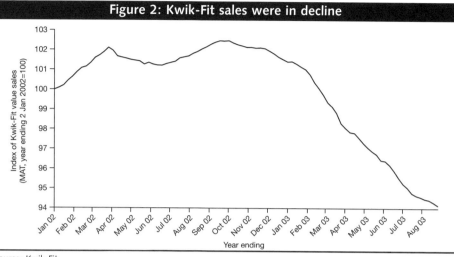

**Figure 2: Kwik-Fit sales were in decline**

Source: Kwik-Fit

These conditions, together with a decline in investment in marketing in previous years, the underperformance of a small proportion of Kwik-Fit centres, and a period of restructuring, had resulted in a downturn in Kwik-Fit's sales (see Figure 2).

The challenge was to:

- stem declining sales and return the company to growth
- increase margins by increasing market share in higher-value products like branded tyres
- increase profitability.

## Our first solution – a 'Price' campaign

In 2003 Kwik-Fit had carried out a survey of competitor prices and realigned its prices – this was what we would talk about in communications.

This fitted in nicely with conventional marketing theory about the fast-fit category, which holds that the majority of the market is already loyal to a garage. Accordingly we needed to target others – non-loyalists. Received wisdom said these people shop on price.

Initial research showed that people had worryingly poor price perceptions of Kwik-Fit. Moreover, people are in the market on average only every 18 months, so price perceptions are very slow to move. It wasn't enough to just lower prices, it was vital to actually tell people about it.

So our communications would address poor price perceptions, using the 'new news' of Kwik-Fit's price realignment. As already noted, the majority of Kwik-Fit's sales come from tyres; however, past communications had tended to focus on budget tyres, which meant that Kwik-Fit had a lower market share in higher-value branded tyres than it would have liked. In order to grow market share in higher-value products, we decided to focus communications on famous-brand tyres.

We took the new price message to TV in July 2003 to maximise impact and awareness; we had an enviable 100% share of voice.

Kwik-Fit had last used television in 2000, using a 'burst' format with limited weeks on air, immediately eliminating a large proportion of its potential audience who weren't in the market at the moments it chose to advertise. MediaCom demonstrated that a continuous presence using a combination of terrestrial and satellite channels would be more effective – we would be there with our price message whenever people were in the market. Our media buyers hand-picked a bespoke range of channels. Our message was that branded tyre prices were coming down and staying down. Our creative was simple and straightforward.

The first execution was so successful it was decided to include exhaust prices as well.

During the 'Price' campaign, MediaCom was commissioned to build econometric models for each of the three key product groups: branded tyres, budget tyres, and exhausts. By analysing how consumers were responding to the price message, econometrics helped determine TV weights and flighting for the rest of the campaign. A diminishing response was identified, where consumers needed to see the ad only once or twice in order to respond (see Figure 3).

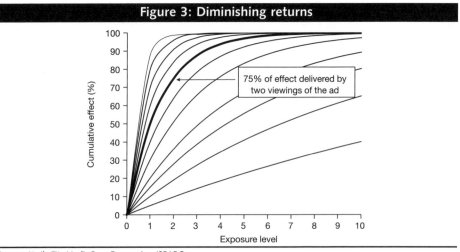

**Figure 3: Diminishing returns**

Source: Kwik-Fit, MediaCom Economiser/SPARC

This response reflects behaviour in the fast-fit category, where people are only in the market for a short period of time. As a result of this insight we were able to run more efficient lower weights for a longer period of time.

## Results of the 'Price' campaign

Figures 4 and 5 demonstrate that spontaneous brand awareness increased and that price perceptions improved. As a result of these shifts, consideration increased (see Figure 6).

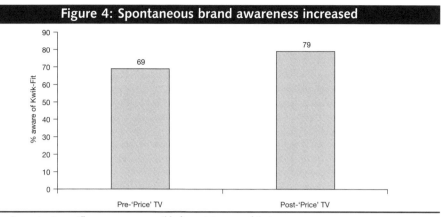

**Figure 4: Spontaneous brand awareness increased**

Source: Synovate. Base: All car owners responsible for maintenance of their car
Pre-'Price' TV (163), post-'Price' TV (247)

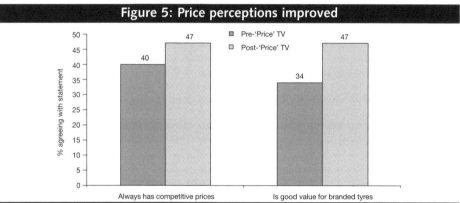

**Figure 5: Price perceptions improved**

Source: Synovate. Base: All car owners responsible for maintenance of their car
Pre-'Price' TV (163), post-'Price' TV (247)

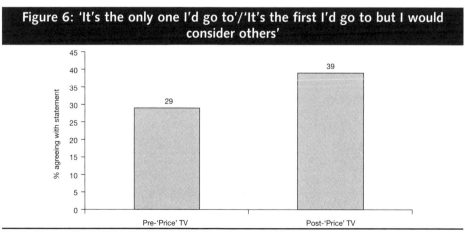

**Figure 6: 'It's the only one I'd go to'/'It's the first I'd go to but I would consider others'**

Source: Synovate. Base: All car owners responsible for maintenance of their car
Pre-'Price' TV (163), post-'Price' TV (247)

And the sales decline was reversed (see Figure 7).

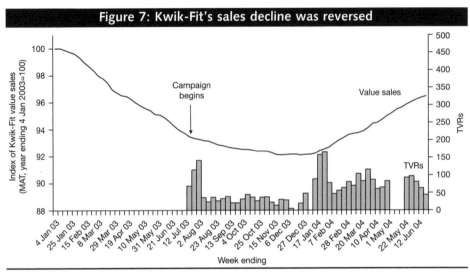

Figure 7: Kwik-Fit's sales decline was reversed

Source: Kwik-Fit, BARB

The 'Price' campaign had a clear effect on sales of branded tyres (see Figure 8).

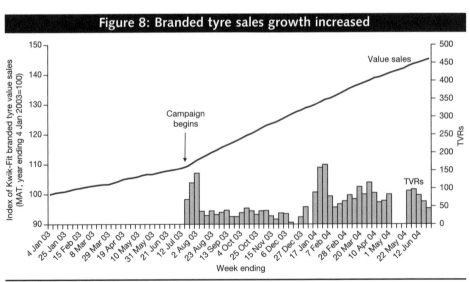

Figure 8: Branded tyre sales growth increased

Source: Kwik-Fit, BARB

Introducing exhausts into communications after the first execution managed to halt the long-term decline in sales (see Figure 9).

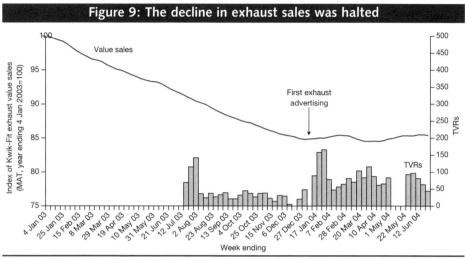

Figure 9: The decline in exhaust sales was halted

Source: Kwik-Fit, BARB

Econometrics identified a strong impact on sales (see Figure 10).

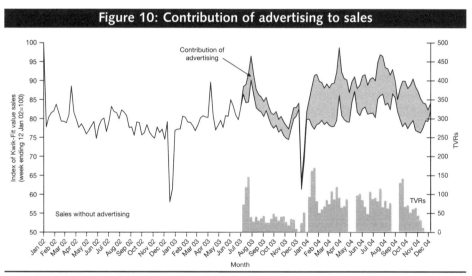

Figure 10: Contribution of advertising to sales

Sources: Kwik-Fit, BARB, MediaCom Economiser

## Worrying signs

However, towards the end of 2004, tracking made clear that, whilst talking about prices coming down had improved price perceptions, there were other, worrying signs emerging. Just talking price was making people think we didn't care about quality (see Figure 11).

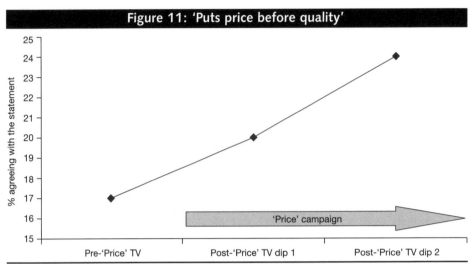

Figure 11: 'Puts price before quality'

Source: Synovate. Base: All car owners responsible for maintenance of their car
Pre-'Price' TV (163), post-'Price' TV dip 1 (247), post-'Price' TV dip 2 (326)

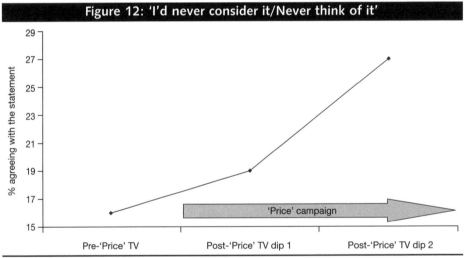

Figure 12: 'I'd never consider it/Never think of it'

Source: Synovate. Base: All car owners responsible for maintenance of their car
Pre-'Price' TV (163), post-'Price' TV dip 1 (247), post-'Price' TV dip 2 (326)

This was leading to a growing proportion of people actually rejecting Kwik-Fit (see Figure 12).

Sales had begun to slow again. The 'Price' message seemed to be running out of steam (see Figure 13).

Modelling also identified a decrease in the effectiveness of the TV activity. Efficiencies had started to fall considerably (see Figure 14).

Our first solution had worked, but only up to a point. Talking about price alone wasn't a sustainable strategy; we were starting to alienate sections of the market.

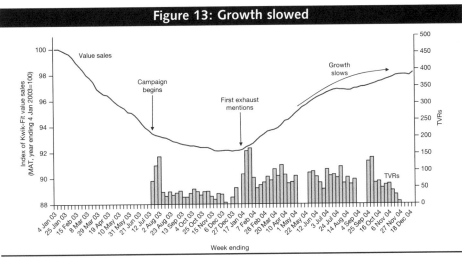

Figure 13: Growth slowed

Source: Kwik-Fit, BARB

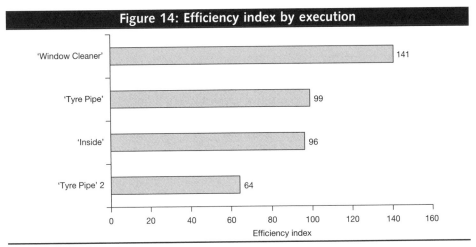

Figure 14: Efficiency index by execution

Source: MediaCom Economiser

## A change in strategy

We took a step back to examine the assumption that in a low-interest category, price is the only thing worth talking about. Focus groups showed we'd got it all wrong. It's not low interest at all – many people feel worried and vulnerable.

In fact, most non-loyalists weren't shopping on price at all – they were desperately looking for recommendations. We discovered this in a twist on the usual way of running focus groups. We ran the groups as usual with non-loyalists, but then invited three loyalists to join at the end to describe why they liked their garage. People began interrogating the startled advocates to within an inch of their lives, scrabbling around in their bags for pens and notebooks to write down the details of the garages and mechanics they were recommending.

| Table 1: Segmentation of non-loyalists | | | | |
|---|---|---|---|---|
| Main reason for deciding where to get repairs done | Convenient location | Ability to do work immediately | Price | Recommendation |
| Percentage of non-loyalists | 16% | 18% | 30% | 36% |
| Gender split | More likely to be male | More likely to be male | Much more likely to be male | Slightly more likely to be female |
| Social grade | BC1 | BC1 | C2DE | ABC1 |
| Income | Moderate (£23–40k) | Moderate (£23–40k) | Low (up to £17k) | Moderate to high (£23–50k) |

Source: TGI PostScript

We carried out a segmentation study to quantify the scale of the opportunity. We discovered that non-loyalists constituted 50% of the market, and recommendation was the biggest single reason for choosing a garage (see Table 1).

We'd discovered a huge segment of the market that no garage had ever spoken to. They were more upmarket and less price-sensitive than price shoppers, and were looking for quality and honest reliable service – attributes Kwik-Fit could offer.

## The creative solution

In research, we discovered what appealed to recommendation seekers most was the fact that normal people had positive experiences at Kwik-Fit. This appeal was heightened when the positive experience was set in the context of a negative expectation. People immediately empathised with these 'negative truths': the sharp intake of breath a mechanic might make as if to say 'That's going to cost you!'; the discomfort many women feel about going to garages. Neither sex enjoys having to organise car repairs, but because men don't like admitting to an 'unmanly' fear of garages, we discovered it was actually easier to address men's fears if they think you're targeting women.

We decided that two of our three executions should feature women. Because garages are pretty much a man's world, women's 'negative truths' tended to be stronger than men's – making for a better story. This encouraged us to do something truly radical: to be the first fast-fit company ever to talk to women sympathetically about their fears about going to garages. Simply acknowledging these negative truths set Kwik-Fit apart from the competition. Using animation allowed us to present relevant but somewhat humdrum situations in an eye-catching way, giving us leeway to exaggerate to make a point and do so credibly.

Media buying was tailored for the male and female 'talking heads', placing them into more male- or female-orientated programming, respectively. Because we were talking to people in a completely new way, we decided to increase weekly weights significantly over the first two weeks, before returning to the more efficient lower weights econometrics had previously identified.

Phase 2 of Kwik-Fit's revitalisation, 'Recommendations', aired on 1 January 2005 and ran throughout the rest of the year.

## Results of the 'Recommendations' campaign

As we have seen, the 'Price' campaign worked well – but 'Recommendations' worked even better. 'Price' TV reversed the pre-campaign decline: advertising the fact Kwik-Fit had cut prices initially stimulated sales but then started to run out of steam. Our service message in 'Recommendations' drove further growth: Kwik-Fit experienced a record-breaking year in 2005 (see Figure 15).

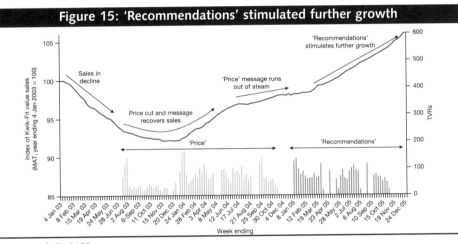

**Figure 15: 'Recommendations' stimulated further growth**

Source: Kwik-Fit, BARB

This was the first time we had talked about brakes on TV so an additional econometric model was created to understand the impact communications were having on brake sales. As with previous TV activity, where the strongest impact was measured the first time we talked about a specific product, 'Recommendations' had a strong impact on brake sales (see Figure 16).

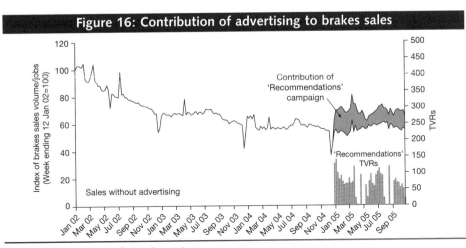

**Figure 16: Contribution of advertising to brakes sales**

Sources: Kwik-Fit, BARB, MediaCom Economiser

## How did we achieve this?

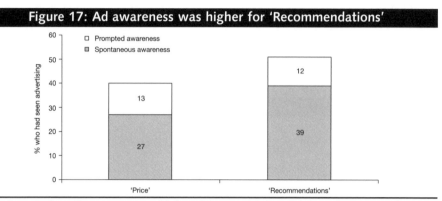

**Figure 17: Ad awareness was higher for 'Recommendations'**

Source: Synovate. Base: All car owners responsible for maintenance of their car. 'Price': weighted average of post-dips for 'Window Cleaner' (239), 'Tyre Pipe' (231), 'Inside' (326). 'Recommendations': post-dip (472)

The ads cut through (see Figure 18).

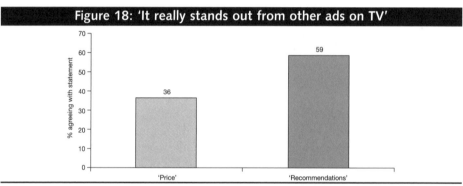

**Figure 18: 'It really stands out from other ads on TV'**

Source: Synovate. Base: All those who recognised the ad. 'Price': weighted average of post-dips for 'Window Cleaner' (100), 'Tyre Pipe' (90), 'Inside' (130). 'Recommendations': post-dip (258)

The advertising communicated simply and clearly (see Figure 19).

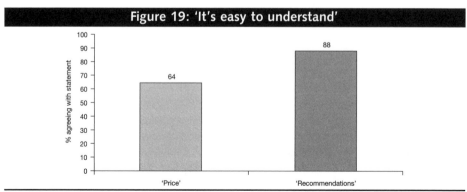

**Figure 19: 'It's easy to understand'**

Source: Synovate. Base: All those who recognised the ad. 'Price': weighted average of post-dips for 'Window Cleaner' (100), 'Tyre Pipe' (90), 'Inside' (130). 'Recommendations': post-dip (258)

The advertising made more people think differently about Kwik-Fit (see Figures 20 and 21).

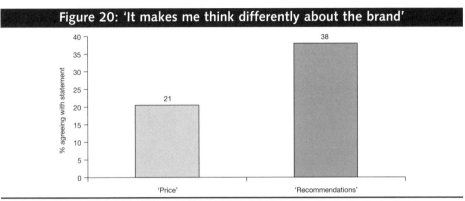

**Figure 20: 'It makes me think differently about the brand'**

Source: Synovate. Base: All those who recognised the ad. 'Price': weighted average of post-dips for 'Window Cleaner' (100), 'Tyre Pipe' (90), 'Inside' (130). 'Recommendations': post-dip (258)

**Figure 21: 'It made the brand seem more appealing'**

Source: Synovate. Base: All those who recognised the ad. 'Price': weighted average of post-dips for 'Window Cleaner' (100), 'Tyre Pipe' (90), 'Inside' (130). 'Recommendations': post-dip (258)

## Proving the effectiveness of communications

It's clear that sales did very well. But was it really our advertising campaign that was responsible? We'll now look at four pieces of evidence to prove that the effect on sales was the result of our advertising, namely:

- sales movements coincided with the timing of our advertising
- sales at Kwik-Fit outperformed those at Tyre Plus (a natural 'control')
- no other factors can explain the sales increase
- econometric analysis proves and quantifies the effect from advertising.

### Timing

Figures 22–24 show that sales of tyres, exhausts and brakes increased when these items were included in the ads during the campaign.

**Figure 22: When we talked about tyres, tyre sales improved**

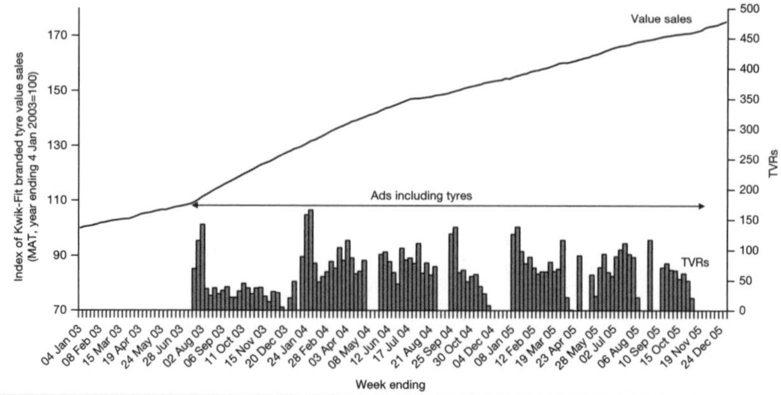

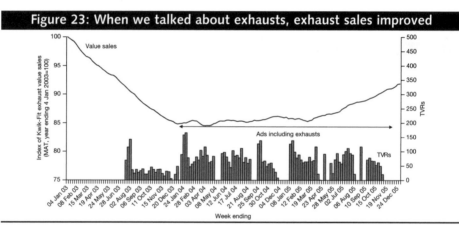

Source: Kwik-Fit, BARB

**Figure 23: When we talked about exhausts, exhaust sales improved**

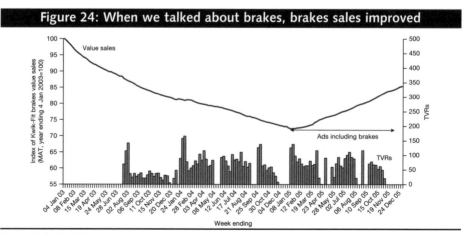

Source: Kwik-Fit, BARB

**Figure 24: When we talked about brakes, brakes sales improved**

Source: Kwik-Fit, BARB

## A natural control

Sales have increased, but could this be explained by market growth? Unfortunately we don't have access to detailed market data. However, one of Kwik-Fit's biggest competitors, ATS Euromaster, submitted an IPA paper in 2005, which shows that its sales fell by about 2% in 2004. Datamonitor forecasts back this up, suggesting that the market as a whole was in slight decline.

Fortunately, we also have a natural control for the state of the market: Tyre Plus outlets. Tyre Plus is the collective name for 95 fast-fit centres owned and run by Kwik-Fit but not Kwik-Fit branded – they trade as local independents or small regional chains. Since January 2004 these centres have had the same products, pricing structure and run the same promotions as Kwik-Fit, with marketing support in local press. The only difference between the two is the Kwik-Fit branding and the lack of TV support for Tyre Plus stores. We can therefore use Tyre Plus sales as a proxy for what was happening in the fast-fit market over this period.

In 2005, Kwik-Fit significantly outperformed Tyre Plus (see Figure 25).

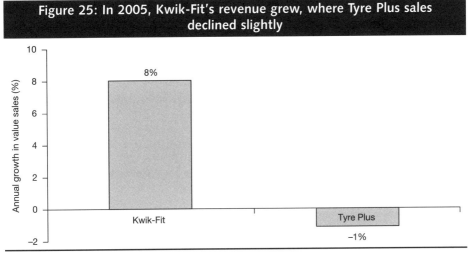

**Figure 25: In 2005, Kwik-Fit's revenue grew, where Tyre Plus sales declined slightly**

Source: Kwik-Fit

The Tyre Plus evidence means that it's safe to assume Kwik-Fit was actually growing market share over this period, rather than merely growing sales.

Furthermore, we can use more detailed weekly sales data to prove that it was the advertising that caused Kwik-Fit to outperform Tyre Plus. Figure 26 shows the ratio of Kwik-Fit sales to Tyre Plus sales over time, a measure of the relative performance of the two store chains. The figure also shows the adstock, a measure of cumulative advertising support. It is clear that these two measures move in synch with one another. When Kwik-Fit advertises, performance relative to Tyre Plus improves. When Kwik-Fit is off air, performance relative to Tyre Plus slips back. The close correlation between these two measures suggests that advertising was the main reason why Kwik-Fit did so much better than Tyre Plus. In other words, if we hadn't advertised, sales at Kwik-Fit would have fallen, as they did with Tyre Plus.

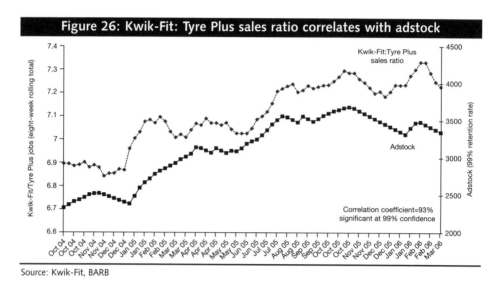

Figure 26: Kwik-Fit: Tyre Plus sales ratio correlates with adstock

Source: Kwik-Fit, BARB

## No other factors can explain these results

Could there be other factors that would explain the sales growth? Here we eliminate five other factors that might cause sales to increase.

### Number of centres

During the period we went back on air, the number of centres actually decreased by 11%.

### Price

Since our price realignment in July 2003, Kwik-Fit prices have tracked the market (see Figure 27). Also, prices were the same in Tyre Plus stores and in Kwik-Fit, so price cannot explain Kwik-Fit's sales increase.

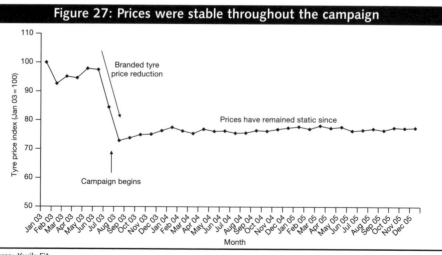

Figure 27: Prices were stable throughout the campaign

Source: Kwik-Fit

## Customer promotions

These were exactly the same for Tyre Plus as they were for Kwik-Fit over the period in question, so we can eliminate them as a reason for the sales increase.

## Product range

The product range has been exactly the same at Tyre Plus as it has been at Kwik-Fit, allowing us to discount it as a reason for Kwik-Fit's superior sales growth.

## Competitors

Again, Tyre Plus faces exactly the same competition as Kwik-Fit, meaning that we can discount changes in the competitive context and the effects of competitive advertising as explanations for Kwik-Fit's increase in revenue.

### *Econometrics*

Ongoing analysis has provided vital accountability across all campaigns. Econometrics has helped drive the shape of the campaigns. By taking account of all key drivers in the market we have been able to understand and quantify the effects of all communications. Figure 28 demonstrates the effects of advertising separated from other factors (such as price, distribution, seasonality, and so on), showing both campaigns were highly effective and played a vital role in revitalising the brand, but that, contrary to all received ideas of how communications work in the fast-fit category, the new 'Recommendations' service message was working more efficiently than the price message. The impact was seen across all key products (see Figures 29–31).

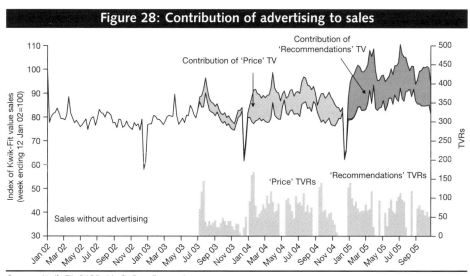

**Figure 28: Contribution of advertising to sales**

Sources: Kwik-Fit, BARB, MediaCom Economiser

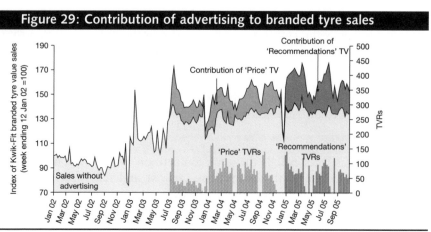

Sources: Kwik-Fit, BARB, MediaCom Economiser

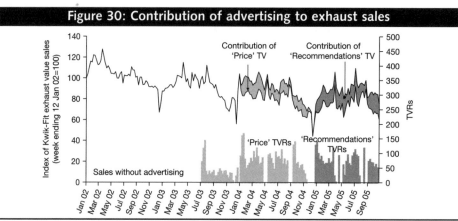

Sources: Kwik-Fit, BARB, MediaCom Economiser

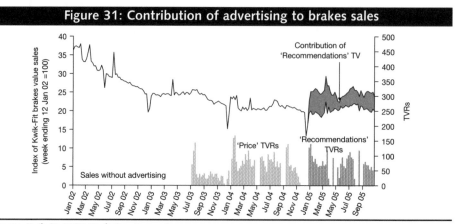

Sources: Kwik-Fit, BARB, MediaCom Economiser

## Proving the efficiency of communications

Econometrics also identified that, as we'd seen with the 'Price' campaign, consumers didn't need to see the ad many times in order to respond. Using this information, we were able to adjust communication weights and flighting as both campaigns progressed, thus increasing efficiencies even further. This meant media spend could be lower for 'Recommendations' than it was for Price (see Figure 32).

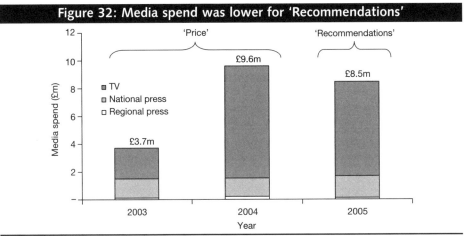

**Figure 32: Media spend was lower for 'Recommendations'**

Sources: MediaCom, Nielsen Media Research

'Recommendations' drove more revenue than talking about price, and did so with lower media spend, so efficiencies were higher (see Figure 33).

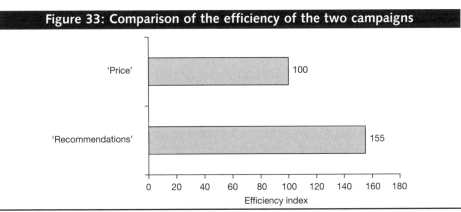

**Figure 33: Comparison of the efficiency of the two campaigns**

Source: MediaCom Economiser

## Payback

Our 'Price' campaign led to an increase in sales, which saw profits increasing from £43.6m in 2003 to £58.8m in 2004.

As the 'Price' campaign started to run out of steam, our decision to change strategy and talk about service rather than price proved even more profitable. Unfortunately the 2005 audit has not been completed, so we cannot quote a figure. The figure being audited, however, comfortably exceeds previous years and represents a record-breaking year for Kwik-Fit.

We have been able to use econometrics to calculate return on investment from our campaign. Overall, across both the 'Price' and 'Recommendations' campaigns, for every £1 Kwik-Fit spent it got £1.55 back as profit (£1.37 for 'Price' and £1.74 for 'Recommendations').

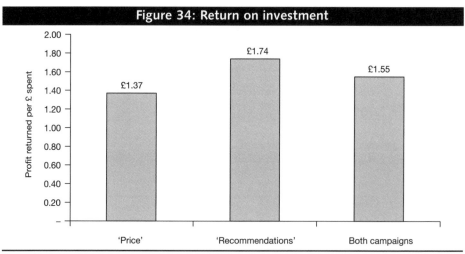

**Figure 34: Return on investment**

Source: MediaCom Economiser

Of all the 2004 IPA Effectiveness Awards winners, just four reported a return on investment in terms of profit generated per pound spent. If we compare these ROI figures with our own, it becomes apparent that this was one of the most effective campaigns you are likely to see in a long time (see Table 2).

**Table 2: Return on investment**

|  | ROI |
| --- | --- |
| Direct Line | £4.11 |
| **Kwik-Fit ('Recommendations')** | £1.74 |
| British Airways | £1.70 |
| Cravendale | £1.30 |
| Bounty | £1.10 |

Source: *Advertising Works 13*

## Conclusion

This paper has shown how communications helped to revitalise Kwik-Fit, turning the business around.

Phase 1: our return to television to tell people about Kwik-Fit's price realignment, helped to correct negative price perceptions and reverse the decline in sales Kwik-Fit had been experiencing.

Phase 2: our service campaign, was based on a strategy never tested before in this market, but focusing on service rather than price proved even more profitable.

## Chapter 20

# Monopoly Here & Now

Pass Go, Collect £1.5 million: how a radical, experiential approach to communications reinvigorated Monopoly – turning it into the best-selling game of 2005

By Georgina Murray-Burton, DDB London; Matt Dyke, Tribal DDB, and Tristram Harrison, DDB Matrix
Contributing authors: Les Binet, DDB Matrix; Sarah Carter, DDB London; Alex Ebdon, OMD UK, and Matt Law, Tribal DDB

This case study shows how one of the oldest board games in the world used a highly modern communications strategy to connect with a new generation of consumers. To celebrate Monopoly's 70th anniversary in the UK, owner Hasbro decided to launch a new limited-edition version of the game – Monopoly Here & Now. The new board depicted London in the 21st century, with features such as updated locations, modern game pieces and even revised property prices.

With ambitious sales targets to meet, it was decided that the media approach should move away from the traditional 'interruption' model of marketing, and instead attempt to encourage consumers to actively engage with brand communications.

This was achieved by turning the streets of London into a giant, real-life game of Monopoly Here & Now, using taxis as playing pieces. By investing in an online platform for the game, Hasbro was able to ensure that people actually played the game for themselves, rather than merely associating it with their childhood memories.

The campaign and the positive word of mouth that followed not only created a buzz around Monopoly, but also persuaded people to go out and buy it. As a result, Monopoly Here & Now became the best-selling family game of 2005, and sold out of stock just two weeks prior to Christmas. By the end of the year, total Monopoly sales had improved by 35% (double the initial target), with analysis showing that communications contributed some £1.5m in sales.

## Introduction

This is a story of success against all the odds. We show how one of the oldest board games in the world recaptured the hearts of a nation and reignited the British public's passion for competing against one another to make money.

It is the story of how a radically different media idea resulted in a massive sales uplift and a return far exceeding the initial investment by Hasbro.

## Background

People love to play and no game is better than Monopoly at fuelling this desire. Launched in Britain in 1935, it has sold over 20 million sets.

In celebration of its 70th anniversary in the UK, Hasbro launched a new limited edition version of the game: Monopoly 'Here & Now', depicting twenty-first century London.

## The marketing objectives

Our overall objective was to increase the total sales value of Monopoly by 15%, by the end of 2005. Specifically:

- to sell all of UK Monopoly Here & Now Limited Edition stock by the end of 2005
- to break from the entrenched seasonality of board game sales and increase sales over the summer by 30% year-on-year from 2004
- create a 'buzz' around Monopoly in its 70th-anniversary year
- broaden the appeal of the brand beyond young families.

## The challenge

A number of barriers stood in the way of success.

- **Saturated brand:** the vast majority of UK families already owned a copy of the game.
- **No licence:** Hasbro has become more and more reliant on variants such as *The Simpsons* and *Star Wars* to sustain market value share. Due to the popularity of the products being licensed, such products sell very well. Monopoly Here & Now did not have a ready-made audience like this, and needed to be launched without such a guaranteed sales avenue.
- **Higher price point:** it was clearly not going to be easy to get people to shell out for an updated and more expensive version of a game they already own.
- **Less family time:** we are all familiar with the increasing pressures on family time.
- **Entrenched seasonality:** Monopoly sales always suffer a predictable slump outside the key Christmas shopping months of November and December (see Figure 1).
- **Lack of category interest outside family target:** in order to meet the ambitious sales targets, we would have to reach a much broader audience than families, an audience that claimed, in qualitative research, to 'have absolutely no interest in board games'.

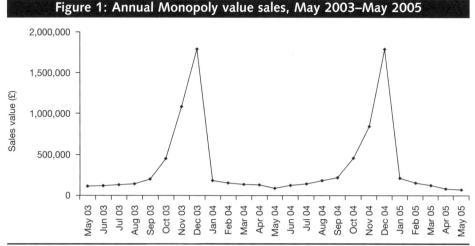

**Figure 1: Annual Monopoly value sales, May 2003–May 2005**

Source: NPD EPOS

## Our startpoint

When talking about Monopoly in research, people had fond memories of playing the game: tales of trying to sneak a couple of extra notes from the bank when no one was looking, humorous Community Chest cards, various theories on playing strategy. However, people also recounted as many *less* positive memories of the game: it's complicated, takes hours (even days) to play, it's a bit boring (when you are losing!).

When we stopped *talking* about the new updated edition and actually put the board down in front of them, people became much more enthusiastic. From research, two things became clear.

1. The interesting news wasn't necessarily just that Monopoly had been updated. Rather, the key to creating a buzz seemed to centre on how *London had changed*.
2. Additionally, we felt that just *telling* people how Monopoly (or even London) had changed would not be enough. Instead, could we get people to discover the new board for themselves? Better still, could we reignite their passion for Monopoly by getting them to actually *play* it?

## The ingenious solution

For one month, we turned the streets of London into a real-life game of Monopoly Here & Now! We called it Monopoly Live.

Real-life locations in London corresponded with the updated locations on the board. We recruited London black cabs, equipped with GPS transmitters to act as our life-size playing pieces, offered a host of prizes, and anybody in the country could play the game via our dedicated website.

## The business case

We worked with Hasbro to project not only how sales success might play out, but also the additional value that the project might bring to Hasbro. We calculated that the additional value from this campaign might come in the shape of:

■ modernising Monopoly in the eyes of the public and the trade, having long-lasting effects on the future of the Monopoly brand (and Hasbro)
■ the accumulation of a database of players who could be invited to take part in future Hasbro marketing activity
■ the novelty of the event might give us leverage to ask for free prizes and incentives from partners
■ the value of text messages (to enhance game play) sent by players to Hasbro during the period of the event
■ the use of the UK event as a test market for Hasbro Global.

## Playing Monopoly Live

Once the additional budget had been signed off, the real fun began. How exactly were we going to pull off a nationwide multiplayer event, which took place live in a real capital city?

*How to play*

■ Consumers were able to participate in the live national event by visiting www.monopolylive.com.
■ Each game lasted for 24 hours and the event lasted one month, so there was an opportunity for people to join in every day.
■ At the beginning of each game every player was handed £15m in virtual Monopoly money (oh yes, that had been updated too!).
■ Each player spent their money on property sets and strategically placed flats and hotels.
■ Finally, each player picked a playing piece.

We had signed up 18 cabbies to act as the playing pieces (three cabbies per piece). As the cabbies went around their daily business, their movements either gained or lost our players virtual money over 24 hours as their passing the locations was logged by the GPS.

*The prizes*

To encourage people to sign up and play in the live event, there were prizes awarded every day of the competition. All prizes were negotiated from other brands in return for being featured in Monopoly Live.

The grand prize (having your mortgage/rent paid for a year) was awarded by a prize draw at the end of the event (one entry to the draw for every £1m made).

## Bringing the campaign to life

Conventionally the toy industry demands television advertising, as retailers need the assurance that the product will be adequately promoted (see Figure 2).

## Figure 2: Conventional communications approach

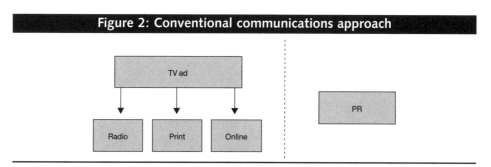

## Figure 3: Our radical communications approach

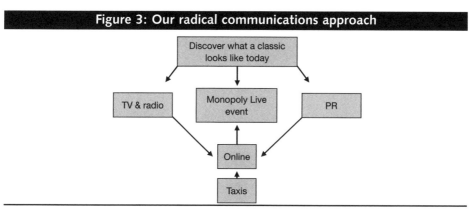

We flipped the model on its head and put the brand experience at the centre, with each media channel both supporting this experience and performing its own key task (see Figure 3). Monopoly Live was to be our central brand experience.

## The communications plan

Figure 4 presents the communications plan, centring around launch activity in June 2005.

### Figure 4: Communications plan for Monopoly Here & Now launch activity

| Event | June | | | | | | | | | | | | | | | |
|---|---|---|---|---|---|---|---|---|---|---|---|---|---|---|---|---|
| | Sun 12th | Mon 13th | Tue 14th | Wed 15th | Thu 16th | Fri 17th | Sat 18th | Sun 19th | Mon 20th | Tue 21st | Wed 22nd | Thu 23rd | Fri 24th | Sat 25th | Sun 26th | |
| Coverage in Sunday press – teaser stories to build up to launch day on 16th June | | | | | | | | | | | | | | | | |
| Hamleys' window goes live | | | | | | | | | | | | | | | | July 3rd |
| Monopoly Here & Now goes on sale! | | | | | | | | | | | | | | | | |
| Prize draw promotion with 'win a trip to Philadelphia' | | | | | | | | | | | | | | | | 1st 200K units |
| My Monopoly Here & Now site goes live | | | | | | | | | | | | | | | | |
| Launch event and charity sale with Cherie Booth | | | | | | | | | | | | | | | | |
| Press coverage from launch event | | | | | | | | | | | | | | | | |
| GMTV Kids Toonatik coverage and competition | | | | | | | | | | | | | | | | |
| Play Monopoly at school week to raise money for Shelter (Monopoly's charity) | | | | | | | | | | | | | | | | |
| Monopoly Live event launches | | | | | | | | | | | | | | | | July 15th |
| Yahoo! home page banner link to Monopoly Live | | | | | | | | | | | | | | | | |
| TV advertising on Channel 4, Five, GMTV, Satellite daytime and selected peak | | | | | | | | | | | | | | | | |
| TV advertising on Big Brother eviction night | | | | | | | | | | | | | | | | |
| Online advertising – Monopoly Live registrations link | | | | | | | | | | | | | | | | |
| Radio advertising | | | | | | | | | | | | | | | | |
| Competitions on local radio across the nation – win a game! | | | | | | | | | | | | | | | | |
| Organised play at key sites | | | | | | | | | | | | | | | | |
| PR coverage | | | | | | | | | | | | | | | | |

*PR*

The key role for PR was to spark the debate around the changes to London on the Here & Now game board.

> *I was amused to read that in the new version of Monopoly devised to reflect the changing face of London, they have replaced the railway stations with London City Airport and Stansted, and Bond Street has been axed for the King's Road. But what have they done about Free Parking?*
>
> Tom Byers, W1
>
> *Evening Standard* letters page, January 2005

*TV and radio*

The key role for TV and radio advertising (TV: 1 × 20-sec execution; radio: 1 × 30-sec execution) was to build awareness of Monopoly Here & Now and entice people to go online and discover the new board for themselves at monopolylive.com.

*Online*

Online advertising was used to further direct people to monopolylive.com.

*Taxis*

Finally we had our 'playing piece' taxis as an outdoor presence, bringing the idea to life!

> *The most exciting thing was seeing a Monopoly cab when I was out in Soho, it made it come to life and all the more exciting.*
>
> Source: DDB qualitative research

## What happened?

The launch of the Monopoly Here & Now board game was an amazing success.

1. Here & Now was the best-selling family game of 2005 and we sold out of stock (see Table 1).

| Table 1: Top-selling games, 2005 | | |
|---|---|---|
| Rank | Game | Sales value (2005) |
| 1 | Monopoly Here & Now | £1,525,546 |
| 2 | Monopoly Classic | £1,303,243 |
| 3 | Scrabble Original | £1,145,987 |
| 4 | Scene It? DVD Game | £941,645 |
| 5 | Simpsons Monopoly | £927,151 |
| 6 | Cluedo | £733,944 |
| 7 | Harry Potter Scene It? | £669,359 |
| 8 | Simpsons Cluedo | £513,533 |
| 9 | Star Wars Monopoly | £363,033 |
| 10 | Risk | £247,187 |

Source: NPD EPOS

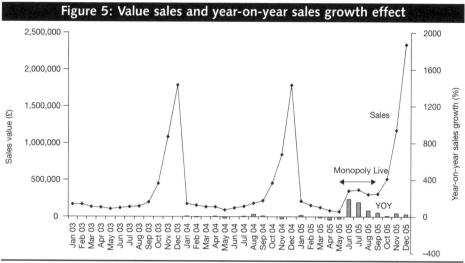

Figure 5: Value sales and year-on-year sales growth effect

Source: NPD EPOS

2. By the end of 2005, total sales for Monopoly were up 35% on the previous year (more than double our ambitious target) (see Figure 5).
3. We countered the seasonal slump of board games with sales of Monopoly up 200% year-on-year in June 2005. This mid-year success was carried through to Christmas.
4. We achieved our target, with Monopoly Here & Now stock selling out just two weeks before Christmas!
5. We created a buzz around Monopoly in its anniversary year.
6. We engaged with and persuaded a broader audience to purchase Monopoly.

## How it all worked

The integrated push clearly encouraged people to get online and play (see Figure 6). Figure 7 shows how each channel played its role in raising awareness of monopolylive.com.

Now we will look at the contribution of each media in turn.

### Online advertising

The key role for online advertising was to direct players through to the monopolylive.com website, to play the game. The advertising was very effective at fulfilling this role, delivering 240,552 visits to the website, resulting in 43,597 registered players (just under one-quarter of the overall total number of players).

### TV and radio advertising

TV advertising was the most significant driver of our core audience (mums) to the website (see Figure 8).

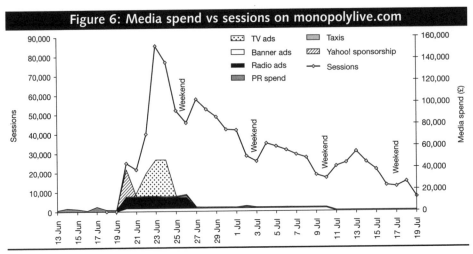

Figure 6: Media spend vs sessions on monopolylive.com

Source: Tribal DDB, MMS

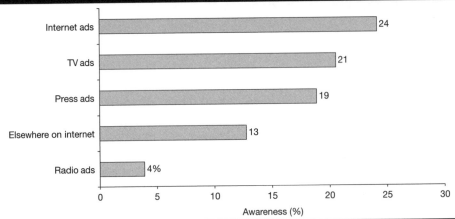

Figure 7: Medium through which players discovered monopolylive.com and Monopoly Here & Now

Source: The Bridge, Online quantitative research. Base: 2789

### The Monopoly Live taxis

Post-event research among the cabbies revealed that they often ended up chatting about the promotion to passengers several times every day, for the whole period of the campaign and were really proud to be part of the event:

*A lot of passengers ask what the campaign is 'all about'. Additionally, more passengers and tourists ask to take pictures of the cab than of any other campaign I've ever participated in!*

Brian Kent

## Figure 8: How core audience discovered the event in comparison to total audience

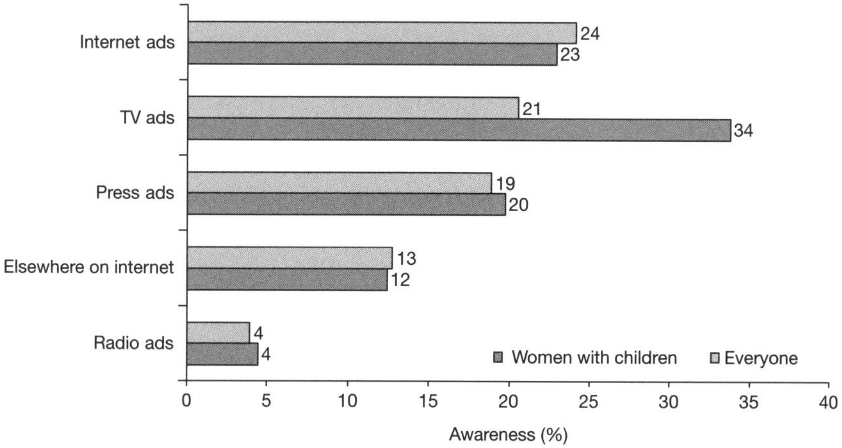

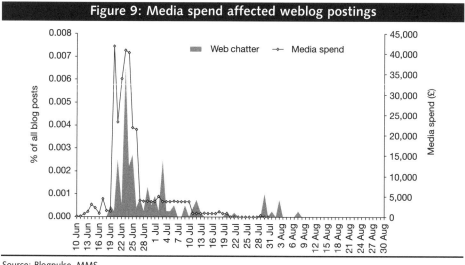

| | Women with children | Everyone |
|---|---|---|
| Internet ads | 24 | 23 |
| TV ads | 21 | 34 |
| Press ads | 19 | 20 |
| Elsewhere on internet | 13 | 12 |
| Radio ads | 4 | 4 |

Awareness (%)

Source: The Bridge, online quantitative research. Base: 2789

*Quite a few have mentioned that they like the advertising and even mentioned going online before they even rode in the cab.*

John Hayes

### PR

PR's role was to alert people to the new Here & Now board game and get people discussing the updates. The calculated value created by the planned PR was £3.7m. The interesting news was the PR or word of mouth generated by the sheer intrigue of Monopoly Live (see Figure 9).

## Figure 9: Media spend affected weblog postings

Web chatter    Media spend

Source: Blogpulse, MMS

*The 'ripple effect'*

The event really caught the imagination of key influencers in the blogosphere, who were primarily drawn to the scale of the live event and the creativity of using GPS in the taxi cabs. These influencers are extremely hard to reach through traditional media and even harder to persuade with traditional marketing messages. The resulting player-generated PR, driven through online chat, ended up being beyond our wildest dreams.

These important players wrote about the game in over 300 well-regarded blogs and websites during the live event, with many more contributing to the online buzz in the shape of chat forum discussions. Whilst the majority of this content was generated by early adopters and the younger internet generation, the readership of that content was a more mainstream audience.

Early on in the campaign, the infamous website Slashdot.org featured the monopolylive.com web address. Then media sites like *Wired* magazine's wired.com picked up on the story, making it their 'Website of the Month', and commenting:

> *That someone had the idea to tag up London taxis with GPS and use them as pawns in a giant interactive board game is Geek++.*

As momentum gathered, more mainstream offline titles then covered the story in detail. It was this ripple effect through media circles that sustained the talk value throughout the duration of the campaign (and well beyond).

## The Monopoly Live game

The game itself was a tremendous success. Over a million unique users visited monopolylive.com in one month. A total of 189,699 of them played the game an average of three times, staying on the site for over 14 minutes.

Although the average number of games played was three, there were also a hardcore group of players who got really carried away, some playing every day of the event! These 'hardcore' players also took advantage of the many enhanced features of the game, collectively sending 45,477 premium SMS text messages to Hasbro for virtual 'Chance' and 'Community Chest' cards (for further chances to win prizes).

Who were these 'hardcore' gamers? No, not the young geeky boys locked away in their bedrooms, but actually the older players (see Figure 10)!

## A positive consumer experience drove sales

Those people that took part in Monopoly Live really enjoyed playing, with three-quarters recommending it to friends (see Figure 11).

We attained the broader audience we had set out to persuade, with people of all ages playing the game.

And the more people played Monopoly Live, the greater their consideration to purchase the Here & Now board game (see Figure 12).

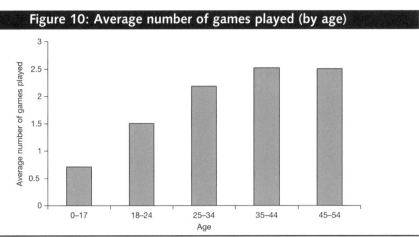

## Figure 10: Average number of games played (by age)

Source: Tribal DDB

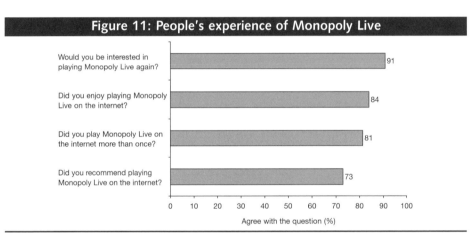

## Figure 11: People's experience of Monopoly Live

Source: The Bridge, online quantitative research. Base: 2789

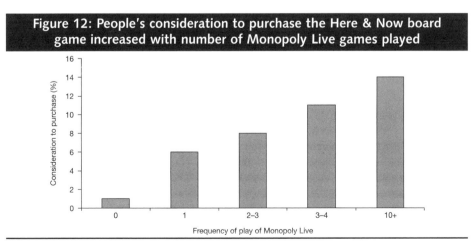

## Figure 12: People's consideration to purchase the Here & Now board game increased with number of Monopoly Live games played

Source: The Bridge, online quantitative research. Base: 2789

The greater the number of people signing up to the website; the greater the sales (see Figure 13).

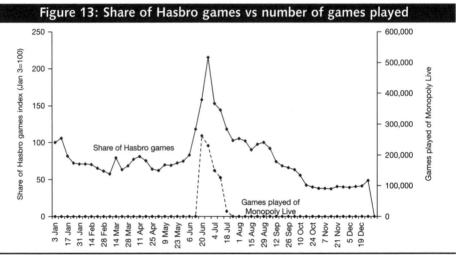

Figure 13: Share of Hasbro games vs number of games played

Source: Tribal DDB, Hasbro UK

## Board game sales success was as a result of communications

Three pieces of evidence demonstrate irrefutably that the sales success was a direct result of our communications.

1. Our market share increased, ruling out overall market growth as the cause (see Figure 14).

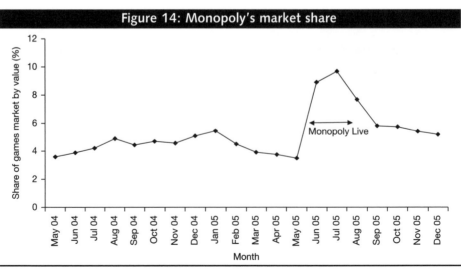

Figure 14: Monopoly's market share

Source: NPD EPOS

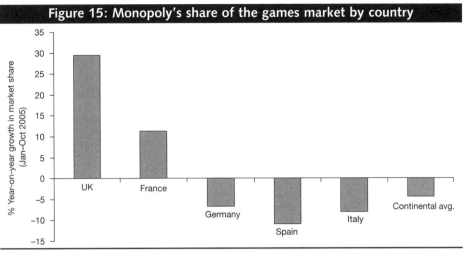

Figure 15: Monopoly's share of the games market by country

Source: NPS EPOS

2. Success was not simply a result of the new Monopoly Here & Now board game being on the shelves. The product was also launched at the same time across Europe. Monopoly Live ran only in the UK. Across Europe, Monopoly's share of the total games market declined, whilst in the UK it increased (see Figure 15).

3. Furthermore, sales in the UK begin to diverge from Europe at precisely the point that Monopoly Live began (see Figure 16).

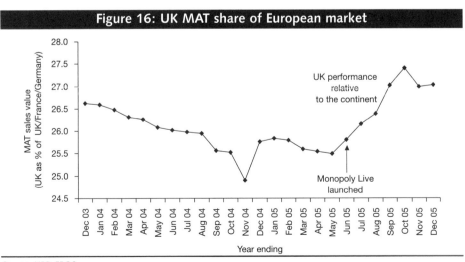

Figure 16: UK MAT share of European market

Source: NPD EPOS

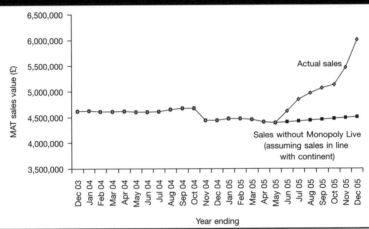

Figure 17: MAT sales value with and without effect of running our communications

Source: NPD EPOS

## The payback

### Sales payback

The launch of the Monopoly Here & Now board game in many European markets at the same time as in the UK created a large regional test. If we had not run our full communications plan, we can assume that UK sales would have grown in line with those of Europe. However, we did, and as a result sales reached an additional £1.5m in value (see Figure 17).

The total cost of the campaign was under £600,000 including media and production (source: Hasbro data and OMD); the profit generated from these extra sales more than covered the costs of running the campaign.

### Wider payback

In addition to the direct contribution to sales, we also:

■ negotiated £30,000 in free prize funds off the strength of the idea, thus reducing the overall operating costs
■ generated a database of 156,115 opted-in consumers for Hasbro marketing activity, calculated to be worth £608,848 over three years
■ generated text revenue in excess of £5,000.

## Conclusion

This case study represents a watershed for the IPA, its member agencies and every marketer looking for solid business proof of the value of new ways of communicating.

It does not sound the death knell for the 30-sec TV ad, nor does it claim the internet is the holy grail. But, what it does prove is the huge payback from ideas that are strong enough to create their own audience.

## Chapter 21

# Nicorette

## Sold not dispensed: the power of consumer brands vs pharmaceutical brands

By Toby Horry and James Miller, Abbott Mead Vickers.BBDO

Pharmaceutical brands generally don't travel well. In particular, their cross-border growth tends to be constrained by cultural attitudes towards health and medicine, which vary greatly by country. Despite this, Pfizer aimed to pursue its ambition of making Nicorette a billion-dollar global brand by 2010. Achieving this objective required a new idea that would drive growth in both new and established markets – especially in the UK, where the sector was in a 3% decline.

In an effort to do so, it sought to replicate the strategies of consumer brands from other market sectors, which connected with consumers worldwide on an emotional – rather than clinical – level. As such, a strategy was adopted that repositioned Nicorette from its traditional placement as a pharmaceutical brand, transforming it into a consumer one.

The creative element of this campaign focused on the individual battles that smokers have with each cigarette, based on the proposition that every craving they beat counted as a personal victory. This challenge was embodied in the 'Cravings Man', a 2.5 metre-high cigarette with arms, legs and a face. His image was used on everything from TV commercials to outdoor and in-store media. As a result, and largely as a consequence of the success of the 'Cravings Man' campaign, from 2000–2004 Nicorette grew from seven advertised countries to 16, and from $194m in sales to $295m, establishing itself as the clear market leader as it did so.

## Introduction

This paper will show how taking Nicorette out of its natural pharmaceutical environment and repositioning it as an integrated consumer brand allowed us to meet our international aspirations. From 2000 to 2004, based largely on the success of the 'Cravings Man' campaign, Nicorette grew from seven advertised countries to 16, from $194m to $295m in sales, and established itself as the clear market leader.

## The challenge of international growth

Abbott Mead Vickers.BBDO was appointed late in 2000 by Pharmacia (later Pfizer), with a brief to establish Nicorette as the dominant player in nicotine replacement therapy (NRT) across Europe in the face of increasingly aggressive competition. Specifically the business objectives were:

- make Nicorette the NRT brand that most smokers are aware of and would consider first
- establish a clear leadership position in perceptions of the brand
- establish sales leadership
- drive double-digit year-on-year growth across Europe.

In a new category or with a new product, these objectives would have seemed very achievable, but Nicorette and other brands of NRT have been available in Europe since the late 70s. Indeed, in 2000 NRT was already a $474m category in Europe.

By 2001 we were established in seven countries: UK, France, Sweden, Ireland, Germany, Italy and Spain.

Growth in established markets presented a real challenge. In the UK, in 2000 the NRT market was worth $188m and in slight decline (–3%). In Sweden, the first NRT market in Europe, the $39m market declined 7.5% in 2001.

## The business challenges

There were four key challenges.

1. All the brands sounded largely the same – Nicorette, Nicotinell, NiQuitin – a dynamic we refer to as 'nico-confusion'
2. All the brands had largely identical products, in pharmaceutical terms 'bio-equivalent'.
3. The only thing to differentiate the products were cosmetic benefits – flavour, size of tablet, colour of patch, and so on, and we were at a real disadvantage vs the competition. NiQuitin had a clear patch, aesthetically better than our patch. Nicotinell had coated gums that tasted better than ours.
4. We also lagged behind competitors on the launch of new SKUs in the period 2000–2004 (see Figure 1).

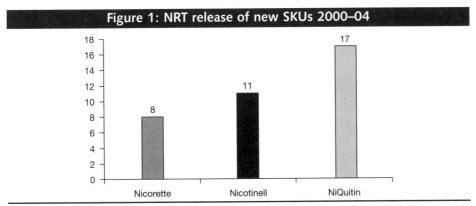

Figure 1: NRT release of new SKUs 2000–04

Source: IRI

## The need for a consumer brand and creative idea

The key to unlocking international growth came from one core insight: pharmaceutical brands don't cross borders, consumer brands built on fundamental human truths and insights do.

Attitudes towards health vary markedly across countries, which makes developing international pharmaceutical brands problematic. This is particularly true when it comes to smoking, where attitudes vary widely across Europe: in some places tobacco advertising is banned, in others there are rigorous government-sponsored anti-smoking campaigns, in some there are smoking bans in public places, in others cigarettes are still advertised and a 'smoke 'em if you've got 'em' attitude prevails. While a general public acceptance of the dangers of smoking and the benefits of quitting pervades large parts of the continent, elsewhere the attitude is more laissez-faire. This variation is exacerbated by regulation that varies across markets; a claim that can be made in one country might not be approved in another.

When we spoke to smokers and learned more about their attitudes towards their habit, it confirmed that we needed to think of Nicorette not as a pharmaceutical brand, but as a consumer brand.

## Smoking: a lifestyle choice not a medical condition

Even those smokers who wanted to quit weren't interested in a typical pharmaceutical brand that would tell them how to deal with their 'problem'. They wanted a brand that felt like it was on their side. The real potential was for a champion of smokers as consumers.

## Developing a consumer brand

To move from the pharmaceutical world to the consumer world:

■ strategically, we decided to challenge the conventions of anti-smoking advertising and establish Nicorette as the brand that helps rather than hectors people to quit

■ creatively we had to develop an idea that championed smokers, would work across Europe, be instantly recognisable and could become synonymous with the category

## The consumer insight that crossed borders

Our breakthrough came in qualitative research. Quite simply, most smokers can't imagine giving up cigarettes altogether. What they can imagine is giving up one or two cigarettes, or at best giving up for a few days. They can imagine winning a battle but not the war.

Brands that focused on the end-point of being smoke free put smokers off because they presented an 'unattainable' goal. We could make smokers feel better about Nicorette and their quit attempt by presenting a more honest and accessible goal. Nicorette will help you fight the battles with individual cigarettes.

In research the proposition seemed to resonate internationally (see Figure 2).

### Figure 2: Checking our emotional proposition

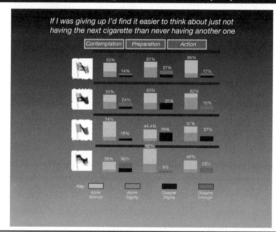

Source: AMV.BBDO Taylor Nelson Omnibus Study. Base: All adults: 1000 UK, Germany, Italy, 500 Australia

## A creative idea that crossed borders

This strategic insight led to the core idea for our advertising, summed up by our end-line 'Beat cigarettes one at a time. You're twice as likely to succeed with Nicorette.'

The creative device developed for all of our communications was 'Cravings Man', a 2.5-metre cigarette with arms, legs and a face.

He represented the cravings for cigarettes that smokers struggle with when they're trying to quit. Each ad showed a smoker literally beating a craving as he appeared. This has the flexibility to be taken through the line to online, PR and point of sale. Pre-testing of our first two executions – 'Cold Turkey' and 'Karate' – in the UK produced promising results, with excellent engagement, branding and an Awareness Index at or above the UK average (see Figures 3 and 4).

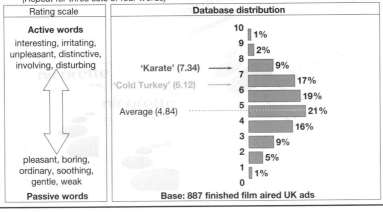

Figure 3: 'Karate' is more actively engaging than 'Cold Turkey' although both are involving executions

Source: Millward Brown

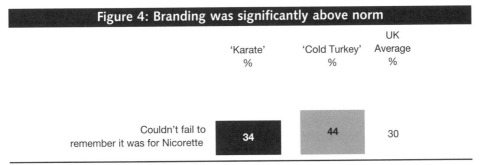

Figure 4: Branding was significantly above norm

|  | 'Karate' % | 'Cold Turkey' % | UK Average % |
|---|---|---|---|
| Couldn't fail to remember it was for Nicorette | 34 | 44 | 30 |

Source: Millward Brown link test 2002 (805 ads)

## Using media like a consumer brand

NRT sales peak around the new year when many smokers finally 'resolve' to quit. Advertising is thus concentrated around the new year, using TV for maximum impact with approximately 40% of yearly media spend at this time. Our competitors spend more than 50% of their budgets at this time of year.

In 2001 we began to invest our media over a longer time period rather than pouring it into the 'quit season'. Figure 5 demonstrates how we focused less of our media spend at 'quit season' than our competitors. Figure 6 demonstrates how we allocated money across the year to ensure we spoke to smokers at different times throughout the year.

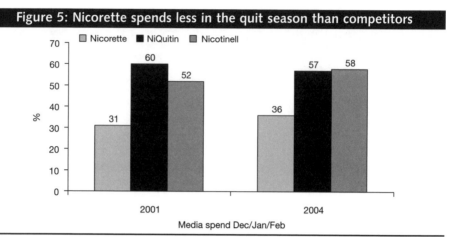

Figure 5: Nicorette spends less in the quit season than competitors

Media spend Dec/Jan/Feb

Source: Mindshare Media Analysis

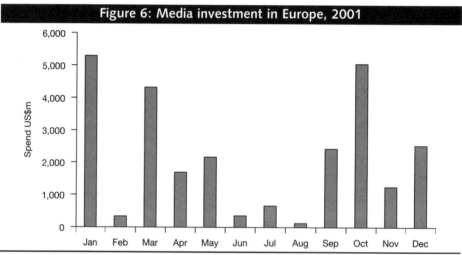

Figure 6: Media investment in Europe, 2001

Source: Mindshare Media Analysis

## Surrounding people like an integrated consumer brand

We worked hard to take the creative idea right through all media channels from advertising to point of purchase.

We've used 'Cravings Man' in TV and press, and we've used him in an opportunistic fashion for PR purposes. When the tobacco advertising ban was introduced in the UK, we had all of the tobacco outdoor posters replaced with Nicorette posters, and used the event to generate PR.

We've used him for pharmasite posters and point of sale, reminding people to buy Nicorette as they walk into the chemist, as well as pharmacist detailing to help pharmacists advise customers. And he's appeared on websites across Europe.

A more extreme example came in 2003 when Nicorette sponsored an 80ft maxi racing yacht, which won the Sydney–Hobart race with a 90 m$^2$ 'Nicorette Country' spinnaker sail.

## But has 'Cravings Man' worked?

From 2000 to 2004, based largely on the success of the 'Cravings Man' campaign, Nicorette grew from seven advertised countries to 16, from $194m to $295m in sales, and established itself as the clear market leader (see Figure 7).

The success story in this paper is very much a European one, but the vast majority of our research is from the UK. This was a conscious decision taken by Pharmacia/Pfizer in order to save money on duplicating research.

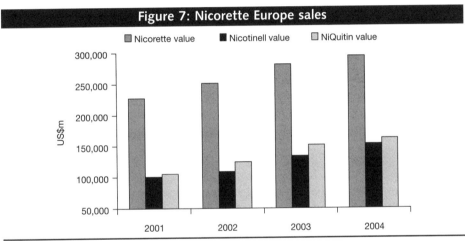

**Figure 7: Nicorette Europe sales**

Source: IMS sales data

## What wasn't driving our growth?

### Media spend

Over the period 2000–2003 our media spend remained largely flat. There was a significant increase in media spend in 2004 due almost entirely to the decision to advertise in 16 markets rather than seven. Our media spend in the seven previously advertised markets remained essentially flat. As 80% of our growth came in the years 2001–2003, then it is clearly not media spend that is driving growth.

### Distribution

Distribution is a key to sales but our distribution levels have remained largely static in key markets across Europe. In some cases we actually lost distribution.

### Salesforce

We estimate that the big three players have sales teams of comparable size and buying power.

*Promotions*

Promotions are illegal in all countries except the UK. In the UK we have the same amount of volume sold on discount as the other major players.

*NPD*

Nicorette didn't launch any new products between 2001 and 2004, and we were at a product disadvantage in both gum and patch. We did launch new SKUs over the period but they were variants in pack counts, packaging, and so on, and they were fewer than our competitors (see Figure 1, page 335).

*Big tobacco*

Tobacco companies retain a large number of marketing tools at their disposal (e.g. price, on-pack promotions), but this effect would impact all NRT firms equally.

*Price*

The products essentially have price parity across Europe.

*Government*

Government initiatives vary wildly by country. For example, in the UK the Government spent £49.3m between 2000 and 2004. By contrast, the German Government spent less than $4m over the same time period. But any benefit from government communications will be spread equally amongst competitors.

## So what did drive growth?

In 2001 when we began the 'Cravings Man' campaign we saw a step-change in TV recognition (see Figure 8). Given the challenge of 'nico-confusion', driving advertising awareness was an important first step.

The percentage of people who recalled seeing 'Cravings Man' in 'any media' increased by almost 50%. Encouragingly, this 'any media' awareness measure has built over the course of the campaign (see Figure 9).

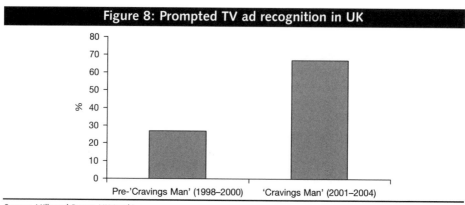

**Figure 8: Prompted TV ad recognition in UK**

Source: Millward Brown UK tracking

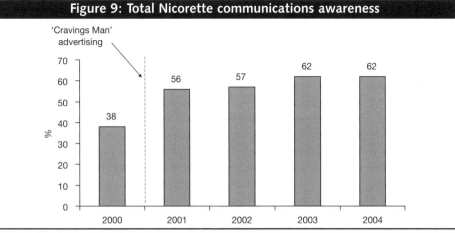

Figure 9: Total Nicorette communications awareness

Source: Millward Brown UK tracking

As Table 1 demonstrates, TV has been the main driver of awareness, but tracking showed that our strategy of surrounding people made a significant contribution to our lead in overall awareness.

From the early days of the campaign, we saw positive shifts in brand saliency (see Table 2). On broader unprompted brand awareness we have maintained a significant gap versus the competition (see Figure 10).

Increased advertising awareness and brand saliency has helped drive a key measure – consideration (see Figure 11). During the course of our campaign consideration of Nicorette has grown 28% whilst consideration of NRT has grown at only 17%.

Tracking in other countries around Europe is less consistent than in the UK (and is conducted to a variety of different methodologies), but it still reveals excellent results. In France, recognition of 'Cravings Man' ads has risen from 66% in 2001 to 89% in 2004 (see Figure 12).

## Table 1: Exposure in all media has raised total awareness

|  | Nicorette | Nicotinell | NiQuitin | Boots |
|---|---|---|---|---|
| Total communication awareness | 62 | 38 | 41 | 10 |
| Seen on TV | 54 | 31 | 33 | 3 |
| In shops | 8 | 8 | 8 | 6 |
| Magazines | 7 | 4 | 4 | 2 |
| Newspapers | 5 | 3 | 2 | 1 |
| Posters | 7 [30] | 3 [19] | 2 [20] | 1 [10] |
| Radio | 2 | 1 | 3 | – |
| Internet | 1 | – | 1 | – |
| Base: | (330) | (330) | (330) | (330) |

Source: Millward Brown UK tracking, January 2005

## Table 2: Market saliency (first mention)

Which products can you think of that can help people to give up, cut down or not smoke at certain times? By product, I mean things you can buy in shops, not treatments like acupuncture or hyponosis.

'Cravings Man' campaign

|  | March/ April 2000 % | October 2000 % | January/ February 2001 % | March/ April 2001 % | October/ November 2001 % |
|---|---|---|---|---|---|
| Nicorette | 45 | 45 | 45 | 47 | 53 |
| Nicotinell | 11 | 7 | 6 | 12 | 6 |
| NiQuitin | 3 | 2 | 2 | 3 | – |
| Base: total sample | (318) | (308) | (324) | (329) | (341) |

Source: Millward Brown

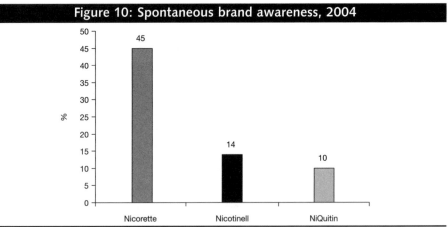

## Figure 10: Spontaneous brand awareness, 2004

Source: Millward Brown tracking, September 2004

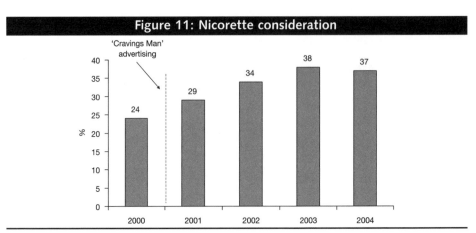

## Figure 11: Nicorette consideration

Source: Millward Brown UK tracking

342

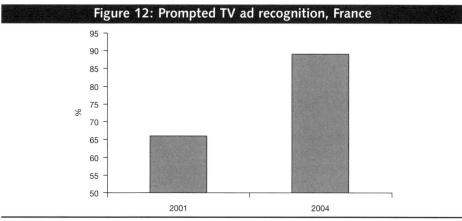

**Figure 12: Prompted TV ad recognition, France**

Source: TNS Tracking France

Overall NRT saliency dropped over this period. Those who claimed to know at least one brand of NRT actually fell from 75% to 70%. In contrast, in the same period, Nicorette's top-of-mind awareness rose by almost 14%.

In Sweden our tracking has been sporadic, but we have seen spontaneous TV advertising rise from 33% in 2001 to 45% in 2004.

## How did we know it was the advertising that was driving growth?

Across Europe there is a distinct correlation between sales when we're on-air vs off-air, as demonstrated in Figure 13, where the relationship between media spend and sales is clear.

In the UK, we had an econometric model for the years 2000 to 2002 so we could help quantify the monetary value that the campaign brought to the brand. The decomposition chart (see Figure 14) clearly shows the positive effect of Nicorette communications on sales.

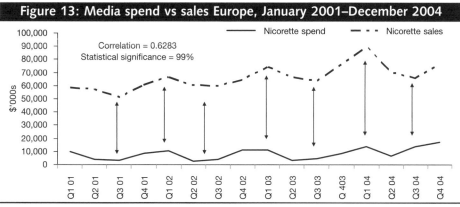

**Figure 13: Media spend vs sales Europe, January 2001–December 2004**

Source: Mindshare media spend analysis and IMS sales data

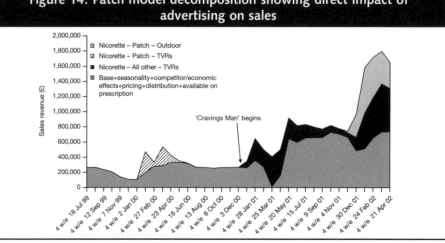

**Figure 14: Patch model decomposition showing direct impact of advertising on sales**

Source: Nicorette, OMD Metrics

The model could not isolate a return on investment for Nicorette patch or gum advertising prior to the 'Cravings Man' campaign but the new work delivered a return of 3.3:1, with individual executions, later in 2002, delivering a return of 14:1. The model also found that when we advertised the patch, the campaign actually drove brand switching, with our competitors losing £1.25 of business for every pound we spent. Given nico-confusion and the competitive nature of the category, this was very encouraging.

In our three biggest markets the results have been nothing short of spectacular.

- **UK:** share has grown from 28.4% to 36.1% between Q1 2001 and Q4 2004. In 2001 Nicorette sales stood at US$61.6m, but had grown to US$88.1m by 2004, growth of 43%.
- **France:** share has grown from 18.1% to 28.1% between Q1 2001 and Q4 2004. In 2001 Nicorette sales stood at US$27.2m, but had grown to US$35.1m by 2004, growth of 29%.
- **Germany:** share has grown from 24.1% to 50.1% between Q1 2001 and Q4 2004. In 2001 Nicorette sales stood at US$14.6m, but had grown to US$20.1m by 2004, growth of 37%.

## Conclusion

Thinking about Nicorette as a consumer brand, we realised there was a fundamental human truth about smoking – namely that giving up isn't a war, it's a series of battles against individual cigarettes, and Nicorette can help you give up one craving at a time.

## Chapter 22

# Teacher Recruitment

## A class act: how communications averted the teacher recruitment crisis, 1998–2005

**By Ric Nicholls, DDB London, and David Bassett, DDB Matrix**
Contributing author: Sergen Ozbek, OMD Metrics

This case study describes the teacher recruitment campaigns that ran from 1998 to 2005. Prior to these, British children were performing badly over a wide range of metrics, and the education system was on the verge of a major teacher supply crisis.

The communications strategy aiming to reverse these trends fell into two phases. The first, from 1998–2003, was based around attracting those who were 'born to teach' into the classroom. The creative aimed to appeal to graduates who were drawn to teaching, but had concerns about entering the profession. The 'No One Forgets' and 'Can teach' campaigns thus emphasised the personal and professional value of teaching. The second phase began in 2003, when increased targets necessitated a change in approach, and was based on an appeal to those who needed reasons beyond altruism to change their career direction and step up to the 'chalk-face'. The 'Headless' and 'Most exciting' ads targeted people who were compulsive communicators, and wanted to discuss, debate, explain and engage in a positive interaction on a daily basis.

Analysis shows that advertising bursts during both phases influenced attitudes and enquiries, while econometric modelling showed that 50% of all enquiries were generated directly by communications. There has been a 70% rise in applications, and an extra 67,000 trainee teachers have been recruited, with numbers for maths and science – among the most difficult recruitment areas – more than doubling. The saving to the tax payer is also estimated to be in the region of £4.9bn.

*To me, the sole hope of human salvation lies in teaching.*

George Bernard Shaw

*Teachers are, more than any other, the guardians of civilisation.*

Bertrand Russell

*Exodus of Teachers and Nurses.*

*Guardian* headline, 1997

## Introduction

This paper isn't about incremental growth. It isn't about brand equity, or gross profit margins, or market share points; nor is it concerned with competitor spends, share prices or quarterly sales targets.

It is about how a dire teacher supply problem was transformed inside eight years, motivating an *extra* 67,000 highly prized graduates to enter teacher training and producing large savings for the tax payer. But the real story goes beyond even that. By averting a crisis in our schools, communications have helped our Government fulfil its electoral mandate and our children's education to get better.

## Education, education, education

1997 was an election year dominated by debates about education (see Figure 1): the Government was elected famously promising that it would be priorities one, two and three.

There were good reasons for this. From literacy rates in primary schools to the academic achievements of 18-year olds, the UK trailed far behind its major competitors (see Figure 2). Largely as a result, productivity rates paled in comparison with those of other OECD countries (see Figure 3).

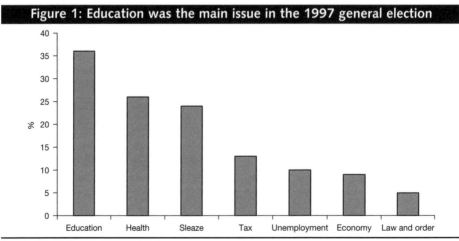

**Figure 1: Education was the main issue in the 1997 general election**

Source: MORI Poll, April 1997. Base: 642
Question: What has been the main issue in the general election campaign?

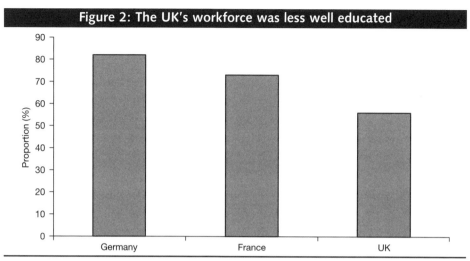

Figure 2: The UK's workforce was less well educated

Source: Department for Education and Skills (DfES). Proportion holding post-16 qualifications

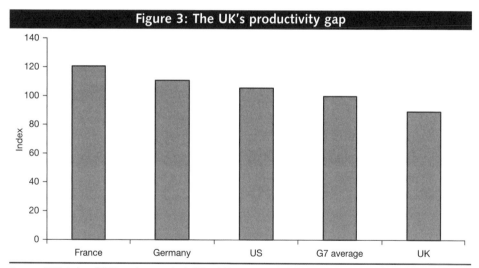

Figure 3: The UK's productivity gap

Source: ONS. Index of GDP per hour worked, G7 = 100

The new Government could and would provide the money required to make schools better, but without enough high-quality teachers in the frontline this investment would be without return. And therein lay the problem.

## The looming teacher crisis

Numbers entering teacher training were falling rapidly (see Figure 4) at a time when retirement rates in the ageing teaching workforce were accelerating fast (see Figure 5); 50% of all existing teachers were due to retire by 2010 – some 200,000 teachers who would need to be replaced.

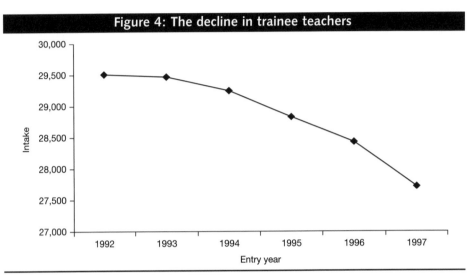

Figure 4: The decline in trainee teachers

Source: DfES. Intake to initial teacher training, 1992–97

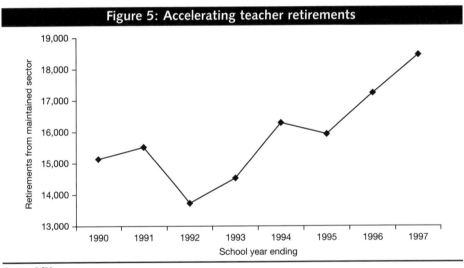

Figure 5: Accelerating teacher retirements

Source: DfES

Fewer teachers would be at the 'chalk-face' just when the number of pupils in schools was growing rapidly (see Figure 6).

If nothing was done, the growth in class sizes (see Figure 7) would continue when a mountain of evidence showed that smaller classes were needed to drive up standards.

If Government education policy was to be a success, a new generation of teachers had to be recruited; thus the communications campaign through the Training and Development Agency for Schools (TDA) was born.

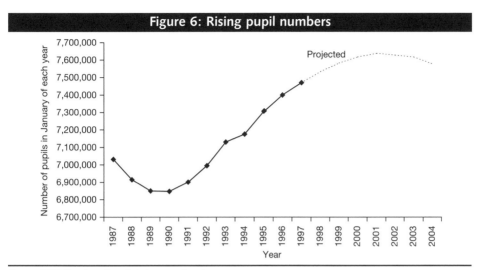

Source: DfES. Number of pupils in January of each year

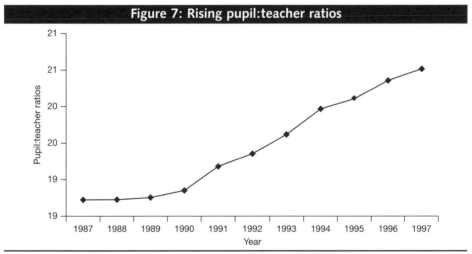

Source: DfES. Pupil:teacher ratios in primary and secondary schools, 1987–97

## The scale of the task

The scale of this task was immense. In 1997, 27,804 people embarked upon a teacher training course; by 2005 there were 42,000 places on these courses each year. To put this in context, filling each place would require 15% of *all* new graduates to enter teacher training each year (see Figure 8).

The magnitude of this task was compounded by the number of allocated places in the shortage subjects of Maths, Physics and Chemistry – 55% of the total numbers graduating in those subjects each year.

Figure 8: The number of places on courses rocketed as projections of trainee numbers declined

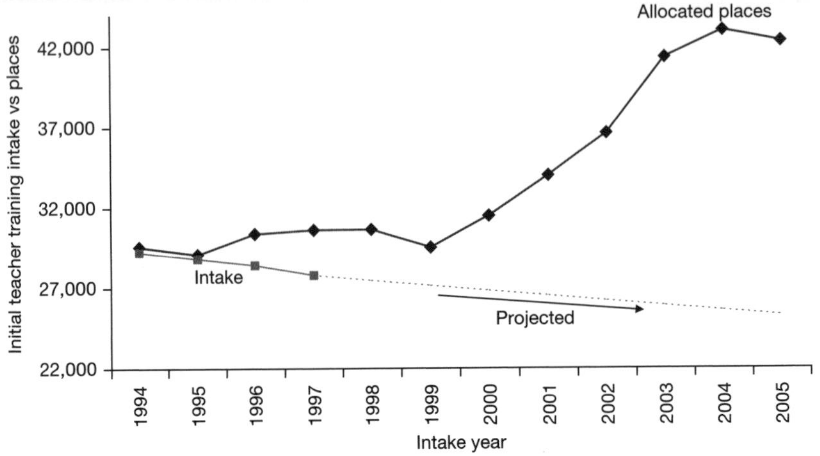

Source: DfES. Projected intake vs allocted places. Projection is based on average decline in intake, 1992–97

To fill these places, a cumulative 78,215 *extra* teachers had to be recruited over and above existing levels.

A ratio of two applications per place was mandated to ensure that improving the quantity of new teachers did not jeopardise their quality. This meant generating 156,430 more applications from highly skilled graduates at a time of virtual full employment.

## What this paper will prove

This paper will prove how communications turned around the teacher recruitment situation, increasing the numbers entering teacher training by over 50% inside eight years, despite operating in an extremely competitive graduate employment market.

It will also show how the investment paid off handsomely, both in narrow financial, and broad social and economic senses.

## The shape of the campaign

The campaign fell into two phases, the shape of which is shown in Figure 9.[1]

## Phase 1, 1998–2003: recruiting 'born to' teachers

This first phase addressed 'born to' teachers: those instinctively drawn to teaching but who were worried that teaching wasn't a 'proper job' any longer.

> It sounds cheesy, but I really do want to make a difference ... when I told my brothers I wanted to become a teacher, though, they laughed – and told me to get a proper job.

Undergraduate, 21

## Figure 9: The shape of the campaign

| PHASE 1, 1998-2003: RECRUITING 'BORN TO' TEACHERS | PHASE 2, 2003-2005: RECRUITING 'CHANGE TO' TEACHERS |
|---|---|
| Objective: Convince those who always thought they might teach to actually apply | Objective: Motivate new audiences to consider a teaching career and help them change to teaching |
| Target: Altruistic individuals who fear that teaching isn't a 'proper job' any longer | Target: Those who see teaching as one option amongst many but who fear teaching won't be a job they will enjoy |
| Comms Model: Surround the audience with communications that appeal to their altruism and raise the status of teaching | Comms Model: Force career re-appraisal by showing the joy of working with children and guide people to the point of application |

*I always thought I would go into teaching – both my parents teach – but I just don't think it's the job it used to be.*

Undergraduate, 20

This problem was recognised in the highest echelons of Government – and echoed by the profession itself:

*Teachers' pay and status has fallen out of kilter with other occupations. Their status is often derided and teaching is seen by many of the well-qualified middle classes as little better than a second-best occupation.*

Peter Mortimore, Institute of Education Director, 1998

*The status quo is not an option. After decades of drift, decisive action is required to raise teaching to the front rank of professions.*

Tony Blair, Foreword to the Teachers Green Paper, 1998

The two campaigns in this first phase – 'No One Forgets A Good Teacher' (1998–2000) and 'Those Who Can, Teach' (2000–2003) – worked as shown in Figures 10 and 11.

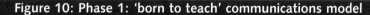

## Figure 10: Phase 1: 'born to teach' communications model

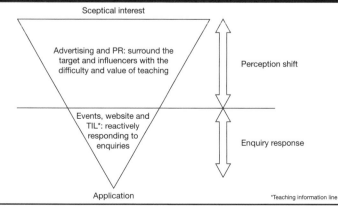

Sceptical interest

Advertising and PR: surround the target and influencers with the difficulty and value of teaching

Perception shift

Events, website and TIL*: reactively responding to enquiries

Enquiry response

Application

*Teaching information line

## Figure 11: Phase 1: 'born to teach' media plan

Total Spend: £31.9 million

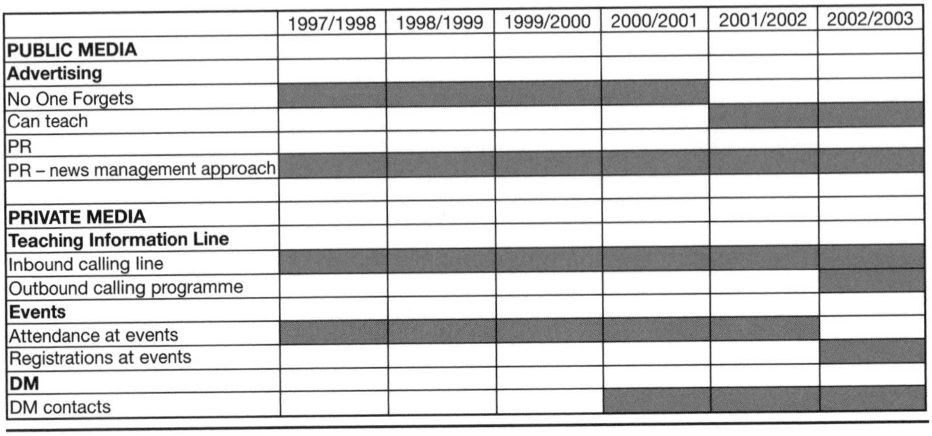

| | 1997/1998 | 1998/1999 | 1999/2000 | 2000/2001 | 2001/2002 | 2002/2003 |
|---|---|---|---|---|---|---|
| **PUBLIC MEDIA** | | | | | | |
| **Advertising** | | | | | | |
| No One Forgets | ▓ | ▓ | ▓ | ▓ | | |
| Can teach | | | | | ▓ | ▓ |
| **PR** | | | | | | |
| PR – news management approach | ▓ | ▓ | ▓ | ▓ | ▓ | ▓ |
| | | | | | | |
| **PRIVATE MEDIA** | | | | | | |
| **Teaching Information Line** | | | | | | |
| Inbound calling line | ▓ | ▓ | ▓ | ▓ | ▓ | ▓ |
| Outbound calling programme | | | | | | ▓ |
| **Events** | | | | | | |
| Attendance at events | ▓ | ▓ | ▓ | ▓ | ▓ | ▓ |
| Registrations at events | | | | | | ▓ |
| **DM** | | | | | | |
| DM contacts | | | | ▓ | ▓ | ▓ |

Alongside these communications – and within some of them – a £6,000 training bursary and 'Golden Hello' payments for those applying for shortage 'priority' subjects (both in 2000), and a scheme to repay trainee teachers' student loans (2002) were introduced.

### What happened?

These financial benefits combined with the advertising campaigns to effect a sea-change in perceptions of teaching as a 'proper job', both amongst young graduates and those who influenced their career decisions. By the end of Phase 1, perceptions of teaching as a career that high-flying graduates would avoid had more than halved. As a result, an IPPR survey in 2001 ranked teaching above the law, banking or management consultancy in status terms – an astonishing turnaround for the profession (see Figure 12).

The decline in numbers entering teacher training was halted, and by 2003 numbers entering teacher training had increased by some 30% – 8,000 extra trainee teachers each year (for more detailed results, see the 'Exam results' section).

## Phase 2, 2003–2005: recruiting 'change to' teachers

By 2003, however, it became clear that maximising the numbers of 'born to' teachers entering the profession would not be enough. The campaign now needed to turn its attention to a more difficult target: those who weren't 'born to teach' but were either considering teaching as one option amongst many or as a change to their current career. Research revealed a sizeable target of 'change to' teachers. They were potentially interested in teaching, but needed to be convinced about the day-to-day enjoyment of the job.

> I have always known that teaching is a way to make a difference to kids' lives, but it has never made me want to be one.
>
> Research chemist

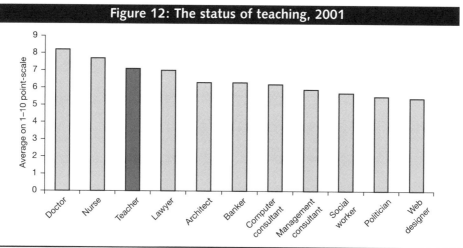

Figure 12: The status of teaching, 2001

Source: ICM Poll for IPPR/General Teaching Council, August 2001. Base: 1002 adults
Question: 'How much status do you think each of the following occupations has in society today?'

*You don't need to sell teaching as a vocation. You have to tell me why I would want to do it.*

Travel agent

*Teaching suffers from a lack of appreciation for the rewarding, enjoyable aspects of the job for the teachers directly, rather than vicariously through their students.*

Research conclusion

Research indicated that they shared a 'teaching personality' with existing teachers: they were compulsive communicators who loved nothing more than to discuss, debate or explain. Importantly, this positive interaction was precisely what their current jobs were failing to provide.

The role for communications was to convince them that teaching was the career that could provide it. Campaigns were needed that presented the target with the joy of working with children in its rawest form. Thus first the 'Headless' (negatively) and then the 'Work with the most exciting people in the world' (positively) campaigns were created.

*It shows you can be so much more than a hamster in a wheel – those classrooms just feel so alive.*

Trainee accountant

*Even when I have an awful day at work I see those kids in those ads and think – yep, that's why I came into teaching.*

Head of RE

The barriers 'change to' teachers faced also demanded a radically different structure of communications. Phase 2 ('change to teach') communications used a sophisticated model of integration that tailored communications along the 'customer' journey (see Figures 13 and 14).

## Figure 13: Phase 2: 'change to teach' communications model

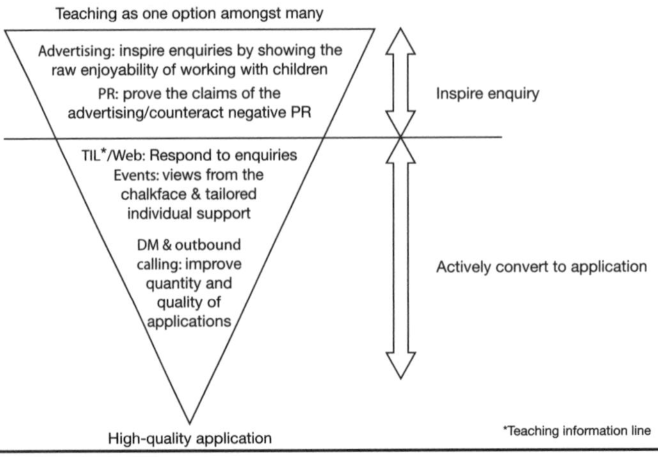

Teaching as one option amongst many

Advertising: inspire enquiries by showing the raw enjoyability of working with children

PR: prove the claims of the advertising/counteract negative PR

Inspire enquiry

TIL*/Web: Respond to enquiries

Events: views from the chalkface & tailored individual support

DM & outbound calling: improve quantity and quality of applications

Actively convert to application

High-quality application

*Teaching information line

## Figure 14: Phase 2: 'change to teach' media plan

Total Spend: £25.7 million

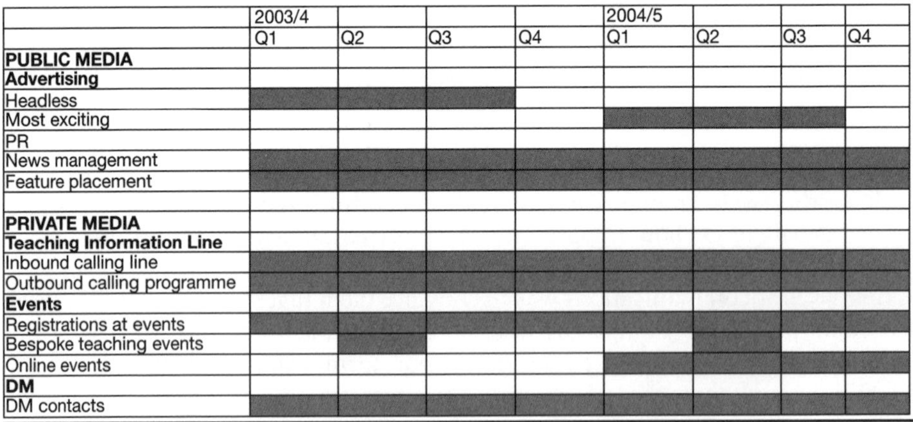

| | 2003/4 | | | | 2004/5 | | | |
|---|---|---|---|---|---|---|---|---|
| | Q1 | Q2 | Q3 | Q4 | Q1 | Q2 | Q3 | Q4 |
| **PUBLIC MEDIA** | | | | | | | | |
| **Advertising** | | | | | | | | |
| Headless | | | | | | | | |
| Most exciting | | | | | | | | |
| PR | | | | | | | | |
| News management | | | | | | | | |
| Feature placement | | | | | | | | |
| | | | | | | | | |
| **PRIVATE MEDIA** | | | | | | | | |
| **Teaching Information Line** | | | | | | | | |
| Inbound calling line | | | | | | | | |
| Outbound calling programme | | | | | | | | |
| **Events** | | | | | | | | |
| Registrations at events | | | | | | | | |
| Bespoke teaching events | | | | | | | | |
| Online events | | | | | | | | |
| **DM** | | | | | | | | |
| DM contacts | | | | | | | | |

## Exam results

Communications have transformed the teacher recruitment situation and averted a major crisis in our schools.

Inheriting a legacy of six straight years of decline, the campaigns have attracted an additional 67,000 trainee teachers and are now recruiting 65% more trainees than one would have expected without communications (see Figure 15).

This has been achieved despite fierce competition for these graduates, and has meant that by 2005 the numbers undergoing teacher training were at their highest for three decades. Here is how it worked.

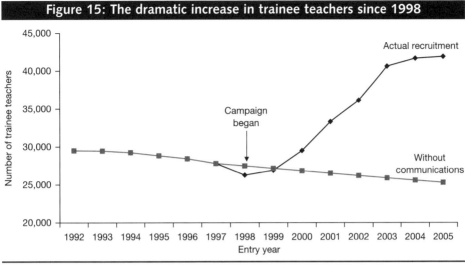

**Figure 15: The dramatic increase in trainee teachers since 1998**

Source: DfES. Without communications figures are based on average decline 1992–97

- **Advertising awareness was consistently high.** Teacher recruitment has remained more top-of-mind than any other recruitment campaign for the years in which we have data (see Figure 16).
- **It made people more positive about teaching** (see Figure 17).
- **The image of teaching improved** (see Figure 18).
- **As a result, interest in teaching grew strongly** (see Figure 19).
- **Thus applications to PGCEs doubled, with even more impressive**

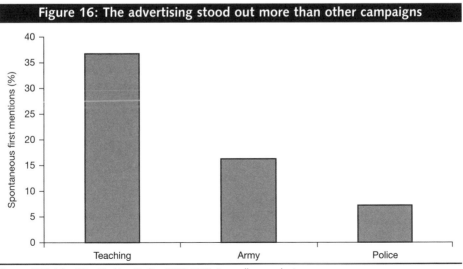

**Figure 16: The advertising stood out more than other campaigns**

Source: TDA Advertising Tracking Studies, 2000–2006. Base: all respondents

## Figure 17: The advertising made people more positive about teaching

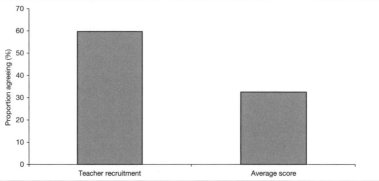

Source: TDA Advertising Tracking Studies, 2000–2006. Base: all aware of the advertising
Average courtesy of Consumer Insight, the TDA's tracking research agency

## Figure 18: The image of teaching was transformed

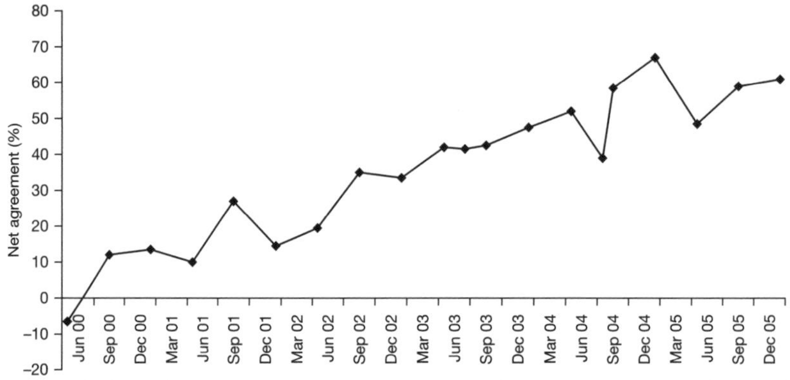

Source: TDA Advertising Tracking Studies, 2000–2006. Net agreement 'that the image of teaching is improving'.
Base: all respondents

## Figure 19: Interest in teaching grew strongly

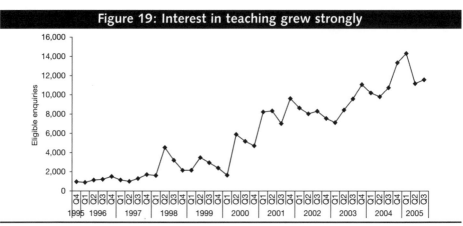

Source: TDA. Eligible enquiries to the Teaching Information Line, 1995–2005

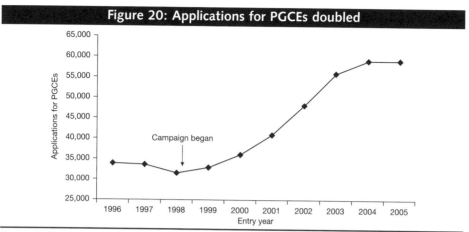

Figure 20: Applications for PGCEs doubled

Source: Graduate Teacher Training Registry (GTTR)

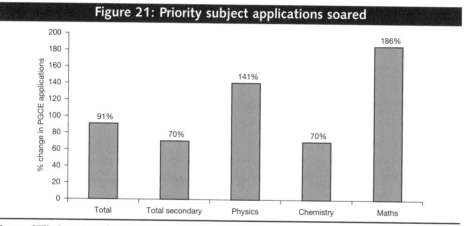

Figure 21: Priority subject applications soared

Source: GTTR. Percentage change in PGCE applications, 1998–2005

improvements in problem subject areas (see Figures 20 and 21).

## Showing the workings

Five pieces of proof collectively point to the specific contribution of the recruitment campaign in delivering these ever-increasing numbers of new trainee teachers.

1. **When advertising messages changed, attitudes towards teaching changed with them.** Attitudes towards teaching have changed in line with the core messages of the campaign. Phase 1 communications were about raising the status of teaching: at the same time, numbers believing that teaching was 'not a career for high-fliers' halved (see Figure 22). Similarly, when Phase 2 communications focused on the day-to-day enjoyment of teaching, the belief that teaching was enjoyable rose substantially (see Figure 23).

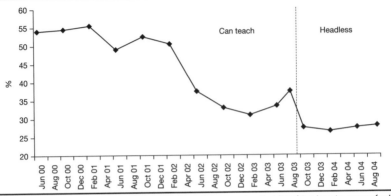

**Figure 22: Belief that 'teaching is not a career for high-fliers' in Phase 1**

Source: TDA Advertising Tracking Studies, 2000–2006. Percentage agreeing that 'teaching is not a career for high-fliers'. Base: all respondents

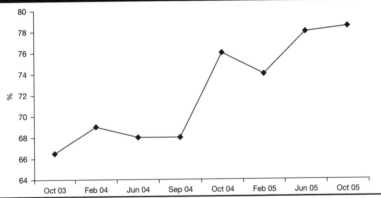

**Figure 23: The perceived day-to-day enjoyment of teaching in Phase 2**

Source: TDA Advertising Tracking Studies, 2000–2006. Percentage agreeing that 'teaching is enjoyable day to day'. Base: all respondents

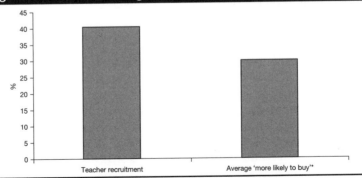

**Figure 24: The advertising made more people consider teaching**

Source: TDA Advertising Tracking Studies, 2000–2006. Percentage claiming that the advertising made them more likely to investigate/buy as a result of the advertising. Base: all aware of the advertising
* Average courtesy of Consumer Insight, the TDA's tracking research agency

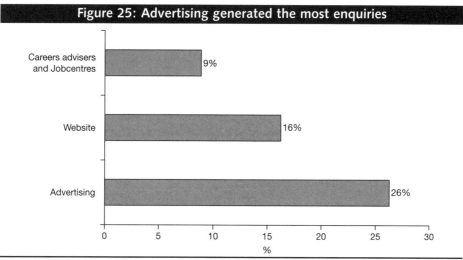

Figure 25: Advertising generated the most enquiries

Source: TDA. Claimed source of phone enquiries to the Teaching Information Line

2. **People claimed the advertising had made them feel more positive about teaching and drove them to enquire** (see Figure 24). When people actually called up the Teaching Information Line (TIL), they were more likely to say that the advertising drove them there than anything else (see Figure 25).
3. **Enquiry spikes correlated with advertising spend** (see Figure 26).
4. **Advertised subjects outperformed non-advertised subjects.** Enquiries for the key priority subjects that have consistently been advertised – Maths, Chemistry and Physics – have increased at a faster rate than those for non-advertised subjects (see Figure 27).

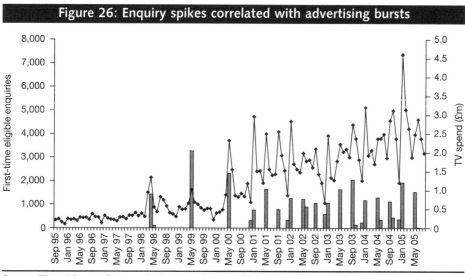

Figure 26: Enquiry spikes correlated with advertising bursts

Sources: TDA, Nielsen Media Research. Correlation between first-time eligible enquiries and TV spend

**Figure 27: Advertised subjects outperformed non-advertised subjects**

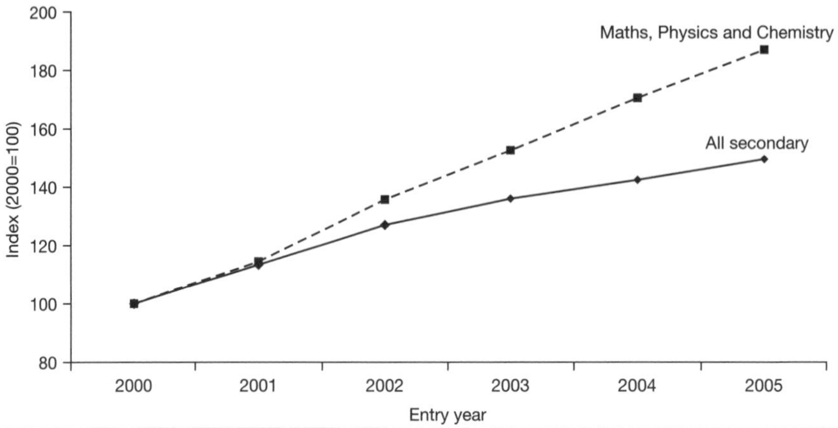

Maths, Physics and Chemistry

All secondary

Index (2000=100)

Entry year

Source: GTTR. Index of PGCE applications (2000=100). 2000 was the first year that specific subjects were advertised

**Figure 28: Those who received DM were more than twice as likely to apply**

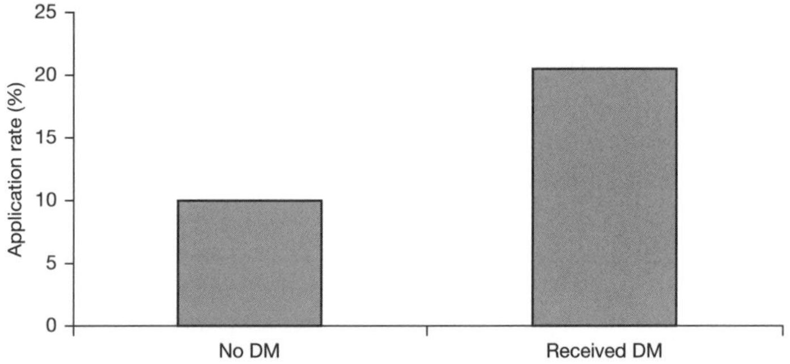

Application rate (%)

No DM          Received DM

Source: TDA. Application rates for those who receiced DM vs those who did not

**Figure 29: Those who received outbound calls were 70% more likely to apply**

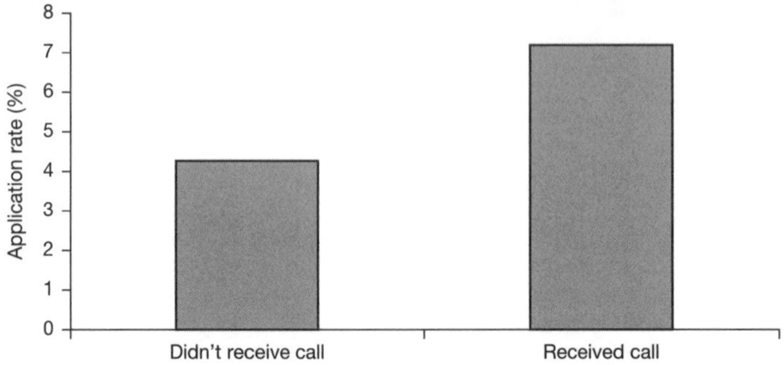

Application rate (%)

Didn't receive call          Received call

Source: TDA. Application rates for those who received an outbound call vs those who did not

5. DM and the outbound calling programme raised application rates significantly (see Figures 28 and 29).

## Eliminating other factors

Communications have had a direct and significant impact on the number of new teachers in our classrooms. However, the decision to teach is potentially influenced by a range of other factors.

### Financial incentives for teacher training

The financial incentives introduced as the campaign evolved have clearly played a role in attracting people to teaching. But the evidence suggests that by themselves they would not have 'done the job'. Significant rises in enquiry levels occurred before these incentives were introduced, and continued rising after they were announced. Indeed, enquiries continued to grow even after one incentive – the repayment of student loans scheme – had been discontinued (see Figure 30).

Furthermore, increases in enquiry and application levels have actually been greater in subjects that do not offer Golden Hello payments than in those that do,

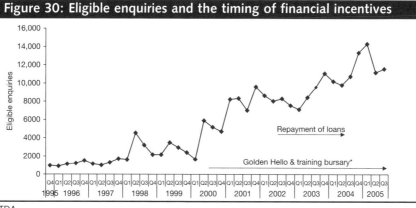

**Figure 30: Eligible enquiries and the timing of financial incentives**

Source: TDA
* These incentives started in Q3 1999 for Maths and Science

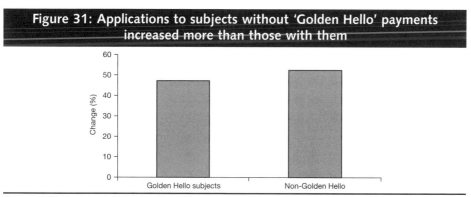

**Figure 31: Applications to subjects without 'Golden Hello' payments increased more than those with them**

Source: GTTR. Percentage change in PGCE applications, 2000–05
Golden Hello subjects are Maths, Science, English, ICT, Design and Technology, and Modern Languages

implying that something other than financial incentives has been driving those enquiries (see Figure 31).

## New routes into teaching

Another potential factor has been the introduction in 2000 of more flexible ways of becoming a teacher: the employment-based routes. These provide better-paid ways of training to be a teacher (a £13,000 salary rather than £6,000) that allow people to train at their local school.

Whilst these routes have proved to be attractive, the majority of the increases in trainee teachers have come via the 'traditional' routes into teaching (see Figure

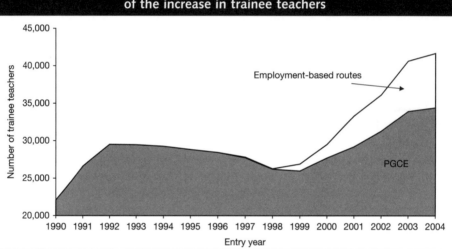

**Figure 32: Traditional routes into teaching account for the majority of the increase in trainee teachers**

Source: TDA. Recruitment to PGCEs and employment-based routes into teaching

32). This shows that the lure of teaching was a general trend and not confined to these new, more flexible training options.

## Teacher pay

Starting salaries for new teachers failed to keep up with the median graduate starting salary between 1997 and 2005, making the recruitment task actually more difficult (see Figure 33). Overall, teacher salaries remained a constant proportion of average incomes over the period.

## The pool of graduates

The number of graduates has increased in the last nine years, increasing the pool of potential applicants. However, a buoyant economy has kept graduate unemployment low compared to the years before the campaign began (see Figure 34), again making the recruitment task harder, rather than easier.

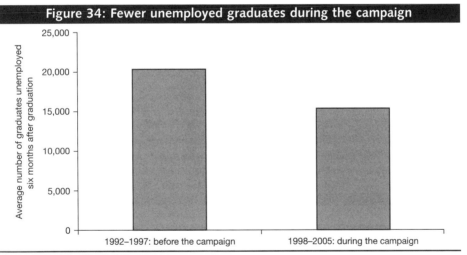

**Figure 33: Starting salaries for teachers decline in relation to average graduate starting salaries**

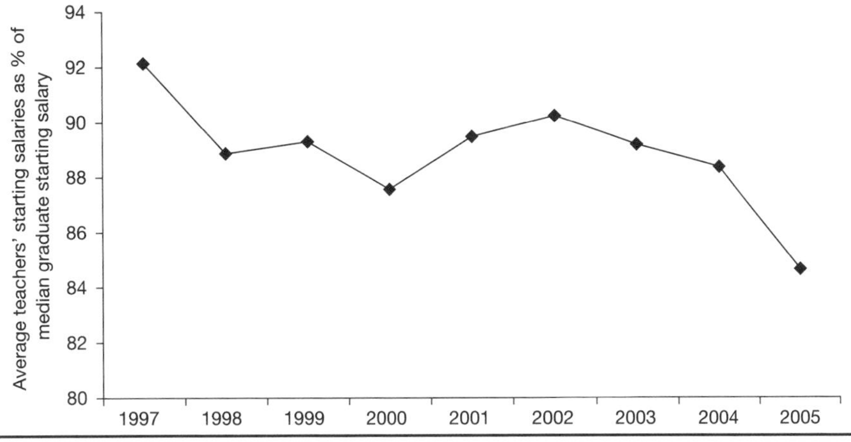

Sources: DfES, Association of Graduate Recruiters

**Figure 34: Fewer unemployed graduates during the campaign**

Source: Higher Education Statistics Agency

The pool of graduates in Maths, Physics and Chemistry has become even smaller as the campaign has evolved, falling 2.5% between 1997 and 2005. This makes the increases in applications for those subjects of up to 186% over the period an even more outstanding achievement.

## Changes to eligibility

This paper has focused on eligible enquiries – those from enquirers with the minimum academic qualifications to become teachers. These criteria have actually got tighter as the campaign has gone on – now all teachers have to have a GCSE grade C in science to teach *any* subject (if they were born after 1979).

*Teaching scare stories*

The campaign has also had to work against a background of consistently negative PR, making the recruitment challenge all the more difficult.

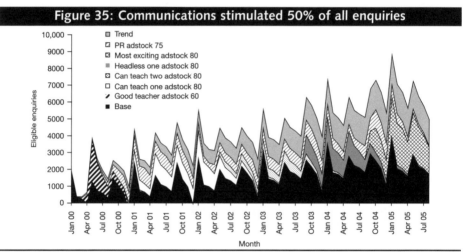

**Figure 35: Communications stimulated 50% of all enquiries**

Legend:
- Trend
- PR adstock 75
- Most exciting adstock 80
- Headless one adstock 80
- Can teach two adstock 80
- Can teach one adstock 80
- Good teacher adstock 60
- Base

Y-axis: Eligible enquiries (0 to 10,000)
X-axis: Month (Jan 00 to Jul 05)

Source: OMD Metrics

*Econometric model*

Finally, the TDA-commissioned econometric model has stripped out the specific effects of different marketing communications activities (see Figure 35). This demonstrates that communications have been responsible for driving 50% of all enquiry traffic.

## Payback

**Table 1: The financial returns to communications, 1998–2005**

| | |
|---|---|
| Extra trainee teachers | 66,829 |
| Attrition rate | 34% |
| **Total additional teachers** | **44,107** |
| Average length of career in teaching | 15 years |
| Average salary of a teacher (2002) | £28,580 |
| **Total costs of additional teachers** | **£18.9bn** |
| Daily cost of a supply teacher (2002) | £180 |
| Average length of school year | 200 days |
| **Total savings from supply teachers** | **£23.8bn** |
| **Net savings from additional teachers** | **£4.9bn** |

Sources: National Association of Headteachers 2002 survey for the costs of supply teachers; DfES Pay data for starting salaries; Teachers Green Paper for attrition rate

*The financial payback*

Since 1997, an additional 67,000 trainee teachers have been recruited. This has saved enormous amounts of money by reducing the need for supply teachers to cover their classes. Taking into account the high attrition rate during teacher training, and the fact that the average teacher stays in the profession for 15 years, the actual savings flowing from the recruitment campaigns will be £4.9bn (see Table 1).

Given a marketing spend of £57m, the campaign has paid for itself 86 times over.

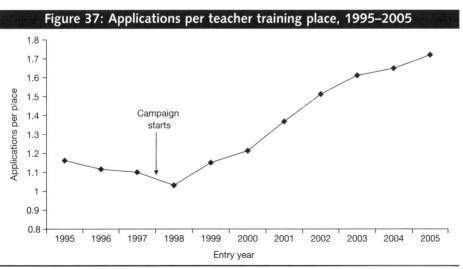

**Figure 36: Pupil:teacher ratios in primary and secondary schools, 1987–2005**

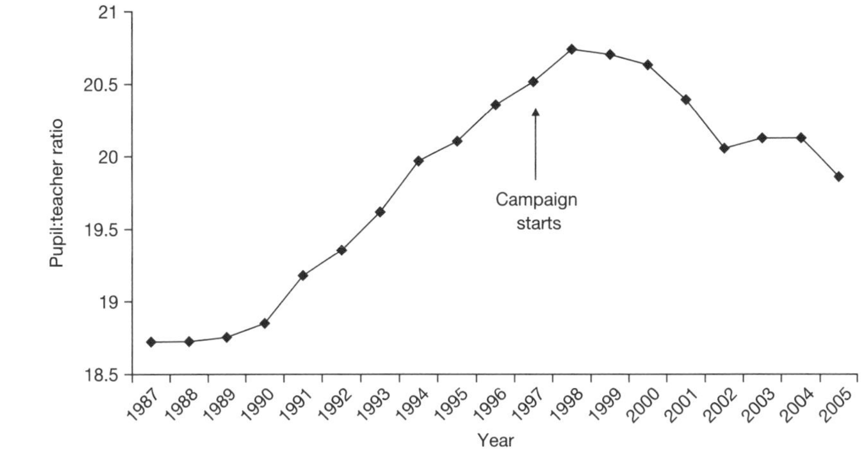

Source: DfES

**Figure 37: Applications per teacher training place, 1995–2005**

Sources: DfES, GTTR

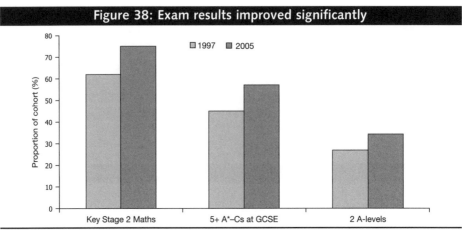

Figure 38: Exam results improved significantly

Source: *Statistics of Education: Schools in England*, 1998 and 2005 editions

### The pupil achievement payback

Reductions in pupil:teacher ratios have significantly reduced class sizes, a vital component in any attempt to improve standards (see Figure 36).

By almost doubling the number of applications for teacher training, the campaign has raised the ratio of applications to places (see Figure 37).

This has given teacher training providers more choice and the luxury of cherry-picking the best candidates – a positive benefit of the campaigns that has been felt even in subjects that have never had recruitment problems, like History.

The campaign has thus led to a sustained increase in both the quantity and quality of teachers in our schools, which in turn has had a strong and direct effect on pupil achievement. Whilst open to influence by a whole range of factors, it is hard to see how the increases in pupil attainment achieved at all levels in English and Welsh schools could have been sustained without the necessary numbers of well-qualified teachers to deliver the curriculum (see the Figure 38).

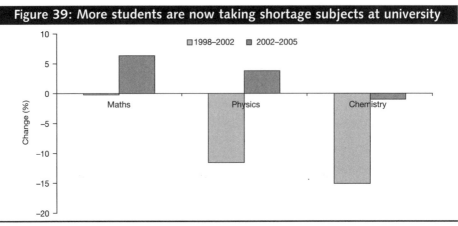

Figure 39: More students are now taking shortage subjects at university

Source: Prospects

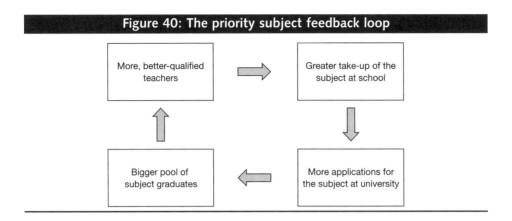

Figure 40: The priority subject feedback loop

## Creating a feedback loop

The improvements in Maths, Physics and Chemistry teacher recruitment have been arguably the biggest achievements of the campaigns. Whilst it is too early to prove conclusively, early evidence suggests that one positive effect of the extra teachers in these subjects could be to raise the numbers actually studying them at university (see Figure 39).

Should this continue, a feedback loop could be sustained whereby the future pool of potential teachers in these hard-to-recruit subjects can be grown, easing the recruitment situation for future generations (see Figure 40).

## The wider economic and social payback

The impressive improvements in educational achievements over the past eight years also benefit society as a whole.

Raising educational achievement has huge economic effects. Academic research has shown a significant link between higher educational achievement – such as that

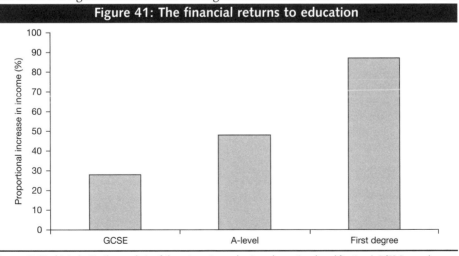

Figure 41: The financial returns to education

Source: S. Mackintosh, 'Further analysis of the returns to academic and vocational qualifications', DfES Research Paper, 2003

witnessed over the last eight years – and earning power (see Figure 41). By improving the quantity and quality of our nation's teachers, the campaign has had a strong, if indirect, role in boosting overall national income.

## Conclusion

Teacher recruitment communications have averted a major crisis in our schools. A situation of spiralling decline has been transformed: 67,000 extra trainee teachers have been recruited at a time when the health of the economy meant they could get far better-paid jobs elsewhere.

In doing so, communications have repaid the investment made in them 86 times over. By increasing the quality and quantity of teachers in our schools, they have allowed many of the Government's, and the electorate's, most cherished goals to be realised. They have left the nation's children better educated and the economy stronger and wealthier.

## Note

1. Current agencies involved in the campaign are: DDB London; Manning Gottlieb OMD; COI; Euro RSCG KLP; Band & Brown; Draft; and EWA. Previous agencies involved were: McCann-Erickson Manchester; Financial Dynamics; Hill & Knowlton; Universal McCann; Delaney Fletcher Bozell; and BJK&E Media.

## Chapter 23

# The Famous Grouse

## Small guys have to think big for long-term success

**By Michael Davidson, Abbott Mead Vickers.BBDO; Sam Dias, ROI Consulting, and Andrew Barnett, The Edrington Group**
Contributing authors: Jane Dorsett, Abbott Meads Vickers.BBDO, and Clementine Webb, ROI Consulting

This case study tells the story of a small brand that was willing to pursue an ambitious, expansive approach in order to succeed. Prior to adopting its new creative strategy, The Famous Grouse was one of many players trapped in the middle of a UK whisky market that presented a number of challenges. Its own sector – blended scotch – was in decline, while single malts and own-label brands were experiencing strong growth. As a small Perthshire-based entity, it also did not have the international reach of many of its major competitors.

Despite this, the brand's owner, the Edrington Group, did have global ambitions, and was prepared to 'think big' to achieve them. As many of its main competitors reined in their advertising, The Famous Grouse 'Icon' campaign was launched: a brand-centric advertising platform that was intended to build brand equity, engage with consumers and make The Famous Grouse stand out from the crowd – helping it, in effect, to out-perform the market.

Benchmarking against Bell's – its biggest competitor – shows the impact of the campaign, which closed the gap in market share by increasing The Famous Grouse's proportion of sales. Similarly, by measuring the impact of communications against Teachers, it is shown that sales value in both the on and off trade was greatly increased. This evidence is corroborated by econometric analysis, and, ultimately, the retail sales value of the brand rose by some £513m in the UK, while simultaneously building the future of the brand in overseas markets.

## Summary

This is the story of a small brand that had to think big to succeed:

■ trapped in the middle of the whisky market in the UK; with its sector (blended Scotch) declining while single malts and own-label brands experienced strong growth
■ trapped in the middle as a corporate entity; a small Perthshire company with global ambitions, but without the scale of its global competitors.

The Famous Grouse had to outperform the market.

This paper will show how our course of action provided retail sales value in excess of £513m in the UK.

## Staring down the barrel of a gun

The father of the Famous Grouse brand, Matthew Gloag, launched the brand on its unconventional path when he hatched the idea of a house-label blended whisky in the late 1800s and named it after Scotland's national bird.

The Famous Grouse entered 1996 facing difficult circumstances for a number of reasons:

■ we were in a market experiencing long-term decline
■ there had been a drop in market volume of 36% in just 16 years
■ the bulk of our consumers were over 50
■ the number of whisky drinkers as a whole was in decline.

The marketplace for whiskies had become highly stratified. In the middle (see Figure 1) you were squeezed:

■ by the growth of the super premium single malt category
■ by highly price-competitive private-label blends
■ by whiskies from North America and Ireland.

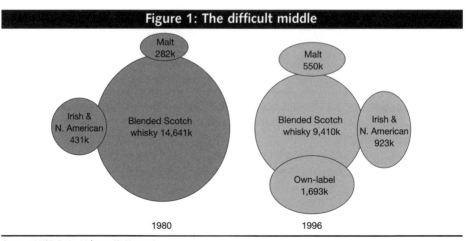

**Figure 1: The difficult middle**

Malt 282k

Malt 550k

Irish & N. American 431k

Blended Scotch whisky 14,641k

Blended Scotch whisky 9,410k

Irish & N. American 923k

Own-label 1,693k

1980

1996

Source: IWSR Data, Volume (8.4l cases)

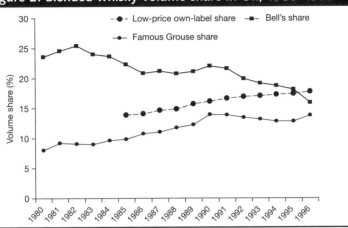

**Figure 2: Blended whisky volume share in UK, 1980–1996**

Source: IWSR

For the market leader, Bell's, the problem was even more acute. The Famous Grouse had the advantage of being able to grow its share in the 80s through distribution gains – something that was much harder for the market leader to achieve (see Figure 2).

By the mid-90s our strategy of gaining incremental sales through additional distribution was no longer working. Alongside increased competition in the whisky category, white spirits were growing and enjoyed sustained advertising support.

The challenge was immense:

■ to grow profits having exhausted our strategy of share gains through salesforce-led gains in distribution
■ to find a low risk way of expanding into new markets in the most cost-effective manner possible.

## Our flight to glory

We could have retreated and turned The Famous Grouse into a cash cow, as others were doing. Teachers, the number two brand in the 80s, largely pulled its advertising support and did just that. We chose a different option.

We needed a campaign idea that would:

■ drive involvement with the brand
■ support a choice made on brand preference not price
■ help us stand out in a cluttered market
■ maintain distribution in the on trade
■ build a price premium against competitors in the off trade
■ travel internationally.

Instead of holding a mirror up to the consumer, we turned to the brand as our source of inspiration. We took the Grouse from our label and turned it into a brand campaign capable of engaging consumers and creating standout at point of purchase.

In the UK, we have invested £15.4m in above-the-line advertising support since 1997. Bell's, the only other brand of blended whisky to invest in significant advertising support, outspent us by 55%.

We launched the Icon campaign in Greece in 1997 and in Taiwan in 2003.

## Success is sweet

Since 1997, we have built value in three ways:

1. Growth in share: on and off trade
2. Increased distribution relative to the competition: on trade
3. Increased price premium: off trade.

### Growth in share: on and off trade

The Famous Grouse has increased its market share steadily over the past decade, managing to close the gap with Bell's (see Figure 3). This is a result of share gains in both the on and off trade (see Figure 4).

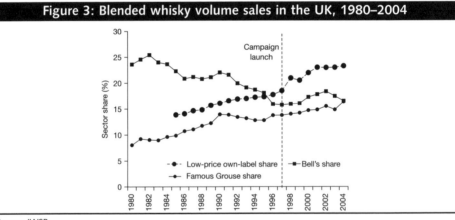

**Figure 3: Blended whisky volume sales in the UK, 1980–2004**

Source: IWSR

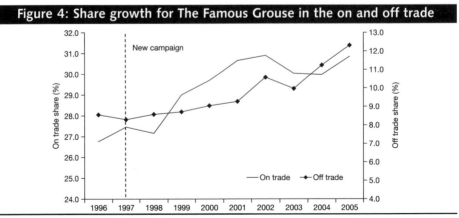

**Figure 4: Share growth for The Famous Grouse in the on and off trade**

Source: Nielsen

*Increased distribution relative to the competition: on trade*

Teachers and Grant's (brands that largely pulled advertising investment) lost distribution in the on trade (see Figure 5).

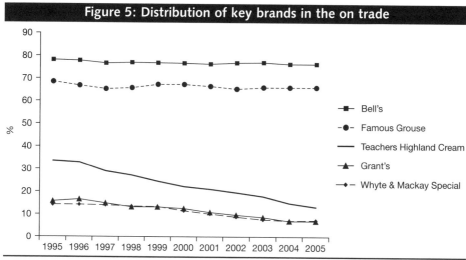

Figure 5: Distribution of key brands in the on trade

Source: Nielsen

The efficiency with which we maintained our distribution is illustrated in a scatter plot, which shows the strong correlation between advertising investment and the ability of the brand to maintain distribution (see Figure 6).

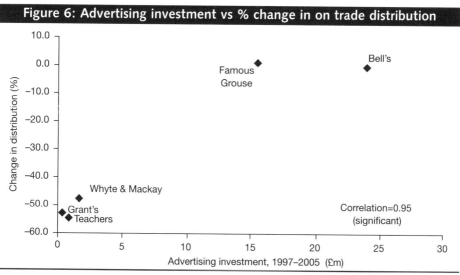

Figure 6: Advertising investment vs % change in on trade distribution

Source: Nielsen

373

*Increased price premium: off trade*

The off trade is more price sensitive than the on trade due to greater price transparency, the presence of more competitive brands, and powerful retailers committed to reducing prices. Despite this, since 1997 we have seen an increase in relative price premium (see Figure 7).

Figure 7: The Famous Grouse price premium in the off trade against Teachers (and off trade share growth)

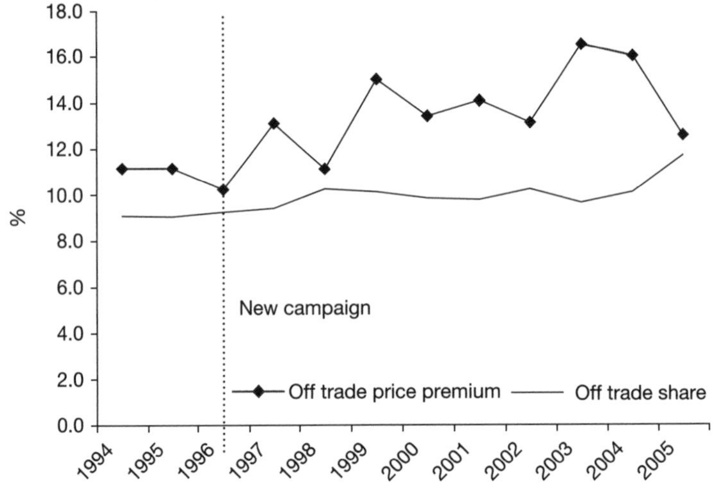

Source: Nielsen

## It had to be the advertising

In order to demonstrate advertising was responsible for share growth we need to eliminate other possible sources of success:

■ price
■ distribution
■ product
■ packaging.

*Ruling out price*

### In the off trade

The Famous Grouse maintained a healthy price premium over other players in the sector, meaning we can eliminate it as a causal factor.

### In the on trade

We have actually grown our price relative to the sector average and can eliminate it as a causal factor (see Figure 8).

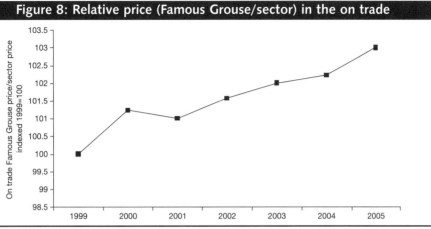

**Figure 8: Relative price (Famous Grouse/sector) in the on trade**

Source: Nielsen

## Ruling out distribution

### In the off trade

Prior to the early 90s, distribution gains in the off trade helped keep Famous Grouse sales buoyant. However, distribution had peaked by 1997 and since then there have not been any significant movements.

### In the on trade

The Famous Grouse's on trade share increased from 27% in 1996 (pre-Icon) to 32% in 2005.

It could be argued that the increase in Famous Grouse sales was inevitable, given the decline in distribution of unsupported brands. To rule this factor out, let us consider The Famous Grouse's on trade share divided by its on trade share of distribution (see Figure 9).

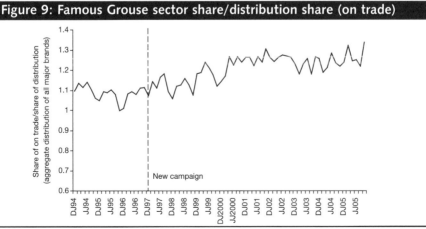

**Figure 9: Famous Grouse sector share/distribution share (on trade)**

Source: Nielsen

The metric we have created increases post-campaign launch, and carries on increasing. This suggests that The Famous Grouse has increased market share faster than the increase in share of distribution.

*Ruling out packaging*

The Famous Grouse packaging changed in 2004. However, this was a minor change – with all the important elements unaltered. In fact, the label design has been developed to better reflect the advertising idea. We have been unable to measure any effect econometrically.

*Ruling out product*

The product has not changed.

Having eliminated all other possible causal factors for our success we can conclude that the Icon campaign was responsible for the growth in share in both on and off trade.

## Success in the UK

We now show the retail sales value built by advertising using the payback model shown in Figure 10.

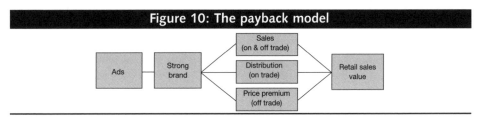

**Figure 10: The payback model**

By benchmarking against Bell's we are able to show the Icon campaign has been critical to our success, rather than just the fact we invested in advertising.

The Icon campaign was successful at building ad awareness and brand image attributes at launch (see Figures 11 and 12).

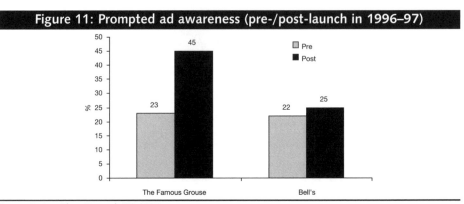

**Figure 11: Prompted ad awareness (pre-/post-launch in 1996–97)**

Source: System Three Research UK, 1997

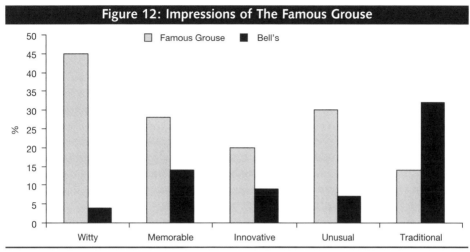

Figure 12: Impressions of The Famous Grouse

Source: System Three Research UK, 1997

By comparing prompted ad recall per £1 of media, it is possible to show our advertising efficiency (see Table 1).

### Table 1: Advertising efficiency

| UK | Prompted advertising recall (average) 2001–2005 | Media spend (£) 2001–2005 | Advertising efficiency: advertising recall per £ media spend index FG=100 |
|---|---|---|---|
| The Famous Grouse | 44% | 7,621K | 100 |
| Bell's | 20% | 13,589K | 25.5 |

Source: Ipsos, Nielsen MMS

### Brand image

As a result of the involvement consumers have with our advertising, we have the highest brand equity score of any whisky in our tracking study (see Table 2).

### Table 2: Brand driver perceptions

| UK | Brand driver perception index 2005 |
|---|---|
| The Famous Grouse | 171 |
| Bell's | 164 |
| Teachers | 94 |
| WM Grant's | 68 |

Source: Ipsos

As Bell's has outspent us by 55% since 1997 while achieving poorer results, it is possible to infer that our creative worked more efficiently.

The benefits of a strong brand affect The Famous Grouse in a number of ways.

**Our sales are less sensitive to short-term declines in advertising support**
Econometric modelling shows a temporary reduction in ad investment resulted in only a small decline in share (0.23 of a share point per 100 TVRs).

**Our sales are less sensitive to Bell's advertising**
Our model also shows that when Bell's is on air there is only a small (negative) impact on The Famous Grouse sales in the short run (0.08 share points per 100 TVRs).

**The Famous Grouse is relatively immune from Bell's price promotions**
A 1% reduction in the price of Bell's reduces The Famous Grouse share by 0.51 share points. This suggests that there is a loyal consumer base for The Famous Grouse who are not tempted by Bell's promotions.

## Quantifying the contribution

We have used modelling to demonstrate the effect of advertising on sales. Advertising from July 2001 to January 2006 has generated incremental sales of 245k 8.4-litre cases. This represents 7.2% of volume sales in the short run (see Figure 13).

To ascertain an estimate of the long-run effect of Icon advertising on volume sales, we have used the model to 'backcast' sales to 1997 (see Figure 14). The model estimates that Icon advertising generated 13% of volume sales in the long run.

When we scale this up from the off trade model to ex-factory sales, this is equivalent to £285m of incremental retail sales from an advertising investment of £15.4m since 1997. This is likely to be a conservative estimate since the on trade has fewer brands, making it a less competitive environment.

**Figure 13: Econometric model – effect of advertising on MAT volume sales**

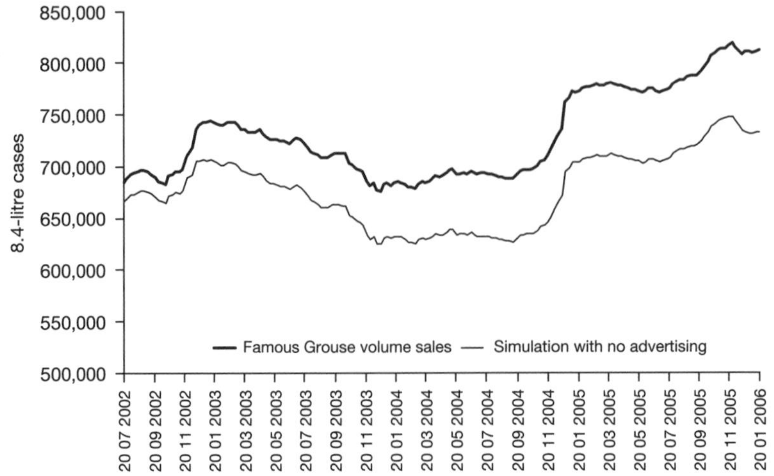

Source: ROI Consulting

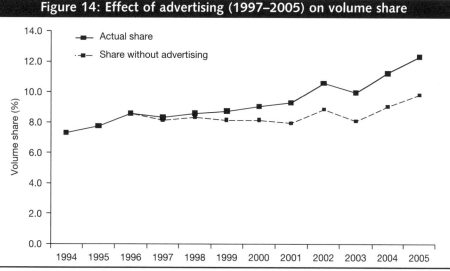

**Figure 14: Effect of advertising (1997–2005) on volume share**

Source: ROI Consulting, Nielsen

## Estimating the impact of distribution (in the on trade)

Let us assume that without advertising our on trade distribution would have declined at a similar rate to that of Teachers. Figure 15 shows the decline we could have suffered without support.

Having worked out the difference between our actual share and the share that would have resulted had we declined in on trade distribution at the same rate as non-advertised Teachers (see Figure 16), it is possible to calculate a value of this advertising effect. A 14% decline in sales would have occurred in the on trade 1997–2005. This is equivalent to £189m of retail sales.

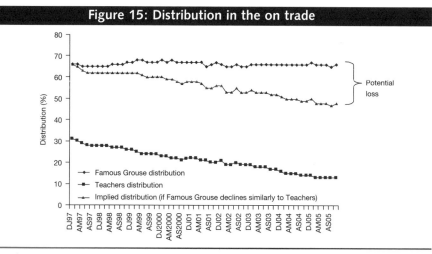

**Figure 15: Distribution in the on trade**

Source: Nielsen

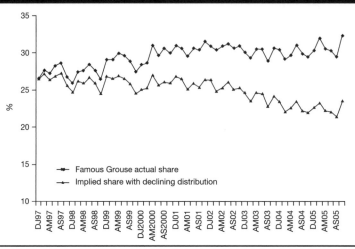

**Figure 16: The Famous Grouse actual vs implied share with distribution decline (on trade)**

Source: Nielsen

Elsewhere we have demonstrated that the share growth was achieved at an off trade price premium to Teachers and at parity to Bell's. In this section we attempt to quantify the financial value of The Famous Grouse price premium by benchmarking against weaker brands, looking specifically at Teachers.

The price premium versus Teachers increased post-advertising (as shown in Figure 7). Table 3 estimates the monetary value of the price premium since 1997 in the off trade. Commanding a price premium is even more important for profitability in the spirits category, compared to other food and drink categories, because of the relatively high excise duty fixed cost.

**Table 3: Value created from a sustained price premium**

|  | 1997–2005 (in off trade) |
|---|---|
| Value sales of The Famous Grouse | £844m |
| Value sales of The Famous Grouse at Teachers price (i.e. without price premium) | £727m |
| **Monetary value created from price premium** | **£117m** |

Source: Nielsen

Given that the price premium over Teachers existed prior to the Icon advertising, a more realistic estimate of premium created by the Icon campaign would be to consider the change in the premium since 1996 and not the absolute value (see Figure 17).

By applying the increasing price premium to off trade volume sales, we estimate that an incremental £39m of sales value was generated. We will apply this number to the third prong of our payback model (see Figure 18).

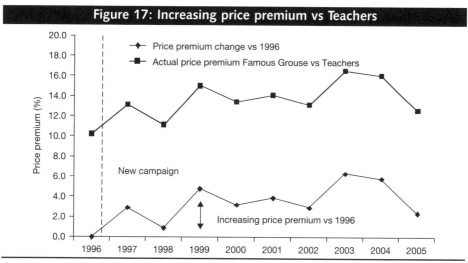

**Figure 17: Increasing price premium vs Teachers**

Source: Nielsen

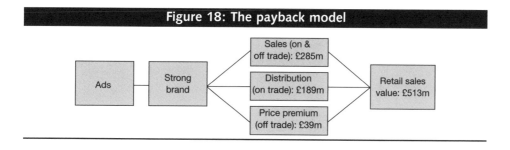

**Figure 18: The payback model**

## Success overseas

Finally, we will look at the international story.

*Market share*

When we compare advertised markets with non-advertised ones, we see markets with advertising fare better. This is partly due to higher distribution, but as our share per distribution point analysis shows, that alone could not explain our success (see Table 4).

While this lacks the rigour of the UK, it is encouraging, especially when looked at in conjunction with strong intermediate measures.

*Intermediate measures*

- **Greece:** strong growth in ad awareness and brand equity (see Figures 19 and 20).
- **Taiwan:** ad awareness and brand equity successfully built (see Figures 21 and 22).

## Table 4: The Famous Grouse market share and distribution

|  | Markets with advertising | Markets without advertising |
|---|---|---|
| Average sector share | 12% | 1% |
| Average distribution | 91% | 40% |
| Share per distribution point, Indexed advertised markets = 100 | 100 | 19.0 |

|  | Sector share: two years pre-advertising | Sector share: two years post-advertising | Share point change pre vs post | Monetary value of share point change |
|---|---|---|---|---|
| Greece | 5.8% | 7.2% | 1.4 | £3.0m |
| Taiwan | 3.0% | 6.0% | 3.0 | £4.2m |

Source: The Edrington Group

## Figure 19: Prompted advertising awareness (Greece)

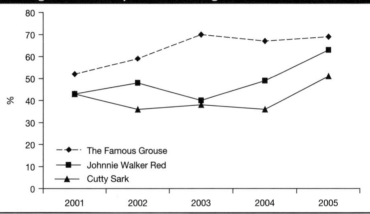

Source: Ipsos

## Figure 20: Brand driver perception index (Greece)

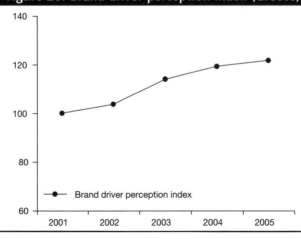

Source: Ipsos

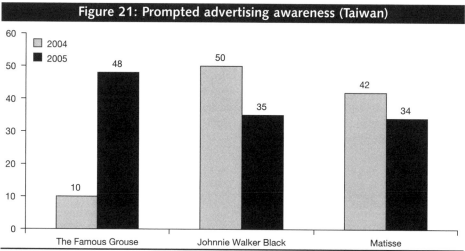

Figure 21: Prompted advertising awareness (Taiwan)

Source: Ipsos

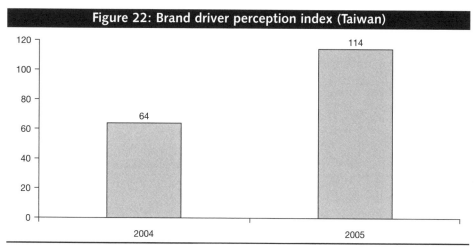

Figure 22: Brand driver perception index (Taiwan)

Source: Ipsos

If the campaign had not been an animated brand-centric advertising vehicle, it would have been necessary to develop separate copy to run in Greece and Taiwan.

Assuming a production to media ratio of 10% and local market retainer fees, it is possible to estimate the additional savings we gained from running Icon in Greece and Taiwan.

The business value to the brand of having a global campaign instead of individual local campaigns can be estimated to be £3m.

## Conclusions

Our Icon campaign, when benchmarked against Bell's – our closest competitor – is shown to outperform it on tracking measures and its ability to build a strong brand. We have eliminated all other causal factors and have proved advertising helped us to close the gap in market share with Bell's, while being outspent by more than 55%.

Using econometrics, we have demonstrated that incremental sales of £285m was generated. In addition, by benchmarking against Teachers – a brand that used to occupy the number two slot in the sector before largely pulling advertising support – we can show that our advertising has added £189m of retail sales value by boosting distribution in the on trade, and £39m of retail sales value by boosting our price premium in the off trade.

# Chapter 24

# Travelocity.co.uk

## Hello World, hello sales: how Travelocity became an overnight success

By Dominic Hall and Andy Nairn, Miles Calcraft Briginshaw Duffy

Online travel agent Travelocity.co.uk launched in the UK in 1998 after the success of Travelocity.com in the US. It enjoyed respectable growth year-on-year, but by 2003 was stilling lagging behind some of the major players in the market. It lacked brand salience, was being heavily outspent by competitors and lacked any sense of differentiation.

To overcome these obstacles, it was decided to pursue a highly alternative targeting strategy. A 'pyramid' of Travelocity's target audience was constructed, with a substantial group of 'novices' at the bottom, and a small group of 'aficionados' at the top. The former group was large in number, but had weaker brand loyalty, and was already being targeted by rival brands. As such, Travelocity decided to aim its campaign at the aficionados, who were young, adventurous and confident about booking online.

The creative expression of this repositioning featured TV personality Alan Whicker in unusual locations around the world, utilising his status as a travel expert to reflect Travelocity's own approach, alongside the tag-line 'Hello World'. These two ingredients were used consistently across all communications channels, including TV, radio, online and PR.

Within days of the start of the campaign, business surged in all the key areas, and in 15 months brand awareness and consideration both greatly improved, as did the number of visits (and unique visitors) to Travelocity.co.uk. Sales and market share also grew, as Travelocity became the most recognised advertiser in the category, with a substantial return on investment reflecting the impact of the campaign overall.

## Introduction

Travelocity started 2004 as a little-known travel brand, overshadowed by its more established, higher-spending rivals, and without any sense of differentiation. However, after just 15 months, Travelocity had boosted brand awareness by 54%, brand consideration by 36%, visits by 123%, unique visitors by 86%, sales by 135% and market share by 44%. All achieved with the most efficient adspend in the category, and a return on investment of £5.60 for every £1 spent.

In short, this paper demonstrates how famous advertising has been responsible for an overnight success story. And it gives hope to fellow upstarts, in fast-moving marketplaces, that you don't always need to wait to reap the rewards of your communications investment.

## Background

Travelocity.co.uk is an online travel agent, which launched in the UK in 1998, following the success of Travelocity.com in the US. At that time, only 9% of UK households had internet access, let alone any interest in booking travel online. However, by 2003, 48% of households were online, and 59% of these had purchased travel, accommodation or holidays over the net.

In fact, travel was one of the fastest-growing categories in the entire e-commerce arena, increasing its share of spend year-on-year (see Figure 1). Travelocity had benefited from this market boom, steadily building up a small band of users (see Figure 2). Sales showed a similar pattern, with a gradual uplift over 2002–2003 (see Figure 3).

However, for all its success, Travelocity was still a relatively minor player in the grand scheme of things. Not only did it have far fewer visitors compared to its competitors (see Figure 4), it was also less likely to be considered by most consumers (see Figure 5).

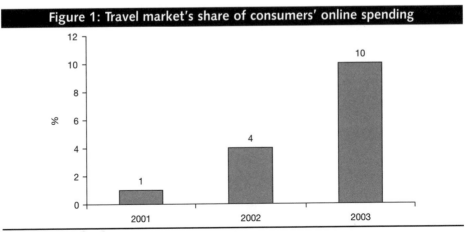

**Figure 1: Travel market's share of consumers' online spending**

Source: Interactive Advertising Bureau

## Figure 2: Unique visitors to Travelocity.co.uk

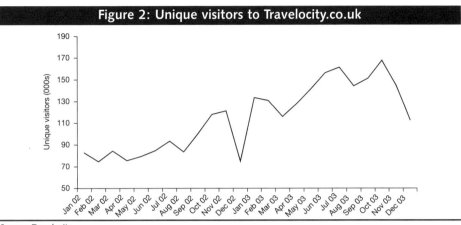

Source: Travelocity

## Figure 3: Travelocity sales

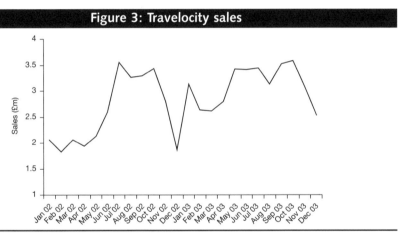

Source: Travelocity

## Figure 4: Ever visited (online travel agents)

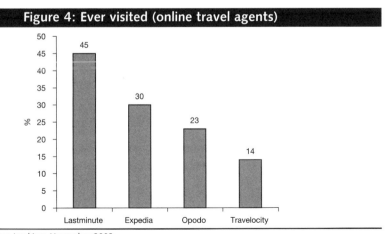

Source: Hall & Partners tracking, November 2003

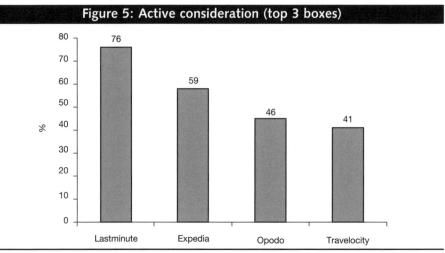

Figure 5: Active consideration (top 3 boxes)

Source: Hall & Partners tracking, November 2003

## Defining the problem

We identified three interrelated problems that were holding Travelocity back – each serious in its own right, but potentially deadly in combination.

### Low salience

There is a strong correlation in this category, between salience and success (see Figure 6). And on this note, Travelocity lagged far behind its competitors (see Figure 7). In a nutshell, Travelocity wasn't famous enough in a marketplace where fame counts for a lot.

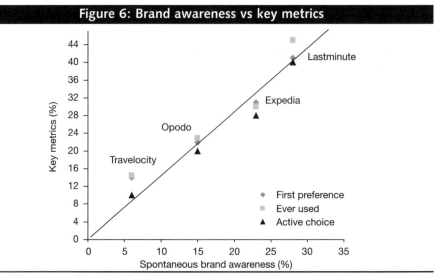

Figure 6: Brand awareness vs key metrics

Source: Hall & Partners tracking, November 2003

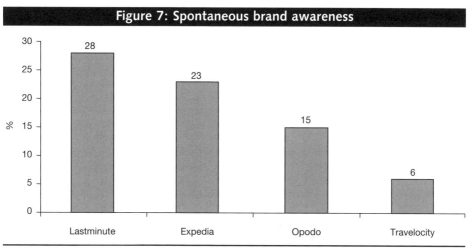

Figure 7: Spontaneous brand awareness

Source: Hall & Partners, November 2003

## Low share of voice

A key reason for this was its low share of voice (see Figure 8). In 2003 alone Expedia spent over seven times more than Travelocity.

## No differentiation

Finally, Travelocity lacked any sense of differentiation. To be fair, this was also true of its main competitors (consumers felt there was little to choose between any of the operators) but Travelocity fared worst of all (see Figure 9).

Now, the other players could arguably get away without any differentiation because they enjoyed greater salience and share of voice. But Travelocity did not have these factors in its favour.

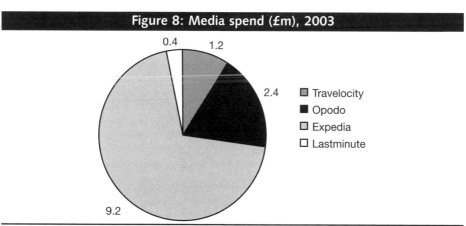

Figure 8: Media spend (£m), 2003

Source: MMS, 2003
Note: although Lastminute spent very little on advertising in 2003, it had spent heavily in previous years. Indeed, in the heady days of the 2001 dotcom boom, it was one of the heaviest spenders of all

## Figure 9: People agreeing that site 'stands out as being different to the rest'

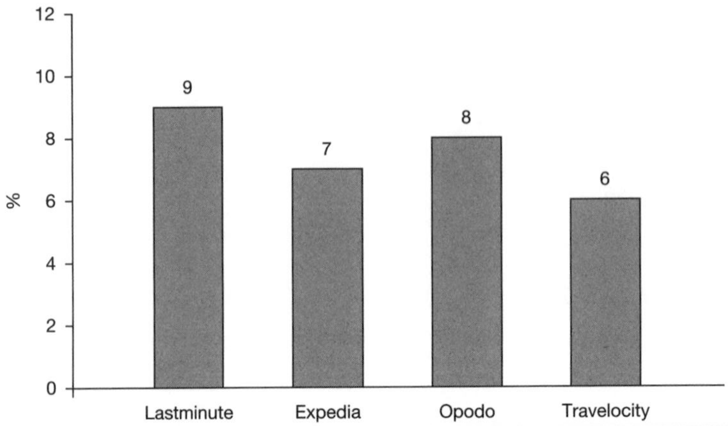

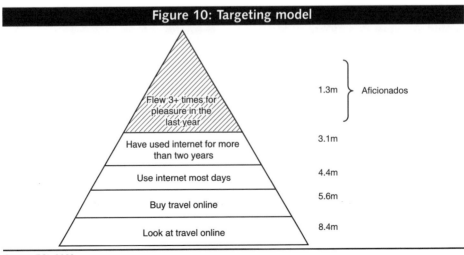

Source: Hall & Partners tracking, November 2003

## Defining the task

Based on the three challenges above, we outlined the task as follows:

- punch above our weight
- dramatically increase Travelocity's salience
- differentiate the brand
- thus force our way onto consumers' shortlists
- and create an immediate step-change in visits and sales.

## Defining an audience

Using TGI, we created a rough targeting model for the marketplace (see Figure 10).

## Figure 10: Targeting model

Source: TGI, 2003

Given our ultimate business objective (create a step-change in visits and sales), the obvious strategy would have been to focus on those 'novices' at the bottom of our pyramid. However, after further consideration, we decided to take exactly the opposite approach, and focus on 'aficionados' instead. These were typically 25–35-year-old urban types with money to spend and the confidence to spend it online. We decided to target them for two reasons.

1. We realised that a focus on 'aficionados' would make our money work harder: not only do they account for a disproportionate amount of sales, they also influence less knowledgeable consumers via word of mouth.
2. We observed that most of our competitors were preoccupied with recruiting 'novices'. In fact, the entire online marketplace seemed to be ignoring experienced users in their desperate quest to reassure beginners.

## Our strategy

Having decided to target 'aficionados', we now needed to position the brand to appeal to this group's adventurous mindset. In a series of dinner parties in city-centre hotels we noted their unbridled sense of confidence, their desire to discover new places and their taste for original marketing approaches. Excited by their attitude, we resolved to position Travelocity as nothing less than:

*The inspirational travel experts*

### Our creative idea

Our creative expression of this positioning was to feature Alan Whicker in unusual places around the world, commentating on Travelocity's expertise. Although, on a superficial level, Whicker's age made him an unusual choice to talk to 25–35-year-old travellers, he was actually ideally suited to this role.

First, he was universally liked and regarded as the original expert in the field. Second, he was seen as a genuine travel 'aficionado', and not a marketing puppet. And, third, precisely because he had been off the public radar for some time, he could acquire a cult cachet that our sophisticated audience would really appreciate.

### Our media approach

With less money than our competitors, it was vital to adopt seamless communications throughout, from the moment of inspiration to the point of booking:

- we used TV (11 ads so far) to drive awareness and reach quickly
- we used radio (31 ads so far) to multiply the effect of the TV, with specific messages about the website's superiority
- we used outdoor (seven executions so far) to build awareness of the brand name and web address in travel-related locations (e.g. around tube/train stations and airports)
- we used the idea online, in everything from customer emails to the website itself, to help clinch the sale

■ finally, we used guerrilla marketing to create a buzz around the campaign; from viral ads, to stunts at airports, to Whicker dolls, we're always looking for new ways to engage 'aficionados' with the campaign.

We launched the campaign on 4 January 2004, spending £3.7m in 2004 and £2.7m in early 2005 (see Figure 11).

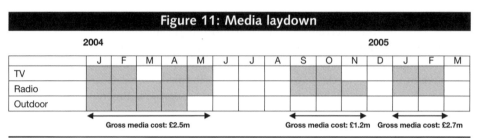

### Figure 11: Media laydown

| | 2004 | | | | | | | | | | | 2005 | | |
| | J | F | M | A | M | J | J | A | S | O | N | D | J | F | M |
|---|---|---|---|---|---|---|---|---|---|---|---|---|---|---|---|
| TV | | ▓ | | ▓ | | | | | ▓ | | | | ▓ | | |
| Radio | ▓ | ▓ | ▓ | ▓ | | | | | ▓ | | | ▓ | ▓ | ▓ | |
| Outdoor | ▓ | ▓ | ▓ | ▓ | | | | | | | | | | | |

Gross media cost: £2.5m　　Gross media cost: £1.2m　Gross media cost: £2.7m

Source: Travelocity/Klondike

## Business results

Within days of the campaign's launch, the business experienced a dramatic surge across all key measures.

### A step-change in visiting

Almost immediately, visits to the website more than doubled. Although the new year is a key season for all travel brands, this was way out of proportion to any 'seasonal' blip: in January 2003, visiting was up 67% on the previous month, whereas in January 2004, we saw an uplift of 168% vs the previous month. By the end of 2004, visiting was up 123% vs 2003 (see Figure 12).

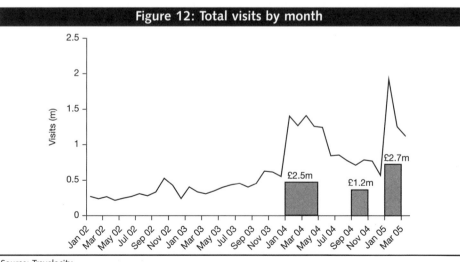

### Figure 12: Total visits by month

Source: Travelocity

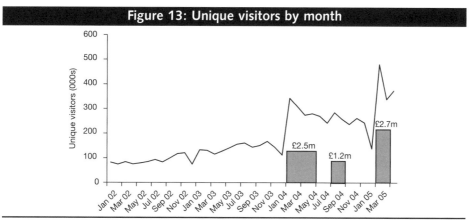

Figure 13: Unique visitors by month

Source: Travelocity

The number of unique visitors shot up even more dramatically, virtually trebling in the first month. In fact, total unique visiting over 2004 was 86% higher than in 2003 (see Figure 13).

The vast majority of these visitors have been new to Travelocity, although we have also held on to our existing customers (see Figure 14).

And as more people have discovered Travelocity, and begun visiting more often, they have explored more of the site too: by January 2005, page views were about eight times the level of two years ago (see Figure 15).

## A step-change in sales

As you'd expect from the preceding charts, there was also a huge and immediate surge in sales. In fact, 2004's sales ended up 135% up on 2003, and continued to rise in 2005 (see Figure 16).

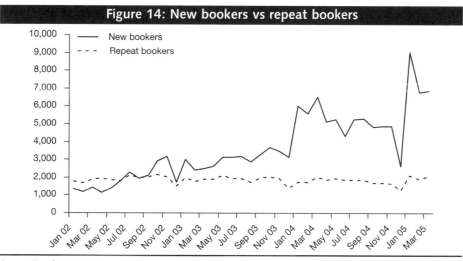

Figure 14: New bookers vs repeat bookers

Source: Travelocity

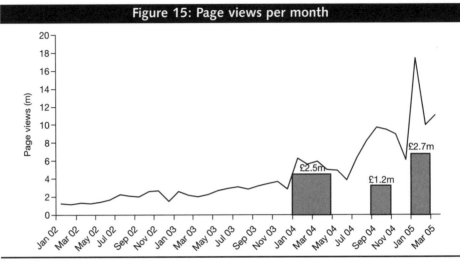

Figure 15: Page views per month

Source: Travelocity

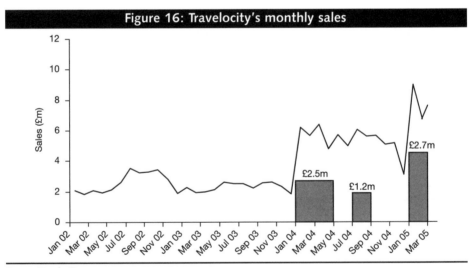

Figure 16: Travelocity's monthly sales

Source: Travelocity

*A step-change in market share*

Given the buoyancy of this market, it is important to emphasise that our massive uplift in visits and sales did not simply reflect category growth.

In fact, Travelocity also saw an immediate rise in market share (from 10% to 18% in the first month). Although this extraordinary surge subsequently receded, our average share still held up at over 13% during 2004, vs 9% the previous year (see Figure 17). This was the biggest shift in market share in the category (see Figure 18).

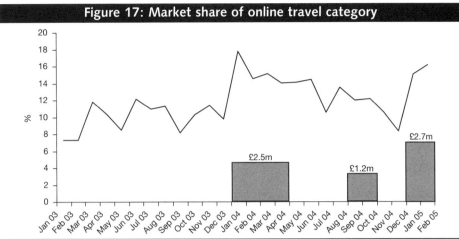

Figure 17: Market share of online travel category

Source: Nielsen

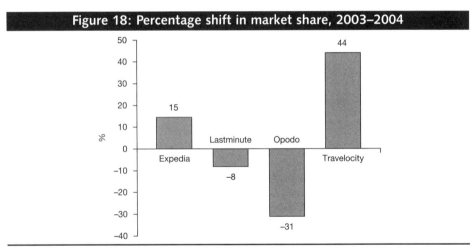

Figure 18: Percentage shift in market share, 2003–2004

Source: Nielsen

## What role did advertising play?

*We punched above our weight*

After the first burst, Travelocity was catapulted from last place in the advertising awareness stakes to first place. We have stayed in that position ever since (see Figure 19). With campaign recognition at 78%, we have by far the best-known campaign in the category.

By comparing advertising awareness against spend, we can prove that our campaign was over four times more efficient than Expedia's in generating cut-through (see Figure 20).

Similarly, we can prove that our campaign was almost twice as efficient in acquiring visitors (see Figure 21).

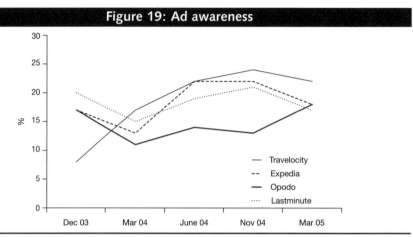

Figure 19: Ad awareness

Source: Hall & Partners tracking

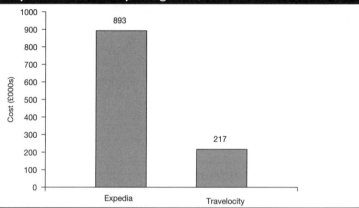

Figure 20: Cost per ad awareness point gained, November 2003–March 2005

Source: Hall & Partners tracking/MMS
Note: this exercise cannot be conducted for Lastminute or Opodo as both saw a decline in ad awareness

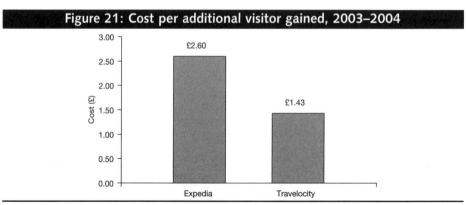

Figure 21: Cost per additional visitor gained, 2003–2004

Source: Nielsen
Note: this exercise cannot be conducted for Lastminute or Opodo as both saw a decline in visitors

*We dramatically increased Travelocity's salience*

The campaign also had an immediate effect on brand awareness (see Figure 22). Again, this increase was far greater than that experienced by our rivals. Travelocity became more famous more quickly than anyone else (see Figure 23).

The campaign has attracted huge amounts of coverage in the consumer world, in titles as diverse as *Heat* and the *Daily Telegraph*.

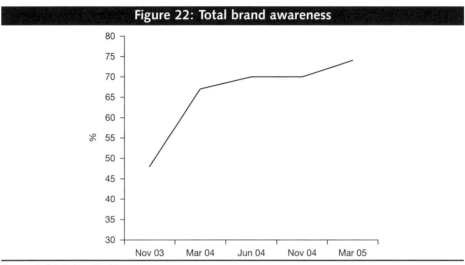

**Figure 22: Total brand awareness**

Source: Hall & Partners tracking

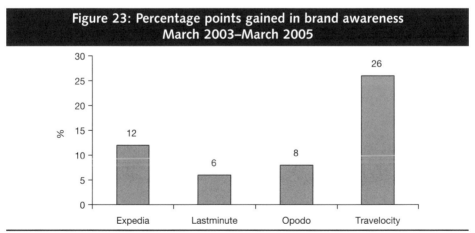

**Figure 23: Percentage points gained in brand awareness
March 2003–March 2005**

Source: Hall & Partners tracking

*We made Travelocity stand out as different*

As we established earlier on, one of Travelocity's key challenges was that virtually nobody felt there was anything different about the brand or site. Again, this situation was changed virtually overnight (see Figure 24).

## Figure 24: Percentage of people claiming Travelocity 'stands out as being different'

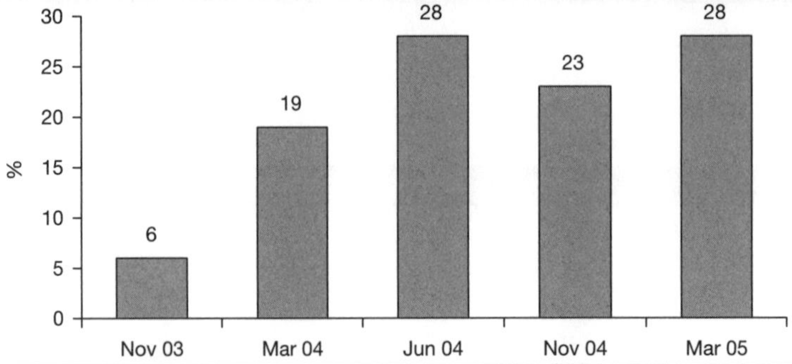

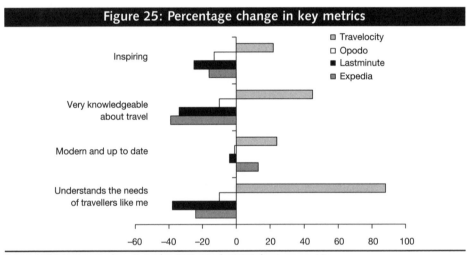

Source: Hall & Partners tracking

## Figure 25: Percentage change in key metrics

Source: Hall & Partners tracking, December 2003–March 2005 in key image metrics

In particular, we have made huge progress in terms of positioning Travelocity as 'the inspirational travel experts' (see Figure 25).

Once again, it's clear that advertising has contributed massively to this sense of differentiation (Table 1).

In particular, Whicker's own role in building our expert credentials is clear. And his contribution continues to grow each year (see Figure 26).

## Table 1: Advertising standout

|  | % agreeing that the advertising: |
|---|---|
| Stands out as different | 60 |
| Makes me pay close attention to it | 61 |
| Really sticks in my mind | 46 |

Source: Hall & Partners tracking

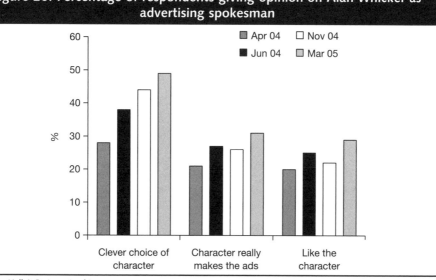

Figure 26: Percentage of respondents giving opinion on Alan Whicker as advertising spokesman

Source: Hall & Partners tracking

## Advertising forced Travelocity onto consumers' shortlists

Finally, by punching above its weight, boosting Travelocity's salience and making the brand stand out as different, advertising immediately increased consumer involvement with Travelocity (see Figure 27). In fact, it was the only brand to increase involvement over this period (see Figure 28).

Boosted by this new sense of involvement with the brand, Travelocity also massively increased active consideration among travellers (see Figure 29).

Yet again, Travelocity increased this measure more than any of its competitors (see Figure 30).

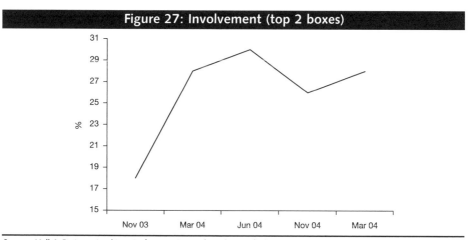

Figure 27: Involvement (top 2 boxes)

Source: Hall & Partners tracking. Definition: 'How close do you feel to the brand'

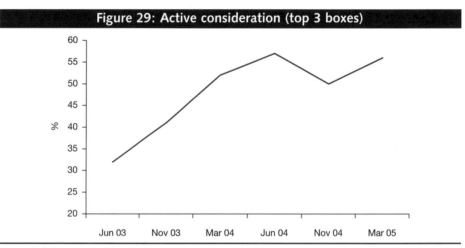

Figure 28: Percentage points gained in 'involvement'
November 2003–March 2005

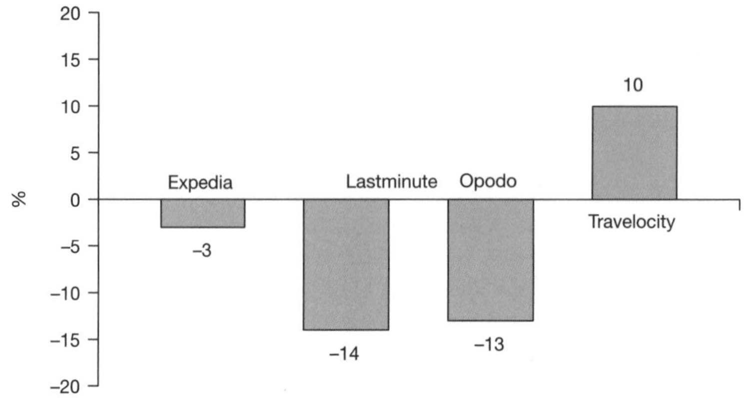

Source: Hall & Partners tracking

Figure 29: Active consideration (top 3 boxes)

Source: Hall & Partners tracking

## Eliminating other factors

### Improvement to the product

While the basic product has regularly been updated (as with any website), these changes have been incremental and certainly no more radical than those made by our competitors.

### Pricing strategy

There have been no major changes to Travelocity's pricing policy over the period. Indeed, during 2004, Travelocity's competitors reduced their booking fees to £4 to

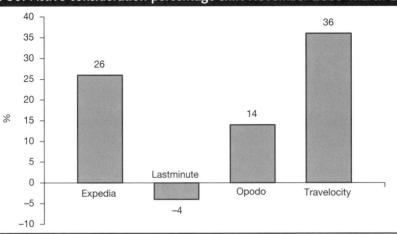

Figure 30: Active consideration percentage shift November 2003–March 2005

Source: Hall & Partners tracking

undercut the £10 fee charged by Travelocity. And even though we have since reduced this to £6, we still operate at a price disadvantage on this measure.

*Promotional strategy*

Travelocity is not pursuing more, or deeper, promotions than in the past. And if anything, as we built a strong, differentiated brand, our association with constant deals fell (see Figure 31).

*Other communications*

As with most websites, Travelocity has an ongoing CRM programme. However, this is relatively limited in scope and, in any case, we have established that growth has come almost entirely from attracting new visitors (see Figure 14).

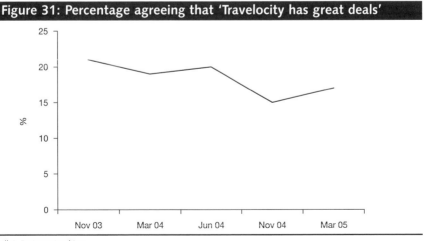

Figure 31: Percentage agreeing that 'Travelocity has great deals'

Source: Hall & Partners tracking

*Market growth*

In such a fast-moving market, it would be disingenuous to discount market growth entirely. As the market grew by 39% over 2004, and Travelocity grew by 135%, it is reasonable to acknowledge that 29% (39/135) of Travelocity's growth may be due to market growth. The remaining 71%, we would argue, is due to advertising.

## Quantifying advertising's return on investment

Based on our calculation that advertising has been responsible for 71% of Travelocity's growth, in sterling terms this equates to £26.3m. On a total spend of £4.7m, this equates to a return on investment of £5.60 for every £1 invested.

Now Travelocity has a strict policy of not disclosing its margins, but it is happy to confirm that, in the words of managing director Ned Booth, 'even in the short term, this has been a very valuable investment'.

## Conclusion

Travelocity has (appropriately enough) been on quite a journey recently. From a bit-player to the market's thought-leader. From a recessive advertiser in its own category to one of the most famous in any sector. From an undifferentiated product to a brand with a distinct point of view. And, finally, from a business that was just doing OK, to one that has grown very dramatically, very quickly. We hope we've proved that, with the right vehicle, advertising can make brands travel at supersonic speed too.

# Chapter 25

# Tropicana

## How the Big Apple helped sell orange juice

**By Alex Huzzey, DDB London, and Julia Wood, DDB Matrix**
Contributing authors: Les Binet, DDB Matrix; Sarah Carter, DDB London, and Marcia Garcia
and Rachel Leaver, ACNielsen Analytic Consulting

In 2003, Tropicana was in a growing market, but as a premium brand was losing share to cheaper own-label products, meaning it was reliant on just 5% of juice buyers for 74% of its volume sales.

Its initial 'Parrots' campaign attempted to reverse this situation by making Tropicana a household name, but met with limited success. A change in approach followed, based on an appeal to more 'foody' consumers who would be prepared to spend more on orange juice. Of the information collected to demonstrate Tropicana's quality credentials, the one that stood out was that Tropicana is the No.1 grocery brand in New York – famous for its breakfast culture and lavish, cosmopolitan lifestyle, something that struck a chord with the aspirations of Tropicana's target market in the UK.

However, tracking research demonstrated that the 'New York' campaign had an AI score of just 3, well below the UK average of 6. While the campaign may have been 'low impact', the music and imagery employed produced a subtle range of positive emotions and associations with the brand. This, in turn, exerted a highly positive impact on Tropicana's rate of growth, more than reversing its decline in market share. Price elasticity decreased by 40% and penetration increased significantly, particularly among the affluent 'foodies' the campaign was aimed at. Econometric modelling also showed that advertising was a significant driver of the sales uplift, giving a payback of £1.83 for every £1 spent.

## Introduction

This is a simple but powerful reminder of what TV advertising can achieve: reversing declining market share, justifying a premium, and driving both penetration and loyalty.

This paper also demonstrates that, despite TV being such a well-established medium, we still have lots to learn when it comes to developing successful campaigns. We show how top tracking scores are no guarantee of sales success, and how a creative idea that underperforms on tracking scores may perform exceptionally well in a live situation.

## Background

The juice market has been buoyant for the past 20 years. However, its naturalness represents a huge challenge for brands in the sector. As it is a totally natural product, what value can a brand add? Orange juice is sometimes likened by consumers to milk – as a similarly commoditised product.

The key challenge throughout Tropicana's history in the UK has been to fight this perception.

## Tropicana launch

When Tropicana was introduced in 1992, it immediately appeared to be distinctively different:

- it was in the chiller cabinet at a time when most juice sold in the UK was long-life
- its packaging was a tall, thin, gable-top carton with a screw top, rather than the squatter long-life packaging
- the juice is processed in a different way to the majority of juices consumed in the UK, which are made from concentrate ('FC'); Tropicana Pure Premium has simply been squeezed, gently pasteurised and chilled, resulting in a fresher and more natural taste (not from concentrate – 'NFC').

Over the next ten years the brand grew steadily, overtaking Del Monte to become the number one UK juice brand in 1999. During the 2000s, however, growth began to stall. Whilst both volume and value sales had continued to increase, the brand had begun to lose share (see Figure 1).

Supermarkets had invested in a range of chilled own-label juices, both copying Tropicana's distinctive carton and undercutting Tropicana significantly on price. Own-label juice was retailing at around 66p a carton, versus £1.62 for Tropicana.

For consumers who weren't aware of the difference between FC and NFC, Tropicana simply looked like a more expensive version of what the supermarket was offering.

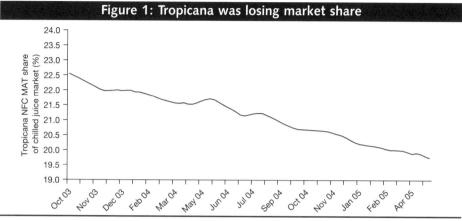

Figure 1: Tropicana was losing market share

Source: ACNielsen

## 2003 marketing objective

In 2003, ambitious growth targets were set for Tropicana. Analysis revealed that the brand still had very low penetration – 74% of volume was bought by just 5% of juice buyers: predominantly over 45, well off and located in the south-east of England; 94% of them were already buying NFC juice, so there was little opportunity to extend penetration within the group. And, as most of them no longer had children at home, there was also little chance of dramatically increasing weight of purchase.

It was unlikely we would make targets unless we could get people outside this cluster to connect with the brand. The key marketing objective was therefore to extend penetration.

DDB was briefed to give the brand personality and salience for a broader audience.

## The 'Parrots' campaign

In March 2004, a trio of all-singing, all-dancing parrots with Latino accents burst onto British television screens, backed by a spend of £4.3m. The campaign delivered on its brief to give the brand some personality. Enjoyment figures were through the roof.

The campaign extended awareness and appeal of Tropicana to a much more downmarket audience, far beyond the well-to-do empty nesters who were the brand's loyal aficionados. However, this revealed a significant flaw in the campaign. Whilst it got the brand noticed by a broader audience, the price premium meant the product was too expensive for most. As the campaign appealed less to the more upmarket audience who could afford it, it did little to drive sales.

Econometrics confirmed that only 1.5% of sales volume in 2004 was attributable to communications (see Figure 2).

Unsurprisingly, penetration failed to increase significantly either, hovering between 3% and 4% throughout 2004.

Figure 2: Contribution of 'Parrots' campaign to 2004 sales volume

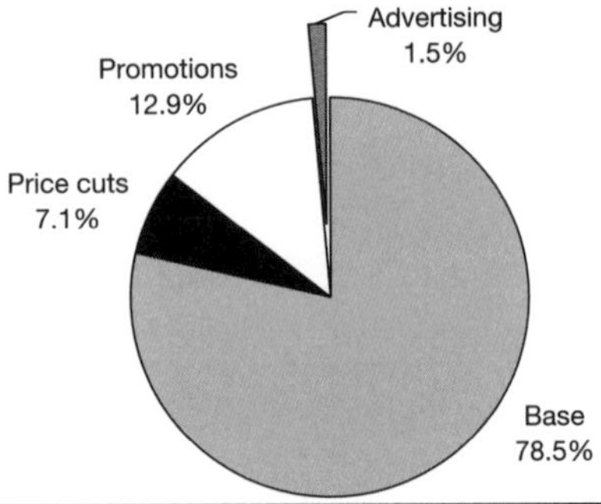

Advertising 1.5%
Promotions 12.9%
Price cuts 7.1%
Base 78.5%

Source: ACNielsen

## 2005: competition looms

Tropicana was still dependent upon a small number of loyal customers for the vast bulk of its volume. Driving penetration was still the key marketing objective.

A new threat was looming. Coca-Cola was going to be launching the first branded NFC competitor to Tropicana, in the form of Minute Maid. The need to justify Tropicana's premium to a wider audience had never been more pressing.

Two key clusters were identified, attitudinally similar to loyalists but younger, where there was still room to grow in terms of penetration: an upmarket audience with a 'foody' inclination that drove them towards premium quality foods and drinks.

## A new approach

We looked at the ways in which other premium food brands had sought to establish their quality credentials. Premium products were often those that could claim to be authentic in some way, via their geographical provenance or authentic company history. Green & Blacks, Waitrose and M&S were all talking to our target market in this way.

### New York, New York

The obvious place to take communications would be Tropicana's provenance down on the groves. However, rather than following in Del Monte's footsteps, creatives found a rather unexpected angle – the fact that Tropicana is the number one grocery brand in New York, outselling even Coca-Cola.

New York also has a strong breakfast culture, with hotels, restaurants and diners offering enormous ranges of eggs, waffles, muffins, coffees and pancakes, all made to order for the most demanding Manhattan clientele. Tropicana was the juice that belonged as part of all those indulgent breakfasts. This became the creative idea for the new campaign.

A TV ad was shot and aired in March 2005, to a backing track of Dean Martin's 'How d'ya like your eggs in the morning'. It was backed up by three press ads, and a total spend of £4.9m.

# The results

## Figure 3: Sales increased as soon as the campaign started

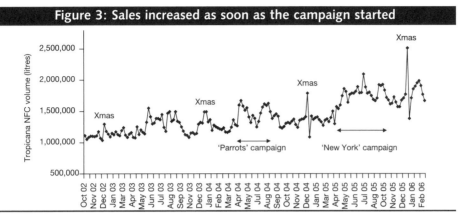

Source: ACNielsen

## Figure 4: The decline in market share was reversed

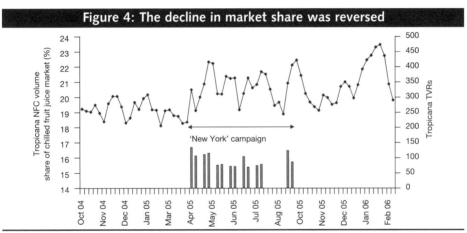

Source: ACNielsen, BARB

## Figure 5: Market share grew in both volume and value terms

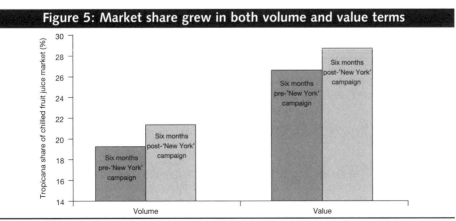

Source: ACNielsen

Tropicana also managed to steel itself against the launch of Coca-Cola's Minute Maid (see Figure 6).

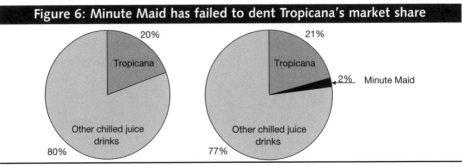

Figure 6: Minute Maid has failed to dent Tropicana's market share

Source: ACNielsen

The campaign delivered on the key objective for 2005, in increasing penetration significantly (see Figure 7).

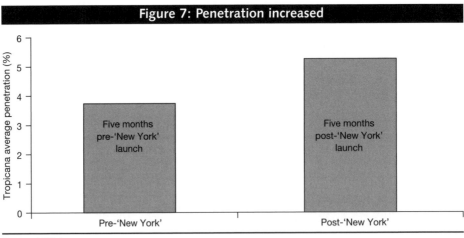

Figure 7: Penetration increased

Source: ACNielsen

Finally, Tropicana's price elasticity fell by 40% during 2005, proving that the campaign had succeeded in justifying the brand's price premium.

## How do we know that the sales increases are attributable to advertising?

As shown in Figure 8, the increase in sales corresponded exactly with the airing of the TV ads. Moreover, regions with more advertising grew faster (see Figure 9).

Econometric analysis demonstrates that advertising was directly responsible for a significant uplift in sales (see Figure 10).

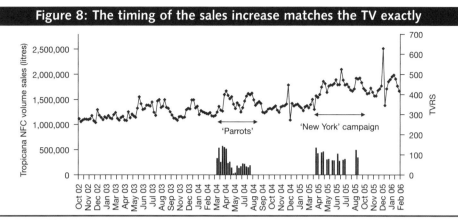

Figure 8: The timing of the sales increase matches the TV exactly

Source: ACNielsen, BARB

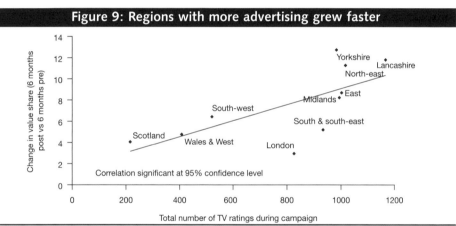

Figure 9: Regions with more advertising grew faster

Source: ACNielsen, BARB

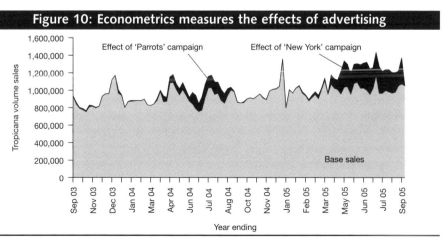

Figure 10: Econometrics measures the effects of advertising

Source: ACNielsen Analytics Consulting

## Figure 11: Contribution of advertising to sales growth in 2005

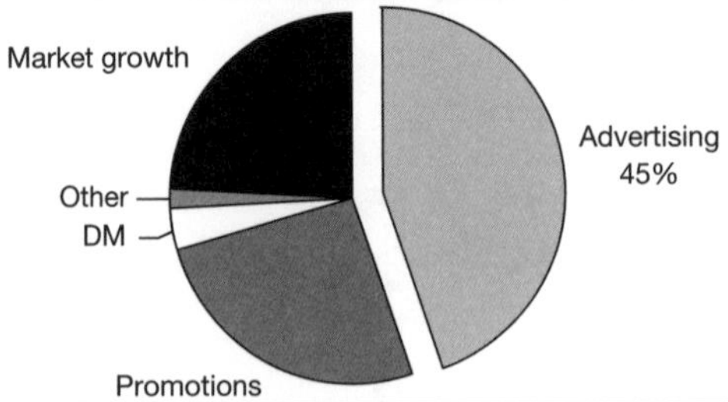

Market growth

Advertising
45%

Other

DM

Promotions

Source: ACNielsen Analytics Consulting

In fact, the model shows that advertising was by far the biggest driver of sales growth (see Figure 11).

## Eliminating other explanations

There is clearly a correlation between the sales uplifts and the timing of the advertising in 2005. However, could any other factor have been responsible?

### Market factors

The market continued to grow in 2005. We can eliminate category-level factors on the basis that Tropicana market share also increased.

### Distribution

Distribution can also be eliminated: it remained fixed at nearly 100% for the entire period.

### Variants

The number of variants increased by only one in 2005, indicating that growth was not simply a result of range extensions.

The new variant was in the Tropicana Essentials range. Essentials remained a small part of overall sales.

### New pack design

A new pack design, launched in January 2005, was very much an evolution rather than a revolution.

Furthermore, the new packaging was introduced several months before the sales uplifts occurred.

ACNielsen's econometric model shows that the packaging change accounted for only 1% of additional volume (see Figure 12).

### Price

Price can also be eliminated as a potential reason for volume increases – the relative price of Tropicana versus own-label NFC increased significantly during 2005 (see Figure 13).

## Figure 12: Contribution of new packaging to growth was minimal

Market growth

Other

New packaging
1%

DM

Advertising

Promotions

Source: ACNielsen Econometrics

## Figure 13: Tropicana's price increased relative to the market

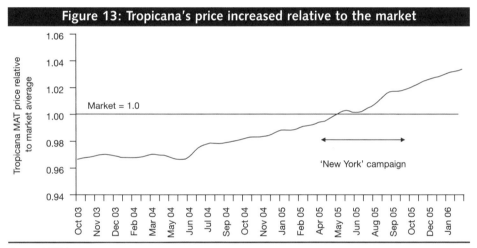

Source: ACNielsen

## Dealing

Econometrics shows that the contribution of in-store dealing is less than that of advertising (see Figure 14).

## Figure 14: Promotions contributed less to growth than advertising

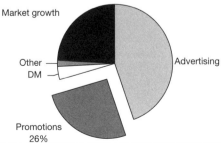

Market growth

Other

DM

Advertising

Promotions
26%

Source: ACNielsen Econometrics

Furthermore, sales promotions were national, whilst the regional analysis cited earlier shows that regions with more advertising saw greater uplifts.

### Direct marketing

Direct marketing played a key role in Tropicana's success in 2006, driving 4% of the sales uplift; '50p off' coupons were distributed to households that fitted the target demographic profile.

However, the majority of the sales increases are not attributable to DM activity for two key reasons:

1. The timing of the uplifts doesn't match the timing of the DM.
2. The econometric model shows that DM was responsible for only 4% of incremental volume in 2006 (see Figure 15).

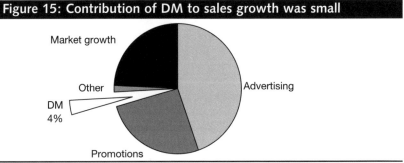

**Figure 15: Contribution of DM to sales growth was small**

Market growth

Other

Advertising

DM 4%

Promotions

Source: ACNielsen Econometrics

### The competitive context

The sales increase cannot be attributed to a decline in competition. Minute Maid, the first ever branded NFC competitor for Tropicana, launched in 2005, achieving 75% distribution from July onwards. Competition from own-label also got much tougher during 2005.

## Payback and efficiency

Econometrics shows ads delivered huge returns in additional sales revenue (see Figure 16).

The campaign considerably outperforms the fmcg benchmark of 37p return for every £1 spent.

### How the ads worked

First, the evidence from qualitative research. Three key elements appear to be driving the success of the campaign:

1. The music.
2. The food imagery.
3. Manhattan.

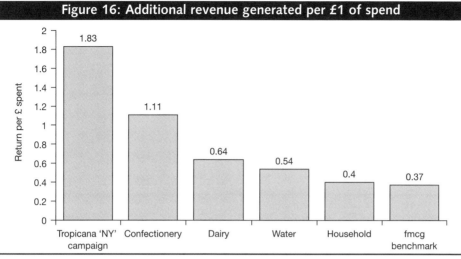

Figure 16: Additional revenue generated per £1 of spend

Source: ACNielsen Analytic Consulting

## Music

Central to the appeal of the ad was the music, Dean Martin's 'How d'ya like your eggs in the morning'. Qualitative research revealed that it gave the ad energy and optimism.

Calls to Tropicana's product helpline went up by 50%, driven solely by people wanting to get hold of the music.

## The food shots

Lingering shots of hollandaise sauce being drizzled onto poached eggs, bacon on a griddle and a fried egg sizzling in a pan got people's mouths watering, and helped conjure up the lavish and indulgent New York breakfast.

## New York

Both Millward Brown tracking and qualitative research conducted before and after the campaign identified the sheer aspirational appeal of New York as key to the success of the campaign.

> *The strength of the story seems to be in this depiction of big, sensuous scenes – the dew on Central Park, an empty Times Square, the sun rising over Brooklyn Bridge, not in a factual thrust about Tropicana being New York's favourite juice.*
>
> Flamingo International, creative development research

## Evidence from tracking

On the whole, the tracking study also shows the campaign working effectively (see Figures 17–19).

## Figure 17: Brand awareness increased whilst the 'New York' ad was on air

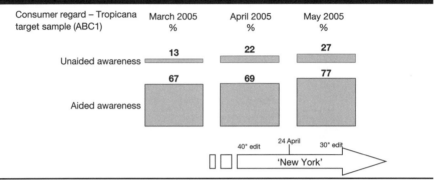

Consumer regard – Tropicana
target sample (ABC1)

|  | March 2005 % | April 2005 % | May 2005 % |
|---|---|---|---|
| Unaided awareness | 13 | 22 | 27 |
| Aided awareness | 67 | 69 | 77 |

40" edit    24 April    30" edit
'New York'

Base: ABC1 sample (140+ interviews per month)
Significant to April data at 95% or above confidence level
March (07/03–03/04/05), April (04/04–01/05/05), May (02/05–29/05/05)
Source: Millward Brown tracking study, 2005

## Figure 18: Brand image improved whilst the ad was on air

Brand health summary – Tropicana Pure Premium
target sample (ABC1)

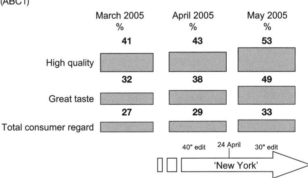

|  | March 2005 % | April 2005 % | May 2005 % |
|---|---|---|---|
| High quality | 41 | 43 | 53 |
| Great taste | 32 | 38 | 49 |
| Total consumer regard | 27 | 29 | 33 |

40" edit    24 April    30" edit
'New York'

Base: ABC1 sample (140+ interviews per month)
Significant to April data at 95% or above confidence level
March (07/03–03/04/05), April (04/04–01/05/05), May (02/05–29/05/05)
Source: Millward Brown tracking study, 2005

## Figure 19: Ad diagnostics also suggested the campaign was improving brand image and driving trial

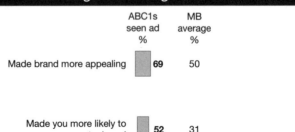

|  | ABC1s seen ad % | MB average % |
|---|---|---|
| Made brand more appealing | 69 | 50 |
| Made you more likely to try brand | 52 | 31 |

Source: Millward Brown tracking study, 2005

## The awareness index

However, certain aspects of the quantitative analysis of the campaign are at odds with the fact that we now know the campaign to have been extremely successful. First, although the ad is enjoyable, it is measured by Millward Brown to be enjoyable in a passive way, particularly in comparison to the 'Parrots' campaign (see Figure 20).

**Figure 20: The 'New York' ad registered as less actively engaging than 'Parrots'**

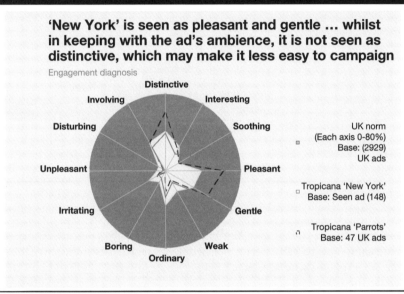

'New York' is seen as pleasant and gentle ... whilst in keeping with the ad's ambience, it is not seen as distinctive, which may make it less easy to campaign

Engagement diagnosis

UK norm
(Each axis 0-80%)
Base: (2929)
UK ads

Tropicana 'New York'
Base: Seen ad (148)

Tropicana 'Parrots'
Base: 47 UK ads

Source: Millward Brown

Millward Brown expects 'pleasant' and 'gentle' ads to have lower cut-through, and therefore to struggle to drive awareness or sales.

The second problem is that of branding (see Figure 21).

The combination of poor branding and poor cut-through leads to a poor AI of just 3, rising to 4 for ABC1s (see Figure 22).

**Figure 21: Tracking data suggested the ad was poorly branded**

| | ABC1 seen ad % | MB average % |
|---|---|---|
| Branding | 38 | 48 |
| Ad could have been for anything | 33 | 18 |

Source: Millward Brown

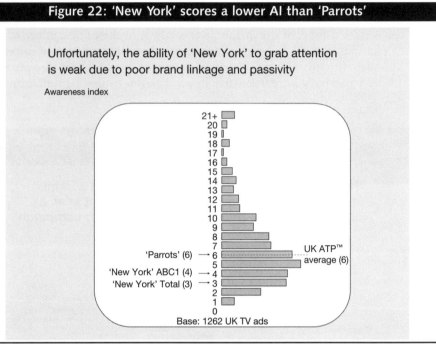

Figure 22: 'New York' scores a lower AI than 'Parrots'

Source: Millward Brown. Base: 1262 UK TV ads

If one were to use the AI as a key indicator of a likely sales effect, one would expect the campaign to have performed worse than 'Parrots' in a real-life setting. How can we explain this discrepancy between sales on the one hand and tracking evidence on the other?

Robert Heath's theory of low-involvement processing suggests that a lot of successful advertising does not need to actively engage consumers, but works by simply creating a set of positive emotional associations around the brand. These then linger in consumers' subconscious minds, and ultimately drive choice.

This is in stark contrast to the high-involvement model, which many agencies and tracking methodologies have subscribed to, which suggests ads need to provoke reaction from consumers, shaking them out of their apathy and forcing them to sit up, take notice, and remember the brand and the message.

'Parrots' and 'New York' are good illustrations of the way in which the two models work.

'Parrots' fits a high-involvement model of advertising, featuring bright, brash and colourful characters that you can't fail to notice. You might not like them, you probably don't find them aspirational, but you definitely remember them. Add to this the catchy Tropicana jingle they sing and it's hard to miss the branding either.

'New York', on the other hand, is nowhere near as obviously intrusive. The city environment does not immediately cue either Tropicana or juice in general, and the focus of the ad is not a rational persuasive message about the product or brand.

However, what the campaign does do is create a whole range of positive emotional associations around the brand. All of which might just push you in the direction of Tropicana as you speed past the chiller, rather than the anonymous own-label equivalent.

Interestingly, if we compare all the campaigns ACNielsen has recently developed econometric models for, with the AI scores Millward Brown accorded those campaigns, we see that it is by no means unusual to see campaigns that have high AI scores failing to translate to real-world effectiveness (see Figure 23).

## Figure 23: Relationship between AI scores and sales uplifts

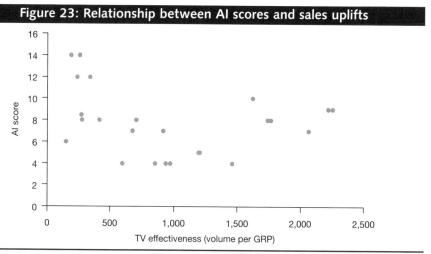

Source: ACNielsen Analytic Consulting

## Conclusions

Our case study of Tropicana's 'New York' campaign casts doubt on two advertising truisms.

At a time when TV advertising is supposed to be on the way out, we have proven how a TV campaign is still able to achieve extraordinary feats. It justified a price premium at a time when own-label equivalent prices were dropping through the floor. It reversed a brand's decline in market share despite a significant new competitor entering the category.

Second, the success of the New York campaign refutes the idea that successful advertising has to conform to a model of active engagement. This paper demonstrates how a campaign, which conventional tracking dismissed as quiet and unengaging, was able to generate positive associations around the brand at a more instinctive, emotional level. Associations that ultimately influenced brand choice, and drove considerable sales success.

## Chapter 26

# Virgin Trains

The Return of the Train: how Virgin Trains became the nation's favourite transport provider

**By Lucy Howard, RKCR/Y&R, and Claire Marker, Manning Gottlieb OMD**
Contributing authors: David Bratt, Jack Bowley and Sally Dickerson, Manning Gottlieb OMD, and Steve Perry, Virgin Trains

In 1997, Virgin Trains took control of the UK's two largest rail franchises: the Cross Country and West Coast networks. By 2002, however, the proportion of respondents stating that Britain's railways had deteriorated outnumbered those thinking they had improved by 13:1. Rail travel was also seen by many as slow, uncomfortable and unreliable.

Consumers' emotional engagement with the Virgin Trains brand also remained low, especially compared with the attachment to, and positive images they had of, travelling by road or by air. The new Voyager and Pendolino trains, which showed that the company was addressing their concerns, also no longer constituted 'new news'.

Despite this, Virgin Trains wanted to encourage travellers to begin to view it as the transport provider of choice. The ensuing 'Return of the Train' TV campaign sought to generate a step-change in behaviour and attitudes by providing a modern take on the 'golden era' of rail travel, when the UK was a nation of train lovers, fusing cutting-edge communications with 'the good old days' of train service. This was backed up by details of innovations such as increased speed, timetable changes and improved on-board facilities.

The campaign met with record tracking scores for awareness, saliency and involvement, and emotional affinity had also greatly improved by the end of 2005. Overall journey numbers also showed a significant increase over the campaign period, and West Coast revenues improved by 32% year-on-year, with incremental revenue from advertising estimated to be £29.7m, or an ROI of £4.20.

## Introduction

Perhaps more than any other brand, Virgin loves a challenge.

Our 2004 IPA paper detailed the first chapter of the journey towards delivering on what Richard Branson called his 'greatest challenge ever': to rekindle the public's enthusiasm for the train.

This is Chapter 2: the story of how the campaign known as 'The Return of the Train' helped to make Virgin Trains the nation's favourite transport provider. By engaging the public on a positive emotional level, we succeeded in making Virgin Trains the transport operator of choice in the UK, thereby driving higher journey numbers, £29.7m in incremental revenue and an ROI of £4.20 on the West Coast line alone.

This step-change was delivered in the face of the dominance of the airlines operating on the same routes, the lack of genuinely 'new news' and, last but not least, the tragic London terror attacks of 7 July 2005.

## Context: from 'grim' to 'good enough'

In 1997, Richard Branson acquired the UK's two largest rail franchises: the Cross Country and West Coast networks. The Virgin takeover had a rocky start. Virgin Trains were seeking to overturn nationally held, deeply negative perceptions rather than a complacent category leader.

After five years of Virgin involvement, the proportion of respondents who believed Britain's railways had deteriorated exceeded the proportion that believed they had improved, by a ratio of 13 to 1. Due to the stature of the brand and the expectations that the public had of Richard Branson, Virgin Trains was disproportionately likely to be criticised.

A new fleet of state-of-the-art 'Voyager' trains, plus a dramatically improved timetable, provided the opportunity to demonstrate progress and to start to correct the negative view that the consumer had of rail travel in the UK. These trains were a world away from the rickety, slam-door trains that used to operate on the Cross Country route, and gave Virgin Trains fantastic 'fuel' with which to address the rational barriers that the consumer had around product experience, speed and frequency.

These new developments were brought to life in the 'New Beginning' campaign of 2002, which used the analogy of a woman giving birth on a train.

The campaign worked to overcome deeply held, negative impressions of trains, increasing the number of people willing to consider travelling by rail and in turn generating an increased return on advertising investment.

## The challenge: from 'good enough' to 'great'

Awareness of the new trains and timetables was good, and rational barriers had largely been overcome. The Cross Country route was performing well. However, the West Coast line was still failing to challenge other modes of transport, and the ultimate goal of rekindling public enthusiasm for rail travel was yet to be realised. Positive emotional engagement was still lacking, as demonstrated by the higher consideration afforded to airline operators and a lack of emotional proximity between the consumer and Virgin Trains. In comparison to the plane and the car, the train still felt like the unglamorous, poor relation; a practical choice, but not a particularly sexy or exciting one.

Our ultimate aim was to be Britain's favourite transport provider. We wanted to encourage consumers to make an active, positive choice to take the train rather than driving or opting to fly – and to keep doing so. Virgin wanted people to feel passionate about their trains, to reignite people's belief in the railway.

It was time to behave like a true Virgin company, injecting some glamour and emotion.

## Some sturdy barriers

After a nine-month roll-out, by June 2005 new Pendolino trains made up the entirety of the West Coast fleet. The new rolling stock featured the same characteristics as the Voyagers, including technology that allows the train to tilt and reach 125 mph.

Generating a step-change in terms of attitude and behaviour was a far tougher challenge in 2005 than it had been two years previously, when the 'New Beginning' campaign celebrated the arrival of the Voyagers on the Cross Country network. Not only were we aiming to meet a more challenging objective – addressing deep-seated emotional barriers rather than rational product bugbears – we were faced with a more challenging environment, as outlined below.

### New trains are 'new news' no longer

The new-style trains, launched in 2002, had now been operating in the UK for almost three years. By the time our campaign launched, new Pendolino trains had been operating on the West Coast route for ten months, although the roll-out had been gradual. Over 75% of the population had some knowledge of the new trains. In short, we did not have the 'new news' story that had been so crucial to changing perception and behaviour in 2002.

### A harsh competitive environment

The West Coast line runs from London to Glasgow via Birmingham, Liverpool and Manchester. These major conurbations are heavily serviced by other modes of transport:

- the M6 links London and Manchester; despite the journey times being longer than the equivalent trip by rail, journey costs are significantly cheaper
- National Express has frequent departures between the major cities along the route, with 25 departures from London to Manchester daily and single fares as low as £4
- there are five airlines servicing the London to Manchester route alone.

### A demanding consumer

The West Coast route attracts a high proportion of business travellers due to the nature of the destinations serviced. When the ticket is not being funded out of the traveller's own pocket, purchase drivers change fundamentally. Price becomes less important, and reliability and the on-board experience become more crucial. Air travel in particular is an enticing prospect due to greater perceived punctuality, speed and comfort.

## An emotive aim, an emotive strategy

Years of underperformance from the nation's rail providers had left a legacy of deep-seated prejudice. Unless we addressed the emotional deficit, train travel would remain the poor relation to other modes of transport, and Virgin Trains would fail to reach its true potential.

In contrast to the 'New Beginning' campaign, this new work would need to do more than simply highlight the new product and the rational benefits thereof. It needed to engage people in the entirety of the train experience, a 'top down' approach, in comparison to our previous 'bottom up' strategy centred on functional improvements to the service.

Recognising that an emotive message without any back-up could be perceived as an empty promise, we sought to underpin our campaign with more rational communications (see Figure 1).

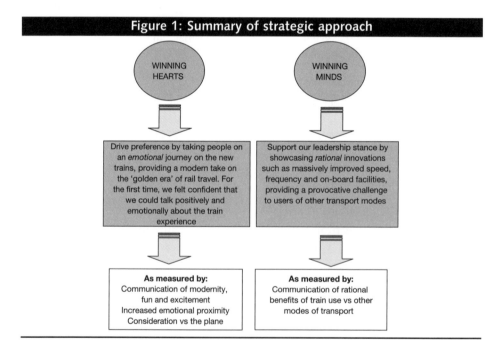

**Figure 1: Summary of strategic approach**

## The creative idea: wooing the consumer

*Injecting emotion*

Our creative idea, 'The Return of the Train', was a romantic celebration of the marriage of cutting-edge innovation with 'golden era' train service, featuring clips from famous train journeys from *The Railway Children* to *North by North West* via *Murder on the Orient Express* and *Some Like It Hot*.

We extended this golden age association by sponsoring weekend matinees on Turner Classic Movies (TCM), and a film season at the Prince Charles Cinema.

### Supporting our stance

The second strand of communication focused on three key areas of rational support that the new trains had brought to the West Coast line:

1. Speed/reduced journey times.
2. Higher frequency.
3. Better on-board services.

At the start of 2006, these ads were replaced by more explicit 'anti-modal' executions, which ran in conjunction with a fresh burst of the TV execution, as a more pointed challenge to users of plane and car.

## Spreading the love: media strategy

National TV and cinema allowed us to get closer to people's hearts. Long spot lengths showcased the creative work, and delivered standout and engagement (see Figure 2).

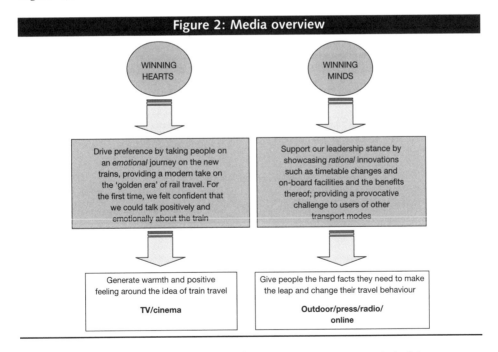

Figure 2: Media overview

Underpinning this emotive strand of communications was a 'minds' strategy.

Track and timetable improvements came into effect in September and December 2004, and June 2005. Coupled with the roll-out of the Pendolino trains the greatest benefits were felt across the West Coast route. The campaign had to work on a national level – making people fall in love with the train again – but with a focus on the West Coast route, to leverage the service and revenue opportunities. This regional upweight also supported and protected the brand in this area against fierce competition from other modes of transport.

Detailed mapping, location and business analysis informed prioritisation. Proximity, type of message (speed, frequency, service), and the message itself, were planned on a micro level, taking into consideration:

- estimated revenue and journey growth by station
- peak and off-peak load factors, by standard and first class
- drive time around each key hub, and the stations within this radius.

Such tailored communications planning delivered the rational 'minds' messages in optimum environments.

Interactive TV highlighted the benefits of the train service and introduced the star of the ad – the Pendolino carriage.

Messages in the press underpinned the outdoor and radio activity. Online activity focused on core travel environments and consideration moments, delivering awareness and ticket sales.

Direct marketing allowed us to send tailored, relevant messages to our current customers, building on the rational messages of the press and outdoor activity.

## Did it work? And how?

**Figure 3: The journey from advertising to revenue**

The advertising was seen and liked

⇩

The advertising communicated emotionally and rationally
(we won hearts and minds!)

⇩

People felt closer to Virgin Trains

⇩

Consideration improved vs the competition

⇩

Journeys increased, including switching from plane

⇩

Revenue increased dramatically

### The advertising was seen and liked

There was a significant shift in both spontaneous and prompted ad awareness for both business and leisure users (see Figure 4).

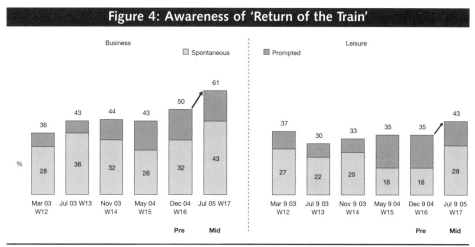

Figure 4: Awareness of 'Return of the Train'

Source: Synovate, 2005

The TV execution generated the highest advertising awareness in the travel industry (see Figure 5). Advertising enjoyment, saliency, involvement and persuasion scores were amongst the best ever seen (see Table 1).

Visits to the Virgin Trains website went up by 43% over the campaign period, from 350,000 visits per week to 500,000.

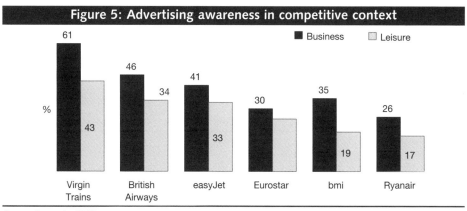

Figure 5: Advertising awareness in competitive context

Source: Synovate, 2005

### Table 1: Tracking scores for 'Return of the Train', % agreement

|                             | Business | Leisure |
|-----------------------------|----------|---------|
| Really good ad              | 84       | 80      |
| Really stands out           | 85       | 81      |
| Can relate to it            | 74       | 73      |
| Makes me want to find out more | 51    | 40      |

Source: Synovate

*The advertising communicated both rationally and emotionally*

As intended, emotional responses dominated (see Figure 6). However, rational messages were still communicated by the TV campaign, despite the relative lack of emphasis on product points in this media (see Figure 7).

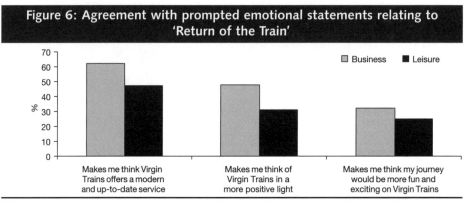

**Figure 6: Agreement with prompted emotional statements relating to 'Return of the Train'**

Source: Synovate

**Figure 7: Agreement with prompted rational statements relating to 'Return of the Train'**

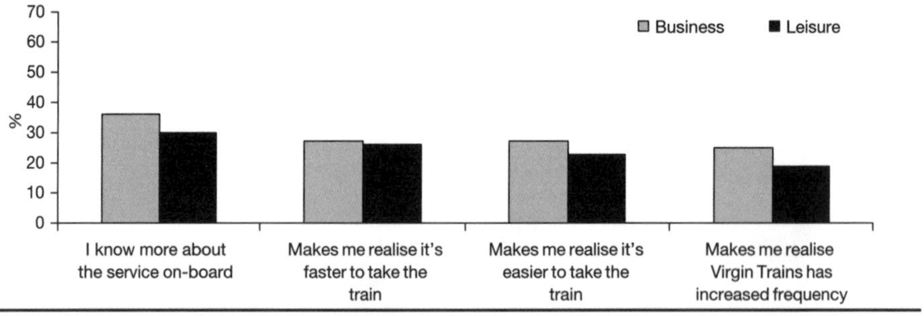

Source: Synovate

*People felt closer to the train*

Emotional proximity has moved strongly, most noticeably amongst business travellers (see Figure 8).

*Consideration improved*

Attraction to using the train increased significantly over the campaign period amongst both leisure and business users (see Figure 9).

*Virgin Trains consideration improved vs other train operating companies*

Opinions of Virgin Trains vs other train operators increased significantly over the campaign period, again most noticeably amongst the business audience (see Figure 10).

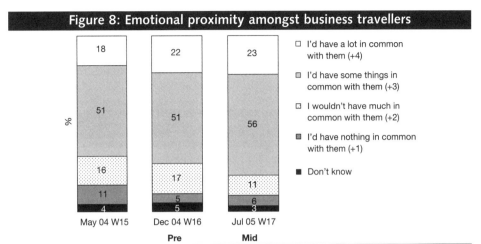

**Figure 8: Emotional proximity amongst business travellers**

- □ I'd have a lot in common with them (+4)
- ▨ I'd have some things in common with them (+3)
- ▢ I wouldn't have much in common with them (+2)
- ▣ I'd have nothing in common with them (+1)
- ■ Don't know

Source: Synovate

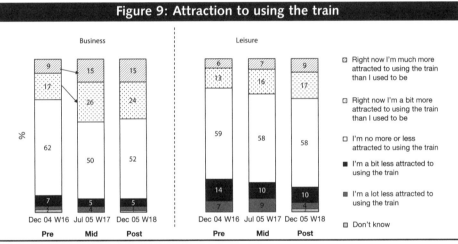

**Figure 9: Attraction to using the train**

- ▨ Right now I'm much more attracted to using the train than I used to be
- ▢ Right now I'm a bit more attracted to using the train than I used to be
- ▢ I'm no more or less attracted to using the train
- ■ I'm a bit less attracted to using the train
- ■ I'm a lot less attracted to using the train
- ▢ Don't know

Source: Synovate

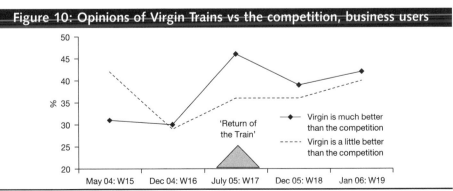

**Figure 10: Opinions of Virgin Trains vs the competition, business users**

- ◆ Virgin is much better than the competition
- - - - Virgin is a little better than the competition

Source: Synovate

*Consideration improved to the extent that we became the nation's favourite transport operator*

At the end of the year, Virgin Trains overtook British Airways as the nation's most considered travel provider for the first time, a gap that has widened following a reprise of the campaign in January 2006.

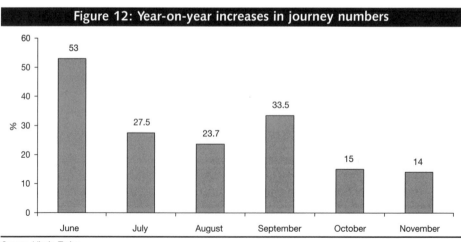

**Figure 11: Consideration of Virgin Trains vs BA, 'Firm favourite or one of my favourites'**

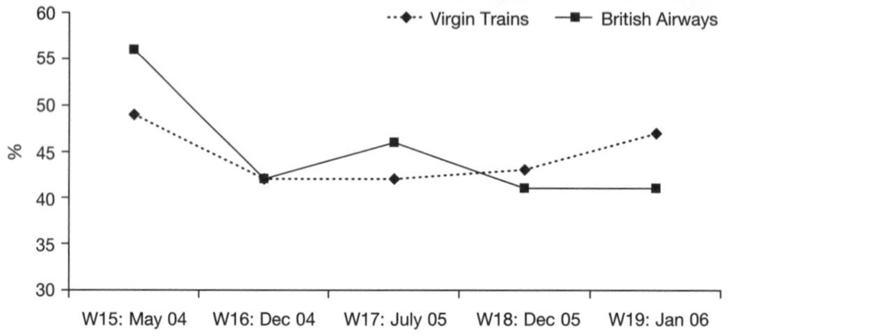

Source: Synovate

*Journeys increased, including switching from plane*

Overall journey numbers increased significantly over the campaign period when compared with the same period the previous year, despite the impact that the London bombings had on the number of people travelling (see Figure 12).

**Figure 12: Year-on-year increases in journey numbers**

Source: Virgin Trains

City reports on domestic airlines suggest that the campaign has been working in an 'anti-modal' fashion, encouraging those who would previously have taken the plane to take the train instead. Airline volumes are down 6.2% between

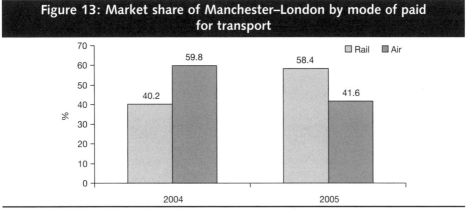

Figure 13: Market share of Manchester–London by mode of paid for transport

Source: CAA

Manchester and London, and Virgin Trains is up 96% over the same year-long period (September 2004–October 2005), according to the Civil Aviation Authority.

As a result, market share for the train overtook that of the plane on the London–Manchester route (see Figure 13).

### West Coast revenues improved

West Coast revenues were up 32% June to September year-on-year despite the impact of the London bombings in July.

## Isolating the effect of advertising

In order to isolate and demonstrate the impact of advertising on revenues, econometric modelling was used. The model quantifies the impact of all drivers and detractors of passenger volumes, and hence can factor out both the influence of the new train product and the impact of the July 2005 terrorism.

To account for the impact of the London terrorism, we analysed the daily rate of sale over the period, quantifying the loss in performance, and then added this to the actual passenger volumes to provide a 'no terrorism' estimate of performance from which advertising performance could be evaluated.

The roll-out of the new rolling stock occurred gradually over a two-year period. We control for this historically by having a variable 'percentage of Pendolinos rolled out' in the model.

In conjunction with the launch of the improved rolling stock, Virgin Train's West Coast line was scheduled a higher proportion of trains in the National Rail Network. To control for this we modelled passenger volumes per percentage point of the West Coast's share of the timetable.

The following factors were also reviewed and controlled for via the analysis:

- growth in the performance of the overall national rail network
- price changes
- engineering activity
- improved running performance of Virgin Trains

- Virgin sales promotions
- public events – sports and cultural
- non-train competitor passenger volumes (e.g. airlines)
- ticket purchase channel changes.

The model gives us the following scenarios, which clearly demonstrate the impact that advertising had on revenue (see Figure 14).

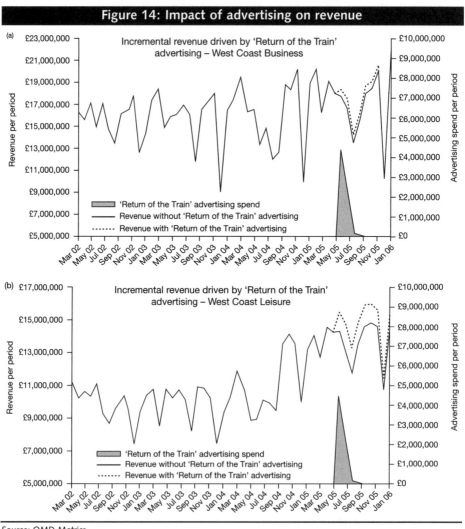

Figure 14: Impact of advertising on revenue

Source: OMD Metrics

Incremental revenue generated by the advertising was sustained well beyond the 'on air' period (see Table 2).

Our campaign ROI is calculated at £4.20, with £19.1m revenue coming from West Coast Leisure and £10.5m coming from West Coast Business.

| Table 2: Incremental revenue generation | | |
|---|---|---|
| **Period End** | **West Coast Business** | **West Coast Leisure** |
| 25 June 2005 | £592,000 | £1,154,000 |
| 23 July 2005 | £871,000 | £1,668,000 |
| 20 August 2005 | £723,000 | £1,514,000 |
| 17 September 2005 | £623,000 | £1,326,000 |
| 15 October 2005 | £654,000 | £1,283,000 |
| 12 November 2005 | £600,000 | £1,166,000 |
| 10 December 2005 | £585,000 | £1,029,000 |
| 7 January 2006 | £270,000 | £680,000 |
| 4 February 2006 | £509,000 | £848,000 |
| **Expected future revenue** | **£5,094,000** | **£8,481,000** |
| **Total** | **£10,523,000** | **£19,150,840** |

Source: Virgin Trains

Within this, online advertising, working from our macro strategy and based on the above-the-line creative, generated an impressive, directly calculable ROI of £8.

Given that the incremental cost of additional passengers travelling on the route is a tiny proportion of Virgin Trains' total cost base, the observed revenue return on investment scores can be viewed as a very close approximation to the real 'profit' ROI of the activity.

## Conclusion

'The Return of the Train' sought to generate real emotional engagement with Virgin Trains. The campaign succeeded in its aim, encouraging more train journeys, delivering an impressive return on investment and helping Virgin Trains to become the nation's preferred travel provider.

## Chapter 27

# Volkswagen Golf GTI Mk5

## The new Golf GTI Mk5: a launch without a car

**By Abe Dew, Tribal DDB, and Tristram Harrison, DDB Matrix**
Contributing authors: Les Binet, DDB Matrix, and Sarah Carter, DDB London

This case study discusses the launch of the Volkswagen Golf GTI Mk5 in 2005. Volkswagen UK was set the target of selling 50% of the annual 2005 volume of the Mk5 six months before any cars would actually be available, and using just 10% of the overall budget. It was also decided that most of the traditional media were not suitable communications channels, meaning that a vastly different advertising strategy was required.

Volkswagen's response was to target the core GTI audience, encouraging them to buy a new Golf GTI before it was officially launched. An online platform was created that allowed people to build a dream Golf GTI Mk5, positively engaging them with the brand experience. This was supported by direct mail and POS communications. If successful, this approach would offer the advantages of delivering the necessary sales and improving the campaign payback, growing both market share and profitability, and also pre-empting the competition.

The GTI micro-site received over 1.2 million visitors in the pre-release period – 179,000 of whom built virtual Golf GTIs online, and 1,700 serious prospects who saved full personal details and pre-ordered a GTI online. Around 16% of these went on to buy a new Golf GTI, and after six months of the campaign, the target for pre-sales was reached, with those who pre-ordered online paying £1,000 more than the average value of cars bought by the majority of GTI buyers. The direct effect of the campaign was estimated to be £4m, while the indirect effect is estimated to be much greater still.

## Introduction: the challenge?

This paper is the story of the challenges Volkswagen UK and its communications agencies faced in the pre-release of the new Golf GTI Mk5. The objective was to pre-empt Golf GTI's competitors and secure the loyalty of hardcore car fanatics by getting them to pay a deposit on a car they hadn't even seen yet.

## Background

### Our heritage: a legend

The Mk1 Golf GTI launched in 1976 as a sporty variant of the Mk1 Volkswagen Golf. Despite an illustrious heritage, Mk3 and Mk4 Golf GTIs became more mainstream and less sporty. (By 2001 the Mk4 Golf GTI represented a quarter of total Volkswagen Golf sales volume.) Aware of Golf GTI's heritage, an improved Mk5 Golf GTI was due to launch in 2005, to reinvigorate Golf GTI's spirit and refocus its halo onto Volkswagen's brand.

### The marketing challenge

The traditional launch media environment was going to be very cluttered when the Golf GTI was due to launch on 28 January 2005. Figure 1 shows how several main competitors were advertising their cars on TV at this time, just prior to the March registration plate change, one of the busiest seasonal spikes in the UK car market.

Volkswagen UK's strategy was to pre-empt its competitors by reaching the core GTI audience first. The objective was to encourage hot-hatch lovers to commit to buying a Golf GTI by pre-paying for a car months before it launched. This radical strategy was something Volkswagen had never done before anywhere in the world. If successful, the benefits would be threefold:

1. 'Time shift' the sales curve to deliver pre-sales before the car was available.
2. Pre-empt competition for high-value buyers and deliver more profit earlier.
3. Secure more market share and improve the campaign's overall payback.

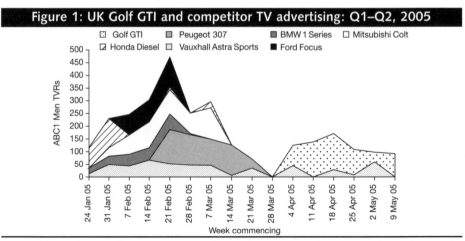

Figure 1: UK Golf GTI and competitor TV advertising: Q1–Q2, 2005

Source: MediaCom London

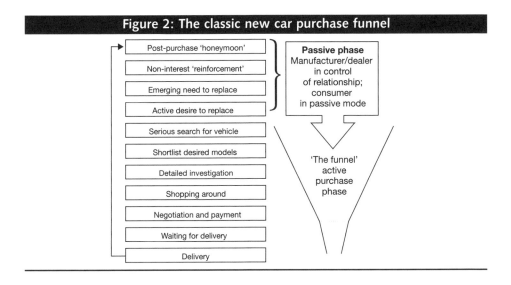

Figure 2: The classic new car purchase funnel

### The scale of this task

As Volkswagen had never done this before, no benchmark for success existed. Volkswagen UK head Paul Willis set an ambitious goal of 3,100 pre-sales (or 50% of the 2005 annual sales target) by the time Golf GTI launched.

### The traditional communications context

Volkswagen wanted to beat the competition and convince 'hot-hatch' lovers to buy a new GTI, but for most new car buyers the decision-making process usually takes three to six months. Figure 2 shows the 'funnel' model used by almost every car maker and car advertiser.

But, a pre-release strategy that encourages pre-sales before a car is available short-circuits this model. The solution had to find new ways to let the right people find out about the Golf GTI. Luckily, Golf GTI appeals to car fanatics who are always in the active mode, and don't require a typical passive media set-up.

## A new communications strategy

### Invert the funnel: active media followed by passive

The answer provided by Volkswagen UK and its communications agencies was to lead the pre-release in active tactical media, the internet supported by DM, PR and POS. Then a traditional mass media launch would follow once the car was available.

### Volkswagen understood GTI buyers

TGI and NCBS data showed that potential GTI buyers were affluent males aged 25–34, and were also heavy internet users. Table 1 shows that they strongly agreed with certain lifestyle and attitude statements.

| Table 1: Potential Golf GTI buyer attitudes | | |
|---|---|---|
| | Index | Target |
| I visit websites devoted to motoring | 100 | 194.6 |
| I like innovative cars | 100 | 153.9 |
| I refer to the internet before making a purchase | 100 | 173.2 |
| People come to me for advice before buying new things | 100 | 206.5 |

Source: MediaCom London, UK, 2002, TGI data (T02UK)

Golf buyer profiling research showed Golf GTI performance buyers earned more than average Golf buyers. They could afford to pre-pay a deposit on a new car and wait for the Golf GTI, if we gave them sufficient reason.

*Volkswagen knew what people want online*

Figure 3 presents the tracking research that showed Volkswagen UK's website users valued research into new cars' details. The communications opportunity was to creatively reinvent how research can influence the desire to buy cars and help people buy them.

**Figure 3: Value of research into new cars' details**

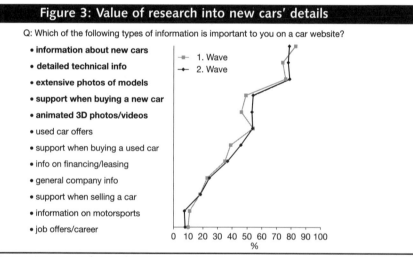

Q: Which of the following types of information is important to you on a car website?

- **information about new cars**
- **detailed technical info**
- **extensive photos of models**
- **support when buying a new car**
- **animated 3D photos/videos**
- used car offers
- support when buying a used car
- info on financing/leasing
- general company info
- support when selling a car
- information on motorsports
- job offers/career

1. Wave
2. Wave

Source: Volkswagen UK. Psyma website tracking Wave 2 (April 2004)

## The creative solution

The creative idea was to let people build a dream Golf GTI Mk5 on a website, a process known as 'online configuration'.

In 2004 several car websites offered basic configurators. They were detail focused, seldom reflected brand personality and all looked the same.

In contrast, the new Golf GTI website is a brand experience that reflects the Golf GTI personality and Volkswagen branding throughout. Only real cash-on-the-table deposits paid to Volkswagen retailers counted as pre-sales. Figure 4 shows the goals for pre-ordering and pre-sales.

## Figure 4: New Golf GTI online pre-ordering and retailer pre-sales process

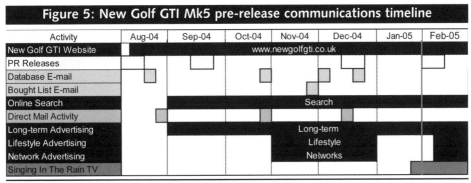

**Internet environment**

GTI prospects    www.newgolfgti.co.uk website

**1:** Identify & inform prospects about the new GTI
**2:** Encourage configuration and saving virtual GTI
**3:** Collect Pre-orders for GTI with personal details
**4:** Build a database of genuine GTI prospects

**Real world**

Volkswagen UK retailer network

**1:** Increased interest in GTI
**2:** Convert online Pre-orders
into earlier cash Pre-sales
**3:** Increase sales of Golf GTI

The Golf GTI campaign used many channels to target potential GTI buyers. Advertising was placed on websites about buying cars like *WhatCar?* and *AutoExpress*, as well as lifestyle-focused websites like *GQ*'s website and network websites like Google and MSN. Emails were sent to the growing Golf GTI database.

Figure 5 shows the activity timeline of the pre-release campaign.

## Figure 5: New Golf GTI Mk5 pre-release communications timeline

| Activity | Aug-04 | Sep-04 | Oct-04 | Nov-04 | Dec-04 | Jan-05 | Feb-05 |
|---|---|---|---|---|---|---|---|
| New Golf GTI Website | | | www.newgolfgti.co.uk | | | | |
| PR Releases | | | | | | | |
| Database E-mail | | | | | | | |
| Bought List E-mail | | | | | | | |
| Online Search | | | Search | | | | |
| Direct Mail Activity | | | | | | | |
| Long-term Advertising | | | | Long-term | | | |
| Lifestyle Advertising | | | | Lifestyle | | | |
| Network Advertising | | | | Networks | | | |
| Singing In The Rain TV | | | | | | | |

Sources: Tribal DDB London Media, DDB London and Proximity London

After six months the pre-release finished and the car launched on 28 January 2004. Internet activity now had a fresh objective: to support a traditional launch with DDB London's 'Singing in the Rain' TV ad.

## What happened?

*The integrated campaign reached millions*

The campaign reached over 5.4 million people, at an average frequency of 3.6 times each. This is a conservative estimate as figures are not available to measure the reach of internet search engines, online PR and traditional press releases. Figure 6 summarises the main results.

## Figure 6: Overall summary of integrated pre-release campaign reach and impact

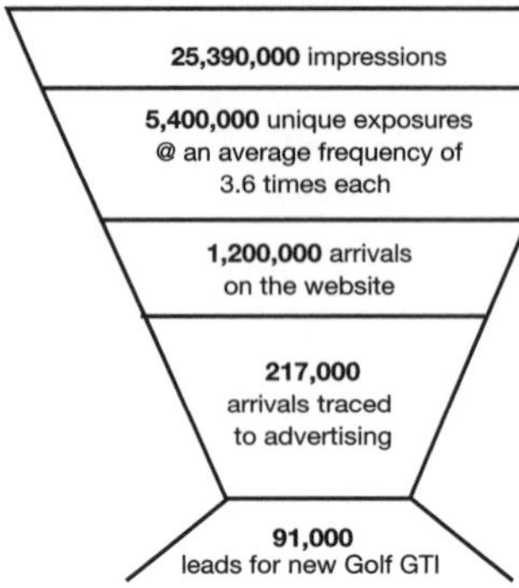

**25,390,000** impressions

**5,400,000** unique exposures
@ an average frequency of
3.6 times each

**1,200,000** arrivals
on the website

**217,000**
arrivals traced
to advertising

**91,000**
leads for new Golf GTI

### Communications drove people to the website

The GTI micro-site received over 1.2 million visitors in the pre-release period. Figure 7 shows that website traffic correlates with the peaks of expenditure and activity in the communications campaign. This figure also shows the internet was extremely cost efficient in generating an active response among millions of car enthusiasts.

In the pre-release period volume of traffic to the GTI micro-site reached over 20% of annual 2004 traffic to Volkswagen UK's main website, which was 5.4 million visitors.

### More importantly, the visitors were Golf GTI enthusiasts

Website tags that measured what people did on the website showed that 75% of GTI homepage visitors went on to visit the configurator in November. This traffic rose to 85% in December.

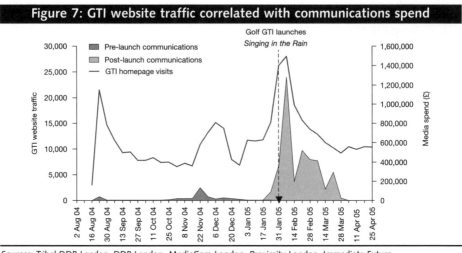

## Figure 7: GTI website traffic correlated with communications spend

Sources: Tribal DDB London, DDB London, MediaCom London, Proximity London, Immediate Future

## They were involved in the experience of building the GTI

The value of the website was shown by over 90% completion of virtual Golf GTIs. Figure 8 shows the high percentage of completed cars. Each person who did this was involved with the Golf GTI for a minimum of four minutes per car.

The website successfully got people to pre-order online (see Figure 9).

## A high proportion of people who pre-ordered online went on to buy

Comparing the online pre-order database and Volkswagen's sales delivery database reveals the absolute minimum effectiveness of the pre-release activity. Volkswagen UK's own sales data show that, of those who pre-ordered on the website, a minimum of 16% went on to buy a new Golf GTI.

Because of the way retailers collect customers' details, it's not always possible to tally sales with pre-orders. It has been estimated that, once this problem is accounted for, the true conversion rate could be as high as 40%.

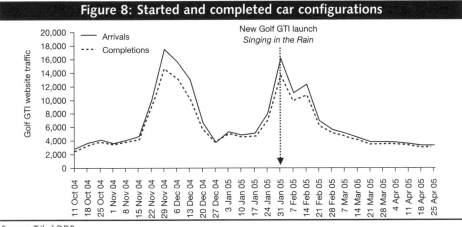

**Figure 8: Started and completed car configurations**

Source: Tribal DDB

**Figure 9: The volume of virtual new Golf GTIs configured and pre-ordered online**

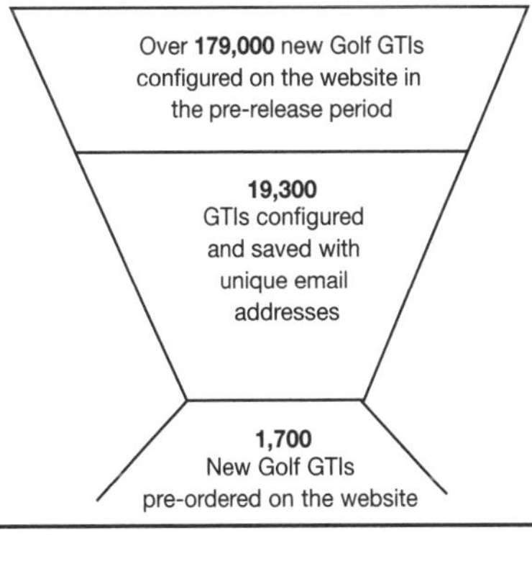

Over **179,000** new Golf GTIs configured on the website in the pre-release period

**19,300** GTIs configured and saved with unique email addresses

**1,700** New Golf GTIs pre-ordered on the website

*Configuration and pre-ordering of cars correlates with pre-sales*

Figure 10 compares the dates for pre-ordered cars online and Volkswagen's pre-sales 'order bank' in the pre-release period. Activity in retailers correlates with website activity from August to December 2004. After this point, online pre-orders decline, but by this stage the launch of the Golf GTI was only a month away, so communications shifted towards the driving of test-drive requests in retailers.

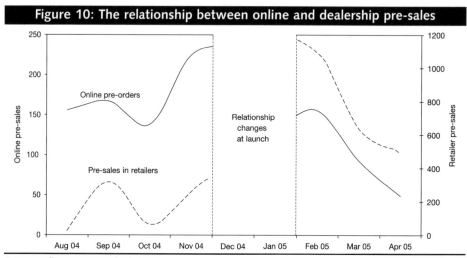

**Figure 10: The relationship between online and dealership pre-sales**

Sources: Volkswagen UK and Tribal DDB

## The results

*The pre-sales goal was met in six months*

Volkswagen order bank totals suggest the goal of pre-selling 3,100 Golf GTIs was reached in early February, exactly six months after the Golf GTI website launched. As car buying research takes three to six months, reaching 50% of annual sales within weeks of launch shows the success of the pre-release strategy. With early pre-sales, the annual 6,200 Golf GTI sales target was exceeded by 2%.

*The GTI pre-release delivered pre-sales earlier*

Figure 11 compares order bank pre-sales data for the new Mk5 Golf launch in January 2004, and for the Golf GTI launch in January 2005. The Mk5 Golf is Volkswagen's most popular and highest-selling model. Its launch was keenly anticipated, but there was no pre-release campaign for the Golf Mk5 in 2004.

*Removing the enthusiast factor*

But could the appeal of the GTI badge have created this early pre-sales curve? The best way to counter this argument is to compare the pre-sales curve of the new Golf GTI against a similarly sporty car with just as fanatical a following among the same active male early-adopter audience.

## Figure 11: Comparison of Golf GTI pre-sales curve versus Golf Mk5 pre-sales curve

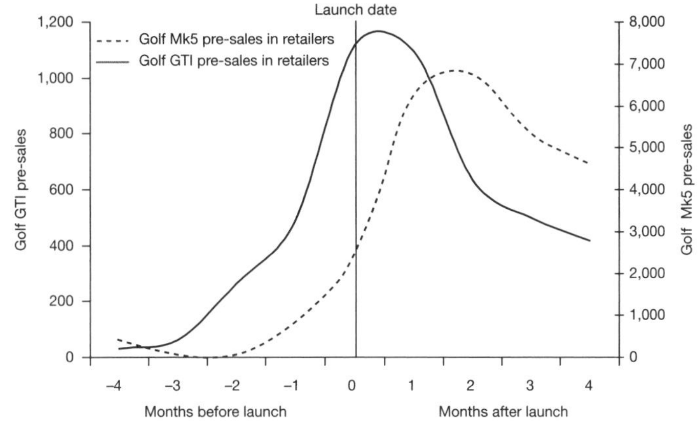

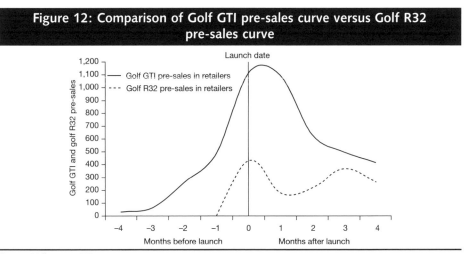

Source: Volkswagen UK

The Golf R32 is a proper race car and the new model launched in November 2005. Golf R32 had a configurator website at launch, but not before the car launched. Figure 12 shows that Golf R32 has the same short pre-sales curve as its domestic parent, the Golf Mk5.

The simplest reason for the lack of Golf Mk5 and Golf R32 pre-sales around the launches of these cars is the lack of pre-release campaigns for both models. As a result they both share a similar lack of pre-sales.

### People who pre-ordered paid more for their GTIs

As shown in Table 2, the audience targeted in the Golf GTI pre-release campaign were a valuable target market that paid more for their cars.

## Figure 12: Comparison of Golf GTI pre-sales curve versus Golf R32 pre-sales curve

Source: Volkswagen UK

| Table 2: Comparative UK prices paid for Golf GTIs | |
|---|---|
| Average price of GTI pre-ordered online and bought 2005 | £22,450.00 |
| Average price of UK GTIs bought in 2005 | £21,423.00 |
| Average difference in value | +£1,027.00 |

Sources: Tribal DDB London, Volkswagen UK and NCBS

### Pre-release activity paid for itself

Let's start by looking at the *direct* effect of online activity – that is to say, those sales that can be directly tallied with online pre-orders from Volkswagen's database. The direct effect contributed £4m of extra revenue. While we cannot reveal Volkswagen UK's profit margins, we can state that these sales alone are quite enough to cover the cost of the activity.

Then there is the *indirect* effect – that is to say, those sales that were stimulated by the activity but can't be directly tallied with pre-ordering. We have argued that the bulk of the GTI's pre-sales were in one way or another stimulated by our campaign, in which case it generated somewhere in the region of £20m. This is enough to pay for the activity eight times over.

### The pre-sales strategy increased cash flow

The campaign paid for itself in terms of simple short-term revenues, but there are further implications for profit:

- by getting people to pay more for their car, we increased Volkswagen's profit margins
- by getting people to pay cash deposits months earlier than normal, we improved cash flow
- by selling cars faster, we reduced the costs of holding cars in stock or paying interest.

### The value of integrated communications

When we consider the combined effect of the pre-release and post-release activity, we see that the total payback was even bigger.

To do this, let's compare the UK with continental Europe. The UK got the same GTI cars as the continent, at similar prices. But only the UK was supported with the pre-sales activity, and only the UK got 'Singing in the Rain'. The result is shown in Figure 13. The sales uplift in the UK was almost twice as big as it was abroad.

If we assume that this difference was due to the communications, then this implies that the UK's unique combination of pre-launch and post-launch activity generated around £53m worth of extra sales. This revenue is enough to pay for the entire new car launch and brand-building communications many, many times over.

### Cost-effective exposure to branded media

The average time taken to configure and save a car on the GTI website is four minutes from start to finish.

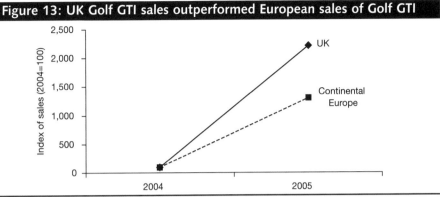

Figure 13: UK Golf GTI sales outperformed European sales of Golf GTI

Note: Continental Europe includes Germany, Spain, Italy and France

- A total of 19,000 cars were configured and saved. At four minutes each, this is 53.6 days spent with the new Golf GTI.
- A total of 1,700 cars were pre-ordered. This process takes seven minutes on average, and this is 8.4 days of exposure for the most dedicated GTI enthusiasts.

*The GTI website continues to deliver above expectations*

The GTI website is still live and attracting traffic 18 months after it launched. Payback from this longevity compares well with the lifespan of TV advertising. The Golf GTI website continues to perform well.

## Summary

The scale of the challenge involved in this pre-release was huge: to convince a discerning and spoilt car-buying audience to pay a deposit on a car that they had not yet seen.

Three clear benefits signal the success of this radical new car launch strategy.

1. A 'time shift' in the sales curve delivered additional pre-sales before the car was available, well above the curves demonstrated for comparable models.
2. Early commitment to buy pre-empted competitors from targeting high-value buyers and delivered profits earlier than a traditional new car launch.
3. This resulted in faster growth of UK Golf GTI sales than in other European markets, improving business profitability and the payback from advertising.

# How to access the IPA dataBANK

The IPA Effectiveness dataBANK represents the most rigorous and comprehensive examination of marketing communications working in the marketplace, in the world. Over the 26 years of the IPA Effectiveness Awards competition, the IPA has collected over 1,000 examples of best practice in advertising development and results across a wide spectrum of marketing sectors and expenditures. Each example contains up to 4,000 words of text and is illustrated in full by market, research, sales and profit data.

## Access

The dataBANK is held in the IPA Information Centre for access by IPA members only. Simply contact the Centre by emailing *info@ipa.co.uk*. Simple or more sophisticated searches can be run, free of charge, by qualified, professional knowledge executives across a range of parameters including brand, advertiser, agency, target market (by age, sex, class, and so on), medium and length of activity, which can be specified by the user, and the results supplied by email or other means as required.

## Purchasing IPA case studies

Member agencies will be allowed a maximum of 25 case studies for download in any given calendar year, after which they will be charged at £17 each. Alternatively, members can sign up to WARC (see overleaf) at a beneficial IPA rate and can then download case studies as part of that subscription.

## Further information

For further information, please contact the Information Centre at the IPA, 44 Belgrave Square, London SWIX 8QS
Telephone: +44 (0)20 7235 7020
Fax: +44 (0)20 7245 9904
Website: *www.ipa.co.uk*
Email: *info@ipa.co.uk*

# www.WARC.com

The IPA case histories dataBANK can also be accessed through the World Advertising Research Center (WARC). Reached by logging on to *www.warc.com*, the world's most comprehensive advertising database enables readers to search all the IPA case histories and case histories from similar award schemes around the world, including the American Marketing Association New York, the Advertising Federation of Australia and the Institute of Communications and Advertising in Canada. WARC also offers thousands of 'how to' articles on all areas of communication activity from sources such as the *Journal of Advertising Research*, *Admap* magazine and the ESOMAR conference series.

# IPA dataBANK case availability

* Denotes winning entries.
** Denotes cases published in *Area Works* volumes 1–5.

**NEW ENTRIES 2006**

| | |
|---|---|
| 2006 | 100.4 smooth fm |
| 2006 | Actimel* |
| 2006 | Anti Drug (Scottish Executive) |
| 2006 | Ariel |
| 2006 | Audi |
| 2006 | Axe |
| 2006 | Bakers Complete* |
| 2006 | Barclays Global Investors (iShares) |
| 2006 | Bendicks |
| 2006 | Bertolli |
| 2006 | Branston Baked Beans* |
| 2006 | British Heart Foundation* (Anti Smoking) |
| 2006 | Brother |
| 2006 | Bulldog |
| 2006 | Cathedral City* |
| 2006 | Daz* |
| 2006 | Dero* |
| 2006 | Disability Rights Commission |
| 2006 | Dogs Trust |
| 2006 | Eurostar |
| 2006 | Felix* |
| 2006 | Halifax Bank of Scotland |
| 2006 | HM Revenue & Customs (Self Assessment)* |
| 2006 | Homebase |
| 2006 | Horlicks |
| 2006 | ING Direct* |
| 2006 | Jamie's School Dinners* |
| 2006 | Johnnie Walker |
| 2006 | Kwik-Fit* |
| 2006 | Make Poverty History (Comic Relief) |
| 2006 | Manchester City* |
| 2006 | Marks & Spencer* |
| 2006 | Mastercard |
| 2006 | Monopoly Here & Now* |
| 2006 | More4* |
| 2006 | Naturella* |
| 2006 | Nicorette* |
| 2006 | NSPCC |
| 2006 | $O_2$* |

| | |
|---|---|
| 2006 | Petits Filous |
| 2006 | Privilege Insurance |
| 2006 | Road Safety – Anti-Drink Driving (DoE Northern Ireland) |
| 2006 | Road Safety – THINK! (Department of Transport) |
| 2006 | Ryvita Minis |
| 2006 | Sainsbury's |
| 2006 | Seeds of Change (Masterfoods) |
| 2006 | Sobieski (Vodka) |
| 2006 | Sony BRAVIA |
| 2006 | Sony DVD Handycam |
| 2006 | Sony Ericsson K750i/W800i* |
| 2006 | Sprite |
| 2006 | Teacher Recruitment* |
| 2006 | The Famous Grouse* |
| 2006 | Travelocity.co.uk* |
| 2006 | Tropicana Pure Premium* |
| 2006 | TV Licensing* |
| 2006 | Vehicle Crime Prevention (The Home Office)* |
| 2006 | Virgin Trains* |
| 2006 | Visit London |
| 2006 | Volkswagen Golf* |
| 2006 | Volkswagen Golf GTI Mk5* |
| 2006 | Wall's Sausages |
| 2006 | Women's Aid* |

**Numerical**

| | |
|---|---|
| 2000 | 1001 Mousse* |
| 2003 | 55 Degrees North** |

**A**

| | |
|---|---|
| 2004 | AA Loans* |
| 1982 | Abbey Crunch |
| 1990 | Abbey National Building Society |
| 1990 | Abbey National Building Society (plc) |
| 1980 | Abbey National Building Society Open Bondshares |
| 1990 | Aberlour Malt Whisky* |
| 2004 | Ackermans (SA) |
| 1996 | Adult Literacy * |

| | |
|---|---|
| 1992 | Limelite* |
| 1980 | Limmits |
| 1999 | Lincoln Financial Group** |
| 2000 | Lincoln Insurance |
| 2000 | Lincoln USA |
| 1980 | Lion Bar |
| 1992 | Liquorice Allsorts |
| 1988 | Liquorice Allsorts |
| 2004 | Listerine |
| 1988 | Listerine* |
| 1980 | Listerine |
| 1998 | Littlewoods Pools |
| 1992 | Lloyds Bank |
| 1984 | Lloyds Bank* |
| 1999 | Local Enterprise Development Unit (NI)** |
| 1990 | London Buses Driver Recruitment |
| 1984 | London Docklands* |
| 1982 | London Docklands |
| 1990 | London Philharmonic |
| 1992 | London Transport Fare Evasion |
| 1986 | London Weekend Television |
| 1980 | Lucas Aerospace* |
| 1996 | Lucky Lottery |
| 1992 | Lucozade |
| 1980 | Lucozade* |
| 2000 | Lurpak* |
| 1988 | Lurpak |
| 2002 | Lynx* |
| 2004 | Lynx Pulse* |
| 1994 | Lyon's Maid Fab |
| 1988 | Lyon's Maid Favourite Centres |

**M**

| | |
|---|---|
| 2004 | M&G |
| 1988 | Maclaren Prams |
| 2003 | Magna Science Adventure Centre** |
| 1999 | Magnet Kitchens** |
| 2004 | Magnum |
| 1990 | Malibu |
| 2001 | Manchester City Centre** |
| 1999 | Manchester City Centre** |
| 2003 | *Manchester Evening News* Jobs Section** |
| 2002 | *Manchester Evening News* (Job Section)* |
| 2003 | ManchesterIMAX** |
| 1982 | Manger's Sugar Soap* |
| 1988 | Manpower Services Commission |
| 1994 | Marks & Spencer |
| 2004 | Marks & Spencer Lingerie* |
| 2002 | Marmite* |
| 1998 | Marmite* |
| 1998 | Marmoleum |

| | |
|---|---|
| 1988 | Marshall Cavendish Discovery |
| 1994 | Marston Pedigree* |
| 2001 | Maryland Cookies** |
| 1986 | Mazda* |
| 1986 | Mazola* |
| 1998 | McDonald's |
| 1996 | McDonald's |
| 1980 | McDougall's Saucy Sponge |
| 1990 | Mcpherson's Paints |
| 1988 | Mcpherson's Paints |
| 2004 | McVitie's Jaffa Cakes |
| 2000 | McVitie's Jaffa Cakes |
| 1992 | Mercury Communications |
| 2005 | Metrication |
| 1988 | Metropolitan Police Recruitment* |
| 2003 | Microbake |
| 1990 | Midland Bank |
| 1988 | Midland Bank |
| 1992 | Miele |
| 1988 | Miller Lite* |
| 2000 | Moneyextra* |
| 1999 | Morrisons** |
| 1988 | Mortgage Corporation* |
| 2002 | Mr Kipling* |
| 1984 | Mr Muscle |
| 1995 | Müller Fruit Corner** |
| 1994 | Multiple Sclerosis Society |
| 1996 | Murphy's Irish Stout* |
| 2000 | Myk Menthol Norway* |

**N**

| | |
|---|---|
| 2005 | Nambarrie Tea |
| 2000 | National Code and Number Change |
| 1996 | National Dairy Council – Milk* |
| 1992 | National Dairy Council – Milk |
| 1980 | National Dairy Council – Milk |
| 1992 | National Dairy Council – Milkman* |
| 1996 | National Lottery (Camelot) |
| 1999 | National Railway Museum** |
| 1996 | National Savings |
| 1984 | National Savings: Income Bonds |
| 1982 | National Savings: Save by Post* |
| 1986 | National Westminster Bank Loans |
| 1982 | Nationwide Building Society |
| 1990 | Nationwide Flex Account |
| 1988 | Nationwide Flex Account |
| 1990 | Navy Recruitment |
| 1988 | Nefax |
| 1982 | Negas Cookers |
| 1982 | Nescafé |
| 2000 | Network Q |
| 1992 | Neutrogena |
| 2003 | Newcastle Gateshead Initiative |
| 1982 | New Man Clothes |

| | |
|---|---|
| 1986 | Post Office Special Issue Stamps |
| 1996 | Potato Marketing Board |
| 1998 | Pot Noodle |
| 1984 | Presto |
| 1980 | Pretty Polly* |
| 1990 | Price Waterhouse |
| 2005 | Progressive Building Society – Financial Services |
| 1992 | Prudential |

**Q**

| | |
|---|---|
| 1984 | QE2 |
| 2003 | Qjump.co.uk |
| 1988 | Quaker Harvest Chewy Bars* |
| 1982 | Qualcast Concorde Lawn Mower* |
| 1984 | Qualcast Mow-n-trim and Rotasafe |
| 1986 | Quatro |
| 1986 | Quickstart |
| 1996 | Quorn Burgers |

**R**

| | |
|---|---|
| 1982 | Racal Redec Cadet |
| 1990 | Radion Automatic* |
| 1994 | Radio Rentals |
| 1990 | Radio Rentals |
| 1996 | RAF Recruitment |
| 1980 | RAF Recruitment* |
| 2004 | Rainbow (evaporated milk)* |
| 1994 | Range Rover |
| 2000 | Reading and Literacy* |
| 1992 | Real McCoys |
| 2000 | Rear Seatbelts* |
| 1998 | Red Meat Market* |
| 1984 | Red Meat Consumption |
| 1988 | Red Mountain* |
| 1996 | Reebok* |
| 1992 | Reebok |
| 1990 | Reliant Metrocabs |
| 1994 | Remegel |
| 1998 | Renault |
| 1986 | Renault 5 |
| 1990 | Renault 19* |
| 1996 | Renault Clio* |
| 1992 | Renault Clio* |
| 1984 | Renault Trafic & Master |
| 2005 | ResponsibleTravel.Com |
| 1996 | Ribena |
| 1982 | Ribena* |
| 2001 | right to read (literacy charity)** |
| 2001 | rightmove.co.uk** |
| 2002 | Rimmel* |
| 1986 | Rimmel Cosmetics |
| 2004 | Road Safety (DoE Northern Ireland)* |
| 2003 | Road Safety (DoE Northern Ireland) |

| | |
|---|---|
| 1999 | Road Safety (DoE Northern Ireland)** |
| 1996 | Rocky (Fox's Biscuits) |
| 1988 | Rolls-Royce Privatisation* |
| 1996 | Ross Harper* |
| 2004 | Roundup |
| 2005 | Roundup Weedkiller* |
| 1988 | Rover 200 |
| 1982 | Rowenta |
| 1990 | Rowntree's Fruit Gums |
| 1992 | Royal Bank of Scotland |
| 1986 | Royal College of Nursing |
| 2002 | Royal Mail |
| 1986 | Royal Mail Business Economy |
| 1997 | Royal Mint** |
| 1990 | Royal National Institute for the Deaf |
| 1996 | RSPCA |
| 1988 | Rumbelows |

**S**

| | |
|---|---|
| 2004 | s1jobs |
| 1994 | S4C |
| 1988 | Saab* |
| 1996 | Safeway |
| 2004 | Safer Travel at Night (GLA)* |
| 2002 | Sainsbury's* (Jamie Oliver) |
| 2002 | Sainsbury's* (Promotion) |
| 2001 | Salford University** |
| 2003 | Salvation Army, the** |
| 1996 | Samaritans |
| 1986 | Sanatogen |
| 1980 | Sanatogen |
| 1988 | Sandplate* |
| 1986 | Sapur (Carpet Cleaner) |
| 1992 | Save the Children* |
| 1988 | Schering Greene Science |
| 2001 | Scholl Flight Socks** |
| 2000 | scoot.com* |
| 1980 | Scotcade |
| 2005 | Scotch Beef |
| 1984 | Scotch Video Cassettes |
| 1998 | Scotland on Sunday |
| 1992 | Scotrail |
| 1992 | Scottish Amicable* |
| 2005 | Scottish Power* |
| 1998 | Scottish Prison Service |
| 2005 | Scruffs Hard Wear |
| 2002 | Seafish Industry Authority |
| 2002 | Seatbelts* |
| 1980 | Seiko |
| 1992 | Sellafield Visitors Centre |
| 2002 | Senokot |
| 2001 | Senokot** |
| 2005 | Senokot |

# Index